THE BOOK OF
ISAIAH

Personal Impressions of Isaiah Berlin

THE BOOK OF
ISAIAH

Personal Impressions of Isaiah Berlin

Edited by Henry Hardy

THE BOYDELL PRESS

in association with Wolfson College, Oxford

First published 2009
The Boydell Press, Woodbridge

ISBN 978-1-84383-453-3

The Boydell Press is an imprint of Boydell & Brewer Ltd
PO Box 9, Woodbridge, Suffolk IP12 3DF, UK
and of Boydell & Brewer Inc.
668 Mt Hope Avenue, Rochester, NY 14620, USA
website: www.boydellandbrewer.com

The publisher has no responsibility for the continued existence or accuracy of URLs for external or third-party internet websites referred to in this book, and does not guarantee that any content on such websites is, or will remain, accurate or appropriate.

A CIP record for this book is available from the British Library

This publication is printed on acid-free paper

Designed and typeset in Garamond Premier Pro by
David Roberts, Pershore, Worcestershire

Printed in Great Britain by
CPI Antony Rowe, Chippenham and Eastbourne

*For Sally Denholm-Young
and Serena Moore*

Contents

This is the place of *Isaiah Berlin*,
The man who is clever & yet without sin;
Who has spent years at Oxford, yet still remains straight
And has never been taken by anyone's bait.

Edmund Wilson
(written on a card from the Ritz-Carlton Hotel, Boston)

Preface

SOME YEARS AGO I lent a copy of Isaiah Berlin's volume of essays on his contemporaries, *Personal Impressions*, to a friend and neighbour, the psychiatrist Bob Gosling. When I later asked him what his own personal impression was of the book and its author, he confessed: 'I did get rather tired of all that praise.' There is certainly a lot of praise in that collection, and it is no doubt partly a matter of taste how one responds to the kind of sustained enthusiasm for humanity in all its teeming multiplicity that was one of Berlin's hallmarks. But Gosling's response also misses a point. The prominence of praise was quite deliberate. Berlin much preferred celebration to denigration,[1] on the whole, and his main purpose in the pieces that make up that volume is to see the point of each of the very various people he writes about – to 'accentuate the positive', as the song has it – and to convey it to the reader, which he duly does, often to spellbinding effect.

When Wolfson College asked me to compile a book about Berlin to mark the centenary of his birth, it seemed natural to turn the tables on the master eulogist and invite a number of those who have encountered him closely, in person or on paper, to provide their own personal impressions of the man, and of the point of his life and work. So there is much praise here too. Indeed, one might issue a warning to readers, along the lines of those announcements that precede radio or television programmes liable to offend their audience: 'This book contains strong laudatory content throughout.' Nevertheless, I think there is also in these pages a sufficient lacing of detachment and reservation to placate Gosling's shade. And even those who find accumulated eulogy indigestible cannot fail to be struck by the power Berlin had to elicit personal love and intellectual and moral admiration in almost every, if not quite every, quarter. The degree to which he did this is surely remarkable and exceptional by any standard, and deserves examination. What manner of man was this? This is the question to which this collection is addressed.

Just as there is wide variety among the subjects of Berlin's own personal impressions, so there is among the impressionists who depict him here, and therefore among their impressions, for all that they also often agree in judgement and sentiment. But it is a central truth for Berlin that variety among opinions need not be a sign of error. Samuel Guttenplan quotes Berlin's excellent remark about the widely differing accounts of Irving Berlin's famous lunch with a Winston Churchill who believed his guest was Isaiah Berlin: 'There are many

---

[1] See, in this connection, the beginning of Noel Annan's introduction to PI.

versions of this story, all true.' In this volume there are many different, sometimes conflicting, impressions of Berlin, all true.

I should say something about the structure of the book, and about my
rationale for choosing the contributors. The text proper begins with reflections
by Evan Zimroth on Berlin's origins, stimulated by her encounter with the
engaging anecdotal history of his family written by Berlin's father Mendel for
his son, and published here, as an appendix, for the first time. Mendel vividly
conveys the very un-English world into which Berlin was born, the world out
of which he was transplanted only at the age of eleven. Berlin's Jewish and
Russian roots are rightly stressed by those who write about his life, and about
its impact on his thought, just as they were by Berlin himself, and this is one
of the most important source-documents for the understanding of those roots,
quite apart from its value as social history. Evan Zimroth's contribution well
displays such understanding, and I shall not trespass further on its territory
here.

In the rest of the volume I have had three main aims. The first was to include
a representative sample of the best personal accounts of Berlin that had already
been published, broadcast or recorded. In the days and months after his death
on 5 November 1997 there was an outpouring of writing and broadcasting
about him, much of it of high quality and great interest. It is no exaggeration
to say that a substantial volume could be constructed from these sources alone.
Indeed, I hope that one day this may happen; even a collection of the longer
obituaries would be valuable (if inevitably somewhat repetitive). But to keep
this book within bounds I have confined myself to some of the fine tributes
delivered in London, Oxford and Washington, with the addition of a few
other items that seemed to shed useful further light from different vantage
points. The tributes form the first main section of the book, and the remaining
material drawn from what was already available is to be found in the next section, entitled 'Isaiah in Person'. (The distinction suggested by the titles of this
section and the next, 'Berlin in Print', is not hard and fast, since many of the
contributors to 'Isaiah in Person' also discuss his work. But all these contributors knew Berlin personally, and this knowledge colours their response to his
writings. As Leon Wieseltier puts it, 'they are the mourners who will remember
the teacher and not just the teaching'.)

My second aim was to provide an opportunity for others who knew Berlin
well to write about him for the first time. As so many of the authors in this
book make clear, Berlin's personal presence and style were wonderfully idiosyncratic, as well as complementing and illuminating his intellectual persona,
and it seemed desirable to gather further testimony about his living personality from his contemporaries while there was still time. He has his Boswell in
Michael Ignatieff, but there is room for other voices too, if as many facets of his

capacious personality as possible are to be captured for posterity. These pieces too are included under 'Isaiah in Person'.

There is admittedly a risk in writing of this kind. To be given the impression that you cannot really understand a man's importance or attraction unless you have seen him in the flesh, or known him personally, can be more irritating than informative. As Berlin himself wrote in his memoir of Felix Frankfurter, 'Nothing conveys less to the reader or (rightly) nauseates him more than such passages as [...] "His irresistible manner and his inimitable wit drew gusts of merry laughter from us all!"' [1] This, however, is not the way to do it. Something is irrecoverable, certainly; but this is a negative way of saying something that can also be compensated for to some extent by exactly the kind of impressionistic writing at which Berlin excelled, and I hope and believe that these memoirs largely follow this latter, more constructive, path. The point is not to wring our hands about what we can't now experience, but to preserve memories of it which have the power to bring the past to life. [2]

I have not included a personal impression of my own (except in so far as this emerges from the interview Kei Hiruta has extracted from me), because I have already published such a piece – originally the obituary that appeared in the London *Independent* newspaper – in the first volume of Berlin's letters, and did not want to duplicate that here. But I remembered that, in the first draft of the first article I published about Berlin, [3] I had included an account of my first encounter with him that I cut from the final version. In the present context it seemed worth resuscitating this as my widow's mite:

> I first met Isaiah Berlin on a Saturday morning early in 1972, at Wolfson College, which then occupied temporary buildings in the Banbury Road. I was due to begin graduate work in Oxford that autumn, and I had been called for a scholarship interview. Interviews were not normally held on a Saturday, but I was at the time teaching at Shrewsbury, and so could not get away on a weekday. As it was, I felt obliged to teach the first period that morning, being my last with my Latin A-level class [on Lucretius], and so I could not offer to arrive until just before lunch. And even so, I was late: I had been up into the small hours the night before, and a few hundred yards from my destination I lost my concentration for just long enough to run my car into the back of another when it stopped at a pedestrian crossing. Luckily the other car suffered no damage, but I burst my radiator: so I ran the car up on to the pavement, and sprinted the rest of the way to

[1] PI2 117.

[2] There are also numerous surviving audio and video recordings of Berlin which have a role in this context, and I hope to make at least some of these more widely available in due course.

[3] 'Editing Isaiah Berlin's Writings', *British Book News*, January 1978, 3, 5; also in the IBVL.

the College, arriving breathless and incapable of organised mental activity. The interviewing panel, who had already put themselves out considerably by coming in that day, were patiently waiting, and a strange, disjointed interview followed as the sweat dried on me.

These circumstances alone would have been sufficient to fix the occasion permanently in my memory, but more was to come. The chairman of the panel (whose name, I am ashamed to say, was then scarcely familiar to me), evidently bubbling over with mental energy, talked so fast that I could catch little of what he said, and so much that my replies had to be virtually monosyllabic, and certainly uninformative. I felt completely witless.

There were two other things about the interview that I particularly remember, and which seem to me now, in their different ways, not insignificant. Isaiah wanted to know, of my proposed topic of research, not so much what I hoped to establish, or how, but whether the subject was currently a live one in the philosophical community. And every two or three minutes he would get up and look out of the window to see whether a taxi that he had ordered had arrived.

It was only later, of course, that I learnt that one of his standard descriptions of his authorial output was 'I am like a taxi: I have to be hailed.'

The last of my three aims was to counter a claim that is sometimes aired (it is related to one alluded to above), namely, that if one meets Berlin only on paper, his impact is critically diluted, so that once those who knew him are no longer alive, he will be forgotten, or thought far less significant than he was in his lifetime. I admit that I have wondered in the past if there might not be more than a grain of truth in this prediction; but the authors in the section entitled 'Berlin in Print', and others like them, have convinced me otherwise. Evidently Berlin's published work, including and perhaps especially his letters, is fully able to speak to new readers in a way that will keep his personality alive and impart his intellectual significance. In this connection I should like to quote part of the synopsis written by one of these authors, James Chappel, for his undergraduate thesis, since it demonstrates perfectly the truth of what I have just said:

This essay [...] is [...] my attempt to answer the following personal question: why is it that Berlin is such a wildly attractive figure to me? I had dabbled in philosophy and intellectual history before encountering Berlin. But when I read him for the first time, I felt like the Piltdown Man stumbling upon New York City. Ideas came to life, and the history of thought became exciting and important. But the army that sprang from the dragon's teeth was not staid and dull. Berlin delights in ideas that flash instead of plod, coming from thinkers more like the warriors of the Old

Testament than the benevolent preachers of the New. And when I began to read Berlin's purely philosophical works, it struck me that these terrifying but fascinating ideas were not absent from his own thought: modified, surely, but not entirely ignored as they were by other liberals, then and now. This essay is my attempt to ascertain how and why Berlin's ideas 'flash' like those of [Joseph] de Maistre, instead of seeming limp and dull like those of John Dewey and Karl Popper, two of the most estimable liberals of the twentieth century. Berlin's wit, which has ever remained his most attractive feature to me, is much closer to the aristocratic hauteur of the conservative Waugh than the bitter acerbity of Bertrand Russell. As the Queen Mother once reputedly said of Isaiah Berlin: he is 'such fun!' [1]

Such fun indeed. Which brings me to the last item in the book. When I showed Berlin's widow Aline a draft of the preface to the second volume of his letters, she observed that it made him sound too unremittingly serious, and failed to mention the enormous fun that his letters contain. She was right, and a similar point is sometimes made about his academic work by those who knew him in person. His principal published writings undoubtedly display great moral gravitas, as George Crowder observes, and taken by themselves they might give the initial impression to those less perceptive than James Chappel that Berlin was a solemn, portentous figure, lacking lightness of touch, humour, mischievousness. The truth is quite otherwise. He had a strongly playful streak, and delighted in what might be called intellectual parlour-games, great riffs of imaginative, often fantastical, speculation that buoyed up the company he was in (and everyone could join in). This, central, aspect of his character was not disconnected from his academic persona: they were two sides of the same coin. The recurrent game of differentiating cads from bounders was of a piece with the more serious, but still playful, exercise of separating hedgehogs from foxes.

Berlin's playfulness is well brought out by a number of the contributors to this book. But I wanted to finish the main text by exhibiting it directly in his own words, in a final course served at the end of the meal, *pour parfumer la bouche*. This could easily be done by citing passages from his letters, but I called to mind an occasion on which his sheer sense of fun spilled over into a published item. 'Elysian Schools' dates from 1958, when it appeared in the *Oxford Magazine*. Although authorship is not formally assigned there to Berlin, it is clear both from the text and from the editorial headnote that precedes it that, even if Berlin is not its only begetter, its paternity is to be laid principally at his door. Evidently Berlin's labours as an examiner in the Oxford Final Honour School of PPE (Philosophy, Politics and Economics) had struck a spark in his imagination that led to this elaborate fantasy about the examination performance

---

[1] http://triceratops.brynmawr.edu/dspace/handle/10066/672, accessed 21 October 2008.

of the historical figures about whom he was lecturing as Oxford's Professor of Social and Political Theory. One can well imagine an after-dinner game taking place along these lines; but for once, somewhat uncharacteristically, a version of it was committed to paper, and here concludes the main agenda.

Kay Graham quotes the end of a letter she received from Berlin in 1974: 'the longer I live the more passionately convinced I become that personal relations are all in all'. The longer I spend in Berlin's company, the more convinced I become that his particular form of delight in the play of ideas is one of the most distinctive and endearing ingredients in his own personal relations.

H.H.

Wolfson College, Oxford

October 2008

Acknowledgements

T HIS VOLUME has been prepared in the midst of much other work generated by the centenary of Isaiah Berlin's birth. That it has reached finished form at all is due in large part to the unwavering patience and support of my Assistant, Serena Moore, one of the authors who appear within. I have dedicated it to her, in both her Berlinian incarnations, with feeling. I also have a particular debt to another author, Jennifer Holmes, now co-editor with me of Berlin's letters, who generously and unstintingly came to my aid when the going was tough; her help, too, has been indispensable.

I should also like to thank the authors for either agreeing that I should reprint their contributions, or writing new ones; and my friend Peter Clifford, Editorial Director of Boydell & Brewer, who has been as understanding and imaginative in his role as my commissioning editor as I knew he would be. I am grateful, too, for other help of various kinds, to Jean Floud, Samuel Guttenplan, Kei Hiruta, John Penney, Philomen Probert, Jon Stallworthy and Josephine von Zitzewitz.

Some of the items in the book have previously been published elsewhere, and acknowledgement is due to the authors and publishers concerned. Details of previous publication are as follows:

The tributes by Noel Annan, Stuart Hampshire, Avishai Margalit, Charles Taylor and Bernard Williams were privately printed in Oxford as a pamphlet (together with an address by Roy Jenkins); with the exception of Charles

Taylor's tribute, and the addition of Aileen Kelly's (first published in the *New York Review of Books*, 18 December 1997), they also appeared in Isaiah Berlin, *The First and the Last* (New York: New York Review of Books, 1999)

Isaiah Berlin: *Oxford Magazine*, 20 February 1958

Joseph Brodsky: excerpt from 'Isaiah Berlin at Eighty', *New York Review of Books*, 17 August 1989

Ian Buruma: excerpt from *Voltaire's Coconuts, or Anglomania in Europe* (London: Weidenfeld & Nicolson, 1999)

Nicholas Henderson: excerpt from *Old Friends and Modern Instances* (London: Profile, 2000)

Michael Hughes: *Twentieth Century British History* 16 no. 2 (2005)

Michael Ignatieff: in *Berlin in Autumn: The Philosopher in Old Age* (*Occasional Papers of the Doreen B. Townsend Center for the Humanities*, 16) (Berkeley: Doreen B. Townsend Center for the Humanities, 2000); repr. with corrections in Alistair Horne (ed.), *Telling Lives: From W. B. Yeats to Bruce Chatwin* (London: Macmillan, 2000)

Anatoly Naiman: excerpts from *Ser* (Moscow: Eksmo, 2001)

Peter Oppenheimer: parts of his memoir appeared in *Oxford Menorah* (the magazine of the Oxford Jewish Congregation) no. 146 (Winter 1997)

Beata Połanowska-Sygulska: 'Isaiah: A Deeper Truth', *Oxford Magazine*, Eighth Week, Trinity Term 1998

Robert Wokler: part of his text appeared in *Proceedings of the American Philosophical Society* 150 no. 4 (December 2006)

Most of the photographs used as plates are by unknown photographers. Known photographers are named in the following list. I am grateful for permission (from the photographer except as stated in parentheses) to use their photographs.

Plate 30: Stephen Spender (Natasha Spender), © The Stephen Spender Photograph Archive
Plate 35: Douglas Glass (Christoper Glass)
Plate 37: Shepherd Building Group Ltd
Plate 38: Alice Kelikian
Plate 39: Sandra Burman
Plate 40: Dominique Nabokov
Plate 41: Billett Potter
Plate 42: Carolyn Djanogly
Plate 43: Mats Lund

The family trees were designed in the Department of Typography & Graphic Communication, University of Reading, by Andrew Twigg and Ross Waters.

Abbreviations

The following abbreviations are used in the notes for the titles of works by and about Isaiah Berlin (IB):

AC	*Against the Current* (1979)
CC	*Concepts and Categories* (1978)
CIB	Ramin Jahanbegloo, *Conversations with Isaiah Berlin* (1992)
CTH	*The Crooked Timber of Humanity* (1990)
FIB	*Freedom and Its Betrayal* (2002)
IBVL	The Isaiah Berlin Virtual Library, ed. Henry Hardy, http://berlin.wolf.ox.ac.uk/
L	*Liberty* (2002), incorporating *Four Essays on Liberty* (1969)
L1	[*Flourishing:*][1] *Letters 1928–1946* (2004)
L2	*Enlightening: Letters 1946–60* (2009)
MI	Michael Ignatieff, *Isaiah Berlin: A Life*
MSB	Oxford, Bodleian Library, [shelfmark]/[folio(s)], e.g. MSB 232/1–3 = MS. Berlin 232, folios 1–3
OM	*The One and the Many: Reading Isaiah Berlin*, ed. George Crowder and Henry Hardy (2007)
PI; PI2	*Personal Impressions* (1980; 2nd ed. 1998)
PIRA	*Political Ideas in the Romantic Age* (2006)
POI	*The Power of Ideas* (2000)
PSM	*The Proper Study of Mankind* (1997)
RR	*The Roots of Romanticism* (1999)
RT2	*Russian Thinkers* (2nd ed. 2008)
SM	*The Soviet Mind* (2004)
SR	*The Sense of Reality* (1996)
TCE	*Three Critics of the Enlightenment* (2000)

The dates in parentheses are those of the first UK editions. The main (arabic) pagination of all editions of these works, apart from the successive editions of PI and RT,[2] is the same. There is some variation, however, in roman pagination. This affects, in particular, Berlin's preface to CC, where the pagination in the first UK edition is used. Unpublished letters are cited by date, where this is known to the editor, who has also added references for quotations, when not already provided, and if he has been able to track down their source.

[1] The US hardback edition omits the bracketed part of the title.
[2] In RT2 a concordance of the old and new page numbering is provided, as in the case of *Four Essays on Liberty* and *Liberty* (the latter collection incorporating the former).

In Search of Isaiah Berlin

Evan Zimroth

I

T O M E, there is something unfathomable in the following declaration, made by Mendel Berlin in 1946 to his son Isaiah:

> I started several times to write down my autobiography [...] for the benefit of my son, but during the war I could not concentrate sufficiently; now when the extinction of nearly all the members of [our] family by the Nazis has been confirmed, I feel the necessity for these records is real; the living link [...] is practically only myself.

I know what he means, of course; there is utter clarity about that. But even though I have read of countless atrocities perpetrated against the Jews in the Holocaust, I still cannot fathom how a father writes these words to his child. How, in what tone, with what explanation, does one say that the murder of one's entire family is confirmed? Something in that long sentence will always remain a deep mystery.

Mendel Berlin's striking sentence is at the start (and at the heart) of a long, fulsome account of the history of the Berlin family,[1] or the Berlin–Volshonok–Schneerson–Zuckerman–Apter family, with all its interrelationships, marriages (good and bad), schooling, religious behaviour, travels, business deals, loves and quarrels, dating back to 1750. The narrative moves around the Pale of Settlement to Riga, Petrograd, Moscow, and back to Riga, and ends in the safe haven of Britain. One surviving remnant of the large family – Mendel, his wife Marie, their son Isaiah – had been refugees in that safe haven since 1921. For the father, it was imperative after the devastation of the war that the son know his heritage.

Isaiah knew that his relatives had died, even if he didn't know exactly how many or in what manner.[2] He has to have been aware that, had his own family remained in Riga rather than emigrating to the UK in 1921, he himself would probably have been murdered along with his parents and the entire Jewish community of Riga.

His death, like that of his relatives, would probably have occurred during one of two 'actions', on 30 November and 8 December 1941, when the Jews incarcerated in the Riga ghetto were marched to the killing fields of Rumbula,

---

[1] Published in the present volume as an appendix.
[2] See 265 below, note 2.

outside Riga, and massacred *en masse*. On those two days alone, about 25,000 Jews were killed. (Thousands more, in smaller groups, were killed at Bikernieki, another killing field on the outskirts of Riga.) The Latvian historian of the Holocaust, Andrew Ezergailis, describes in more horrifying graphic detail than any other I've encountered what those murders were like and how they were carried out.[1] It makes for unbearable reading, and I cannot bring myself to describe it any further. As Isaiah said, 'What can one possibly say about so great a horror?'[2]

Mendel's response is as tight-lipped as his son's, but his urge to pass on to his son details of the family's heritage is his way of anchoring the Berlins to history. The first thing this hard-working, modest father does in his memoir is to swell with pride in his *yikhes*, the Yiddish term for ancestry, DNA. Mendel clearly values his *yikhes* – the intelligence, learning and achievements of his own and his wife's ancestors – and wishes to bequeath appreciation of this heritage to his son. From a Jewish point of view, it is a glorious heritage. In fact, had he been so inclined, Isaiah could have claimed descent from Jewish aristocracy. Mendel traces the family back to the great eighteenth-century religious leader Rabbi Shneur Zalman of Liadi, the founder of Lubavitch Hasidism, a religious movement that, as Mendel accurately says, 'drew hundreds of thousands of pupils and admirers, and which split [...] Jewry into two sects, the Misnagdim and Chassidim'. Rabbi Shneur Zalman thus pitted himself against, and was greatly persecuted by, that era's other great religious leader, the (Lithuanian) Vilna Gaon, who tried, unsuccessfully, to diminish and eradicate the Hasidim as heretics.[3] Mendel's own grandfather, called the Lubliner Rav, was also a *gaon*, a man of such prodigious Talmud learning that he was considered one of the greatest scholars of his generation. Mendel hopes – indeed, assumes – that Isaiah has inherited his great-grandfather's intelligence and capacity for scholarship.

The most famous descendant of Rabbi Zalman of Liadi (other than Isaiah) is the seventh Lubavitcher Rebbe, Menachem Mendel Schneerson of Brooklyn, who died in 1994 and was promptly proclaimed the Messiah by a breakaway Lubavitch group who still await his resurrection and the ingathering to Jerusalem of the exiles of the Jewish diaspora. He and Isaiah were distant cousins and perhaps had more in common than Isaiah thought: Schneerson,

---

[1] *The Holocaust in Latvia 1941–1944* (Riga and Washington, 1996).

[2] CIB 21.

[3] For a thorough account of the controversy, which continues to some extent to this day, see Immanuel Etkes, *The Gaon of Vilna: The Man and His Image* (Berkeley, 2002). For the theological underpinnings of the controversy, I recommend the outstanding account by Allan Nadler, *The Faith of the Mithnagdim: Rabbinic Responses to Hasidic Rapture* (Baltimore, 1997). See also the introductory chapters of Michael Ignatieff's probably unsurpassable biography, *Isaiah Berlin: A Life* (London, 1998).

far from being intellectually narrow or cloistered, studied mathematics at the Sorbonne and worked in Paris as an electrical engineer. He was greatly revered not only for his towering talmudic learning but also for his practical wisdom. As a Lubavitcher Rebbe, he did not, of course, assimilate to the common culture, but then neither did Oxford dons.[1]

Mendel describes his own childhood as drenched in traditional Jewish learning. Sent to *cheder* from the age of 3 or 4, and then, as he got older, educated by private tutors, he divided his time into systematic study of Talmud and rabbinics and the traditional pattern of synagogue attendance and thrice daily prayer. Luckily for Mendel, though, his mother had a strong interest in secular European culture, especially music and literature, interests she was allowed to follow because she was only a girl and therefore not required, as Jewish men traditionally were, to devote herself to Talmud only. She had a particular love for Russian literature and studied the language to read novels in the original. She passed on these interests to her son Mendel, who also learned to love Russian literature (and read it on the sly when he was abroad), and who was the first in the family to learn and use English. In this way Mendel acquired the linguistic skills that allowed him to emigrate with his family in 1921. It is interesting to think that, had Mendel's mother not been passionate about Russian literature, Mendel would not have acquired fluency in so many languages, and the Berlin family would have been less able to leave Riga when the political and economic situation had made it increasingly desperate for Jews. In a sense, the Russian novel saved Isaiah's life.

Isaiah's mother was also fiercely Jewish, but in a political rather than a scholarly way. Lacking the classical Jewish training of Mendel, Marie Berlin was an early and ardent Zionist, a fan of Jabotinsky, and more committed to Jewish practices than either her husband or her son. It was important to her, for example, that her family observe *kashrut*, the Jewish dietary laws; so while Marie visits the Riga relatives and Isaiah and his father are on their own, Isaiah reassures her that 'so far all our meals have been Jewish and not "exotic" ' – presumably not *treif* or non-kosher.[2] Marie also diligently observed the Sabbath and holidays. When Isaiah returned briefly from New York to England in 1940, Mendel greeted him in Oxford, but Marie 'stuck to her principles and would not travel' on the Sabbath or the Jewish holiday of Simchat Torat, and so joined

---

[1] For a full discussion of the split within the Lubavitch movement caused by those claiming messiahship for Schneerson, see David Berger, *The Rebbe, The Messiah, and the Scandal of Orthodox Indifference* (London, 2001). It would have been amusing to hear Isaiah's reaction to the claim that his distant cousin was the Messiah and would be resurrected after death.

[2] Early September 1937, L1 253.

them later. Mendel, despite his earlier intense religious training, was by this time apparently completely unobservant.

With these parents, as he observes in an unpublished letter[1] to his biographer Michael Ignatieff, there was no way Isaiah could evade his Jewishness, even had he wanted to. That was true: it's highly unlikely that anyone ever took him for something other than what he was. In the same letter, Isaiah claims he was always and for ever completely comfortable with his Jewishness, that it never provided him with a moment's anxiety at being a cultural outsider in Britain, and that, as far as he knew, it never evoked the slightest derogatory comment in the ultra-WASP circles of Oxford and London in which he travelled. As for those British and American Jews who try to 'pass', Isaiah mocks them with the acronym OTAG, members of 'the Order of Trembling Amateur Gentiles'. He acknowledges this might be a tad anti-Semitic of him, but so be it. It's an inside joke Isaiah is comfortable enough to share with the *goyim*. You can see his disarming smile and politically incorrect shrug.

He is charmingly confessional in this letter about how, from the moment he arrived in Britain in 1921, he'd always felt comfortable and easy in his new culture. Aside from a refusal to change his name from Isaiah to something less Jewish – John, Robert and Henry were suggested – in his early days, at least, he did everything he could to assimilate and fit in. If this is indeed the case, then he could thank, at least in part, his father's Anglophilia. According to Isaiah, Mendel was 'a fanatic Anglophile'.[2] From the time he stepped off the boat as a pudgy twelve-year-old, Isaiah was schooled by his father to be a proper English child. Mendel tells of teaching him English slang by treating him to a toffee apple to illustrate the meaning of 'swop'. Mendel also goes out of his way to use an English word in his memoir when the Jewish idiom would have been just as clear and even more accurate. When Mendel describes his grandfather, the revered talmudic authority, he says that the man was so dedicated to scholarship he barely left his study even for the synagogue, 'or as one would say now the Chapel'. Even the most acculturated British Jew is unlikely to call a synagogue a chapel. But, according to Mendel, this eminent grandfather, the Lubliner Rav who held 'the most illustrious position among Polish and Lithuanian Jews', attended not *shul* but 'Chapel'. Not quite OTAG, but close.

Aside from passing on his Anglophilia to his beloved son, a gift that obviously helped the young Isaiah acculturate quickly to his new surroundings, Mendel, as his memoir shows, was gifted in other ways that Isaiah was less quick to acknowledge. An obviously excellent linguist, Mendel writes a perfectly fluent and serviceable English, only occasionally lapsing into Yiddishisms ('I could not get so quickly the visa to London'). He was also an extremely savvy

[1] Dated 10 January 1997.
[2] CIB 6.

businessman. Initially, Mendel entered the family timber-export business, and early on, with his linguistic and other skills, became the manager for international exports, especially to England. Later, with inherited money and his general business acumen, he was able to take control of the business, which had become 'one of the leading timber firms in Riga'. He branched out into the Russian railway business, invested in plywood, shipped it to London, and thus was able to convert roubles to sterling, a very shrewd move that enabled the Berlin family, years later, to live comfortably as soon as they arrived in the UK. Mendel's international timber business continued to flourish ('It became a very lucrative business right until the beginning of the war in 1939'), and as a 'financier' he then started a bristle business.

As a businessman, Mendel followed some Jewish practices that would have seemed strange at Oxford, and probably to Isaiah as well. After his marriage, for example, and as he prepares to expand his business dealings, Mendel pays a visit to the current Lubavitcher Rebbe 'to consult him whether to travel round Europe to sell timber. I got the Rebbe's consent to do so.' To the non-Orthodox world, this visit sounds odd and suggests that Mendel was a *shtetl* Jew, hopelessly immeshed in piety. But whether Isaiah understood it or not, his father's visit to the Rebbe was not mere sentimentalism. The Lubavitcher Rebbe was probably extremely well versed in international trade, would have known both the legal regulations and what we would call the 'players', and would have been able both to advise Mendel and probably even to network for him. Through his secretary, he probably arranged letters of introduction for Mendel, as he would have for others seeking his counsel. This is not an uncommon practice amongst the ultra-Orthodox, even today.

Isaiah, however, left his biographer with the clear impression that his father was timid and unprepossessing, and he labelled the memoir (which he read only late in life at Ignatieff's urging) 'pure sentimental return to roots'.[1] To read Mendel's memoir, however, reveals something different. Perhaps Mendel had a low tolerance for financial risk (which would have certainly been justified by the historical circumstances). Nevertheless he was far-sighted and creative enough with his business deals and investments to ensure the family's well-being, even when they were refugees in England. This is a clear example of a son not crediting his father's achievements.

Isaiah seems to have been deliberately clueless about his father's skills, and for all his acumen in the history of ideas, seems not to have wanted to examine his own history critically. In interviews, when talking about his family's experiences in Petrograd during the Russian Revolution, Isaiah paints a comfortable picture. 'My family [...] was not touched,' he says; '[...] we did not starve, we

---

[1] MI 13.

had just enough food and fuel to continue.'[1] In the memoir, however, Mendel tells a different story: to bring home food for his son he once walked three miles in melting snow in the middle of the night, carrying a heavy sack of food 'on which our survival depended'. Routinely, too, both parents went without food to feed Isaiah, so much so that people in the food queues 'used to make offensive remarks [...] like "With such a fat boy you can scarcely need more food."' It is true that no one literally starved (and in later photos both parents look prosperously fat), but that the Berlin family experienced deprivations there's no doubt. These deprivations Isaiah apparently was fully shielded from, and later he seemed never to want to know about them. It could not have been pleasant, though, for Isaiah to find out what a fat little boy he was while his parents went hungry.

These discrepancies aside, Mendel's portrait of the family, its tribulations and its wholehearted assimilation into British culture keeps its bright focus on the brilliance of the son. Isaiah is the classic beloved Jewish son – cosseted, fed, over-protected, doted on – almost to parody. They loved him to death, and while Isaiah seems to have repaid his mother's devotion with his own, he appears to have kept his distance from his father. In the one photo I've seen of the two men together (taken in 1947, the year after Mendel began the memoir, and reproduced in Ignatieff's biography), Isaiah walks slightly ahead of his father, as if embarrassed to be seen with him. And maybe the father was indeed embarrassing (at least to the first-generation son, eager to assimilate). Mendel was short, even shorter than Isaiah; he was very fat, and probably at home spoke with Yiddish inflections ('Oy vey'). Isaiah seems to have dislodged his father rather easily. Mendel, for one thing, always had to earn a living, and so his attentions to Isaiah were necessarily limited. But Marie attached herself to her son like a barnacle and worries in her unpublished diary about whether she should leave Oxford (where she hovers over Isaiah) to spend more time with her husband.[2] (Yes, she should have.)

Mendel's portrait of the family *yikhes* is certainly rich, fully detailed, and (to me, if not to Isaiah) terribly endearing. Mendel obviously laboured over his memoir (he must have used notes brought from Riga, since his descriptions of family connections are so elaborate), and he deliberately uses a formal, almost stilted and old-fashioned (but perfectly functional) prose style. Isaiah inherited some of these virtues, somewhat modernised and changed: he, too, has a seemingly voluminous memory for detail (like his great-grandfather, as Mendel hoped), and, like his father, composes in long, complex sentences that mimic the meanderings of thought. One easily 'hears' each man thinking.

Mendel, too – like Isaiah – has a gift for the small, telling detail. He tells

[1] CIB 10.
[2] Entry dated 13 September 1939.

us that he was afraid of dogs (it was 'unbecoming' for a religious boy to play with dogs, so he never learned how), and was at first hopelessly inept at courting Isaiah's mother. (Unlike his son, who seems to have been a bit retarded in these matters, Mendel was married and therefore presumably fully sexually active by the time he was twenty-three.) On his first journey 'abroad' in 1904, he visits Germany and is naive enough to be shocked that urbane German Jews employ *goyim* to open and close their umbrellas on a rainy Sabbath, it being forbidden to construct an abode (as, by rabbinic analogy, opening an umbrella is deemed to do). Mendel, I'm sure, quickly learned that many Jews – particularly in large, urban centres, as much in nineteenth-century Odessa as in twenty-first century London or Manhattan – can be both religiously observant and quite fully integrated into modern life. In any case, by the time he brought his family to London, as Isaiah reports to Ignatieff, Mendel was 'totally emancipated'.

So although Mendel's memoir is sometimes confusing (all those relatives!) and even often tendentious, still, it's a great gift to his son. I am a little disappointed in Isaiah that he didn't value it more, blinded perhaps by the usual father–son discomfort and the often-seen indifference of the 'new' generation to the 'old country'. There may have been another reason, though, for Isaiah's unease with the memoir: it is overwhelmingly anxious. There are so many stories of business deals won and lost and won again, of fires wiping out investments, of families on the run, apartments searched, interrogations and arrests. And of course the Holocaust is always in the background: the world that vanished in the ghettos, massacre pits and concentration camps hovers in a ghostly way behind even the most charming of anecdotes. Always Mendel shows himself to be one step ahead of disaster. Even in England he never loses the sense that a pogrom (or worse) is just outside the door: 'That psychological state of getting nervous at the sound of a car stopping outside at night continued for many years afterwards in the security of London,' he writes, 'and I used to be drawn to the window to investigate.'

II

Even though I think Isaiah is unjustly dismissive of his father and the family history, I've become quite captivated by him – and Berliniana are, for me, a new and marvellous adventure. Aside from the dynamics of Isaiah's Anglo-Jewish identity and his fervent, long-standing support of Zionism, I am also very taken by his personal charm (like practically everyone who has ever come across him) and also by something his biographers don't often mention: his sense of humour. Witnessed in person it must have been much more wicked, but even in print the humour comes across. Mocking over-assimilated Jews is both funny and an example of politically incorrect bravado, almost shocking after the Holocaust.

Even Isaiah's separation of people into hedgehogs and foxes started as a sort of intellectual game.

But what I think has affected me the most in my brief acquaintance with Berlin's thought is what both infuriates and impresses many people who knew him: Isaiah's capacity, even obsession, always to see the other point of view and accord it validity. Whether you call him 'emollient' (Ignatieff's well-chosen word), a 'fence-sitter' (I've often heard this) or, more philosophically, a liberal, Isaiah's generosity of spirit and avoidance of dogma seems to be a good way to live your life and conduct your intimate friendships. Even though there's a tinge of anxiety here (inherited from his father?), this ability to see the other side might even get you through (as it did Isaiah) to a prosperous, congenial old age.

His tolerance had limits – Hitler, the Gulag – and this I appreciate as well. (Isaiah died before suicide bombs, 9/11 and Islamic fanaticism, which would have further tested and strained his tolerance.) His Zionism is unwavering.[1] As is his support for the Second World War. By 1940, without much information, Isaiah is aware that the Jews of Europe are in peril, and by 1941 he is unequivocal about wishing to be involved. Complaining that he is being held back from posts where he might be useful to European Jewry, he says, 'I passionately wanted to be identified in some way with this war', and then again, 'I wish to help to win the war.'[2] Some issues don't lend themselves to ambiguity. For all his chronic introspection, anxiety and self-criticism, Isaiah had no trouble discriminating between civilised behaviour and outright murderousness.

These are just the introductory thoughts of a newcomer to the Berlin archive. But because of the 2009 centenary, I've had to read in the capacious Berlin library, and by now I've begun to hear Isaiah's idiosyncratic tone and to place his writings within his autobiography. I particularly enjoy his letters, which are quirky and intimate, richly anchored in his complex social and political worlds. In the letters is enough commentary on politics and literature to fill volumes, and they are stylistically impressive as well. Isaiah must be one of the twentieth century's great letter-writers; I hope others come to see him this way. I've also had generous access to unpublished material and have even been invited to sit at kitchen tables, listening to correspondence, personal anecdotes and stories. I've begun to think that everyone in Britain has a personal Berlin story, often delivered dramatically, with impersonations. Unlike his father, who comes across in the memoir as a solitary figure – he truly was a refugee – working

---

[1] See his wonderful defence of Zionism in the essay 'Zionist Politics in Wartime Washington', L1 663–93. About Zionism, Berlin is enormously resolute and intensely personal, even as his gratitude to England leads him to try to exonerate Britain from anti-Semitism.

[2] L1 355, 357.

desperately to keep his wife and son afloat and comfortable, Isaiah was gregarious, even garrulous. He had torrents of friends on several continents, and kept all of them abreast of his whereabouts via his voluminous letter-writing, not to mention his lectures and essays. You could play a parlour-game with his name: I've done it and discovered that half the people I know were either his students at Oxford, or had lunch with him at Headington, or knew him at Harvard or in Washington or in New York City. Isaiah's reach is incredible, and the world is apparently full of his Hasidim, his followers. His father would have been pleased but not surprised. Just like his great-grandfather, he might have said, the Lubliner Rav.

TRIBUTES

When the annual Isaiah Berlin Lecture series at Wolfson College, Oxford, was inaugurated in May 1991 by Stephen Jay Gould, Berlin took the stage beforehand to thank the College, and told the audience of his reaction when he was invited to the lecture:

When I first received the invitation, I misread it: it seemed to me to say 'Sir Isaiah Berlin Memorial Lecture'. At this point I said to myself 'Déjà? They don't expect me to live to the end of May?' But then I read it again: I'd read the word 'Inaugural' as 'Memorial'. At this point I remembered a story which I should like to tell you.

Once upon a time there was a beggar – a very persistent beggar who was rather good at extracting sums of money out of kindly or gullible people, which enabled him to live. There was a man in his town of extreme hard-heartedness, a heart of stone, who never gave anything to anybody. The beggar went to see him and told him the story of a widow who had six children who were bare-foot and starving – the widow herself suffered from every known disease. The squalor, the poverty and the misery of the home was something unbelievable. Even this man, even his hard heart, was touched, and he gave the beggar a sum of money. At some point he decided to find out how the money was spent, so he made enquiries about the widow. He found that the widow was in fact the beggar's wife. He then sent for the beggar and said, 'You said she was a widow, but she is your wife!' To which the beggar said, 'Why should you mind my still being alive?' Those are precisely my feelings now. When I read the invitation again and saw it was not 'Memorial', I breathed again. But I must say I couldn't have asked for a more distinguished body of mourners.

Noel Annan's address was given at a Memorial Service in the Hampstead Synagogue in London on 14 January 1998; the addresses by Stuart Hampshire, Avishai Margalit and Bernard Williams at a Commemoration in the Sheldonian Theatre, Oxford, on 21 March 1998. The remaining tributes were delivered on 28 January 1998 at 'An American Remembrance' of Berlin held at the British Embassy in Washington.

Noel Annan

WHEN I HEARD that Isaiah Berlin had died, I sat down and read the letters we had written each other since 1950, and he lived again. He wrote as he talked, and he was the most dazzling talker of his generation. Strangers might hardly understand a word because his tongue had to sprint to keep up with the pace of his thoughts. Ideas, similes, metaphors cascaded over each other. His talk was sustained by a fabulous memory for names, events and the motives of the participants in his stories. It was like watching a pageant. As Dr Johnson said of Richard Savage, it was 'in no time of Mr Savage's life any part of his character to be the first of the company that desired to separate'.[1] At New College and All Souls he talked until his exhausted guest tottered to bed, only to find Berlin sitting on the end of it, unwilling to bring the evening to an end. On the historic occasion when he called on Anna Akhmatova they talked straight through the night.

No one else was remotely like him. Of course he had charm, but he had more than that. He was a Magus, a magician when he spoke, and it was for his character and personality as much as for his published works that so many honours fell upon him. The *Evening Standard* spoke truth when it said 'it is heartening to see the wave of respectful sadness that has met the death of Sir Isaiah Berlin [...] The enormous regard in which he was clearly held shows that intellectuals can still be prized as civilising influences in modern Britain.'[2] He was loved by people with whom he had nothing in common – millionaires, obscure writers, world-famous musicians, public figures and young unknown scholars, to whom he listened. Whatever the circle, he civilised it; and the world is a little less civilised now that he has left it.

Generosity came naturally to him. He was never sneaky or malevolent as a critic. Indeed he tried too hard, perhaps, to avoid giving offence. 'I enjoy being able to praise,'[3] he said. He never intrigued to meet the geniuses of his time – Freud, Einstein, Virginia Woolf, Russell, Pasternak, Stravinsky – and he had no shame in admitting that he was greatly excited when he did meet them. His oldest friends, Stuart Hampshire or Stephen Spender, were especially dear to him. Yet he had an eye for human failings and noted feet of clay, even of people he esteemed. He did not censure, but he did not condone ungentle behaviour or sexual exhibitionism. 'I was acutely uncomfortable,' he wrote to me, 'in the presence of [...] Beaverbrook, Cherwell, Radcliffe and [...]

---

[1] Samuel Johnson, *An Account of the Life of Mr Richard Savage, Son of the Earl Rivers* (London, 1744): in Johnson's *The Lives of the Most Eminent English Poets*, ed. Roger Lonsdale (Oxford, 2006), iii 133.

[2] 'Berlin's Legacy', *Evening Standard*, 7 November 1997, 11.

[3] Letter of 2 October 1978.

Driberg.'[1] People who rejected equality as a goal were deeply unsympathetic to him. Equality had to give way often to liberty, but so did liberty sometimes to equality. For instance, he thought that the price England paid for the public schools was too high.

Nicolas Nabokov accused him of liking bores too much. But then Isaiah was meticulous in obeying the obligations of a scholar. No one was ever turned away who came to him genuinely wishing to discuss a problem. To watch him at Mishkenot Sha'ananim in Jerusalem, spending hours with those who queued to seek his advice, was to realise that he honoured anyone in search of truth. Those who have never believed, he wrote of the days when the young Oxford philosophers met with Austin and Ayer, that they were discovering for the first time some new truth that might have profound influence upon philosophy, 'those who have never been under the spell of this kind of illusion, even for a short while, have not known true intellectual happiness'.[2]

Very few people are able to write unforgettably about liberty. Rousseau did; John Stuart Mill did; and, in our own times, Schumpeter and E. M. Forster did. But, as Forster once said of himself in a parody of Landor: 'I warmed both hands before the fire of life; / And put it out.'[3] Isaiah made it blaze. He took the unfashionable view that liberty meant not being impeded by others. He distrusted Rousseau's and Hegel's theory of positive freedom as a perversion of common sense. To deny free will – to believe in the inevitability of a historical process – to portray man as imprisoned by the impersonal forces of history – that ran against our deepest experience. He believed that the creation of the State of Israel proved history is not predetermined. Israel owed its existence to Weizmann, yet all Weizmann's schemes were swept away by fortuitous events. And what could be less inevitable than the survival of Britain in 1940? To Berlin, the very methods that Marxists, economists and sociologists used prevented them from discovering what is at the heart of men and women. He distrusted technocrats in government and sapient Reports with their self-confident proposals for restructuring institutions. That was why he did not pontificate on daily issues. Monetarism, social security schemes were not for him. He disappointed President Kennedy by not advancing views on the number needed of ICBMs.

But there was one public issue on which he left no one in doubt. Above all, Isaiah was a Jew, and never forgave those who forgot to conceal their anti-Semitism, the nastier ways of snubs, pinpricks, acts of exclusion which we Gentiles inflict upon Jews, and in so doing defile ourselves. He was a Zionist

[1] Letter of 3 January 1979.
[2] PI2 145.
[3] E. M. Forster, 'Landor at Sea' (1938), in *Turnstile One: A Literary Miscellany from the New Statesman and Nation*, ed. V. S. Pritchett (London, 1948), 16.

precisely because he felt that, however well Jews were treated and accepted by the country they lived in, they felt uneasy and insecure. That was why they needed a country of their own where Jews could live like other nations. As he lay dying, he declared that the partition of the Holy Land was the only solution to give Palestinians rights to their land and give Israel Jerusalem as its capital city with the Muslim holy places under a Muslim authority, and an Arab quarter under UN protection. He never felt the smallest difficulty in being loyal to Judah and loyal to Britain. When he worked during the war in Washington, he told American Zionists that he was the servant of the British government – but its servant, not its conscript. At any time, he could resign if he decided British policy was unforgivable. He was proud to belong to Britain, to that country which Weizmann had praised for its moderation, dislike of extremes, a humane democracy.

There was another claimant for his loyalty – Oxford. He thought he owed it a debt. He paid that debt when, against the advice of his most intimate friends, he agreed to become head of a new Oxford college. Who can doubt that it was Isaiah's personality that convinced Mac Bundy of the Ford Foundation and Isaac and Leonard Wolfson, renowned for their princely generosity, to build and endow a new college with Isaiah as President? President, not Master. The Master of Wolfson sounded to Isaiah too much like a Scottish laird, and he did not fancy himself in a kilt. Many of the chores he left to the faithful Michael Brock; but it was Isaiah who negotiated the deal with the University and strangled some dingy proposals for shackling the new place. And it was Isaiah who travelled 4,000 miles to interview architects, select materials and convince the sixty Fellows with barely a dissenting voice.

He was a man of invincible modesty. But for Henry Hardy we would never have had his collected works. He genuinely believed that he was overrated and deserved few of the honours he was given. He had a dislike, 'amounting to pathological hatred, of personal publicity,' he wrote to me; it was 'like a terror of bats or spiders'.[1] 'I am not a public figure in the sense in which, say, A. J. P. Taylor, or Graham Greene, or Arthur Schlesinger, or Arnold Toynbee, or Kenneth Clark are'; nor 'a kind of ideologue, identified with a movement, like Laski or Tawney or Cole, or even Oakeshott – more like Butterfield (at most), not quite as bad as what Crossman and a good many others thought and think me to be – a well-disposed, amiable rattle'.[2] For years he had no entry in *Who's Who*, until he found the entry form he had left lying about had been filled in by Maurice Bowra, with scandalous fictitious achievements. Then he gave in.

To have lived without music would have been to him a nightmare. Unthinkable to live without Bach, unendurable without Beethoven and Schubert. He

[1] Letter of 27 March 1979.
[2] Letter of 12 May 1979.

loved Verdi for the uninhibited tunes and for Verdi's hatred of aristocratic bru-
tality and tyranny. No one, he thought, had ever played the Beethoven posthumous quartets like the Busch ensemble. He admitted that Toscanini was not
the man for the thick brew of Wagner; but when one saw Toscanini as well as
heard him the authority was such that, so he wrote to me, 'this and only this
was the truth – the intensity and the seriousness and the sublime *terribilità*
totally subdued one'.[1] Walter, Klemperer and Mahler and the luxuriant valleys
of Furtwängler, yes – but Toscanini was Everest – compared with him he said
the rest were not fit to tie his shoelaces, mere Apennines covered with villas. Yet
in his later years he found a friend, an intellectual as well as a profound musician, in Alfred Brendel; and he and his old friend Isaac Stern have honoured
him today.[2]

He was at his happiest in a small group of intimate friends in Oxford colleges
or sitting in a corner of the Russian Tea Room on 57th Street a few blocks down
from the offices of the *New York Review of Books* with Robert Silvers, Stuart
Hampshire and the Lowells. In Oxford as a bachelor – in the days before the
war he was always called Shaya, renowned as the most amusing young don in
Oxford – in those days his door was always open. Colleagues, pupils, friends
from London dropped in to gossip. He loved gossip. An election to a chair in
Oxford or Cambridge would inspire him to give a dramatic performance of
the proceedings. The treachery of Bloggs, the craven behaviour of Stiggins, the
twitterings of the outside electors, and when it came to the vote, the volte-face,
the defection of those you had imagined were your closest allies. Brought up
to imagine that such proceedings were sacred and secret, priggish Cambridge
visitors such as myself reeled.

What made those excursions into fantasy all the more enchanting was
Isaiah's irrepressible sense of humour. It was not English humour. It came from
the Russian part of his make-up; from Gogol, from Chekhov. He loved jokes.
He loved games. Who was a hedgehog, who was a fox? What is the difference
between a cad and a bounder? When others were maddened by the perverse,
egoistic, self-satisfied speeches in a college meeting, Isaiah revelled in them – to
him they revealed the perennial eccentricity of human beings. Let none of us,
however, be deceived. The lot of human beings, he saw, was tragic. And why?
They are made of crooked timber.

As the years pass, bachelor life in college becomes exhausting, and in 1956 the
greatest stroke of good fortune that ever befell him occurred. He married Aline.
She transformed his life without changing it – if the contradiction be permitted.

---

[1] Letter of 17 October 1974.
[2] Isaac Stern played the Sarabande from Bach's Partita for Violin no. 2 in D minor,
   BWV 1004; Alfred Brendel the second movement (*andante sostenuto*) of Schubert's
   Sonata in B flat major, D 960.

She gave him what he had always needed: love. As solicitous as she was beautiful, she caressed his existence in Albany, in Portofino and in Headington. Like him, she disliked ostentation. Aline had been a great competitor when she was golf champion of France, but she never competed with Isaiah. She was there as the setting in which he shone – perpetually anxious that all should go well for him, not for her. She brought him a family, her children Michel Strauss, Peter and Philippe Halban, and her young Gunzbourg cousins, for whom he was a new uncle. To the delight of Isaiah's friends, they created a new persona, calling him 'Ton-ton Isaïe'.

And now he is gone. If I have not spoken sufficiently of his defence of liberty or pluralism, or of his detestation of cruelty and ruthlessness, it is because I speak of him as a friend. Political thinkers and intellectuals, so I believe, have not yet understood how disquieting is his contention that good ends conflict. Isaiah Berlin was original, and he is as hard to come to terms with as Machiavelli or Hume. All I can say is that he seems to me to have offered the truest and most moving interpretation of life that my own generation made.

And I must add this. I owe everything to my teachers. They taught me to learn and, if I got above myself, how much more I had to learn. I was never, of course, one of Isaiah's students, but I never failed to learn from him. He taught me to think more clearly, to feel more deeply, to hope, and to put my trust in life.

Stuart Hampshire

I N 1935 IN LLANDUDNO, North Wales, in Boots' Circulating Library, I came across Kafka's *The Great Wall of China, and Other Pieces*, just translated by Edwin and Willa Muir,[1] and I was overwhelmed. Isaiah had mentioned Kafka in the magazine *Oxford Outlook*, which he had co-edited with Richard Crossman.[2] An undergraduate friend, Benedict Nicolson, introduced us so that we could talk about Kafka.

After that we persisted in talking, more or less continuously, for sixty-two years, except for four war years, when Isaiah was in America. We gradually, in those pre-war years in All Souls, formed the habit of discussing anything interesting that either of us experienced and of checking up on any changes in our opinions and in our loyalties, right up until the last week of his life. In the 1930s there existed among politicians, writers, intellectuals, in Britain and in Europe,

---

[1] London, 1933.
[2] I have not been able to trace such a mention in any of IB's contributions to this magazine, which he co-edited in 1931–2 with Richard Goodman. Richard Crossman was co-editor (not with IB) of the *New Oxford Outlook* 1933–5, but there are no (signed) articles by IB in this successor magazine. Ed.

a culture of paranoia, a feeling of being haunted by a spectre of catastrophe, of a final settling of accounts that was to come. Kafka had diagnosed this mood of anxiety very exactly. But Isaiah, in his room between the Hawksmoor Towers of All Souls, with his old-fashioned HMV gramophone with its immense horn for better sound, sharpening his fibre needles, playing the overture to Rossini's *La scala di seta* or *La gazza ladra*, or Schnabel's Beethoven or the Busch Quartet, Isaiah certainly did not share this sad fear of the world, whether the Marxist forms of fear, or the Freudian forms, or in the subtle form of philosophical scepticism. It soon emerged that he loved England, Oxford University, Salzburg, Italy, the London Library and All Souls College. He was boundlessly benevolent, approachable, gentle, constantly telling stories, and sweeping one along with them. In his All Souls rooms he kept over the mantelpiece a painting, the work of an undergraduate friend, Giles Robertson, which showed him as a small child dangerously perched on a windowsill over the street. Far away from Riga he was utterly at home in pre-war Oxford, happily involved in College affairs and with devoted pupils. In his thought he was at that time, and he remained, a convinced and calm empiricist, who insisted that the stuff of our day-to-day experience, whether in personal experience or in politics, is the true stuff of reality, and that behind the phases of history there lurks no hidden plot either of punishment or of redemption. He took the furniture of the world, both the natural and the social furniture, medium-sized objects on a human scale, to be entirely real and to exist more or less as we perceive them. The Nazis, steadily advancing towards us in those years, were just a manifest and unmitigated evil, and the evil was not for him a sign of something beyond itself, needing to be interpreted, but simply a hideous reality to be resisted. The appeasers, both of the left and the right, with their different theories of history, were for him just wrong, wrong through ignoring natural feelings.

Apart from the Nazis and Zionism and socialism, we talked, for much of the time, about the new analytical philosophy. Typically, it was in Isaiah's room that a group of younger philosophers met on Thursday evenings during term. He was the co-ordinating, animating centre. He always resisted the schematisation of language, and of the sources of knowledge, which logical positivism required. He was always a pluralist in epistemology as later in the theory of politics and of morality. At least two of his journal articles, strikingly original in their time, are still important half a century later. There was no great discontinuity when after the war he turned away from academic philosophy to the history of ideas. To reconstruct and to reanimate the images and fantasies that lay behind the arguments of abstract thinkers was a constant passion of his, and in lectures on Russian thinkers and on the Enlightenment and the Counter-Enlightenment, both in Oxford and on the BBC, he created his own public. I remember standing with him on the lawn at All Souls reading some of the letters, unprecedented in number, which the BBC had received from listeners who had been fascinated by the very various personalities he had conjured up for them in his headlong style. This response to his lectures was repeated in universities all over America as well as in Oxford. Like William James, whom he greatly admired, his thought was naturally rhetorical and declamatory, and he liked to let himself go in his eulogies, and particularly in celebrating the oddities and insights of unconforming minds. He enjoyed those cascades of proper names which I am sure all who heard his lectures will remember: the names were the lights from the other shore that he felt should always be kept alight.

Finally, I must come to the person, to the man of feeling, in one sense of that phrase, which I think was his essence. He responded immediately to tones of voice, to the quality and to the intention of a person's smile, and to the lilt of his or her sentences, and to the displays and disguises of a conversation and of a personality. In speech he could make himself become David Cecil or Henry Price or Maurice Bowra, three friends among many whom he was delighted to impersonate. But his life was reconstituted, started all over again, when he married Aline in 1956. He effectively had two lives enclosed in one, pre-Aline and then with her, and the second life, in its wholeness and completeness, realised for him an undreamt-of happiness. Because of his unalterable modesty, he was surprised by his destiny, just as he was later surprised by the accumulation of honours and titles and prizes, and by the fame and acclamation of all sorts, that came to him in these later years. I can speak here, among his friends, about the uncounted trails of affectionate memory in so many directions that he left behind, in London, Jerusalem, Washington and elsewhere, the many people who enjoyed the sense of having some special intimacy with him – in some cases, an intimacy as with no one else. How did this come about? What was the peculiar quality that explains this multiplication of friendships, quite apart from his evident brilliance and virtuosity and the astonishing range of his knowledge?

One feature of his character which greatly contributed, I believe, was his deep-seated unvarying patience – patience in attending to people, in constantly thinking about them, and about their needs. For example, from the pre-war years onwards he was a kind of consul general to foreign scholars visiting Oxford for the first time, who steadily over the years, and even before the war, found their way to his rooms in All Souls and later also to Headington House. This generous quality of his in giving time to people was connected with a complete absence of self-importance. He always refused to divide his time into measured bits and then to allocate it appropriately. This same habit of unhurriedness caused him to reject philosophies and theories that are in a hurry to explain, right now, the relation of the mind to the body or the movements of history, problems that probably still require a century or two of continuous thought, at

the very least. Lastly he was tirelessly patient in overcoming the many obstacles
to the foundation of Wolfson College, a project that was originally conceived
as a kind of thank-offering to Britain when he was visiting Princeton. This was
perhaps the greatest of all his many achievements. Finding first the endowment,
then the site and the architect, winning the support of the University and also
of the Colleges, not easily but step by step – he seemed to possess the worldly
skills and flair of a medieval Archbishop, of an Archbishop Chichele. The completed Wolfson vividly reflects in its structures and in its customs the unstuffy
personality of its founder and its first President.

I therefore celebrate with you the very happy and the immensely constructive
life of an extraordinary person, an extraordinary human being: and I mourn
also a particular friend, an almost lifelong, and life-creating, friend.

Avishai Margalit

'YOU HAVE BEAUTIFUL BLACK EYES,' Greta Garbo once said to Isaiah
Berlin. His eyes were indeed remarkably expressive. They were full of mischievous cleverness, childish inquisitiveness and sceptical soberness. Today
these eyes appear in framed photographs: glassy and formal. The spark is gone.

In recent years the conversations between us turned more frequently to the
loss of the spark – to death. In one letter he asks: 'Do you think about death?
In my situation,' he writes, 'I naturally find myself thinking about it.' He goes
on to say, 'I believe in what Epicurus said: "Where I am, death is not, and where
death is, I am not."'[1] 'I am not afraid of death,' he used to say, 'but what a
waste!' This mention of Epicurus was not accidental. Isaiah believed the name
Epicurus to be the source of the word 'Apikores', the traditional Jewish label for
one who doubts the afterlife, divine revelation and the authority of the rabbis.
A sceptic, not a heretic.

One streak in Judaism which Isaiah was definitely very sceptical about is the
idea that we are not here to enjoy ourselves. Isaiah enjoyed his life thoroughly,
and made it his business to make others joyous in his presence. This business, of
making others joyous, had its price. Or so Isaiah thought.

Every year, the *Frankfurter Allgemeine Zeitung* asks famous people questions
like 'Who or what would you like to have been?' Isaiah's answer: Alexander
Herzen. To the question 'The main trait in your character?' Isaiah replied
'Anxiety to please.'[2] This was not a coy confession about a cute character flaw,

---

[1] Letter written in 1996. More literally: 'When we exist, death is not present, and when
    death is present, we do not exist.' Epicurus, *Letter to Menoikeus*, in Diogenes Laertius,
    Lives of Eminent Philosophers, 10. 125.

[2] 'Fragebogen' (Proust's questionnaire), *Frankfurter Allgemeine Magazine*, 22 January
    1993, 27.

designed to extract denials, or to fish for double compliments. I want to talk about what Isaiah regarded as a flaw in his character, because I believe that it relates to an issue of importance in Isaiah's life: it relates to his concern with fellow Jews and with his Zionism.

There's a wonderful lecture of Berlin's entitled 'Jewish Slavery and Emancipation'. In it, he spells out a parable for the state of the Jews which is eminently pertinent. He tells there of 'travellers who by some accident find themselves among a tribe with whose customs they are not familiar'. They don't know what to expect. 'The strangers, [...] being alien to this mode of life, find little they can take for granted.' They 'do everything they can to find out how their hosts "function". They must get this right, otherwise they may easily find themselves in trouble. [...] But then this is precisely the reason for which they are felt to be outsiders – [...] they are experts on the tribe, not members of it.' 'They are,' Berlin added, 'altogether too anxious to please.'[1]

For Berlin, as for Tolstoy, the distinction between being natural and being artificial and affected is basic. Natasha in love, stung by a nettle in the field, is for Tolstoy an epiphany of the natural, while Natasha watching French opera, with a stage setting of a phoney moon, is an emblem of the artificial. Isaiah, the avid opera-worshipper, never considered the opera as artificial. He tied his own sense of the natural and the artificial with Friedrich Schiller's distinction, which was most meaningful to him, between the naive and the sentimental. The natural that is the naive is the one who is not conscious of any rift between oneself and one's surroundings, and who is not conscious of any rift within oneself. The artificial that is the sentimental is the one who is being painfully conscious of such rifts. Being at home for Isaiah meant the possibility of being natural, naive and socially at ease. The Jews lost the sense of home by being in exile.

If anyone was at home in Oxford, Isaiah Berlin was the one. He was immensely grateful to English society for accepting him. Yet he sensed that, because of his experience as an immigrant Jewish child, he retained the anxiousness to please. This gave him, the great *Versteher*, the key for his imaginative leap, for understanding what it is like to lack home. Zionism, for Isaiah, had one supreme goal: to endow the Jews with a sense of home. 'Home,' Isaiah liked to quote Robert Frost, 'is the place where, when you have to go there, / They have to take you in.'[2] This is how Isaiah saw the notion of a National Home for the Jews in the land of Israel. In spite of his criticism of Zionist politics, when it unnecessarily deprives Palestinian Arabs of their homes, he saw Zionism as a success story with regard to his central concern, the revival for the Jews of the sense of home.

[1] POI 166–7.
[2] Words spoken by Mary to Warren in Robert Frost's 'The Death of the Hired Man': *North of Boston* (London, 1914), 20.

Of the three sides of the revolutionary triangle – liberty, equality and fraternity – Isaiah is known most for siding with liberty. But I believe that no less at the centre of Isaiah's thought and feeling was the idea of fraternity, or human solidarity. He felt a basic, unapologetic solidarity with Jews everywhere. And this made him think about solidarity in general. For Berlin the Jews were not the carriers of a philosophy called Judaism. Isaiah never believed in the religious idea of the Jews as the chosen people, nor in secular versions of this idea. He believed even less in the idea that the long history of oppression and torment of the Jews attests to their being chosen. There was for him nothing sublime or redemptive in suffering. Suffering is suffering is suffering.

Once he put me to the test. That is – he tested me with a thought-experiment. Suppose, he said, that you have at your disposal an Aladdin's lamp. When you rub it, miraculous things happen. You can rub it in such a way that the Jews, all the Jews in the world, will instantaneously become Scandinavians, without any historical memory, no martyrology, no nothing. They may become a boring people, perhaps, but they will be a happy one. Would you rub the lamp? No, I answered promptly. He did not like the speed with which I replied. He took this as an unbearable lightness towards Jewish suffering. For him suffering could never be a blessing, it was always a curse.

Basically the Jews were for him an extended family. An interesting family, possibly even a neurotic family, but by no means a 'chosen' one. And, in a family like in a family: there is an adored uncle. There was indeed an uncle whom Isaiah loved. He was Isaac Landoberg, who later became Yitzhak Sadeh, the Jewish Garibaldi, as Isaiah referred to him. Like Garibaldi, who founded the Redshirts, Sadeh founded the Palmach, the striking units which eventually played a decisive role in Israel's War of Independence in 1948. Sadeh was not only a general, but also a writer and an essayist, and also – in his early days in Russia – a boxer, a wrestler and an avid footballer, as well as a painter's model and an art dealer. In short, a pagan. During the Russian Revolution he came to Petrograd, as a Socialist Revolutionary officer, to visit the Berlins. Berlin's mother was so terrified of his huge Mauser pistol that she took it from him and put it away in a bowl of cold water, lest it explode. Sadeh ended his life in Israel as a romantic socialist. In Isaiah's eyes he remained a dazzling adventurer.

Isaiah's own family is old and intriguing. He was a direct descendent of Shneur Zalman of Liadi, the founder of the Hasidic dynasty of Lubavitch at the time of the Napoleonic wars. And in a family like in a family, there are also black sheep. A fourth cousin of Isaiah's was the late Lubavitcher Rebbe Menachem Schneerson, the one whose followers in Brooklyn and elsewhere declared him to be the Messiah. Though secretly proud of his illustrious Hasidic lineage, Isaiah felt acute embarrassment with a Messiah in the family. Aline, too, has a long and no less fascinating pedigree. She was born into the family of the

Barons de Gunzbourg, who distinguished themselves for three generations, up until the Russian Revolution, as grand bankers in Russia and in Paris, and were prominent in Jewish diplomacy during the pogroms against the Jews in the days of the tsars; they were also among the most pre-eminent philanthropic families in the modern history of the Jews.

And so Isaiah's family branches in all directions and it extends to the whole of the Jewish people. When Isaiah gossiped about the family it was social history at its best. And when Isaiah talked about social history it was as intimate as family gossip. It is this sense of solidarity that shaped him as the tribal cosmopolitan that he was. He had a vision of a world where people will have a sense of belonging and of identity, and in virtue of this they will have a natural sense of home so that they will be able to express their own humanity to the full. If Jews for Isaiah meant family, what was Isaiah for the Jews? For many Jews he was Resh Galuta, Prince of the Exiles. They wanted to pay him tribute, which on many occasions meant a visit to the great man. Isaiah did not mind that in the least, not even when they were bores. He made room for everyone in his dense little diary, then met them, and enchanted them off their feet with his warmth, with his instant sense of familiarity, and above all with his mesmerising stories.

Isaiah was a master of adjectives. He could get at the gist of one's character by a string of nuanced adjectives. There is no point in my trying to encapsulate him by adjectives: only he could have done that. So I shall end with a reminder. While remembering to mourn his death we should not forget to celebrate his life.

Bernard Williams

I SAIAH HAS BEEN much praised and discussed in the past months, and so he will be in the future. Today is itself an occasion, of course, for recalling what Isaiah did and what he stood for: and I shall try to say a little about his relations to philosophy, and to some other things as well. But we are in Oxford, where he and Aline lived for so many years and shared the warmth of their life with many other people. Here specially, when we speak of his work or his attitudes, we think first of them, and of his home, and of the way in which he was uniquely able to extend his friendship widely but not thinly.

About his relations to philosophy, the best known thing that Isaiah said was that he gave it up – philosophy, that is to say, to use his words, 'as it is taught in most English-speaking universities, and as I believe it should be taught'.[1] He said that this was the result of a conversation during the war with the Harvard logician H. M. Sheffer, who persuaded him that in philosophy one could not

---

[1] CC xi.

hope for an increase in permanent knowledge. 'I gradually came to the conclusion,' Isaiah wrote, 'that I should prefer a field in which one could hope to know more at the end of one's life than when one had begun; and so I left philosophy for the history of ideas.'[1] He would sometimes tell a further story of how this conclusion began to force itself on him, shortly after the conversation with Sheffer, during a flight across the Atlantic in an unpressurised aircraft: he could not read, and he could not go to sleep because he was wearing an oxygen mask, and so for nine hours he had nothing to do except think, something which (he claimed) he always found exceedingly painful.

He did think that philosophy was an important and fascinating subject, which could claim transforming achievements, but he thought that they were achieved only by thinkers of genius. 'Genius' was one of Isaiah's favourite words. He himself took it to be a rich and vague Romantic idea, but he applied it and withheld it with an assurance worthy of Dr Johnson: 'Wagner? Undoubtedly a genius, historically a disaster'; and of almost any contemporary figure outside the sciences or the creative arts, 'Genius? Certainly not.' In any case, he did not regard himself as a genius. Indeed, he did not see himself as a scholar or a professionally learned man, either. When he said that he turned to the history of ideas because philosophy did not produce cumulative knowledge, he did not mean that he wanted to make great scholarly discoveries in that field or be famous for his research. He meant what he said, that he himself hoped to know more at the end of his life than when he had begun.

In fact, I do not think that he did leave philosophy. He merely left what he took philosophy to be. His conception of the subject had been formed originally by those discussions in Oxford before the war which were shaped by the agenda of positivism; and, very broadly, he stuck with that conception. The most important thing about that conception, though, so far as Isaiah was concerned, was that it saw philosophy as a timeless study, with no interest in history (except perhaps, marginally, in the history of philosophy itself). If what Isaiah wanted to do was really history, then, on this view, it could not be philosophy. Isaiah agreed with this himself, and that is why he said that he had left philosophy, and why he did not notice that he had discovered or rediscovered a different kind of philosophy, one that makes use of real history.

Analytic philosophy has been much taken up with defining things. But as Nietzsche said – not actually one of Isaiah's favourite thinkers – 'one can define only things that have no history'.[2] Because that is true, all the things that Isaiah found most interesting – liberty and other political ideals, Romanticism, nationalism, ideas of individual creativity – such things do not have definitions

[1] ibid. xii.
[2] '[D]efinierbar ist nur das, was keine Geschichte hat.' Friedrich Nietzsche, *Zur Genealogie der Moral* (1887), 2. 13.

or analyses but only complex and tangled histories, and to say what these things are, one must tell some of their history. This was what Isaiah believed, and it was expressed straightforwardly in the style of his work, in which he offered narration rather than dialectic, preferred tendencies to laws, and, in many cases, liked illustrative details best of all.

This was not just a manner or an idiosyncrasy, but expressed a quite basic idea, and it may be because of this that people have been frustrated in trying to get hold of some essence of his thought. Coming to his writings, still more to Isaiah himself, with an academic or journalistic receptacle in which they hoped to pack his principal ideas, they usually found that they had come out with too little to fill it, or too much to get into it. He, and the myriad images in his head of past worlds, of people living and dead and their thoughts, were not the right shape for receptacles.

The concrete sense which he had of the special character of different historical times was not just expressed in his philosophy. It shaped his reactions to many other things he cared about. He was notoriously impatient with opera directors who shift the historical period of the production, and just as cross when, supposedly staging the piece in the right period, they got the manners wrong. If his taste was in these ways, as the opera directors grimly pointed out, conservative, it did also conserve, and it kept alive for him materials which to a modern taste might seem psychologically or morally unconvincing. We used to discuss that crucial scene in *Traviata* in which the father tells Violetta that she must give up her affair with Alfredo because the family's reputation is being ruined by it, and she, touched by his appeal, immediately agrees; if I suggested that this does not show either of the characters in an altogether favourable light, Isaiah would have none of it, and returned me firmly to the expectations which people had in that time and place.

Isaiah's taste in opera was broad and hugely enthusiastic. What he loved most in it was sheer melody. It was Rossini, Wagner said, who had installed melody as the absolute sovereign of opera, and Isaiah's passion for Rossini was just about limitless. His relations to Wagner himself were somewhere between distant and hostile, but he did not get over-excited about the subject or give elaborate explanations of his attitude. When he invited us once to go with him to *Parsifal*, I said something to the effect that it was going to be a particularly bad evening for him: 'No worse than all the others,' he said.

One reason that Wagner displeased him was that his music, as Isaiah put it, 'acted directly on the nerves'. There were other works that also fell under this criticism, and they were in quite various styles: *Tosca* and *Turandot, Wozzeck*, Britten's *Peter Grimes*. I think that what these pieces had in common, and what really upset Isaiah about them, was something that always upset him very deeply, that they were too directly expressive of cruelty.

His special affection for Verdi was connected with a quality that Verdi had, which, in a famous article,[1] Isaiah called 'naivety', in Schiller's sense: although his works very recognisably came from a particular time and place, they expressed, directly and unselfconsciously, feelings which have been experienced and understood at all times. Isaiah believed both that interesting and significant expressions of human experience are irreducibly local and peculiar, and also that in order to understand them, and to recognise the most important among them, you have to see them as rooted in understandings and powers and aspirations which in some sense are common to everybody.

These two lines of thought wound round each other in some complex ways, for instance in his attitudes to the Enlightenment. He had a basic loyalty to its reasonable ideals, which were supposed to appeal to humanity as such, but just for that reason he wanted to understand some of its darker critics and subverters. He came back continually to ways in which such conflicting ideas had shaped the experience of Russia. His favourite hero of the Enlightenment outlook was not one of its philosophers, but a man who represented it in relation to that country, offshore, Alexander Herzen.

With most things that interested him very much, such as political ideas, it was their history that concerned him first, the particular circumstances in which they flourished. This was true, to some extent, of his interest in works of art. But when it came to the art that meant most to him, and to the works that he loved most of all, it was not true. In their case, historical relativity finally gave up, and all merely local considerations melted away. To him the works of Bach and Beethoven, Mozart and Schubert, spoke in ways to which their history, however interesting, was external and irrelevant. They were simply there, for ever, for everybody.

He shared that feeling with other people in an entirely direct and unassuming way. We shall remember his talk, and the generous way in which he talked, so that people wanted to listen to him, not simply because he was brilliant and amusing and had many things to tell them, but because he enjoyed letting them into his thoughts, and, unlike many clever talkers, had no desire to bully them or make them feel at a loss. But we shall remember him, too, when he was not talking but listening intently to this music. It will be hard, perhaps, for his friends ever to hear some of these pieces again without thinking of him, slightly bent forward, his head a little on one side, sometimes humming a bit or beating time, absorbed without a trace of self-consciousness in what for him was beyond any talk, any arguments, any history.

---

[1] 'The "*Naïveté*" of Verdi', in AC.

Katharine Graham

HOW LUCKY TO HAVE any sort of friendship – continuous, intimate, joyous and invigorating from beginning to end – for fifty-six years, much more to have that relationship with Isaiah Berlin.

It started in Joe Alsop's garden one morning at breakfast in the summer of 1941. My principal memory is of Isaiah's trousers, hastily pulled on, at the bottom of which his pyjamas showed.

A friendship started immediately among Joe and Isaiah, and Phil and me. It later included many others, but the principals in the beginning, besides us four, were Ben Cohen of the famous Corcoran and Cohen team, then under Roosevelt; Edward Prichard, known as Prich, Phil's brilliant and funny and fat Harvard Law School friend; Felix Frankfurter (for whom Phil was then clerk-ing at the Supreme Court and Prich had clerked the year before), and Felix's wife Marion.

Our friendship was carried on in both the United States and England, in person and by mail. Luckily some of Isaiah's letters were dictated and then typed. Most of the others, the handwritten ones, are as indecipherable as his speech was hard to understand.

The Frankfurters met and befriended Isaiah when they spent a year's sabbati-cal from the Harvard Law School at Oxford. When Marion learned that Isaiah would be coming to New York in 1940, she told him: 'Shaya, when you come to the United States, you will have to speak more slowly or people will not under-stand you.'

'Yes, I know, I know, I know,' responded Isaiah, 'but if I did, I should be quite a different person, quite a different person.'

That was absolutely true – his rapid speech was part of who Isaiah was. He will be increasingly hard to describe as time goes by because his magnificent personality was so unique. How could this man, an immigrant from Latvia, become a great English philosopher, thinker, a ground-breaking mind, an artist of prose surpassing those in his adopted country?

At the same time, he was modest to the point where he never published his work. It was left to his colleague, Henry Hardy, to publish volume after volume for him.

Isaiah's friends stretched from scholars at Oxford to great musicians, poets, writers, artists, social figures, royalty, politicians and several of us here who had quite simply known him for ever and with whom he joked, gossiped and played games – games such as what people in the New Deal might have been in the Court of Louis XIV.

He once said, 'I wish I could be idle all day & read newspapers: I adore gossip about the others: when *I* am mentioned, I die.'[1]

He was loyal to the extreme, but could be ironic or critical. Sometimes his general disapproval of someone changed over the years into either tolerance or enthusiasm. 'Well,' he once said of someone he had criticised in the past, 'the one issue on which he's absolutely reliable is Israel.'

In a letter from Harvard, where he was teaching briefly some years later, Isaiah wrote: 'I don't believe, I say sadly, that anything will ever replace 1941–45 as an enormous last oasis as far as I am concerned after which youth is finally over & ordinary life begins.'[2]

'Those American friendships were wonderful,' Isaiah later told me.[3] 'We had a very good time. I never felt so free in my life. I felt absolutely in my element [...] I wasn't an imported foreigner somehow. I was one of the boys and that worked very well.'

Isaiah's world of friends broadened to include, in Washington, besides Arthur Schlesinger, Chip and Avis Bohlen, Margaret and John Walker (director of the National Gallery), Joe Alsop's brother, Stew, and his wife Tish, and others.

We all thought of Isaiah – a single man and our particular friend – as our possession. So we were initially put out when he told us Aline had come into his life and he was bringing her over to meet us.

We couldn't imagine this would work. She must be an intruder. Then she appeared: stylish, intelligent and athletic, the golf champion of France, an aristocrat in the best sense of the word. In no time we thought of Isaiah and Aline as one.

It was unimaginably perfect. The beautiful house, perfectly decorated and run, but always somehow right for Oxford and the other don friends.

Aline shared Isaiah's interests, but was her own person at the same time. She became our friend separately as well as together. She lived with him in Oxford, London and Italy. She went around the world on their travels, sharing his intellectual interests, his humour, his gossip, and quietly seeing to his comforts. She was his companion in every way and, at the same time, created the scaffolding which enabled him to function well and perform at his best.

Somewhere along the line, of course, incredibly, Isaiah was knighted. He was pleased, in an embarrassed way, and sort of laughed it off by saying he felt like a child at a birthday party wearing a paper hat. He later quietly rejected becoming a lord. That was really too much.

The Berlins' visits here never ceased to occur with some regularity. And many

[1] Letter of 5 March 1965.
[2] Undated letter (mid-January 1949).
[3] In an interview conducted in 1988.

of us went there and always spent time in Headington House, which, like Isaiah and Aline, astoundingly never changed. There was a huge clamour to see them when they came here, because so many people loved and admired them.

In a 1959 letter from Oxford, Isaiah says whom he wants to see on his upcoming visit. He wrote: 'This opens the way to a whole classification of (*a*) persons one wishes to see but does not mind not seeing, (*b*) persons one wishes to see and minds very strongly not seeing, (*c*) persons one does not wish to see and minds very strongly seeing, (*d*) persons who one does not wish to see but minds very strongly not seeing, etc., etc., etc. [...] these are our cards and we place them on the table.'[1]

Later in that letter he admitted to having 'taken to tranquillisers in a big way', saying 'they assuage my guilt quite considerably these days. Flying aeroplanes and getting into the wrong relationship with persons – that is what worries me most, tranquilliser quite good against both.'

Before a late-1959 trip, Isaiah wrote that he was to address 3,000 historians in Evanston, Illinois. Then he and Aline would come East and, he wrote, 'I shall try and get in touch as soon as humanly possible.' As Diana Cooper once said to him, he went on, 'when you arrive in Paris, first the loo: then telephone me'.[2]

In the course of discussing the common, often irritable, reaction to letters asking for things involving money, Isaiah suddenly said: 'Saints might react differently, but annoyingly enough, they are unlikely to be subject to such letters and I must confess that I have never wished to be a saint, nor, I suspect, have you: moreover, those who do, disqualify themselves automatically [...] We might one day discuss what it is that characterises saints, whether we have ever known any (I am quite clear that I have not, though I could mention some who would be much offended by this observation), and so on.'[3]

In 1970 he wrote about going to Italy, where he temporarily acquired arthritis and came home in a wheelchair, about which he said: 'there is no more agreeable method of travel', adding, 'Let me strongly urge this upon you if you can swallow your pride' (which I'm afraid I still can't) '[...] you acquire a kind of serene detachment from the turmoil around you, and become the object of sympathetic and passionate respectful looks while you peacefully read *The Naked Ape* or whatever it is.'[4]

Isaiah was always involved intellectually with Israel. He went to Jerusalem in 1970 and met with Prime Minister Golda Meir. About her he wrote: 'Mrs Meir is like a mother in Israel, stout-hearted, tough, suspicious, her arms akimbo with the air of one who says "We know them, the Gentiles, there is nothing

---

[1] Letter of 7 December 1959. [Should (*d*) end 'but does not mind seeing'?]
[2] Letter of 18 November 1959.
[3] Letter of 13 December 1974.
[4] Letter of 15 January 1970.

they haven't done to us or are ready to do. We don't trust nobody, we would rather go down fighting than be fooled once again." Yet there is a kind of simple appeal about her which goes to the heart of her fellow citizens, although as a policy it does not seem to me at all productive.'[1]

Some five years after this letter, Isaiah ended another with: 'the longer I live the more passionately convinced I become that personal relations are all in all'.[2]

For the last decade of his life, Isaiah ceased to like travelling. But whenever I went to England, I would spend a weekend with Isaiah and Aline. The last time was in May of 1997, just this past year, and before Isaiah's final illness set in.

I remember him from that visit as absolutely unchanged – vibrant, interested and interesting, full of gossip and fun. He was unusually lucky never to have suffered an old age in which he declined in intellectual and physical strength.

Once the illness did take hold at the very end, Aline reported that Isaiah could no longer do the two things he loved most: reading and talking.

Although he had said on past occasions that he never wanted to die – and most of his friends, certainly including me, still thought of him as in his prime – surely he would not have wished to live without these two things which he found so enjoyable and which gave his myriad friends, who loved him, so much pleasure.

Arthur Schlesinger, Jr

I T IS FELICITOUS, it seems to me, that this American remembrance is taking place here at the British Embassy in Washington. For it was in this city, well over half a century ago, that Katharine Graham and I and many others met the brilliant young Embassy attaché who, to so marked a degree, thereafter changed our lives.

I first encountered Isaiah in the winter of 1942–3. He was then only thirty-three years old. One was startled from the beginning by the glittering rush of words and wit, the dazzling command of ideas, the graceful and unforced erudition, the penetrating assessments of personalities, the passion for music, the talent for merriment and, most remarkable of all, the generosity of spirit that led him to treat all of us as his intellectual equals. He had the exciting quality of *intensifying* life so that one perceived more and thought more and understood more.

Isaiah had arrived in Washington by bureaucratic accident. He spoke Russian, and in 1940 the Foreign Office sent him to New York *en route* to the British Embassy in Moscow as press attaché. But the Moscow embassy decided

---

[1] ibid.
[2] Letter of 4 November 1974.

it had no need for Isaiah's services. Stranded in the United States, he did some jobs for the Ministry of Information in New York before going back to Oxford.

There, in November 1940, he was surprised one day by a notice from the Ministry that he had overstayed his home leave. He discovered to his astonishment that, though no one had bothered to inform him, he had been appointed to the Ministry's New York office. He returned to New York and in the spring of 1942 was transferred to the Washington embassy and charged with writing weekly reports on political developments in the United States.

He protested his lack of qualifications, but in fact, long before he first came here, he had shown a sympathetic interest in America. This may be the time and place to say a few words about Isaiah and the United States. He had greatly enjoyed the American pupils who had come his way at Oxford, recalling 'the openness, the responsiveness, the warmth, the uninhibited natural candour, the unblasé attitude of American students and colleagues'.[1] He also had, in his words, an 'unbroken addiction [to American magazines], perhaps somewhat rare in England in those days, particularly in academic circles'.[2] He had been a subscriber to the *New Yorker* and *Time*, the latter since his first term at Oxford in 1928. He was by temperament an Americanophile.

I once asked him whom among all the philosophers of the ages he would most like to have known. He answered promptly, 'David Hume and William James.' As a philosopher, he was of course in the Humean tradition of empiricism, scepticism, genial irony and historical reference. And he shared with William James not only verbal lucidity and elegance but a profound aversion to monism in all forms, a rejection of the idea that there is a single system of value and knowledge in which all conflicts are harmonised and resolved.

His years in Washington confirmed him in his view of the benefits of pragmatism in political affairs. He was delighted by the young men and women of the New Deal and exhilarated by the spirit and effectiveness of Franklin D. Roosevelt's humane experimentalism. The New Deal, he later said, was 'the most constructive compromise between individual liberty and economic security which our own time has witnessed'.[3] He regarded FDR as 'the most genuine and unswerving spokesman of democracy of his time, the most contemporary, the most outward-looking, the boldest, most imaginative, most large-spirited, free from the obsessions of an inner life, with an unparalleled capacity for creating confidence in the power of his insight, his foresight, and his capacity genuinely to identify himself with the ideals of humble

---

[1] PI2 152.

[2] Introduction to H. G. Nicholas (ed.), *Washington Despatches 1941–45: Weekly Political Reports from the British Embassy* (London and Chicago, 1981), vii; cf. L1 654.

[3] L 84.

people'.[1] As Roger Hausheer writes in the introduction to the recently published Berlin anthology *The Proper Study of Mankind*, 'Berlin has always been an enthusiastic New Dealer – a natural allegiance, surely, for an objective pluralist.'[2] His love and hope for America survived even the vicissitudes of the post-war years.

An 'objective pluralist' – this phrase refers to Isaiah's conviction that human values are objective but pluralistic; that is, that they are real, public and authentic but they are diverse and very often incompatible, clashing, irreconcilable. The delusion that ultimate ends can be merged into a single majestic monolithic architectonic philosophical bloc – this, he believed, is the perennial source of fanaticism, destruction, bloodshed and misery in human history. From this standpoint he attacked the other great delusions that have bedevilled humankind – relativism, that values are subjective, mere matters of taste, more or less equally valid; and determinism, that the individual is the slave of vast anonymous historical forces.

Because ultimate ends are so often in conflict, human beings are confronted by the agony of choice. Here Isaiah added a darker dimension that one misses in those other great anti-monists, the ironical Hume and the ebullient James. 'If you choose one value, you must sacrifice another,' Isaiah said.[3] 'No gain [can] be made without a corresponding loss.'[4] Choice imposes costs.

The ineluctable clash of values is tragic in its implication and its effect. At the same time, it places a premium on tolerance and compromise in human affairs. But tolerance and compromise, Isaiah emphasised, do not enjoin appeasement and capitulation. In the sentence he liked so much from Joseph Schumpeter: 'To realise the relative validity of one's convictions and yet stand for them unflinchingly is what distinguishes a civilised man from a barbarian.'[5]

Isaiah was above all a most civilised man in this horribly uncivilised century – 'the most terrible century in Western history,'[6] he called it. Wise, brave, kind, unaffected, an exemplar of moral courage, unalterably committed to the politics of decency, he was himself a stirring prediction of what a truly civilised world might be.

---

[1] PI2 11–12.

[2] PSM xxxv.

[3] 'Isaiah Berlin in Conversation with Steven Lukes', *Salmagundi* no. 120 (Fall 1998), 101.

[4] TCE 233.

[5] Joseph Schumpeter, *Capitalism, Socialism, and Democracy* (London, 1943), 243; cited at L 217.

[6] This is true to IB's views, but not an exact quotation, so far as I can determine. In an unpublished interview with Ramin Jahanbegloo on 7 July 1997, he said, in reply to a request for a comment on the end of the twentieth century: 'It's the worst century in Western history – it is the most terrible century we've ever had, nobody disagrees with this.' Cf. TCE 355, MI 301. Ed.

Now he is lost to us. But in a way we can never lose him. He is imperishable in memory. Those who are loved are never entirely lost. As for myself, I would borrow a phrase from President Kennedy and say only, 'Ich bin ein Berliner.' [1]

James Billington

T HE AMAZING MAN we remember and honour tonight populated, loved, exemplified and enriched at least four distinct worlds: four concentric circles into each of which he radiated powerful waves of thought.

The inner circle was Oxford and the microworlds within it: old ones like Corpus, New College and All Souls; the new one he created with Wolfson; the special one he created at Headington with Aline.

He enlivened Britain, and Isaiah's broader, second circle – its academy, its opera, both its traditions and its scepticism, and its enduring decency.

His third circle was even wider – encompassing all of Europe – its many languages and literatures, its varying forms of art and modes of philosophising.

He was a one-man European community, his own simultaneous translator, the creator of an expansive pantheon that stretched from Vico and Verdi in the Mediterranean to Hamann and Herder in the Baltic, from the young Marx to the old Maistre, from fragments of the Presocratics to the undeconstructed Jane Austen.

He brought the third and first circles together with characteristic brio in his great set piece comparing Oxford colleges to the countries of Europe.

The fourth circle, enriching all the other three, was his modern Jewish sensibility. The Europe of Moses Hess, the Britain of Benjamin Disraeli, the Oxford of Isaiah Berlin. Unique perspectives and the hidden burden of great names: Moses, Israel, Isaiah.

He was a very sunny son of Britain, the only great power that fought against Hitler from the very beginning to the very end of the Second World War; and a believer in the New Israel that emerged from that war: a secular but moral State which like the Old Israel was meant to realise justice in time in a world too long preoccupied with extending power in space.

To have affected all four of these circles would be an amazing accomplishment even for a relatively long lifespan. But Isaiah also deeply touched two other worlds on the periphery of Europe: Russia and America.

I was fortunate to have him as my doctoral supervisor, meeting with him about every three weeks for two-and-a-half years during and just after the last days of Stalin. He sat by a great stack of shillings with which he periodically fed the inadequate and flickering heating element in his tower room at All Souls.

---

[1] 'I am a Berliner.' From a speech by US President John F. Kennedy in West Berlin on 26 June 1963, shortly after the erection of the Berlin Wall.

He often graciously cut me in on part of the conversation he had just had, or was about to have, with the continuous procession of gloomy Europeans, displaced Russians and itinerant Americans who were forever tramping up that cold staircase to see him.

But how did this extraordinarily generous, totally unpatronising teacher have such an extraordinary impact on his time that reached so far beyond those who knew him personally? Not, of course, through any traditional academic *magnum opus* and not just through the extended essays and sparkling conversation that we all treasured. But, I would contend, in four rather unique ways that connected learning with life and that have left a lasting legacy and, like all these words, began with the letter L.

First: the Lectures. Diana didn't need a title; Isaiah didn't need a professorship. But he couldn't resist a name like Chichele, and he turned a chair into a fountain that had already overflowed in his lectures on Russian thought at Harvard in the late 1940s, and on the broader issues of freedom at Bryn Mawr in 1952, and was to do so again in the Mellon Lectures here in Washington in 1965. I first discovered Isaiah through someone else's notes of Isaiah's Harvard lectures, in which he brought back to life the creative and individualistic Russia of Herzen and Tolstoy.

That, unfortunately, was not the Russia of the late Stalin era, as Isaiah warned in his second vehicle of outreach: his Letters – a series of them in the early 1950s through which, once again, I met Isaiah *in absentia*. The letters were not addressed to me, then a very junior Army officer, but to some very senior US Government officials whom I was serving as an aide and a filter. These letters provided the best description of the inner dynamics of the Soviet system I have ever read, helping key Americans of that time understand that the Soviet system had a certain logic and inertial force that could not be easily rolled back but should not be accommodated and would not last for ever.

The third L is that through which the great teacher reached people inside Russia itself. Isaiah, not exactly as the prophet, but as the great storyteller who revalidated in our time, even amidst all its indecencies, the Legend of Liberty. He did this in different ways through the BBC lectures in 1952, his famous essay on two concepts of liberty, his own blend of Mill's reasoning with Schiller's spirit of play and his continuing link with the best in a Russia that he knew as a boy; the Russia that produced probably the greatest constellation of poets in this century.

As with his lectures and letters, I discovered his legend *in absentia* sitting in the Moscow kitchen of the widow of the poet Osip Mandel'shtam in the late 1960s and listening to her describe what Isaiah's celebrated long evening with the other great poet Anna Akhmatova had meant to both of those senselessly bereaved women – and how fascinated with Isaiah had been the old Pasternak and was the rising young Brodsky. As I listened to Nadezhda Mandel'shtam that evening tell me things I never knew about a man she'd never met, I realised that good Russians inside Russia were happy – even proud – that Isaiah had lived the life they might have had – rather the way Russians a century earlier were grateful that Herzen in London had seen so much for all of them and helped keep a culture alive in difficult times.

This brings me to my last letter L – the living links Isaiah forged in recent years with some of the godfathers of the new Russia: Isaiah was a guest scholar at the Library of Congress in the fall of 1988 at a time when Andrey Sakharov was also in Washington. Sakharov was ill and tired when he met Isaiah but was revived and seemed exhilarated by Isaiah's stream of elegant St Petersburg Russian, which was itself a kind of poetry.

Just a few months ago in St Petersburg, I had a long conversation with Dmitry Likhachev, Sakharov's main defender within the Soviet Academy of Sciences and, in many ways, Sakharov's successor as the conscience of Russia. Likhachev is a lonely survivor of the first of the twentieth century's death camps, Arctic Solovetsk of the 1920s. He is today, at ninety-one,[1] the last living representative of the pre-revolutionary culture of the city in which Isaiah was born – just as Akhmatova was its last great lady.

Likhachev became highly animated as he described a long conversation he had with Isaiah at Oxford last year, smiling as we all do when recalling meetings with Isaiah. Likhachev spoke warmly of Petersburg's creative and cosmopolitan past and of the new Russia which he believed would better honour the variety of peoples who had always been there. Isaiah had clearly started off another wonderful train of thought, and as I left Likhachev's flat, a new student generation was climbing up the unheated staircase to meet with him. It reminded me of earlier processions up the stairs long ago at All Souls. It gave me the warm feeling that Isaiah, who helped us understand so much of the twentieth century, was still sending out rays of light and liberty and hope for the twenty-first.

Alas, the champagne with which we toast the passing of time – the pink champagne, I like to think of a Jerusalem sunset – has lost for ever the sparkling effervescence of this great and good man.

---

[1] Likachev died in 1999.

Robert Silvers

When I was told of this memorial in Washington, I thought of the first long
talk I had with Isaiah not far from here at the old Wardman Park Hotel when
he was giving the Mellon Lectures nearly thirty-three years ago. The *New York
Review* had fairly recently been started, and I'd asked him to review a book, and
he replied that he knew the author much too well for that, but that if I came
to Washington, we could meet. So around four o'clock on a spring afternoon
I went to the Wardman Park to see Aline and Isaiah, and found him reading
an article on Trotsky in the *New York Review* by Philip Rahv, then editor of
the *Partisan Review*, and it turned out that Isaiah knew Rahv and had an acute
knowledge of the ex-Trotskyists and other intellectuals of the *Partisan Review*
circle.

And did I realise, he said, that Rahv was one of the few people in that circle
or indeed in America who had a close sense of the life and work of the Russian
critic Vissarion Belinsky, and that if one was to understand Rahv's radicalism
and his frustrations with American political life, and his interests in Henry
James and T. S. Eliot, one would do well to understand the radicalism and frustrations and aestheticism of Belinsky in the 1840s?

And how different Rahv was, Isaiah said, from such a pure and sublimely
learned scholar and critic as his friend Meyer Schapiro; and how different they
both were from Edmund Wilson, with his wholly justified dislike for current
literary theory, and with his marvellous ability to see works of literature as
coming out of a social setting and out of a writer's personal history that he
had himself brilliantly reconstructed. And, as he went on, I realised that Isaiah,
from his Washington days and Harvard days, and his own original insights, had
put together one of the most penetrating accounts of the very different intellectual and political elements of the American scene that I had ever heard, or
would, I rightly suspected, ever hear; and suddenly four hours had passed, and
it was nearly eight o'clock, and Aline mentioned that they would be late for
dinner.

As with so many others, I had been caught up in a flow of observations so
interesting and instructive and funny, and so patient with my own ignorance,
that they seemed indescribable, until some time later I read Isaiah's own comments on Alexander Herzen, the writer and thinker he admired perhaps
more than any other – for his bravery, and his moral idealism, and his absolute scepticism about all political formulas and slogans, and for his luminous
prose.

Of that prose, Isaiah wrote that it was 'a form of talk [...] eloquent, spontaneous, liable to the heightened tones [...] of the born storyteller' – the storyteller, he said, 'unable to resist long digressions which themselves carry him

into a network of intersecting tributaries of memory or speculation, but always returning to the main stream of the story or the argument'. Above all, he said of Herzen, 'his prose has the vitality of spoken words'.[1]

The prose of the born storyteller – that seems to me quintessential in comprehending Isaiah's immensely various work. I felt this most directly the following autumn when he was in New York, and a book appeared on the work of the Russian poet Osip Mandel'shtam, and Isaiah agreed to write on it. The days passed, and he told me that he was soon to leave, and we agreed he would come to the *Review* offices one evening after dinner, and he would dictate from a nearly finished draft. As I typed away, I realised that he had a passionate, detailed understanding of the Russian poetry of this century. Towards the beginning of his review, he wrote as follows:

> Nikolay Gumilev, Anna Akhmatova and Mandel'shtam [...] founded the Guild of Poets, the very title of which conveys their conception of poetry not as a way of life and a source of revelation but as a craft, the art of placing words in lines, the creation of public objects independent of the private lives of their creators. Their verse with its exact images and firm, rigorously executed structure was equally remote from the civic poetry of the left-wing poets of the nineteenth century, the visionary, insistently personal, at times violently egotistic art of the Symbolists, the lyrical self-intoxicated verse of the peasant-poets, and the frantic gestures of the Ego-Futurists, the Cubo-Futurists and other self-conscious revolutionaries. Among them Mandel'shtam was early acknowledged as a leader and a model. His poetry, although its scope was deliberately confined, possessed a purity and perfection of form never again attained in Russia.[2]

And he went on to describe two photographs of Mandel'shtam, one taken around 1910, the other around 1936. The first, he wrote, 'shows a childlike, naive, charming face, with the dandyish, slightly pretentious sideburns of a rising young intellectual of nineteen; the other is that of a broken, tormented, dying old tramp, but he was only forty-five at the time. The contrast is literally unbearable, and tells more than the memoirs of his friends and contemporaries.'[3]

When he finished and we walked out on 57th Street, with huge, black garbage trucks rumbling by, he looked at his watch and said, 'Three in the morning! Mandel'shtam! Will anyone here know who he is?!'

That Isaiah was capable of such powerful and evocative critical prose was not at all surprising. In *The Hedgehog and the Fox*, his study of Tolstoy's fierce, unresolvable quarrel with himself, which made him, as Isaiah put it, 'the most

---

[1] AC 188.
[2] SM 41–2.
[3] SM 45.

tragic of the great writers,'[1] he had already shown that he was a critic of the highest order. And if we read the full range of his works, looking back as far as a schoolboy story he wrote when he was twelve, and to his early Oxford days when he could explain recent Russian poetry to older scholars such as Maurice Bowra who had difficulty understanding it, and to his translation of Turgenev's *First Love*, and to his friendships with Auden, Stravinsky, Anna Akhmatova, Edmund Wilson, Joseph Brodsky and Alfred Brendel, we can see that he was in some fundamental sense an artist. An artist who saw history, as he put it in an essay on Vico, as partly a matter of understanding 'what men made of the world in which they found themselves, [...] what their felt needs, aims, ideals were'. Such a Viconian understanding of history, Isaiah wrote, 'is more like the knowledge we claim of a friend, of his character, of his ways of thought or action, the intuitive sense of the nuances of personality or feeling or ideas'. And to arrive at such understanding one must possess, he said, summarising Vico, 'imaginative powers of a high degree, such as artists and [...] novelists require'. And without this power of what Vico 'describes as "entering into minds and situations",' he wrote, 'the past will remain a dead collection of objects in a museum for us'.[2]

Without his ever saying so, for he refused to make any claims for himself, I think Isaiah in his Vico essay was describing something of himself and his own genius for entering into other minds, whether in his accounts of the ideas of such different thinkers as Machiavelli and Maistre, or of such different political leaders as Weizmann and Churchill. I have no doubt his works will last for their wisdom and their original ideas in defence of negative liberty and political and cultural pluralism; but I believe that his writings on these and other subjects will also last because among them are genuine works of art.

If we are lucky, we find a friend whose sense of life is so intelligent and original and has such authority that we can't help thinking constantly of what *he* would think. We want to walk, so to speak, in the corridors of his mind. And then a panicky moment comes, as it did with Isaiah, when it seems the friend is no longer there. But he is.

---

[1] RT2 92.
[2] AC 105–6.

Charles Taylor

WHAT DOES Isaiah Berlin's life and work mean for philosophy, or more broadly, for thought? What will its meaning be? What did he leave us?

Well, first, he kept his head in this terrible century when so many of the best minds lost theirs. Isaiah was a supporter of the Enlightenment, committed to the Enlightenment values of freedom, reason, of the primacy of rational discourse over violent means. And yet he very early realised that the Enlightenment left to itself as a single-minded project can bring about the very opposite of itself. Very young he had a ringside seat as one of the most titanic attempts in history to realise freedom, equality and rationality turned into a terrible nightmare.

He understood that the Enlightenment needs to be aware of the complex and contradictory human matrix in which its projects are to be made real. And where else to find a list of what Enlighteners often forget than in the writings of their enemies? And so the paradox that Isaiah, a great friend of the Enlightenment, did more than anyone else to make the thought of its critics – even its bitter enemies, think of Maistre – available to us.

Once they see the limitations of the Enlightenment, a lot of people have been tempted to go over to the Counter-Enlightenment. Indeed, in this age of absolute allegiances, it was often very hard not to go whole hog for one or the other. That's where Isaiah kept his head. He taught us that the best way to further the cause of the Enlightenment was to understand more fully what its critics have been saying. And this he did to no small degree.

The next thing we owe him is that he drew the lesson from all this. The problem with the unruffled boosters of the Enlightenment as well as its unreconcilable enemies is that they can't get their minds around the idea that a value may need its opposite not to become dangerous. For them, all good things cohere together, in one single consistent package. Perhaps the doctrine for which Isaiah will be mainly remembered is the denial of this too facile, Panglossian assumption. The things which we inescapably find good often conflict, sometimes tragically. The attempt to hide this from ourselves is not only an intellectual failing, it is also a source of catastrophically destructive action, as we try to dragoon reality into our narrow conceptual net. That was Isaiah's trenchant critique of certain theories of positive freedom, that they tried to pretend that freedom was compatible with a whole lot of other good things, by the simple expedient of including them in its definition.

But it is not just wishful thinking which tempts us to do this. There is something in the modern rationalism, so deeply anchored in philosophy, which pushes us to believe that all morality can be derived from a single source. Both Kant and the Utilitarians believed this, though their single criterion differed.

The real plurality of value, and the potentially tragic conflicts this generates, was not allowed on to their conceptual screen.

Here we can appreciate the complex relation of Isaiah to academic philosophy, which was in a sense his native intellectual turf. After being one of the participants in the exciting new developments of the 1930s, Isaiah in a certain way left philosophy. He emigrated. That is, he called what he then went on to do something else, perhaps the history of ideas. But it went on being extremely relevant to academic philosophy, albeit in a negative way, because it challenged the unitary assumptions which hold so much moral philosophy in their grip. The moral thinking he studied in the authors he wrote about, that which he developed himself, couldn't find a place in the narrow structures of principles and deductions which defined the horizon of much academic moral philosophy. But since he had officially 'emigrated' the challenge could lie unnoticed.

I think Isaiah thought that philosophy had to be done within this horizon, and that's why he lost some of his original interest in it. I still hope this is not so, but here, as so often, Isaiah is probably being more realistic than I am.

So this man told us truths, important truths, which we had trouble hearing, because of our partisan commitments, or our too narrow understanding of reason. He told us about the moral complexity of our world, and the tragedy, the sadness of dashed hopes that this can occasion. But he also offered another kind of hope, that this world need not be intractable, if we could just hold on to the complexity, the paradox, hold together in sympathetic understanding the incommensurable moral goods which clash in our lives, and in the history we are living through.

And this is where we have to move beyond the content of the message to the timbre of the voice which carried it, and beneath the voice, the human being. There is another too neat philosophical dichotomy which distinguishes the logical content of a philosophy from its rhetorical clothing. But in moral thought the convincing power of an idea also comes, and rightly, from the quality of the human life it inspires. Isaiah not only taught us the importance of broad human sympathy, he lived this sympathy, he was this sympathy. He touched all of us, and that is why we were so moved by what he taught us, why we are all here today, and why his message will go on resonating for us and for those who come after us into a new century which will more than ever have need of his wisdom, understanding, and what Herder called *Humanität*.

ISAIAH IN PERSON

Before he gave his inaugural Isaiah Berlin Lecture (see 10 above), Stephen Jay Gould told the audience, and reminded Berlin, of an earlier meeting of theirs:

I MET Isaiah Berlin once before. I doubt he remembers it – there is no reason why he should – but I wish to record the incident because I think it says something not only about his scholarship but especially about his humanity. I was here on a sabbatical term in 1971; I was an absolute assistant professor, nobody at the time. [...] One day, on one of my weekly or monthly trips to London, I got on the train [...] and into the same compartment walked Isaiah Berlin, whom I knew as a legend in the history of ideas, and we started talking. I think it was the most wonderful hour I ever passed during that year here. He was on his way to a meeting in Covent Garden – the Board of Directors, if I remember correctly. And I was just enchanted – I think the conversation was mostly opera but it ranged very widely – not only by his erudition and the interest of everything he had to say, but by the fact that he was obviously taking *me* seriously and listening and having a real conversation. I was so touched by it.

About a week later I was just about to leave – it was the end of the year – and I received a postcard. I didn't even know you'd recorded my address or how to get in touch with me. It was so sweet. It just invited me to come up and have lunch and I remember you said you'd be very sorry if I'd left without our meeting again. As it happened – I think I was leaving two days later – we never did have that meeting. I just wanted to say that I thought that was such an enormous act of kindness towards someone who was an absolute nobody, and I've always appreciated it, I've never forgotten it.

Isaiah As I Knew Him

Bryan Magee

I HEARD OF ISAIAH BERLIN more than twenty years before I met him. When I went up to Oxford at the age of nineteen, in 1949, there was a handful of luminaries in the humanities who were known to us all and thought to be stars. In history, vying with one another, were A. J. P. Taylor, A. L. Rowse and Hugh Trevor-Roper. Taylor, the outstanding lecturer of the three, and perhaps the best in the university, used to perform in the largest hall at the most unpopular hour and day (nine o'clock on a Saturday morning) to demonstrate that he could fill it when no one else could. In the English faculty the comparable figures were Lord David Cecil, C. S. Lewis, and, just beginning to come into his inheritance, J. R. R. Tolkien. But in philosophy there was only Isaiah Berlin. In our little world these were glamorous figures, public intellectuals whose reputations had spread beyond their subjects. They were known not only outside Oxford but outside the academic world altogether, and this gave them a special prestige in our eyes. Unlike nearly everyone else in the University, these were people whom *other* people had heard of. It was as one of the stars in this firmament that I first became aware of Isaiah.

The difference between him and the others was that they had all published what were considered to be distinguished books, and their striking personalities came on top of that. Berlin had indeed published what was to be his one and only full-length book, but it was a lightweight affair that did not pretend to be anything else, a popular biography of Karl Marx in a non-academic series. This meant that his reputation rested on nothing but his personality. He was perceived as hyper-bright – brighter, perhaps, than the others – and the most brilliant of conversationalists. It was this, we supposed, that had gained him his reputation in the outside world. However, his talk was said to be not so much entertaining as formidable, even daunting.

As a student I did not lead a primarily academic life, and did not move personally in those circles. But I saw these rare individuals around the place, and heard anecdotes about them, and read some of their books, including Berlin's biography of Marx. I found it, as people said, lightweight. This made me think of him as no doubt a good talker but not a figure of very great substance.

This view was changed permanently in my last year. On BBC radio, Berlin delivered a series of six one-hour lectures devoted to thinkers who were enemies of personal freedom, for instance Rousseau and Hegel. I found these lectures spellbinding, incomparably superior to any I had heard from any-one else, whether in the flesh or otherwise. When I was told that they were unscripted – that Berlin just sat at a microphone with nothing in front of him and poured out this compelling material for an hour without a pause – I was impressed beyond words. Actually, I later discovered that what I had been told was not quite true – he did have some notes. But from then on I regarded him as a heroic figure intellectually. It was still to be many years, though, before I met him.

In my early forties I was making a series of one-hour television programmes each of which was a head-on argument about a major issue between two public heavyweights. Was democracy compatible with communism or was it not? Did we or did we not want a federal Europe? Should we as a society, or should we not, pursue economic growth? There were thirty-nine of them altogether, and I wanted to make one about nationalism. In general it was taken for granted among liberal intellectuals that nationalism was a bad thing, an immature and harmful stage of psycho-political development that mankind should and would grow out of. But I had noticed that Isaiah Berlin was not only a dedi-cated Zionist but spoke up in general terms for nationalism. So I televised an argument for and against nationalism between him and Stuart Hampshire. It was in arranging this that I met him.

It turned out that he was already an enthusiastic viewer of the series, and had seen nearly all the programmes. He had also listened to a series of thirteen radio programmes about contemporary British philosophy that I had broadcast a couple of years before. It was typical of him to construe situations in terms of the history of ideas, and he saw me as doing the same thing in the Britain of that day as Diderot had been doing in eighteenth-century France, namely present-ing high-level discussion of important ideas to a wide audience without dumb-ing it down. This seemed to me a grandiose way of looking at what I was doing, though I was unquestionably doing it. Isaiah also seemed sensitively aware of the fact that, because of television and radio, I was more widely known than he was, although I had none of his prestige. So – I am embarrassed to say – a certain amount of mutual admiration was expressed at our first meeting. But it made for the immediate establishment of a warm personal relationship with strong interests behind it, and this quickly became a friendship that went on deepening until his death.

It was he who proposed me for a visiting fellowship at All Souls College, Oxford, where I began work on my book about the philosophy of Schopenhauer. This meant that we both had lives divided between Oxford and London, so we took to meeting in both cities for lunch. Our lunches became more frequent, until in the last fifteen years of his life they were about every six or eight weeks. The venue we used most often was the Garrick Club, of which we were both members. Towards the end of each lunch Isaiah would fish out that little black diary of his and say with relish: 'Now when shall we do this again?'

For most of our first twelve years I was a Member of Parliament, and he visited me at the House of Commons. He said I was the only MP with whom he was on terms of personal friendship, and I think this was true at that time, though it could not have been so earlier. We also met as guests at other people's dinner tables in London and Oxford, and at various kinds of party in London; and at opera first nights. He would be there because he was on the Board at Covent Garden, and I because I was a regular judge for one of the awards. Occasionally we would go to performances of other kinds together. In Oxford I quite often went to his home. So we saw one another a good deal, and in different surroundings. As the years went by I came to think of him as one of my most loved friends. I was never conscious of the twenty-one year gap between our ages, nor did he ever show any sign of that himself.

Taken together, our conversations were the most enjoyable I have ever had – though not only enjoyable, also nourishing. Sometimes we met literally just to talk for a couple of hours in some convenient place. Our common interests covered huge areas. But what was so special was the immediacy of mutual understanding, as a result of which things could move fast between us, though unhurried. With some people I seem to spend half of each conversation explaining what I mean. But Isaiah immediately saw the point of everything I said – the assertions, the arguments, the references, the allusions, the connections, the jokes – and took each utterance for neither more nor less than what it was. For instance, if I made an assertion that was a generalisation, he would take it for precisely that, a generalisation, to which naturally there were exceptions, of which both he and I were aware, and to which neither of us needed to waste the other's time referring. And he would either agree interestingly or disagree interestingly with the generalisation. There are so many other academics, perhaps a majority, who would respond immediately by bringing up the exceptions when they are irrelevant, and the conversation would then follow a barren path: I would say I was aware of the exceptions but they did not invalidate the illuminatingness of the generalisation, and the other person would argue with that, and the main point would be abandoned. In that direction no worthwhile conversation can lie. But one never went in that direction with Isaiah. Actually, he loved generalisations, because if they have an interesting amount of validity, and we retain our awareness of the exceptions, they give us serious help in understanding large-scale issues, and in perceiving connections; and it is only lesser minds who disallow them, partly to get out of confronting big questions.

Isaiah was not, to any significant degree, an original thinker, but he was a superlative understander. He understood alien points of view not only at the level of conceptual thinking but at an emotional level. At the conceptual level I have made a small reputation in that line myself. Given a little notice, I am able to provide a clear, reasonably accurate exposition of the main ideas of a number of thinkers in the Western tradition; and the many years of hard work that were required to develop that ability taught me how difficult it is to acquire. Isaiah could do that too, of course, but he went much further. His understanding was existential as well as intellectual. He could illuminate what it was like to *be* a Marxist, or a Romantic rebel against the Enlightenment, or a Christian opponent of Darwinist thought, or innumerable other kinds of people. He could get inside their skins and look out at the rest of the world from their point of view and see it through their eyes. So it was not only a question of his giving you, say, a scintillating exposition of the central tenets of Marxism, he could also get you to understand how all sorts of other things would look to you if you were a Marxist. He had this gift – the gift of self-identification with the outlook of holders of widely differing, sometimes incompatible points of view – to a degree unique among philosophers. We associate it with playwrights and novelists, but in Isaiah's case it was set to work in the service of the history of ideas. There were times when his understanding of what it was like to have a particular set of beliefs had such existential depth that one was tempted to think that he must himself have had the perceptions he was describing, otherwise he would not have been able to acquire such a profound understanding of them; but it was seldom so. An example of this that made a lasting impression on me concerned Tolstoy's belief in the transcendental. Isaiah's insight into this was so profound that I found it difficult to see how he could possess it without himself at least partially sharing it; yet I knew from many years of discussion with him that he did not.

No one else has done this to anything like the same extent. It is as if Isaiah invented a new subject, or at least opened a new branch of the history of ideas, an existential branch. The activity lent itself naturally to case studies; and case studies lent themselves naturally to short forms: essays, articles, lectures, book reviews. It was common for decades to hear people say of Isaiah that he was brilliantly clever but had produced scarcely anything. However, now that Henry Hardy has gathered together all these essays and other pieces into no fewer than thirteen published volumes it is not possible to go on saying that. Berlin's is a big œuvre. And it reveals him as one of the outstanding essayists in the English language. In the twentieth century, only George Orwell can be counted in the same league. The reason why Berlin was belittled for so long was that people were measuring him against the wrong yardstick. They perceived him as a philosopher; and then they said, rightly, that he was not a great philosopher. However, he was a great essayist. And his essays were different in kind from anyone else's.

For several decades scarcely anyone knew that most of these essays existed. They were published in obscure journals very often, not only in his own country but in a large number of others. It was quite easy to know him well and still not know about all these articles appearing in unheard-of publications in far-off foreign lands. He never, so far as I know, drew attention to them. It was as if he was publicity-shy about his work, just as he was publicity-shy about his private life.

When it is seen where his real value as a writer lies his limitations as a philosopher lose most of their relevance. His originality consists not in producing new ideas but in understanding, with the kind of insight a creative writer has, the existential import of ideas for the human beings who believe them, how they are caused to feel and behave, the choices they are led to perceive and make. The gift that enabled him to do this was not a philosopher's brain, or a scholar's mind, but the ability to extend our shared powers of emotional empathy into the sphere of conceptual thinking. Most of us can empathise with other people's feelings, but Isaiah could empathise with how their minds worked. And he could do this not only with people he knew but with the dead, provided they had written on subjects that engaged him.

Much of his conversation was about what it was like to be a certain person, or in a particular situation, or a member of some special group; and his usual way of finding illumination was to compare one thing with another, sometimes across great distances. His main field of interest was Europe in the last three hundred years, so a lot of literature and history came into it, especially social history, above all gossip. His fund of startling stories about the private lives of the eminent dead was without parallel; and the stories were always told with bounce, crisply and well. He was a dedicated gossip himself, famously so (he once said to me, scowling accusingly: 'You never gossip'), but his gossip about our contemporaries was funny without being malicious. I am not sure how he kept this up, but it had something to do with the exactitude of his pointedness – a feature that characterised all his perceptions about people. In any case, his powers of empathy were too strong for him to be malicious in the way gossip usually is. In fact the outstanding characteristics of his conversation were emotional involvement and warmth.

His human curiosity was stronger than his intellectual curiosity. If you were sitting with him in any room he would be alert to the other people in it, and to the room itself, and to whatever the institution was; and he would raise interested questions about all of these, and make sharp observations. It was this lively curiosity that was the motor of his best published work. The only times I felt him to be in danger of boring were when he launched into one of his detailed descriptions of the backstairs politics of the Senior Common Room in New College or All Souls during earlier decades. He would recall each detail of some half-century-old petty intrigue as if it were yesterday, and with an intensity of interest that was abnormal.

Another area of undying fascination for him was what he used to refer to as 'the Jewish question', the question being what it was like to be a Jew in this, that or the other set of circumstances; or how other people looked at Jews. In the House of Commons he would quiz me about MPs who were Jews, and whether this made any perceptible difference to their activities as MPs. If we went to a concert he might start speculating about why so many musicians were Jews, or so many of the music critics, or so many of the concert agents. At the theatre he might start wondering why there were so few Jewish actors. Of fellow Jews who were embarrassed by references to their Jewishness he would say: 'They've got Jewish trouble.' He was constantly telling Jewish jokes. His fascination with Jewishness, what it was and what difference it made, went right down into his foundations; and being the near-genius he was he was perpetually saying things about it whose insights were profound and unexpected.

At the root of this lay the fact that until the creation of Israel Jews had no alternative but to be to some extent outsiders in whatever society they lived in, even if they had been born in it. Growing up in such circumstances affected not only one's relationship with society as a whole but also the formation of one's sense of one's own identity. The unavoidability of this disturbed Isaiah, and he showed the subtlest understanding of the extent and intricacies of its ramifications. It was because of this that he believed in the necessity for a society in which Jews would not be outsiders, and he was therefore a committed Zionist even though I do not think he ever seriously considered living in Israel himself. It goes without saying that he did not talk about the Jewish question all the time; but in all the years I knew him it was rare for us to have a conversation that it did not come in to at some point, if only glancingly.

Over those years I learnt a huge amount about all this from him. Yet it was not something I could share easily. In all the various circles in which I then moved it was unacceptable for me as a non-Jew to tell Jewish jokes, however funny, or make a general remark about Jews that contained any element of critical intelligence, no matter how pertinent. It would have caused people to suspect my motives. Only with Isaiah could I have conversations like this, or even raise such questions.

A word here about my own background will clarify the situation. Until I was about thirty I sincerely held the conventional liberal view that it simply does not matter whether someone is Jewish or not, and makes no difference. But in my late twenties, and for most of my thirties, I was on terms of close friendship with a Jewish man called Val Schur, with whom I held long, absorbing conversations. One day his exasperation with me on this point broke out. 'Look,' he said. 'You've simply got to drop all this. There's not a single Jew in the world to whom being a Jew doesn't make any difference. It makes a difference to me. And if you're going to understand me you've got to understand that.' This took the lid off a Pandora's box of questions about the differences that being a Jew makes. I came to find the subject a fascinating one – partly, I suppose, because it had been in some way suppressed up to that point in my life; but also because of its significance for Val, who was my closest male friend for a long time. He and I went on having various discussions about it until his death in his mid-forties, which were my late thirties. So by the time I came to know Isaiah I had already developed an interest in the subject, and reached a fairly sophisticated level of understanding in it. It was as if I received my undergraduate training from Val, and then moved up to the postgraduate level with Isaiah.

Isaiah was not at all a religious person. He believed that this empirical world of ours is the only reality that exists, or at least is the only reality whose existence we have any grounds for believing in or bothering about. He was not open to the conjecture that we survive our deaths in any way at all, and he did not believe in God. He would often cite the view of Herzen, with whom he identified more than with any other thinker or writer, that the meaning of life is life itself. But none of this caused him to fear death. He once said to me, when he was very old: 'I find the prospect of death not frightening but frustrating: it's like being forced to leave a theatre before the end of the play.' What all this unquestionably meant was that he did not believe the Jewish religion. Yet he considered it a matter of the first importance that Jewish observances should be kept, because they had become the only thing that gave the Jewish people its identity – not race, not country, not language; not, any more, religion: only the shared traditions. Unless these were preserved, Jews would dissolve into their surrounding societies. So he made it clear that he wanted a traditional Jewish burial, with a full service in a synagogue – something that surprised many people, and was misinterpreted by some.

I once made a series of television programmes that consisted entirely of (for once on television) intellectually serious arguments about religion, and I wanted to include one about Judaism. I telephoned Isaiah and asked if he could recommend someone who would put the case for it really well and respond formidably to sceptical questioning. I stressed that I wanted someone really intelligent, and really good. Isaiah thought for a few moments, and then said: 'You've got an insoluble problem.'

'Why?'

'Because there isn't a really intelligent Jew in the country who believes the religion.'

This reply was frustrating for me, and I said: 'Well I suppose that means I'll have to fall back on a professional God person, which in this case would mean one of the rabbis. But I wanted to avoid that if I could. Who would be the best rabbi to do it?'

There was an ominous silence. Then Isaiah said, in a mock-baleful voice: 'You know what the Church of England bishops are like intellectually?'

I laughed. 'Yes.'

'Well the rabbis are worse.'

Although Isaiah had a powerful interest in political ideas, and plenty to say about them, he had almost no interest in practical party politics, the sort reported and discussed in the daily newspapers; and he made no pretence of keeping abreast of them, except perhaps in foreign policy. It all seemed to him so fleetingly evanescent that unless you were actually involved there was no point in trying to keep up with it. All his life he was a Labour voter. This may come as a surprise to some, given that he was at one time possibly the most famous 'liberal' thinker in the world; but it has always been the case that most Labour voters are liberals rather than socialists. In any case, Isaiah was a 'liberal' in the American rather than the British sense of the term. For all I know he may have voted once, even twice, for a Liberal or a Liberal Democrat. I have it from his own lips that he voted Conservative on one occasion. But I also have it from his own lips, and near the end of his life, that he had 'always' voted Labour. I find this easy to understand, being in much the same boat myself, and knowing that millions of other people are too. Those who find it difficult are, I think, being misled by labels.

He once told me that between the two world wars it had caused him much difficulty that so many of his close friends, who were in broad agreement with him about British political and social affairs, had absurd illusions about the Soviet Union, illusions which they took seriously and had strong feelings about. His accurate view of that regime was seen by them as an aberration caused by the fact that as a child he and his parents had fled from it. He, like most of the rest of the world, knew that it was currently murdering millions of people – and what is more he had relatives still living there – but his friends inhabited some sort of cloud-cuckoo-land with regard to it. When our conversation turned to comparing the Soviet and Nazi regimes he said: 'No one could accuse me, of all people, of underrating the Holocaust. But the Soviet regime must be the worst regime there has ever been.' In unpacking this he talked about the way Stalin's regime had calculatedly used terror and mass murder as instruments against the population as a whole, whereas Hitler's had used them against minorities. Stalin had murdered something like three times as many of his subjects as Hitler did, partly to terrorise the rest. Isaiah also thought it had to make a difference to our evaluation of the two regimes that the entire population of the Soviet Union, except for Communist Party members, had been living not only under this terror but in truly hideous economic and social conditions, whereas in Nazi Germany such conditions had been good for most of the population.

Being an odd man out on an issue of such importance over so many years had contributed, I think, to his general feeling of being an outsider. And although he was an academic himself, it also contributed to his feeling that many if not most academics did not understand the basic realities of the world they were living in. When I returned to Oxford to work in a university environment again after many years out of it he asked me how I was reacting to living among academics. I said I liked them on the whole, and got on easily with them, but was a bit shocked to find intelligent people with so little understanding of the society they were living in. I finished by saying, in tones of discovery: 'They're just not men of the world.'

Firmly, and with a lot of personal feeling, he said: 'They never were.'

It was essential to him that half his life should be lived outside academe, mostly in London. There, he was active not only in meeting other sorts of people, going to different sorts of parties, making using of clubs, and so on, but also as a consumer of the performing arts. He had a positive thirst for concerts, recitals and opera. I never knew him to show much interest in the visual arts: his greatest aesthetic pleasures came from music, theatre and reading. But in all the arts he was an enjoyer, and he loved what he enjoyed. His relationship to it was not like that to an academic subject: he did not take a scholarly interest, or set himself to master this or that field. He just let go and enjoyed himself, and largely ignored what did not spontaneously engage him. *Knowing* about the arts did not seem to him all that relevant for his own purposes, although he respected scholarship about the arts in others. The pleasure he derived from music was considerable and real, but I became sceptical about how deep his musicality went. We were once at a piano recital at which Richter played Brahms, and then an encore which I did not recognise. During the applause I asked Isaiah if he knew what it was, and he said: 'Well Brahms, I suppose. But I don't know what.' It could not possibly have been Brahms: the harmony spent much of its time on the border of atonality. I found myself wondering how Brahms sounded to Isaiah: it could not have been very specific. The composer in question turned out to be Scriabin. Another time when I realised that there was something limited about Isaiah's ear was when I saw a good stage production of his translation of Turgenev's play *A Month in the Country*. The characters were not talking as if the language was coming out of their bodies spontaneously, created by them as they spoke. And there was one line that was so cumbersome that no one would actually have said it in real life. Next time I saw Isaiah I mentioned just this one line, and suggested an alternative. He looked at me with an expression of astonishment at himself, and said: 'Do you know, when I translated that play I don't think I stopped to wonder what the lines were going to be like for the actors actually to say.' I had a reaction of equal astonishment: how could anyone translating a play *not* think about what his lines were going to be like for the actors to say? What did he imagine himself to be doing? Both in this case and that of the Scriabin, something was being perceived in an insufficiently distinct, over-generalised way; one thing was being assimilated to another when the differences ought to have been obvious and significant to someone in Isaiah's position.

Not that there was anything at all artificial or insincere about his attitude to the arts: all his reactions were genuine. But the truth is, I think, that in every field his approach was more that of an artistic than a scholarly person: that is to say, it was based on feeling before thought; and when that happens, intellectual enquiry follows up on emotional response, and does not concern itself greatly where there is little or no emotional engagement. He took an interest only in what he cared about, and picked out from it what he needed for his own work, disregarding the rest. Creative artists do this. And in Isaiah's case it was true even of his involvement with philosophy. His knowledge here was exceptionally wide, far wider than that of most of his fellow professionals, and included a detailed acquaintance with the writings of a number of minor figures, some almost unknown to his colleagues. But it all had the character I have described. And for a professional philosopher his ignorance was likewise exceptional. For instance, he made plentiful, apt references to Kant's ideas in ethics, politics, law, history and the social sciences, while remaining not only ignorant but uncomprehending of Kant's central philosophy as expounded in *Critique of Pure Reason*. He once told me that in a determined attempt to master the contents of that book he had taken it on a sea journey so that he would be able to settle down to it for several hours of each day with no other demands on him. But he found himself struggling, getting more and more bogged down, until eventually he gave up. He simply could not understand it, he said. And I can attest from many years of discussing philosophy with him that he did indeed not understand it, even though the conventional wisdom has long regarded it as the most significant contribution to philosophy since Plato and Aristotle.

His relationship to the work of his own contemporary Karl Popper was similar. He told his biographer, Michael Ignatieff, that Popper's political philosophy as expressed in *The Open Society and Its Enemies* had had an enormous influence on him. In the second edition of his biography of Marx he said of Popper's book that it was 'a work of exceptional originality and power. The second volume provides the most scrupulous and formidable criticism of the philosophical and historical doctrines of Marxism by any living writer.' But even with these views, and having been so influenced, he made no attempt to read Popper's central philosophy, the epistemology that is fundamental to all Popper's work and is set forth in two seminal books: *The Logic of Scientific Discovery* and

Conjectures and Refutations. Popper wrote to Berlin trying to interest him in these ideas, but Berlin, to the end of his days, remained in ignorance of them. He was not interested. To Popper this was exceedingly frustrating, and exasperating. I tried to explain to him that Berlin was interested only in doing his own thing, and that it was a thing worth doing; but Popper was unreconciled: he could not understand how someone of Berlin's ability could choose to remain in ignorance of such fundamental developments in his own field. To him it seemed culpable, the more so because Berlin had made his reputation partly on the back of ideas taken from Popper's work, and to Popper it seemed self-evident that Berlin should want to deepen his understanding of the ideas he himself was propounding. There appeared to him to be a touch of charlatanry in Berlin's uncaringness. I knew with certainty that this was not so. What was involved was a form of intellectual limitedness that was outside Popper's comprehension. As the only person who was a good friend of both I made some attempt to mediate; and there was one occasion when I managed to bring all of us together. But the conversation skirted too gingerly around things; and when I tried to bring it to a focus the others became untalkative. With Berlin I could never overcome the fact that he was not sufficiently interested in Popper's epistemology to study it; and Popper could never be persuaded that this was understandable, let alone defensible, in someone who had been as influenced as Berlin had by *The Open Society and Its Enemies* and was propagating so much of its contents in his own work. Inevitably, the fact that Berlin was more intellectually fashionable than Popper, and more widely known, made this rankle somewhat, though Popper was resentful rather than jealous.

Unlike Popper, Berlin had no belief in his own philosophical importance – so both men assessed themselves accurately in this regard. Isaiah once said to me: 'I've been given far more than my due. But I'll tell you one thing: it's better than getting your due.' There was no false modesty about this: he was only telling the truth. But he had a disenchanted view of himself altogether. He once told me that in his forties he had woken up to himself and said: 'What is all this? What are you doing, playing the English gentleman, wearing Savile Row suits of noisy Prince of Wales check and all the rest of it, when everyone can see you're a fat little Jew? This is entirely ridiculous. You must stop all this, and start being yourself.' And, he said, from then on he did. On another occasion he told me that he had been so convinced of his own physical unattractiveness that until his forties he had remained a virgin. In this conversation he used the phrase 'dark, ugly little Jew'. People reading these phrases now, and together, might get the impression that there was some sort of self-hatred in Isaiah to do with his Jewishness, but this was never so. It was an exactitude of vision. It is just plain true that he was ugly, in addition to being of no more than average height, dark and Jewish. One of his favourite quotations was a remark of the eighteenth-century Bishop Butler, which he usually shortened to: 'Things are what they are, and their consequences will be what they will be. Why should we desire to be deceived?'

He took an accurate view of his gifts, too, just as he did of his shortcomings. He knew – he could not help knowing – that he had rare intelligence and a dazzling conversational gift that made him almost universally attractive, in a non-sexual way, to intelligent people. He was avidly sought after, a social lion; and he enjoyed this, playing the part to the hilt. Even so, there remained a personal shyness under the social success, and he was quick to resent it if people expected him to perform, or tried to show him off to their guests. In such cases he would switch off suddenly, and perhaps leave. He wanted just to go on being himself. However, he had a shrewd understanding of the influence his popularity and imposingness gave him, and would press it to its limits. Not only in academic life but in outside bodies, such as the Royal Opera House, he could get his way to a far greater extent than would be justified by his knowledge of the matter in hand. People seldom wanted to argue against him, perhaps because he argued so much more brilliantly than they. But it did make him too used to getting his own way.

This linked up with his only unforgivable defect of character, which was cowardice. He would never fight unless he was sure of winning – and even then not if he thought fighting would make him unpopular. He dreaded being on the losing side in any practical dispute, and would go to ignominious lengths to avoid being so, even when he strongly agreed with it. To take a trivial but revealing example, someone whose research fellowship at All Souls was about to come up for reconsideration asked Isaiah to back his request for its renewal. Isaiah, who thought highly of his abilities, said he regretted being unable to do so, as he would be in America when the committee met. The young man then asked him to write a letter of support to the committee, saying it was bound to influence their decision. Isaiah assured him that there was no need for any such thing as the fellowship was bound to be renewed anyway, the merest formality; and he did nothing. But to me, not knowing that the story up to this point had been related to me by the worried young man, Isaiah said he was almost sure that the College was not going to renew the fellowship, because the young man had been researching for several years already without publishing anything. I had it from other sources, too, that this was how things looked at that time. So what Isaiah was actually doing was ducking out of backing a loser. It was made all the more shameful in this case by the fact that the fellowship was, in spite of Isaiah's desertion and against all expectation, renewed, and the young man went on to publish distinguished work. He probably never knew how Isaiah had betrayed him.

Everyone who knew Isaiah closely knew this sort of thing about him. They loved him in spite of it, but it was the hardest thing about him to swallow. It is now being revealed more widely by the publication of his letters, which sometimes say incompatible things to different people with the obvious aim of keeping in with them all. But again, characteristically, he knew it of himself. I once asked him what he regarded as his worst fault, and he said at once: 'Cowardice.' I think the cause of it lay in an almost pathological need for acceptance and approval, and a radical insecurity about them. It was a jolt to find this in so big a man: I was used to seeing it in smaller ones. It may have had something to do with his origins as an outsider in so many different ways at once: not only a Russian from Latvia, not only a Jew, but someone who first came to England as a well-grown child not knowing a single word of the language or a single person outside his family.

Because of this insecurity in himself he sometimes urged the wrong sort of caution on other people. When I told him I was going to write a book about Schopenhauer he tried to dissuade me on the ground that no one was going to want to read a book on Schopenhauer, so my career would not be advanced. But when he realised I was going to do it anyway, he helped me. Years later, when I told him that in a book that I was then about to write I was going to launch an onslaught on what had become known as Oxford philosophy he said: 'I shouldn't advise it', on the ground that this would turn people in Oxford against me. But when he realised that I was still going to do it he put me up (at his own suggestion) for a visiting fellowship at Wolfson College, Oxford, in order to write the book. In both cases he was seriously concerned for my success without any consideration of my relationship to the substance of what I was doing.

In many ways what appeared to be different characteristics of his, some bad but some wonderful, came down in the end to the same thing, a hypersensitivity to other people's reactions, and an understanding of how to engage successfully with them. It was this that made him the best of all conversationalists. People often described him as witty, but he was not actually a wit. Although his humour was marvellous and non-stop – there cannot ever have been a more entertaining companion – he made people laugh not by coining witticisms but by drawing attention to something that was already there, the funny side of people and situations, of which he was perpetually aware. It gave his humour an in-group character, repeatable as funny only to third parties who knew the same people and situations, not to others. It was rare for him to say something funny in its own right, regardless of context or audience. He was given to making trenchant remarks that others would quote as aphorisms, but, again, this is different from wit: for instance 'the surest way to turn a first-rate institution into a third-rate one is to appoint second-rate people to it'. That is highly apposite in Oxford, and is a penetrating observation, but it cannot be called funny. When he thought of a good remark like that he would repeat it as often as it could relevantly be used, so he was all the time saying the same memorable things to different people. (Indeed, if someone made such a remark to him he would repeat that too, and frequently, without attribution. One – though only one – of his widely quoted bons mots is a remark made to him by me.) The result was that in his circle of friends there was a rich fund of Isaiah-lore that was passed around generally, to be quoted or referred to. He also, like the rest of us, told his best stories to different people, and sometimes repeated them to the same person; and these too would be added to the common fund. The mix was so rich that I have never known anyone more often or more enjoyably quoted by his friends. However, this was something going on within their private world – and there were occasionally others who resented that.

He had tricks of speech that were widely imitated. One was serial negative qualification: '*Rigoletto* is the most enjoyable opera ever written – not the most deeply moving opera, not the best opera, not even Verdi's greatest opera, and certainly not the most popular opera, but ...' Often, to drive a point home, these qualifications would be tautological: 'He was a medium-ranking courtier – not one of the magnates of the court, not someone with great influence, not a power in the land, but not insignificant either, not just a minion, etc., etc.' Because of their colourful use of language, and sometimes their use of distinctions, these riffs gave pleasure. He loved categorising individuals in the spirit of a party game. Philosophers, he would say, could be divided into four levels: in descending order these were the empire-builders, such as Plato and Aristotle; the great philosophers; the geniuses; and the bright boys. The game was to agree on which level so-and-so belonged. It provided mischievous fun about contemporary and recent philosophers. But most often there were two categories and two alone: either you were, when it came right down to it, a conservative or a radical, shall we say; or you were either a hedgehog or a fox; or you were either a bishop or a bookmaker – he was inexhaustibly fertile in his 'two sorts of' distinctions. It gave rise to a joke against him: 'The world is divided into two sorts of people: those who think the world is divided into two sorts of people and those who don't.' He was, it has to be admitted, continually saying things that would have subjected anyone else to accusations of simplemindedness: making large-scale generalisations, or applying a single distinction to everything – but no one ever thought Isaiah was simple-minded. There was always a kernel of truth that was interesting truth, thought-provoking. And there was always a dimension of ironic play as well.

A lot of good things were said about him. Stephen Spender's remark that Isaiah, all his life, had the shape of a baby elephant was brilliantly right. Perhaps the best observation was that he was not one-third English, one-third Russian and one-third Jewish but wholly English, wholly Russian and wholly

Jewish. That truly hit the mark. I several times heard him described as an ideal Englishman.

I loved him as I have loved few people. And I miss him as I have missed few people. The human warmth that radiated from behind his breastbone evoked a matching response. If only I could be sure we had souls I would say he had a beautiful soul. When he died I was not, alas, able to go to the memorial held for him in London: I read Noel Annan's magnificent tribute later, while travelling on a bus between London and Oxford – and found myself sitting there with tears streaming down my face. That is more than ten years ago now, but he still comes into my mind at some time on most days.

It is impossible to tell how well his writings will survive. The best of his essays deserve to last. Already most of these have been selected from their various volumes and reprinted together under one title: *The Proper Study of Mankind*. But it could well be that his longest-lasting achievement will prove to be something quite different, namely Wolfson College, part of the University of Oxford. This is an entirely postgraduate college, very international, covering all subjects. The basic idea for it as it now exists was Isaiah's, and it was he who raised the money to get it built. He played a decisive role in the choice of architect, and then kept a close watch at every stage as the building came into being. On one important point he persuaded the architect to alter his plans – a wall whose shape he insisted on is now referred to as The Berlin Wall. Isaiah became the College's first President, and held that job for nine years. So he is altogether its creator. By rights it should have been called Berlin College. Since most of Oxford's colleges have survived already for hundreds of years, it would seem to require no more than average luck for this one to do the same. Throughout as many future centuries as it lasts, everyone who studies there, or teaches there, or carries out research there, or writes books there, will owe a personal debt to Isaiah.

So Much There

Anthony Quinton

M Y FIRST IMPRESSION of Isaiah Berlin was not all that personal. Some time in the academic year 1948–9 I was a regular attender at a series of lectures he gave in Oxford on what he called 'logical translation'. I always arrived in time to get a good seat, since he was not all that audible at a distance because of the rapid, torrential style of his delivery. He was talking about what was a widespread practice among philosophers of the early mid-century, that of interpreting statements about some more or less unobvious type of entity in terms of a more obvious, or at any rate more unproblematic, kind. An example would be the theory memorably advocated by Gilbert Ryle in his *Concept of Mind*, that statements about the human mind are reducible to statements of a hypothetical kind about human behaviour. Thus 'George is angry' means the same as 'If you surprise George, he will shout and throw things about', a device which turns something inward and rather mysterious into something public and straightforward.

Isaiah would have none of this. Applying himself to this and other examples of translation – objects into sense-impressions, past events into present traces and recollections, nations into individual people – he set about them in a somewhat idiosyncratic way, urging that the statement being translated just did not *feel* like the statement into which it was being converted. For a philosopher, particularly at that time, this was an unusually emotional or aesthetic way of going about things.

In the autumn of 1949 I was elected to a Prize Fellowship at All Souls. Since I was single, I immediately went to live in the College. Not very long afterwards, Isaiah came back to All Souls from his Tutorial Fellowship at New College to be a Senior Research Fellow. The proposed topic of this research was the Russian thinker Vissarion Belinsky, one of the Russian thinkers of Isaiah's 'remarkable decade', along with such better-known figures as Alexander Herzen and Turgenev.

He moved into a noble set of rooms in between the two towers in the Great, or Hawksmoor, Quadrangle, immediately above the dire A. L. Rowse. Still single, he became, as I was, a full-time resident, eating most of his meals in, as I also did. The result was a quite marvellous opportunity to observe him in action, to splash about like some small fish in the magnificent fountain of his discourse. Looking back, I feel I may have been intolerably adhesive. My para-sitism did not begin until lunchtime, but in that period the midday break had a very indefinite termination. I remember an occasion when, after talking at great length over coffee, we headed out into the High Street. 'Shall we go and browse in Savory & Moore's?' he enquired, referring to a fine old pharmacy. He was a dedicated hypochondriac.

Like most great conversation, his is not easy to bring to life a long time after its delivery. Its most notable feature was a wonderful abundance of near-synonyms, and in the style of *Roget's Thesaurus*: 'delightful, highly unedifying, altogether disgraceful' or 'worldly, sophisticated, horribly corrupt, like a tango-dancer'. Then there was the subject matter, which was an intoxicating mixture of the socially and publicly important, the locally chatty and gossipy, and the excitingly highbrow. Although a voluble talker, he was in no way an overpowering one; everyone else in the group was given a fair chance to express himself. A particular form his humour took was the highly structured analogy. One I immensely admired was a comparison between the colleges of Oxford and the main nations of the world. New College was England, both centres of gruff reticence and (at that time) appalling food. Magdalen, of course, with its beauty and somewhat disdainful attitude to the rest of the University, was France. Christ Church was India in the last days of the British Raj, with A. J. Ayer, then a lecturer there, as the resident Anglo-Indian Babu, and the Canons being the hereditary Princes. After that, my recall becomes hazy. Was Balliol Germany, with its unattractive appearance and grim dedication to learning? Was All Souls Switzerland, made unlike other colleges by its freedom from undergraduates? (I have since learnt that Isaiah identified his own old College, Corpus Christi, with Denmark, on the ground that it was decent, thoroughly respectable and unimportant. He may well at times have identified Christ Church with the United States: both being large, rich and fairly silly. I have also heard the suggestion that All Souls should be linked with the Vatican, but this is really cruelly diminishing: Switzerland would be altogether more suitable.)

Isaiah knew a great deal about many important things in history, philosophy, music and literature. He was equally catholic in his taste for people. Certainly he liked important people and brought quite a number of them to the College as his guests. The one who impressed me most was Edmund Wilson, the great man of letters and Anglophobe, who managed to contain his hostility during his visit. Isaiah once gave as his considered opinion about Great Men, that the best show of being great put on by anyone he had met was that provided by André Malraux, leaving such world-historical figures as Churchill, Weizmann and Roosevelt cowering in the shadows.

But much as he liked important people and revelled in their company, he did not confine himself to them. He had a vast constituency of friends and acquaintances of which by no means the majority were ordinary Oxford academics. His lunch guests at All Souls were frequently of Slavonic origin. One recurring guest was a Dr Katkov, who hung obscurely on the outer edges of the University without in the least being led to abate the curiosity of his appearance and habit. I have the feeling that he was originally a philosopher, of Husserlian or phenomenological leanings, but he did not enter the active Oxford philosophical scene of the day. I seem to recall that Isaiah fixed him up with some post in the field of Modern European History.[1] When everyone else had left the smoking-room after lunch, Isaiah and Dr Katkov would fall to talking Russian together. Often when I called on Isaiah in his room between the towers, he would be talking on the telephone in Russian and I would sit there listening to the liquid and completely unintelligible music of his side of the conversation.

Dr Katkov was by no means the only survivor of the sinking of the great ship of European culture by Hitler to wash up on the shores of Oxford, or, more precisely, to come to inhabit remote bedsitters in the northern part of the city. The most luminous of these, thought of at the time to be a wine merchant, was Theodor ('Teddy') Wiesengrund Adorno. Some time later he reappeared under the stripped-down designation of T. W. Adorno as one of the leaders of the Critical Theory movement, a form of slightly jazzed-up Marxism, which flourished in the United States in the closing decades of the twentieth century. I think it was Isaiah who overheard him ask one of his lesser refugee colleagues, 'Essen Sie an dem High Table?'

At the end of Isaiah's first year back at All Souls, an important event in my life occurred at the wedding reception of another Fellow of the College (Keith Joseph) at Claridge's. I fell irreversibly for a delightful young woman in a dark blue coat dress. Isaiah was present, unforgettably, in a top hat and frock coat. As the summer proceeded, the young woman in question and I became engaged and she returned to finish the final year of her degree course at Bryn Mawr College near Philadelphia. In the second semester of the ensuing academic year, Isaiah went over to Bryn Mawr to deliver the Flexner Lectures there. His subject was a series of more or less irrationalistic and emotional eighteenth- and nineteenth-century thinkers. Reading through the transcript of the lectures, I was naturally delighted to discover Saint-Simon represented as Sam Seymour, an altogether more American name. As I went on, I seemed to recognise behind the historic masks the menacing features of A. L. Rowse. Thus J. J. Rousseau turned out to be Rowseau and Joseph de Maistre, de Rowstre. (The lectures were finally published as *Freedom and Its Betrayal* in 2002, half a century after their delivery.)

The lurking presence of Rowse behind the ostensible subject matter of these

---

[1] George Katkov (1903–85); Research Lecturer in Philosophy, Oxford, 1947–50; BBC Russian Service, 1950–9; Fellow, St Antony's, and University Lecturer in Soviet Institutions and Economics, 1959–71. Ed.

lectures shows that Isaiah's widespread interest in, and particularly his tolerance of and friendliness towards, wildly different kinds of people was not without a few exceptions, of which Rowse, perhaps by reason of constant propinquity, was most notable. It was a very proper response. Not to have reacted unfavourably to Rowse would indicate total insensitivity.

When my future wife told her parents in New York that she planned to get married to me, they became extremely agitated at the thought of their only child marrying a Gentile. I got Isaiah to act as intermediary on my behalf and to assure my impending mother-in-law that I was not altogether horrible. He came back reporting that he had not made much headway and was strongly aware of my mother-in-law-to-be's large imploring brown eyes.

Around this time All Souls was in a state of turmoil, precipitated by the death of the nervous Warden Sumner, who was always urging the younger Fellows to take up permanent positions in the United Kingdom and even the Commonwealth. In one case, that of a rather fastidious and quite distinguished philosopher turned English literature scholar, he succeeded. The unfortunate man was projected to an assistant lectureship at Aberdeen. Isaiah was very interested in the obscurity of this man's social background. After much reflection, he came to the conclusion that the man's father must have been, in his stately phrase, 'a turf accountant'. Later, the subject of these speculations published an autobiography in which he plainly stated that his father was a hospital stoker whose hours of work almost precluded contact between them. Another hardier spirit offered a post in Saskatchewan (pronounced by the Warden as two spondees with much emphasis on the final syllable) stood firmly out against the proposal and went on to academic glory in Oxford.

Isaiah was, in a constitutionally self-effacing way, a candidate for the Wardenship and in this he was strongly supported by the younger Prize Fellows. Rowse ran a campaign for the election of an unknown and unimpressive lawyer. He had the support of the Old Guard, the elderly ex-Fellows who by achieving public distinction of some sort had been re-elected to fellowships. The third constituent element of the governing body was the middle-aged Professorial Fellows. Isaiah was not a combative person, to put it mildly, and he did not like the idea of being personally involved in what was going to be a fairly sulphurous contest. He may also have suspected that there were some residues of comparatively mild Edwardian anti-Semitism – the sort of thing you find in John Buchan – in the Old Guard. (They were, by and large, Buchan's contemporaries.) The matter was resolved by the election of Sir Hubert Henderson, a decent old economist with impeccable Bloomsbury and liberal credentials. He, a few days later, reignited the crisis by having a heart-attack at that most melancholy of Oxford social occasions, the Vice-Chancellor's garden party on Encaenia Day. He lingered for a while in the Acland Home, receiving constant visits from Rowse urging him to resign, which he duly did, only to die soon afterwards.

This time Rowse appeared as a candidate on his own account. He had the support of the professoriate. John Sparrow, another active homosexual, was supported by the Old Guard. (He was, after all, a Chancery lawyer and not too insistently academic, although by no means unscholarly.) That left the younger Fellows, with a few exceptions, frustrated by Isaiah's unwillingness to run, to support the excellent Australian Professor of Government, Kenneth Wheare. We were persuaded to drop him by urgent pleas from some Sparrow supporters that the supreme priority was to keep out Rowse. They were probably right. At any rate, Sparrow was elected.

Rowse was not entirely unique in his low standing in Isaiah's eyes. An aged businessman, one of the senior Fellows, called Sir Dougal Malcolm, was given to fairly categorical pronouncements. One evening after dinner, somebody mentioned T. E. Lawrence, perhaps one of the College's most celebrated former Fellows. 'Aargh, I knew him, he was a bugger. Can't stand buggers.' A slightly devastated pause followed this statement until Isaiah piped up in a high, innocent voice, with the question, 'I imagine that that sort of thing was very common in the College in those days?'

He was an artful and indefatigable intriguer. 'Who is going to get that post?' is a permanently leading topic of conversation in Oxford. Isaiah took his full part in this and in the machinations to which it was related. On the whole, there was a certain similarity between those whom Isaiah favoured to fill vacant appointments and his more exotic lunch guests. In fact he was succeeded in the Chichele Professorship by a real Montenegrin, John Plamenatz. Coming from where he did, he was ideal for Isaiah's purposes, but he was in fact one of the least Montenegrin of men. Mild in manner, self-effacing, with a quiet devotion to French culture, he was the last person likely to succeed as a mountain bandit in the Balkans. He had, however, lived in England since he was five.

One moderately debatable case was that of the succession to Lord David Cecil as Goldsmith's Professor of English Literature, a chair that had been deliberately founded for a colourful and not too grindingly scholarly exponent of that specialism. The chair was attached to New College and there was an ideal candidate in the College already, John Bayley, no doubt best known as the husband of Iris Murdoch. He had the required scope of interest and lightness of touch while carrying rather heavier scholarly armament than the charmingly amateur David Cecil. Isaiah succeeded in getting the job for Richard Ellmann from a college near Chicago. There was nothing wrong with Ellmann, a fluent and copious writer, principally on the subject of Irish writers, most notably Joyce and Wilde. It all turned out well enough, since a chair was contrived for John Bayley at another college in Oxford.

I myself felt the cold breeze of Isaiah's manoeuvrings. When Plamenatz gave up his chair, I entertained, perhaps hubristically, but encouraged by the apparent absence of obviously suitable candidates, the idea of applying for it myself. In pursuance of his generally respectable agenda of leavening the lump of Oxford with some interesting import from the wider world, Isaiah arranged for the job to go to Charles Taylor, a Canadian, a thoroughly able man but who had written little about the field of the chair.

What I have now come to feel is that these exoticising operations were just another expression of a fundamentally aesthetic drive behind all Isaiah's activities. It helps to explain the peculiar, idiosyncratic character of his writings on past thinkers. After my initial total subservience to his style of thought, some little yellow shoots of criticism began to grow in me. He was clearly not, and had clearly stated that he was not, a philosopher in the ordinary local sense of the word. As an astoundingly clever man, he could make a perfectly good fist of appearing to be a philosopher. The principal products of this effort are to be found in his volume *Concepts and Categories*. The story he put about was that he had been persuaded by the logician H. M. Sheffer to give up the subject, since he was not any sort of expert in formal logic – a necessary discipline if genuine progress was to be made in philosophy. That advice, if generally followed, would thin the ranks of philosophers like bubonic plague. The fact is that Isaiah did not much like standard analytic philosophy with its persistent argumentation, its distinction-drawing and its general commitment to nit-picking; he was not very good at it, and he knew that he was not very good at it. He was really more a Monet than a Braque or Paul Klee.

What he claimed to be, after the change, was a historian of ideas. But this is not quite right. It is not easy to see him getting on well with A. O. Lovejoy and other exponents of the full-blooded American style of intellectual history. His relation to ideas, I came to realise, was not that of a historian, seeking explanatory connections between ideas in different manifestations and the circumstances in which they were expressed, but that of a connoisseur, lovingly and pertinaciously savouring the thought of particular thinkers in the effort to identify their distinctive particularities. When I first formulated this notion, I took it to be of negatively critical import, and may well have made some mildly disparaging remark about intellectual connoisseurship in conversation or casual writings. Whatever may have carried the message, Isaiah, always extremely sensitive to criticism, got wind of it, and so a certain mild, but happily not Arctic, chill descended on our relationship. I now think that although my conception of what he was up to was perfectly correct, it was philistine and puritanical to regard his way of doing things as in the least objectionable. In fact, it greatly enhances our appreciation and understanding of the thinkers of the past to be made to come to them as distinctive and irreducible individuals, as we come to works of art.

The engagement I mentioned earlier followed its destined course and in August 1952 we married and moved out to the top floor of the fair-sized house of some friends living a few miles out of Oxford. This meant that I was no longer so much in College and could spend less time bathing in the fountain of Isaiah's discourse. But I was usually there for lunch and able to see and meet the variegated flock of Isaiah's guests. Indeed, I was not really conscious of this reduction. In due course (1956) Isaiah himself married and set up in Aline's fine house in Headington. Here a Parisian level of elegance prevailed, far removed from the rugged, slightly boarding-school atmosphere of All Souls. I was always deeply appreciative of the way in which butter was served at meals in little balls in silver dishes. When, at the end of his stay at Bryn Mawr, my wife packed up his stuff for him for his return to England, an entire case was left empty, not because he had disposed of much of what he came with, but because it had now been properly folded. But marriage, generally, did not have a diminishing or taming effect on Isaiah, it simply made him happier and more serene. The conversational cascade continued to flow, like some great East African waterfall, with only creditably infrequent repetition.

In the middle 1970s, we acquired a small flat in central London, and, as soon as we could get in there, a set in Albany. Isaiah and Aline were then in the second of their series of Albany residences. With its staircases, porter's lodge and general sequestration from the life around it, Albany is quite like a college. A slightly odd one: the undergraduates have all disappeared on vacation, a large number of extremely old Fellows is still in residence (as in some Cambridge colleges), the college head is nowhere to be seen. Here Isaiah and I frequently ran into each other. As I reached the bottom of the stairs he would suddenly appear in the archway beyond with his brown trilby hat and a heavy blue overcoat he seemed to wear whatever the temperature. It was wonderful to have such opportunities to exchange vital, red-hot, often rather trivial information. Thinking about him now, it seems to me astonishing that there was so much there, so much knowledge, of all imaginable degrees of importance, so much fresh and original comment on everything from the overall shape of world history to the latest disastrous appointment of a college head in Oxford.

Akhmatova and Sir

Anatoly Naiman

I

I FIRST HEARD ABOUT HIM during conversations from which I found myself suddenly excluded, just at the moment when he was mentioned. It was always and only ever Akhmatova who mentioned him, always lightly, jokingly, cheerfully, with a hint of irony, always as if in the flow of the conversation, as if incidentally, as if she wanted to illustrate the conversation with one of his remarks, statements, actions, in short, *with him*. 'Nina,' she turned towards her friend, 'this reminds me of how *Sir* ...' Or: 'Lida, you said your father received a letter from Oxford – how is our *Sir* doing there? ...' Or: 'Lyubochka, I have to tell you something, I've been sent a greeting from Salomea,[1] direct from London – *Sir* is on characteristic form ...' And her friends, sharing in her secret, smiled understandingly, as if they wanted to confirm that *Sir* really was on characteristic form, and above all, that this wasn't a joke or a fairy tale, that somewhere there was a real *Sir*, of a certain age, with certain manners, living at a certain address. Sometimes they referred to him as *Lord*.

Despite the obvious reality of his existence – even after she had begun to talk to me about him openly, and after I had found out all the details of the story that is now familiar to anyone who has read the most rudimentary biography of either one of them – while Akhmatova was alive, he remained to me a fictional character, partly out of Walter Scott, partly out of Evelyn Waugh. Even partly out of Shakespeare, such a *special* 'Sir', as if one side of him belonged to the circle, or, more widely speaking, to the entourage of Henry IV in Part 1, and even more so in Part 2, but at the same time also to the society of *The Merchant of Venice*, since *Sir* was, in addition to everything else, a Jew. This perception of him was not in the slightest the product of a lively imagination, or literary inclinations, or a romantic nature, if these were ever part of my personality. It was evoked by the fact that Akhmatova had placed this man once and for all in a reality that lay *beyond* the one we were seeing, one that Akhmatova saw better than anyone else. Never mind his postal address, age and title, for Akhmatova

---

[1] Salome Halpern (1888–1982), wife of Alexander Halpern, had belonged to the literary and artistic worlds of pre-revolutionary St Petersburg and inter-war Paris. After the war the Halperns lived in London. See IB's 'Alexander and Salome Halpern', in Mikhail Parkhomovsky (ed.), *Jews in the Culture of Russia Abroad: Collected Articles, Publications, Memoirs and Essays*, vol. 1: *1919–1939* (Jerusalem, 1992) – as yet published only in Russian translation in this Russian collection.

the reality he and we were seeing (and she herself better than anyone else) was for her also a *raison d'être*, and possibly the only *raison d'être*, for a different reality, her own, in which to be a 'Sir', and even more so a 'Lord', meant what it meant in Walter Scott and Evelyn Waugh as they were being read in Russia.

In that other, *her own*, reality her friends Nina, Lida, Lyubochka, Marusya were no longer 'citizen this or that', 'comrade this or that', worn out by the Soviet regime and the burden of every single hour, or yet another illness. Here they were rare, colourful beings, who playfully carried on within their carefree society a ladies' conversation in which he figured as a 'Lord'. The place that was appropriate to this man – a Sir, a Lord among the mediocrity of secret agents, passport officers, shop assistants that were hiding 'doctor's' sausage[1] under the counter, the day shift that was forming an endless queue at the bus stop, and really everything which was then called Russia and which held Akhmatova and her friends confined – smacked of the exotic. Recognisable because of Shakespeare and therefore almost one of them, but nevertheless not from this world, a character from the stage, from a play.

As my relationship with Akhmatova grew closer and more confidential and she began to talk about *Sir* more often and more openly, his role in their shared history gradually assumed a clearer shape. He had appeared in autumn 1945, six months after the end of the Second World War. He was a foreigner in a country gripped by spy-mania. He was Russian, born in Riga, which was provincial in comparison to St Petersburg and Moscow. He was Jewish. He was European, in the full sense of the word. He was English. He was a Western intellectual, ranking among the first on that list of theirs, a list which here in Russia inspired vague speculation but also a certain awe. His surname was Berlin, a most fitting confirmation of all that he was, although in Russian the stress is on the first syllable. His first name was Isaiah, a mighty name.

Everything that was known about him, and to a much greater degree what was not known about him, rendered his figure boundlessly capacious and enigmatic. When we finally met and spoke for the first time, a quarter of a century after my conversation about him with Akhmatova, that is, almost half a century after their meeting, I mentioned at some point during our long, easily flowing conversation that in my book I had referred to him as a 'philosopher and philologist'. His immediate reaction was: 'I'm neither one nor the other.' – 'If you want I'll change it to "historian and literary scholar".' – 'That's not me, not me.' – 'Researcher into ideas, political theorist, ethicist ...?' – 'No, no, no.' – 'Well, at least you're not a mathematician!' – 'That's it: not a mathematician – that's me.'

---

[1] A popular make of cheap sausage.

And not a poet either. 'Oh no! I've never written verse in my life ...' In 1962 Akhmatova had used a line by a certain IB as an epigraph for her poem 'The Last Rose': 'And you'll write about us on a slant.' Those among her readers who were intelligent enough, but not too well versed in her poetic taste, decided that it was a quote from Ivan Bunin. However, all those who had heard the story of 1945, even if in a distorted version, ascribed this almost intimately touching and confident phrase to Isaiah Berlin. (At that time only his friends knew about the twenty-two-year-old Joseph Brodsky, the actual author of the line.)[1] This guesswork was fuelled by Akhmatova's own poems addressed to Berlin: the cycles *Cinque* and *A Sweetbriar in Blossom* and the dedication of her *Poem without a Hero*. A line from 'The Last Rose', 'To fly up with the smoke from Dido's fire', had a distinct ring of 'For a brief while only you were my Aeneas' from the poem 'Dido speaks',[2] which was addressed to Berlin.

Did this man of whom she said 'Two voices only, yours and mine',[3] 'Unpronounced speeches, / Silent words',[4] and finally 'You came here as if following a star / With your long steps you crossed the tragic autumn / To join me in this devastated house / From which burned poems rose up like a flock'[5] write poetry himself? Whose poems had risen up – only hers, or theirs?

– When I was a boy in St Petersburg, in Petrograd, I studied Hebrew. I didn't learn it as well as I should have. But I was still able to write little poems. They were called 'Morning News'. Of course I've forgotten everything, everything.

– So you wrote poetry as a boy?

– In Hebrew.

– Regularly.

– Every morning.

– For how long?

– Oh-oh, I think about six or seven months.

– And not once in Russian.

– Never. And those weren't real poems. They were doggerel. I've never written poetry. I've never written anything like that, I've never worked with poetry.

– But you must admit that it is nevertheless part of your biography – the daily practice of poetry.

– That's not important, it was merely a technical exercise.

[1] From 'Roosters crow and bustle', a poem dedicated to Akhmatova by Brodsky in 1963. In Russian Brodsky's initials are IB (Iosif Brodsky).

[2] 'Don't be startled', *A Sweetbriar in Blossom*, 11.

[3] 'Sounds decay on air', *Cinque*, 2.

[4] 'First Song', *A Sweetbriar in Blossom*, 4.

[5] 'You have invented me', *A Sweetbriar in Blossom*, 8.

II

'He'll never be my dear husband,' wrote Akhmatova about Berlin.[1] He'll never be my *dear husband*, but he and I will achieve something that will embarrass the twentieth century. These words have been repeated, declaimed, muttered a hundred, two hundred times – and suddenly, at the two hundred and first time, you see *who* this '*dear husband*' is. In 1922, one of the last years in this brief interval of time when it was still possible for a limited number of people, including the Berlin family with the eleven-year-old Isaiah, to leave, emigrate, get across from revolutionary Russia to the West, Akhmatova wrote 'Lot's Wife', a poem about Lot's flight from the doomed city of Sodom with his family. It is an autobiographical piece – the comparison is transparent – through the outlines of the abandoned city the images of Petrograd or Moscow are clearly visible. Lot's wife, ignoring the prohibition, turns round to look 'at the red towers of her native Sodom'. Perhaps they are red because the fire is already raging, perhaps because they are the walls of the Kremlin. The name of the place – Sodom – is almost as common as Gehenna. The heroine doesn't close her eyes to the disgrace of her city's depravity, but they are the disgrace and depravity of her *native town*, her *home*. Is it possible not to turn round for a last look at 'The square where she sang, the yard where she spun / The empty windows of the tall house / Where she bore her *dear husband* his sons'? And *he*, the one who came back, the one who was destined to return to the site of the conflagration, who 'turned left after the bridge',[2] will never be this 'dear husband', will not pull her from the fire, will not save her. And once more, in a different poem so as to dispel all doubts about the reasons for such an impossibility, as well as about the non-accidental comparison with Lot, Akhmatova removes the circumstances of that meeting from the closed world of bare facts, from the dictates of merely earthly relations – 'Let the passions, seeking answers / Strangle lovers – we, *my dear*, / Are just souls who stand together / At the edge of the known world.'[3]

Akhmatova rendered the story of their meeting in verse, Berlin in his memoir in *Personal Impressions*. I've heard this story with added commentaries and clarifications from both of them; I think I am the only one who has. Her version is more multi-layered, universal and interesting, his is more definite, documentary and concrete, but both are equally authentic. The generally known facts are these: that one day in late autumn in Leningrad he, at the time First Secretary at the British Embassy, thirty-six years old, was taken by mutual acquaintances to visit her, fifty-six at the time; that this visit was interrupted by a friend of his from Oxford who happened to be in town and had drunkenly sought him

[1] 'Third and Last' dedication to *Poem without a Hero*.
[2] *Poem without a Hero*, part 1, chapter 1.
[3] 'Another Song', *A Sweetbriar in Blossom*, 5.

out; that he had returned to her later in the evening and that they talked from midnight till morning. He visited her again at the beginning of January to say farewell; his diplomatic stint was coming to an end; this meeting was brief. Akhmatova subsequently linked their encounter to some of the most serious political events that followed over the next several months, the most personal and painful of which was her public condemnation by the authorities. Berlin did not confirm this link but agreed that it was not impossible, to say the least.

The scheme of Akhmatova's version looks like this. On a lower level: the First Secretary of the British Embassy, who in the eyes of the official authorities was by definition an agent of a foreign intelligence service; she herself a non-Soviet (if not anti-Soviet) poet; her reputation – as the former wife of an executed counter-revolutionary and the mother of a son convicted of counter-revolutionary statements and acts – that of the quintessential enemy of the regime. On a higher level: Berlin's drunken acquaintance from Oxford, who arrived in the courtyard of her house accompanied by a tail of NKGB agents – Randolph Churchill, the son of Stalin's especially hated temporary ally; Stalin's personal interest in the 'English spy's' visit to 'our nun', as he used to call Akhmatova; Winston Churchill's Fulton Speech that marked the beginning of the 'Cold War' with the Soviet Union; the Central Committee's Decree on Akhmatova and Zoshchenko that constituted her public death.

Above these two stage platforms, known to the whole world, a heavenly vault was positioned, much as in the ancient world, from which the ancient gods directed and observed this Greek tragedy. Six months before Berlin's death, during a conversation which we had agreed to record on tape and which lasted several days, I asked him about the unchanging heavenly realm, or, in Akhmatova's words, 'the starry fittings' between which the two heroes of *Cinque*, and later the *Sweetbriar*, find themselves. 'We were walking high, like the stars.'[1] 'The sounds in the ether are dying.'[2] 'The fleeting glitter of crossing rainbows.'[3] 'I walk with a sun in my body.'[4] 'The whisper of birches in corners',[5] which accompanies the conflagration and passing of the material world. 'Under which star signs'[6] and the quatrain that follows this line. 'The invisible glow',[7] 'The fragments of a flock of stars',[8] 'The deep mirror of the moon'[9] ... Does he know what all this is about?

---

[1] 'As if on a cloud's edge', *Cinque*, 1.
[2] *Cinque*, 2.
[3] ibid.
[4] 'From early days, I never liked', *Cinque*, 3.
[5] 'You know I shall not sing praises', *Cinque*, 4.
[6] 'We did not breathe the poppies', *Cinque*, 5.
[7] ibid.
[8] 'Burnt Notebook', *A Sweetbriar in Blossom*, 1.
[9] ibid.

– I have no idea.

But in his last letter to me, his very last letter to another person, as it were, in which he comments on my interpretation of the poems of the *Cinque* cycle in terms of *The Divine Comedy*, he definitely accepted the closeness of Akhmatova's poetic landscape to that of Dante, not of this world, yet clearly recognisable.

III

Immediately after Berlin's death several articles appeared that were not only harshly critical of him, but unkind and downright hostile. Essentially, the critics deplored the fact that there was not a single field, whether in science, politics or simply human relations, in which Berlin had proved himself to be on a level with the unauthorised position that he occupied in the intellectual and social hierarchy of his epoch. That he had failed to create a philosophical system, that he had not discovered new ideas in history, that his contributions to literary scholarship were not of the same weight as the authority of his name. That he had not influenced the course of events, that he had not set an example of responsibility or devotion, let alone selflessness, never mind passion or morality. That he did not startle the public with a creative output or intellectual prowess to match the fame he was enjoying in all these fields. That his lectures, interviews, essays and books contained factual errors, and banalities too. In short, that he had received recognition that he did not deserve.

In the article Brodsky wrote for Berlin's eightieth birthday[1] the reader also feels a slight lack of focus and what might be called a shortage of material: it is not enough, in a decent essay, simply to write that the main achievement of the person whose birthday is being celebrated consists in the indomitable liking he inspires in the writer. One must cite merits that are generally accepted; one must explain *why* he is loved. (To be honest, it would be sufficient to say *how* he is loved, and if one did that successfully it would explain everything wonderfully well, but that would be a wholly different genre. Certainly not an essay. Perhaps a poem.)

For all who believe in the existence of an objective price-list of achievements, and rewards given in return for them – or simply for Berlin's adversaries – there remained the issue of what they considered the injustice of the recognition he had received. However, receive it he did, and by no means only from people who were dependent on prevailing opinion. And this is one of the few imputations of 'injustice' which indirectly point out, and at least in some way rectify, the injustice of life – for life is seen by most people as just. People with a more or less independent view of the world could see with their own eyes that life kept

---

[1] Joseph Brodsky, 'Isaiah Berlin at Eighty', *New York Review of Books*, 17 August 1989, 44–5. An excerpt from this essay appears in this volume.

changing whenever Isaiah was around, that he positioned mirrors at unusual angles that reflected life's most unusual sides – and that life was deadened, boring, extinguished as soon as he left. People who believe in and think in terms of the price-list usually talk about the topics they write about, and converse in the same manner they use for their books – which, although they are respected in line with some unspoken agreement with other members of the same guild, are not really alive – and also for their irrefutable but somehow weary lectures, which induce weariness in the listener too.

In 1965 Berlin gave six lectures on Romanticism in Washington. The lecture theatre was packed, and the lecturer, in the words of a contemporary critic, was not only on his best form, but surpassed himself. Recordings of these public appearances were broadcast several times by the BBC, and painstaking transcripts were published as a separate book eighteen months after Berlin's death. It is better to read them than to listen to them, one critic writes, because the written word creates the necessary distance from Berlin's bold intellectual constructs and reveals that in these lectures, if anything, Berlin was merely bold. The choice of the word 'bold', with its overtones of insolence, is significant here.

What follows is the analysis of an expert. Some of his conclusions can be challenged, with others one has to agree, but the criticism, dispute and agreement smack of criticism, refutation or acceptance of the actual Romanticism, of, let's say, Lord Byron, his *Childe Harold*, and Childe Harold himself. All three give us enough reason to adopt whatever attitude we fancy towards them, from rapture to indignation. Romanticism is the substance of the lively decades which included the creative work of such and such artists, their personal life, their private enterprises – but only them and those whom they affected or touched, then or after their death. Of course, Romanticism in the narrow sense of the word is also an object of special interest, and the focus of the scholarly career of people who are studying – as far as that is possible, that is in a necessarily fragmented and distorted manner – the details of life at this time and its historical, literary and ideological context. And while they are doing so they are quarrelling among themselves and handing out certificates that assert the degree of correctness of each other's judgements. But Romanticism belongs to them in the same way that the world's oil reserves belong to the laboratory assistant who conducts a chemical analysis of an oil well. We used the word 'necrophilia' to refer to a volume of research on Lermontov's biography that had just appeared in Russia when we were in our twenties.

More than anything else, Berlin in his lectures managed to communicate the spirit of the Romantic era, that which the man in the street, having picked up nothing but a vague idea of the fascination of Romanticism, intuitively feels and expects to hear from someone, but cannot formulate for himself. People did indeed flock to the lecture theatre, but not because they were a herd that loved the sound of the flute and the crack of the whip, or because Berlin had become a fashionable shepherd at the time. The dazzlingly intense presentation of the material, the ingenuity of his speech, the magic of its rhythm, the hypnotic effect of his repetitions and of his flowing enumerations – this was precisely what Romanticism was all about. It was shattering, paralysing, and in a good way numbed the critical capacity of his listeners, who had come not to study Romanticism in a class setting, but to enjoy it with their whole being. They were lucky, the lecturer was not just on his best form, but indeed surpassed himself.

IV

When I asked Berlin whether Akhmatova's solemn words, 'I am happy to have lived during these years and witnessed events that were without parallel', were also an accurate account of what he himself had lived through, his answer made me smile: 'No. I am happy, but not because I lived during that time.' Soon afterwards, in a conversation about something else, he added: 'Generally speaking it has been a terrible century. But it didn't touch me. I've been lucky.'

It is almost impossible to apply Akhmatova's statement to one's own life without sounding affected. Anyway, in essence it is not so much a statement as a motto. As an inscription for a shield, for example, I find Akhmatova's 'happiness' much more impressive than Berlin's 'luck'. For her as a Christian, 'life during these years' was embedded in the perspective of eternal life, a context in which the sum of trials withstood is diametrically opposed to the sum of trials avoided. But even from her these words sound to me too conventional a poetic hyperbole. Why 'happy'? Does seeing the enormity of the terror in the queue for the prison window, or the enormity of the hunger in the queue for the bread ration, as she had seen them, really fall into the category 'happiness'?

Let us stop there. It does not matter which fate Sir Isaiah Berlin *managed to avoid*. What is unique and irreversible – and therefore invites comparison with other, similar fates – is the fate that was conferred on him; in other words, the one he *did not avoid*. When one talks about fate rather than biography, or fate rather than nature, character or talent, events and facts change their interdependence and their scale, and the entire colourful, dense, diffuse, panoramic picture of a life condenses into one single shape –though this shape may be highly complex – one single symbol or hieroglyph. The multitude of lines and details gather to form one exquisite and imposing sign, like iron filings in a magnetic field. When Joseph Brodsky died in January 1996 I rang Berlin from Moscow and told him in the emotional shock of the moment that I felt very much like seeing him so that he could tell me about the deceased's first days and years abroad. He answered that he too very much wanted to talk to me about

Brodsky, but about 'the past, the Akhmatova years, when the seeds of every-thing were planted and it all happened. What came afterwards, in the West, was just the harvest.' When Berlin went to Russia in 1945 he gently tried to convince the people he met that their assumptions about the great flowering of art and literature on the other side of the impenetrable Iron Curtain were mis-taken. On the contrary, he saw that the Russian interest in art and literature, the specifically Russian thirst for culture (or, in the words of Mandel'shtam, 'the longing for world culture'), and the creative potential of Russian artists, poets and writers that constituted the answer to this thirst and longing, were quali-ties of which their Western contemporaries should be envious. At a distance – the geographical one remains the same in 1945 and 2000, but as far as historical distance is concerned, the impression grows stronger as time passes – Berlin's fate, once the preparatory sketches and compositional designs have been erased, is shot through with Russia.

In Russia it is often simple everyday life – a life that is identical with the one next door in its ordinariness and obscurity – that turns into fate, because such innocent activities as milking the cow or ploughing the orchard can easily be raised to the level of a significant act or martyrdom, if your milking or ploughing coincides with collectivisation. In very much the same manner, Berlin, without having done *anything special*, found himself among the initia-tors – or, in the language of official propaganda, instigators – of the Cold War, a member of the Doctors' Plot against the government, an ideological enemy of the Soviet State. It would be easy to ascribe all this to the regime's paranoia, if Russian poetry had not itself raised him to the rank of Aeneas, hero of some of its best and most beautiful poems. As I understand it – and there are first-hand observations that confirm my version – this meant more to him than anything else. While he took the attacks of his critics, even those that were unjust, as something normal to which he replied with appropriate counter-strikes, and while his attitude to the recognition he enjoyed remained ironical, he jeal-ously guarded his role in Akhmatova's cycles *Cinque*, *A Sweetbriar in Blossom* and *Poem without a Hero*, though invariably, for etiquette's sake, accompan-ied by the reservation 'What kind of Aeneas am I?' He was profoundly aggrieved by any encroachment upon his place in Akhmatova's poetry, and pro-foundly upset by the unceremonious intrusions of amateur scholars into their relationship.

When I understood that a letter addressed to me was the last letter of his life, sent to Russia – about Akhmatova – about the end of all that had been, the realisation sent a piercing sensation through my body, but I was not surprised.

His first letter I had received in August 1979; it had been travelling for two months. It was a response to my translation of 'The Troubadours' Songs', which I had sent him.

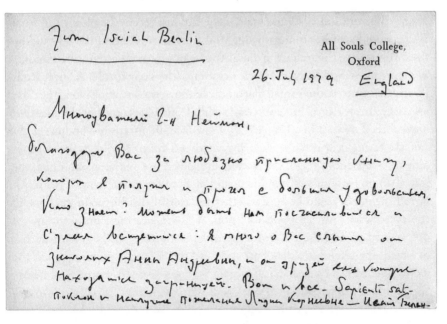

Dear Mr Naiman, I wish to thank you for the book you sent me, which I have enjoyed reading very much. Who knows? Maybe, if we're lucky, we'll meet one day: Anna Andreevna's acquaintances and friends abroad have told me many things about you. That's it, really. Sapienti sat – regards, and please give my best wishes to Lidiya Korneevna [Chukovskaya] – Isaiah Berlin –

The note, reproduced here, was written on a rectangular white card with the letterhead 'All Souls College, Oxford' in the upper right-hand corner. What this All Souls College might be like – where one casually drops *sapienti sat* into a conversation; where Sir is sitting in his extravagantly furnished monk's cell and, at the height of Soviet rule, styles me Mr instead of Comrade; where, changing to Russian, he uses '-eya' in the nominative and accusative case and inserts an apostrophe after 's' before a labialised vowel – I could imagine only in the terms of the literature I knew. *Sapienti sat*, enough for a wise man, also meant that 'abroad' was not an impossible thing and that there were people who might take an interest in me if I were there. Maybe Berlin himself, to some degree.

He rang me in early spring 1988. It was still cold, and snow was lying in the streets. He was in Moscow. He said he was in town for a few days only: could he visit me tomorrow, around midday? Yes, of course. Is this the correct address? Yes, let me explain how to get here – in which hotel are you staying? I am here as the Ambassador's guest, his driver will bring me. In that case let me explain it to him. Not necessary, he'll do a test run today, everything will be OK. See you tomorrow, then. See you tomorrow. Immediately afterwards I received a phone call from Lidiya Chukovskaya: she had just received a phone call from Sir, he would visit her tomorrow night, the driver would find the way and do a test run today. The following day at twelve noon my children were standing at the window. Suddenly a cry: He's coming. I looked outside. A silver Rolls-Royce, the Ambassador's small flag on the bumper, was crawling along the dirty ice-covered track into the courtyard behind our block, formed by identical nine-storey boxes. When I looked up I saw faces in dozens of windows opposite, all staring at this fairy-tale being, neither fish nor fowl. It was the beginning of Gorbachev's reign, the Soviet regime had not yet been abolished, the Iron Curtain had not yet been lifted, and none of the inhabitants of our block, myself included, could be sure whether the royal Rolls-Royce in our squalid courtyard wasn't just an optical illusion. A driver wearing a uniform cap got out, walked around the car, and opened the front door on the other side, out of which a passenger in a dark coat and a red fur cap stepped on to the ice: the driver opened the back door, an elegant young woman appeared, and before she got into the front seat they said goodbye to each other. The silver swan was off, and Isaiah Berlin disembarked from the lift on our floor.

On entering our flat he immediately set the tone for our conversations of the following ten years, during which we would meet regularly and, during my year in Oxford, frequently, and thus gave my wife and me permission to adopt the same tone – ordinary, friendly. It was as if these ten years were already lying behind us and not in the future. And because of this he felt no need carefully to define the degree of irony about topics requiring irony, but behaved as if we had all agreed on it, simply by adopting it. Irony and confidentiality. He told us that he was accompanying his close friend Alfred Brendel, a famous pianist who was to give a concert in Moscow, and Brendel's wife. I asked whether she was the woman I had seen in the courtyard, and he confirmed this, much more quickly than I had expected, and then added, jokingly, as if my question had aimed at something altogether different, or as an excursus that had arisen naturally: She's German, but she was born in 1945 and bears no responsibility for the crimes of the Nazis. Just like that.

When I casually mentioned that Wellesley College, USA, had invited me, as a specialist, to give a series of lectures on Old Provençal poetry – 'but what kind of a specialist am I?' – he interrupted me with the same decisiveness, answered with the same immediacy: 'Trust my experience, you are much more of a specialist than they need ... And how is it going, will they let you out of here?' I would have to conduct a total of thirteen separate negotiations, but when this conversation took place I had got only half way. And he said, 'Why don't you come over to us, if you can manage?' After that we met on several occasions when I attended conferences in England, and he asked me again: 'Would you like to live in Oxford for a while?', and every time he managed to say it before I

had time to ask. And then I received a phone call. An elderly gentleman introduced himself as Professor Soandso from Oxford, said that he was in Moscow,
that he was a friend of Isaiah's and that Isaiah had given him forms for me to
fill in, so that I could apply to All Souls College for the position of a Visiting
Fellow. When? Well, tomorrow.

V

In Russia the figure of Isaiah Berlin is part of two equally convincing landscapes.
The first was created by the cycle *Cinque*, and does not try to hide its closeness
to Dante's landscape, with elements from all three parts of *The Divine Comedy*.
The second is biographical, and linked to Riga. Neither of them takes into
account any of the factors peculiar to Berlin's life in Oxford. It took me some
time to discover Berlin in his natural surroundings – at home, so to say – but
once climate and topography had finally focused my vision and it became normal to see him in the street, inside the College walls and Headington House, in
our flat in Iffley Village and in a café, I caught myself thinking that none of this
cancelled out the other two pictures, created by a mixture of Russian imagination and Russian reality.

'Not to the secret pavilion / The flaming bridge leads these two: / The gilded
cage now awaits him./ At her end, the red scaffold is erect.'[1] Akhmatova wrote
these lines after she had seen the real Headington House, and sat through the
sumptuous dinner organised in her honour. The pathos of this quatrain stems
from the contrast between happiness and disaster, but only at first sight. The red
scaffold – red from blood, the shadow of the Communist flag and the reflection of flames – throws its shadow on to the gilding, too. But it is the bridge
that most clearly embodies the indivisibility of these two fates – there is only
one bridge for the two of them. The drama lies not so much in the antagonism
of the hero's and heroine's respective positions as in the fact that there can be
no third option, no pavilion, but cage and scaffold are the only choices left to
characters of their standing, and through them to humanity as a whole. This
fits the Oxford context just as well as any other.

One day when I was walking towards the lawn in front of Headington House
I turned round and saw a red fox cross the path next to the gates, jump on to the
stone boundary-wall and slip off on the other side: a fiery vision. I asked Isaiah
whether this happened often in these parts and he replied: 'Yes, there are foxes
here. No hens, but quite a few foxes.' – 'What about hedgehogs?' – 'We have
hedgehogs here, too ... But I wrote that without thinking of live hedgehogs and
foxes' ... We were both talking about his book *The Hedgehog and the Fox*.

I had planned to visit my mother in Leningrad during my Oxford year. On

[1] 'Not to the secret pavilion', 1965.

the day before my flight a Fellow of the College who had been to Serbia told us over lunch that a Serbian saying asks: 'Croatia, where is that?' In the common room I read in the papers about Ingushetians hijacking the hostel of the Institute for Railway Engineers, about the hunger Moscow was facing in the next ten days, about −16° centigrade (this I was told by the up-to-date *International Herald Tribune*), about the fact that one Russian rouble was now worth one US cent. All this I read while having coffee, and when I shared the news with Isaiah he just replied: 'Stay here, don't go.' I went to Leningrad, came back, and was again having coffee with the same brown sugar in the same armchair by the window when I read in *The Times* about a radioactive leak that had occurred yesterday in one of Leningrad's nuclear power-stations. At this moment a former Fellow named Butler asked me: 'Is it right that Leningrad used to be more liberal than Moscow?' I replied: 'From time to time. But not while I was living there', which caused general amusement, which I hadn't meant to provoke with my literal description of the circumstances.

Isaiah was capable of simply saying 'Stay here, don't go' when he heard about the concrete threats a person might face in Russia, but he never looked at Russia as an observer. He could not have asked whether life was more liberal in Leningrad or Moscow, because he had first-hand experience of this *liberalism* and was perhaps the only liberal in Oxford – in England, in Europe – who knew why this concept could not be applied to the Soviet regime in any way or to any degree. It is impossible to imagine him taking an interest in some random person's opinion of the new leader, President, Party Secretary, or just the politician who'd made it to the top, because he had seen them in reality, was on the receiving end at first hand – at their own hands. To this extent it did not matter that it happened in 1945 or 1956 and not in 1991, that at the time it was Kaganovich or Stalin and not Brezhnev or Andropov or Zyuganov: a breed doesn't change merely over time, or because of a single litter.

VI

I asked him: How do people exist in the hereafter? Are they middle-aged; young; old? He replied: They don't exist at all. This was before our serious conversation about his 'problems with God' and about 'the difficulty that the word "God" means nothing at all to me'. I tried to make a joke, to be conciliatory: Well, in some way or other they probably do exist. He raised his index finger and declared: They don't exist at all. 'The hereafter' doesn't exist. There is no such thing as a 'hereafter'. There was a smile on his face, but he left me in no doubt that he was being utterly serious. At that moment, though, I decided to go with the smile.

How could he be so sure about this? This was a man whose life consisted in socialising, who was permanently engrossed in conversation and hungry for the news of every new day, who was constantly observing the crowd in the street – 'watching their heads, their faces'. This was a man who told me: 'Other people always cheered me up: whenever I was bored, people came to me and everything became more or less cheerful'; who 'was never bored in the company of other people' – 'I simply can't imagine that there will ever be a day just as light, noisy and happy as this one but without me.'

It does not follow that he collected people. On the contrary, what follows is that he did not collect them, for what is the point of a collection when 'hereafter' there will be nothing left because 'hereafter' itself does not exist? He did not collect people, but he condensed them within himself, probably in the same way he condensed within himself the light, noise and happiness of each new day. His book *Personal Impressions* does not contain biographies, portraits or analytical essays, but remarks that are doubly unstable, doubly 'softer than bronze', doubly prone to slip away, vanish, be erased: first, because they are, literally, impressions, the imprints of light touches, and then because they are personal. He applied the same method of gaining insight in his scholarly work, and it is characteristic of his knowledge in general. His descriptions of a person, a phenomenon, an abstract category are encyclopaedically exact and complete, but at some moment the volume of the encyclopaedia snapped shut and gave way to the impression, or, rather, allowed the impression in: a living episode, an anecdote, a witticism, an aphorism.

VII

Once, in one of those moments of unperturbed morning clarity (I was in New York, where I was teaching at the time), I suddenly experienced a burning desire to ask Isaiah about all the things I am writing about (more or less) at the moment. About what a Russian can gain from Europe, about what Europe can do to a Russian and what happens when the Russian is Jewish and Europe is specifically England, and when the setting is the twentieth century from beginning to end, and when the Russian in question is Isaiah Berlin. Something like this.

My desire to see and hear him that very minute was so strong that the memory of it remained with me for the next day and the day after that, too. Three or four days later I received a letter from him. It was a breathless monologue about the feeling he had had when reading the third volume of Lidiya Chukovskaya's *Notes* on Akhmatova. The letter finished with the words: 'Oh dear. I will not go on about it. Is there any chance of your coming to this side of the ocean? The three volumes of *Neva* create an agenda on which we could talk and talk and talk for days and days and days. Do let me know.' I rang him to tell him about my own desire to see him, similar, as it seems, to the one he had experienced, just as urgently, on the same day and at the same hour.

There are few people to whom world poetry has devoted so many poems, and poems of such quality, as the addressee and inspirer of *Cinque*, *A Sweetbriar* and the dedication to *Poem without a Hero*. Moreover, he occupies the special position of 'the Guest from the Future', alive among the dead. I asked him when he found out that Akhmatova wrote these poems for him.

– Only when Zhirmunsky arrived.

– At the end of the 1960s, that late?

– That late. She had read them to me. But I didn't understand that they were about me.

– When did she read them to you?

– I am telling you: she read them to me in January 1946.

– That is, during your last meeting?

– Yes, yes, during our last meeting.

– You met twice.

– Yes, and this was the last meeting, quite a short one.

– She read them to you, but you did not understand that they were for you?

– Yes.

– Can you explain why they are called *Cinque*?

– No. It means five.

– Yes, but why in Italian?

– Well ...

– Why not *Cinq* or *Five*?

– Well yes, of course. I don't know.

– ... and 'the cigar's blue smoke', what does that refer to?

– That's me.

– You used to smoke?

– Yes, I used to smoke. Long Swiss cigars. Weak Swiss cigars. I had these long weak cigars from Switzerland which I was constantly smoking.

– And when did you stop smoking?

– When I fell ill; I can't remember the name of the illness, not even in English; somewhere in Persia I must have caught something. I came back here, lay down, and, well, they despaired of my life, but I survived in the end. That's why I didn't smoke while I was ill. I only took it up again when I got better, but even then I wasn't too keen on smoking. Well, I was ready to smoke. And then I decided, maybe I should try *not* to smoke. And I've never smoked again, never had the desire to smoke, smoking held no attraction for me.

– Did you smoke cigars or cigarettes?

– Before the war I smoked cigarettes, during the war I smoked cigars. Real ones, Dutch. Cuban ones. Big ones.

– But when you were at Akhmatova's, you weren't smoking real cigars?

– No, they were real cigars. Long Swiss cigars. There is a straw inside them,

you need to pull it out and then you can light the cigar. No, no, she was definitely talking about me.

– (*I answered jokingly.*) As you know, I don't doubt that.

– I know. And the same thing when I talked about love. That I was in love
with someone. About another woman's love. Remember, she says at some point
'that you had no time to finish your tale about a stranger's love'.[1]

– That did also happen?

– Yes. I told her. That I was in love, and how – where and how.

– Did she ask you?

– No, I think I simply started to tell her, just like that.

– And was there an atmosphere of magic in your encounter?

– Of course. Of course. The whole evening was filled with a magic atmosphere. As soon as we were alone, after that lady had left – the Assyriologist,
probably a student of that man Shileiko, I think – as soon as she left us alone,
around midnight, the magic began. I've never spent an evening like that with
anyone.

– And what about an erotic charge ...?

– There wasn't any. Nothing at all.

– Did it occur to you that her first husband, Gumilev, who had pretensions
to being a Russian Livingstone, and you, an outsider, the traveller in cultural
territories and strange universes, were finishing a mission he had begun then, in
her youth?

– No. No. I didn't know a thing about Gumilev.

– And why 'Sweetbriar'?

– I have no idea.

– OK. I'm enjoying all this very much, that you know nothing. But still –
why Bach's Chaconne?[2]

– I don't know that either. Well, Richter or someone probably played her
Bach's Chaconne. No, Bach's Chaconne, that's a piece for violin.

– Well, yes, people have already researched that, so that's not interesting
now ... What does 'You did not give me that present which you had brought
from afar'[3] refer to? Did you bring her something from someone?

– No, nothing, from no one. No, I only gave her the books I had with me.
English books.

– Do you remember which ones?

– I can tell you. I gave her Kafka, one book by Kafka, I don't remember
which one. And then some poetry by the Sitwells, who were bad poets and

---

[1] *Cinque*, 4.

[2] Mentioned in 'A Dream', *A Sweetbriar in Blossom*, 6; and in the 'Third and Last'
dedication to *Poem without a Hero*.

[3] 'In a Broken Mirror', *A Sweetbriar in Blossom*, 9.

whom I shouldn't have given to her. But still, I had them with me and I decided
it would be best to leave them with her. The Sitwell brothers, the brothers and
Edith Sitwell, who was a poetess. Not an important one. All these beautiful
emotions. That's what I gave to her, and later I was embarrassed about it – they
were not for her. Kafka, that was right.

   – Did you ever have the impression that you had missed something, not
reciprocating the feeling Akhmatova had for you?

   – Only afterwards. When I heard that she had become angry when I married,
I understood. Before that, no. I never had the impression that I betrayed her
in any way. (*He pronounced the following sentences with a mixture of seriousness
and light irony.*) I realised that between her and me there was ... – some kind of
mystical relationship, which I cut short by my vulgar step of marrying. Indeed,
what massive vulgarity on my part, to marry. The two of us were bound by a
mystic thread, which I severed suddenly. After that, I think, I stopped being her
Guest from the Future. Afterwards I suddenly became *Sir* Isaiah: you remember, when she is talking to Chukovskaya I am always *Sir* Isaiah – that is ever so
slightly ironical.

   – Yes, it is. When I met her and she began to tell me about you I was given
a dual impression of you: on the one hand all that you've told me just now, on
the other hand, nevertheless, a figure of considerable significance.

   – She made me up, I wasn't the person she saw in me. I was something ... she
constructed me in some way.

VIII

In his *Personal Impressions* Berlin lists the topics of his nocturnal conversation
with Akhmatova and sometimes also mentions *what* is being said on this or
that topic, mostly by her. In addition to the ways in which it enriched their
encounter, from the concrete and individual to the magical and historical, this
conversation also quenched Akhmatova's thirst for what Mandel'shtam had
called 'world culture'. The remark she once let slip about 'a foreigner' who on
one occasion told her that which can be 'neither forgotten nor remembered'
inspires an irrepressible desire to reconstruct Berlin's part in their duet, at least
approximately. Of course, at the time many of the things about which he used
to talk towards the end of his life hadn't yet happened, but the topics themselves, and the way in which he discussed and elaborated them during our conversation in April 1997, which lasted several days, can, with all due reservations,
give a sufficiently close idea of that night in November 1945. Berlin's manner of
drawing broad comparisons and contrasts, sometimes laid out for the conversation partner to see, sometimes left to be guessed at, a manner that was close
to Akhmatova's own, but most importantly his way of calling things by their
name were undoubtedly characteristic of him even back then. Even then his

fascination consisted not so much in his knowledge and gift for observation as in his manner of combining his knowledge and his observations and his ability to express these combinations in a human language, understood and welcomed by all.

IX

Around that time, it seems, I found the answer to the question why the cycle of poems is called *Cinque*. The analogy with Dante's imagery would seem forced, as is often the case with interpretations of Akhmatova's poetry, if it weren't for the space in which the two lyric heroes of *Cinque* are placed. This space is the starry cosmos, on to which the cosmos of the *Divine Comedy* is projected.

In September 1997 I wrote a letter to Berlin mentioning this. On 5 November he died. On 10 November I received a letter from him in reply to my own. He had dictated it on 31 October.

> I was delighted to receive your letter, and am full of admiration [...] you weave lines from the *Divine Comedy*, which AA, of course, knew intimately. [You have] made a marvel of this complex of interwoven attributions. So I [...] am proud to be the first owner of this masterpiece.
>
> I cannot remember if there is anything you asked me to do, in your letter, as I have been very ill and am not recovering fast. This is no surprise. [...]
>
> In the meanwhile, warm good wishes – there is not much likelihood of my coming to Moscow, Washington or New York – so you must come here.
>
> My wife sends you both her warm greetings, as indeed how could not I?

The passages I have left out here (as well as those I have included) are personal. Well, the entire letter is like that, and I wouldn't want to publish it here if I was convinced that it was addressed exclusively to myself. Given that the letter is not just addressed to a *concrete person*, but also sent *to Russia*, the omitted middle paragraph – 'If there is something I can do for you from my literal bed of sickness, I shall of course try to do it – you have but to say' – speaks of his readiness to do something, not just 'for you', in the singular, but for 'all of you'. You who are *over there*.

In life in general, in such a full and expressive life in particular, and in its last gesture before death most of all, nothing appears accidental, and these last few phrases of a conversation with other people that lasted almost a hundred years inevitably attract the spotlight. This light finds that they constitute his final utterance to the place where it all began, and where everything then reached its acme in two dozen poems that were not foreshadowed by anything and not in any way caused by the general order of life.

In such a light every single one of the one hundred and fifty or so words sounds like a word of conclusion. The towns and cities he will not see again. The illness from which he will not recover. Warmth, cordiality. The desire to serve and give. Emotional generosity. His wife. Akhmatova. Poetry.

And the signature. 'Isaiah', in Russian. Perhaps the first word he learned to write, and now the last one he was ever to write.

X

This man, Isaiah Berlin, was, as he had himself admitted when we first met, 'neither the one nor the other'. Neither philosopher nor philologist. Not a historian, or a literary scholar, or a researcher, or a political scientist, or an ethicist. Not a poet. In one word, a typical 'non-mathematician'. Very sharp-witted, but not Bernard Shaw. Intelligent, but both he and I have met more intelligent people. A kind man, but not as kind as, say, Mother Teresa. A man of great learning, but not an academic type. And so on.

We always wish we could explain a person in a single word, and we always use a hundred or a hundred thousand words instead, and the essential always remains unsaid. However, if I had to do it on the condition 'Either one word or none at all', I would call my protagonist *normal*. He embodied the standard of the human norm, not in the contemporary sense of the word, according to which it is equivalent to 'OK' or 'all right', but in the sense of the axis around which the definitions of humankind, more often than not framed unconsciously, revolve – definitions of intelligence, goodness, talent, extravagance, exception-ality, banality, vulgarity, baseness, stupidity. The norm in the sense of the core that supports all these human phenomena. The norm not as an average, not as a limit, but on the contrary, as offering itself in the fullness and clarity of all that it contains. The rabbi – we have to suppose that this is how Isaiah Berlin's parents wanted to see him – reclining at Plato's Symposium at Agathon's house; the Eternal Jew in the company of the Knights of the Round Table. These are the extremes of the amplitude which the pendulum of the norm traverses so as not to limit the abundance of life on earth and not to slow down its march, yet at the same time not to force the whole mechanism to the point where it breaks.

The well-known entomologist Miriam Rothschild, Berlin's contemporary and close friend, once tried to convince me, in her lightly ironic manner, that the civilisation of ants was in equal measure older and wiser than the human one – that is to say, more lively. That when the human race has disappeared from the face of the earth, the ants will continue to live on it, just as they lived before the appearance of man. Perhaps. In a way this was confirmed recently when I discovered that tiny light-brown city ants were nesting in my computer.

Perhaps the ants will really take the place of the human tribe. But they cannot replace it. And neither will the computers.

This man spent his entire life turned towards the past. He never forecast the future. He only ever lived in the present moment, although never according to its fashion. And now we discover that despite all this he did not confine himself to 'his own time'. By his own nature or instinct he defined it (his time) through his way of participating in life and in culture. His perception of reality and his devotion to it were categorically non-systematic, and complete only in so far as they appropriated fragments of the whole. In some sense, as they would say today, like film clips. In other words, contemporary.

Looking at people rather than insects, and taking a pen in his hand rather than a computer, he nevertheless went from his century into the next, as a 'contemporary man', open to and respectful of every novelty. As an amusing, absolutely genuine, living person.

Translated by Josephine von Zitzewitz

Run Over by Isaiah

Peter Oppenheimer

OUR FAMILY'S FRIENDSHIP with Isaiah began with the Russian connection: my mother-in-law Lydia Pasternak-Slater and her sister Josephine. But I personally first encountered him some six years before my marriage, when I came up to Oxford as an undergraduate in Michaelmas Term 1958. Berlin gave his Inaugural Lecture – 'Two Concepts of Liberty' – on 31 October of that year. Everybody knew that this was one of those lectures that one had to go to (like Edgar Wind's lectures on Michelangelo, or J. L. Austin's on the theory of perception – I still kick myself for not having gone to the latter). I duly joined the spellbound throng in the South School, at first straining to catch every syllable of that inimitable basso cantante, and then gradually realising that one didn't need to catch every syllable, because the important points were repeated several times from different angles and perspectives.

A few weeks (or was it months?) later I was cycling into Radcliffe Square from Catte Street – in those days a motorised thoroughfare, not a pedestrian walkway – when a small car overtook me and drew up opposite the side gate of All Souls. The driver opened his door without looking and knocked me off my bicycle. Fortunately there was no other traffic coming up behind. The front-seat passenger alighted in anxious haste to make his apologies. It was Isaiah. Being totally unhurt, I scrambled to my feet, unable to resist a piece of undergraduate chutzpah. 'Please don't worry, Sir Isaiah. It's an honour to be run over by such a distinguished personality!' It made me one of the – surely – very few people ever to see Isaiah at a loss for words.

In 1966 Isaiah was named founding President of Wolfson College. I saw something of him in that context. Wolfson did not yet have its charter as an independent foundation. In approaching the question of investing the embryo college's initial endowment, Isaiah sought the help of his former All Souls colleague, the economist Ian Little, who was now a Fellow of Nuffield and one of those responsible for that college's outstandingly successful performance on the stock exchange. At Ian's prompting I was also brought in, being at that time a Research Fellow and Acting Investment Bursar of Nuffield.

The creation of Wolfson College is one of the notable events of twentieth-century Oxford. Its gossipy aspect, however, remains to be chronicled. An obstacle which had to be overcome was the element of mutual contempt which coloured relations between the Wolfson family and the University, notwithstanding the interest of both sides in reaching a deal. 'Astonishing to visit Universal House [then headquarters of the Wolfson business empire, Great Universal Stores],' one member of the University's hierarchy confided to me on a train journey from London, 'there's hardly an educated man in the place!' Leonard Wolfson (now Lord Wolfson of St Marylebone) was equally forthright on the subject of the University rattling the begging bowl and knowing not the first thing about how to earn a living. He also insisted before long, incidentally, on overriding Ian Little and myself as investment advisers, regarding us as low-grade speculators. If there was any huxtering to be done, that was his job. What he wanted from us was a portfolio of unquestionable probity – gilt-edged and blue chips only, if you please. In such circumstances, Isaiah's combination of distinction and bonhomie, of status both in British academe and in the Jewish community, of seeming unworldliness and shrewd judgement of personal qualities, was surely significant in nursing matters to a successful conclusion.

Music formed Isaiah's most frequent cultural enthusiasm, particularly chamber and piano music, but also opera. He was an ultra-regular at Wigmore Hall recitals. He relished his years (1954–65 and 1974–87) as a Board member of the Royal Opera House. Lord (Garrett) Drogheda, who even before becoming Chairman had brought Isaiah on to the Board, describes him in his memoirs as 'mercurial, hypersensitive, with antennae stretching far out in every direction, omniscient, prejudiced, funny, human and lovable'.[1] At Covent Garden Isaiah was often ready with suggestions for a particular conductor or (less frequently) singer to fill a vacant slot in the calendar. Occasionally he played a key role in overcoming some episodic crisis. Drogheda reproduces *in extenso* the masterly letter which Isaiah wrote to Georg Solti to persuade him not to abandon his musical direction of Schoenberg's *Moses and Aaron* in 1965.[2]

Isaiah's Jewishness was another of his cultural commitments. Of course it was more than that. Asked by the UK Union of Jewish Students to contribute his thoughts on 'Why be Jewish?' to an edition of the Haggadah – that extraordinary compendium of liturgy, narrative, wisdom and sing-song around which Jewish families celebrate the Eve of Passover – Isaiah wrote:

> I am quite incapable of writing even a short passage on what being Jewish means to me [*sic*!]. All that I think is that I am a Jew, in exactly the sense in which I have two legs, arms, eyes etc. – it is just an attribute, which I take for granted as belonging to me, part of the minimum description of me as a person. I am neither proud of it nor embarrassed by it – I just am a Jew, and it never occurred to me that I could be anything else. The question

---

[1] Lord Drogheda, *Double Harness: Memoirs* (London, 1978), 240.
[2] Letter of 10 February 1964, ibid. 306–7.

'Why be Jewish?' is something that I cannot answer any more than 'Why
be alive?' or 'Why be two-legged?' [1]

Religion remains, however, a crucial aspect of the Jewish heritage. Jewish
religious practice centres on scriptural awareness and on obedience to a code
of law (*halakhah* in Hebrew) covering all aspects of existence from high moral
principles to mundane details of diet and dress. Rabbinic tradition identifies
not ten, but no fewer than 613 commandments to be obeyed by an observant Jew. Isaiah's attitude to Jewish observance had much in common with his
approach to political philosophy. Moderation, kindness, the rule of reason
and the appreciation of human qualities and of societal and cultural achievements were the great virtues. Purely mechanical compliance with regulations
did not appeal to him. Rather, one should be honest about one's choices
and shortcomings, and not seek probably specious justification for them.
Associated or consequent inconsistencies did not trouble him. Life is full of
them.

'I don't fulfil many of the 613 commandments,' he would say about his
preference for Jewish orthodoxy over reformist modernism, 'but I don't want a
rabbi to tell me that it's in order not to.' In the same spirit he resigned his membership (and Vice-Presidency) of the Old Paulines – the old boys' club of his
school, St Paul's – when the school's Jewish quota became public knowledge,
even though he himself had known about it long before.

Isaiah adopted positions of this kind without forfeiting respect, because
people recognised that they stemmed not from moral carelessness but from a
strong instinct about moral priorities. When is compromise in order and when
not? At what point does discretion become hypocrisy, and why? Isaiah did not
attempt to give general, abstract answers to such questions, but he felt able to
answer them in (almost) any specific instance. And he judged people first and
foremost by their moral qualities, not by whether they were clever or interesting. His descriptions of people he knew usually began with a moral dimension –
'Not an evil man', or something of that sort. Nor would he shrink from a little
malice if he thought it deserved. 'Under that crusty, disagreeable exterior is a
real shit trying to get out,' he remarked (or quoted) of an All Souls colleague.
And of course he had his academic *bêtes noires*, especially when he thought
them politically tainted, such as (for very contrasted reasons) Hannah Arendt
or Isaac Deutscher.

Isaiah himself always said – and obituarists and others duly stressed the
point – that conversation rather than writing was his preferred means of
self-expression. He wrote not from inner compulsion, but when circumstances obliged or people pestered him: a distinguished lecture here, a

[1] *The UJS Haggadah* (London, 1996), 68.

contribution to a symposium there, even his book on Karl Marx. But that did not stop his human concerns and preoccupations from being apparent in his writings.

In his work on Russian thinkers and writers (Belinsky, Herzen, Turgenev) he highlighted the glimmers of liberal reason and tolerance in that politically tortured country. It is as an authority on Herzen that he is most admired by scholars in Russia. In relation to the eighteenth-century Enlightenment he was drawn not merely to mainstream figures, like Montesquieu or Hume, but still more to those less widely known (Hamann, Herder, Vico) whose thought suggested the fragility of the rule of reason, the chaos beneath the surface, and presaged its supersession by nineteenth-century Romanticism. And not least, Isaiah's Zionist convictions informed his portraits of Moses Hess and Chaim Weizmann, as well as of Lewis Namier, and also his view of nationalism in all its manifestations – subject only to his utter rejection of violence as a political instrument, whether by those in rebellion or those in power.

Isaiah had married relatively late – he was nearly forty-seven – and had three stepsons but no children of his own. One would never have guessed. As husband and stepfather and domestic host he radiated family warmth by a kind of natural add-on to the conversational agility and humour that had long captivated academic colleagues and wider audiences.

A younger generation is the best witness to this. When the Oppenheimers began in the mid-1970s to be regular guests of Isaiah and Aline at the annual Passover Eve celebrations – known as the *seder*, meaning 'order', in Hebrew – our own children were not yet ten years old. Our son Daniel remembers those evenings as

> splendid occasions [...] with various august Jewish members of the 'Great and the Good' as a floating cast of extras. Isaiah would read the text [of the Haggadah] with great relish and greater speed, pausing only to add the occasional comment, most of which would be repeated verbatim every year. I say 'comment', but future students of Isaiah's thought, pricking up their ears at the notion of hearing the great thinker's ideas on the festival of freedom, will have to be disappointed. Though utterly typical of Isaiah these comments were made very much off-duty. To take the two most usual – when we reached Psalm 114, 'Be-tzet Yisrael mi-Mitzrayim' (When Israel went forth from Egypt), Isaiah would pause after reciting it and say, 'There is a most splendid setting of that by Mendelssohn, in Latin – "De exitu Israel ...", describes the Jordan being driven back – "reversus est retrorsum, retrorsum, reversus est retrorsum ...". Very fine

setting ...'.[1] Later in the evening, when we reached the phrase 'Even ma'asu habonim hay'ta l'rosh pina' (the stone rejected by the builders has become the cornerstone), he shook his head doubtfully and remarked, 'A most mysterious verse.'

Isaiah also took particular delight in the aftermath of the hunt for the Afikoman [a portion of matzo hidden for the children to compete in finding it, the winner then returning it to the family head in exchange for a reward]. Whichever child it was would shyly approach Isaiah, Afikoman in hand. 'Now you must bargain with me,' the eminent historian of ideas would inform them gleefully. 'I have something here which I can offer you in exchange. Are you willing to accept it?' In the closing stages of the evening Isaiah would delegate singing of the prescribed songs to my family, as we knew the tunes; but he beamed at the company as we bellowed our way through the familiar melodies.

Now no more, alas. But at Jewish occasions the past tends to leave its mark, and this one is no exception. Visitors to my family's Seder may have noticed a peculiar *minhag* [ceremonial custom] we have. Often, when we reach Psalm 114, one of the company may mutter a strange phrase in Latin: 'reversus est retrorsum, retrorsum ...'.[2]

---

[1] Mendelssohn's setting (his Opus 51) is indeed memorable. That aside, Isaiah allowed himself a bit of latitude on the detail, though just how much remains intriguingly unclear. Op. 51 is familiar in German ('Da Israel aus Ägypten zog'). A Latin version is additionally listed in Mendelssohn's complete works, but as unpublished. So did Isaiah hear it performed? Most unlikely, yet not impossible. Certainly he was no student of musical manuscripts. Vivaldi among others composed a specifically Latin setting (where the Psalm is numbered 113), which Isaiah may possibly have had in simultaneous mind. He was in any event creative with his Latin prepositions and prefixes. The actual text in the (Clementine) Vulgate begins '*In* exitu Israel de Aegypto'; and the river Jordan '*con*versus est retrorsum' (italics added). I am grateful to Henry Hardy for enlightenment (and amusement).

[2] A shortened and edited version of these remarks appeared as 'A Fine Setting', *Jewish Chronicle*, 14 November 1997, 31.

Working for Isaiah

Patricia Utechin in conversation with Humphrey Carpenter

An interview conducted by Humphrey Carpenter for BBC Radio 3 soon after Berlin's death, for a programme on IB broadcast on 8 December 1997

CARPENTER How did it all begin?

UTECHIN Well, I was in Oxford. I'd been working for a couple of other senior people in the University, and then my future husband, Sergei, came over direct to Oxford from displaced persons camp in Germany. He was Russian, so obviously Isaiah was one of the first people he was taken to see. I was looking for a new job, Isaiah was looking for a secretary. He knew of me on the grapevine and via my future husband, and there it was.

CARPENTER What sort of date was this?

UTECHIN I worked for him for two or three years in the early 1960s. Then Sergei got a job in Glasgow University and we went off to Glasgow. I came back to Oxford in 1972 after separating from Sergei, and worked for Isaiah for twenty-five years, until he died.

CARPENTER So you'd worked for academics before. Did you have any idea what you were in for?

UTECHIN Absolutely not.

CARPENTER I asked Henry Hardy if Isaiah was actually quite organised – you're starting to giggle already ...

UTECHIN He knew very, very clearly what he wanted to do, just on the level of the work he and I used to do. He'd buzz me on the telephone in my office on the top floor of Headington House: 'Can you come down?' When I arrived he'd say, 'Now, we've got a lot of work to do this morning', and he'd produce a pile of letters or, in the old days, when he was still in the full vigour of writing, he'd want to dictate a review or some other piece. But the detail was extremely chaotic. Everything would get changed: we can't catch that flight after all, we want to go on *that* flight; I can't manage the concert *this* night, could you switch the tickets? Could you move paragraph C from page 6 to page 5, and paragraph B from page 1 ... And what used to amuse me a lot, endlessly shuffling language around. For somebody who used language and words as marvellously as Isaiah did that's perfectly understandable, but he sometimes insisted on changes of adjectives that seemed to me absolutely synonymous: 'lovely' for 'beautiful' or 'beautiful' for 'lovely' or whatever it might be, but there was some nuance, Isaiah wanted this adjective and not that one.

CARPENTER That's also surely because he was very unsure of himself. He never believed that he was doing things to the best of his ability, did he?

UTECHIN People say this. I've read this. But he never, certainly when talking to me, put it quite that way. He did always firmly believe that he was overestimated. I know he said that very often publicly, but he used to say it in private too. He can't, though, surely, really not have thought that what he was doing was valid?

CARPENTER The indecision, or the fondness for changing his mind about details, fits in with his pluralism. The whole point of pluralism is that you've got a mass of choices; but he wasn't very good at making the choices?

UTECHIN I think that changing his mind so often was very much a case of a sudden new alternative or new perspective, if it was moving paragraphs about. Something would suddenly present itself to him and he'd think: Oh yes, it would be much better to do it that way than that way, whatever it was. And the other big problem he and I had was things getting lost: bits of paper, or letters, or whatever; and he'd accuse me of losing it and I would stoutly deny that I had lost it, and I have to say that quite often it had been misplaced by Isaiah.

CARPENTER He was absolutely determined to answer all letters, wasn't he?

UTECHIN He was *wonderful* – above and beyond the call of duty. That was one of the very many, if less important – although still important – things that I admired him so much for. The scruffiest little letter from somebody who'd studied with him thirty years ago, or somebody whom he'd met in the street. He was absolutely marvellous; sometimes for my sake almost too marvellous. I'd say, 'We don't *really* need to write a thank you letter *for* a thank you letter, Isaiah.' And he would say, 'Yes, I think we must write.'

CARPENTER You mention dictating reviews: would anything be drafted by him on paper before he dictated to you?

UTECHIN Sometimes he drafted on paper. Reviews he would normally dictate on to cassette or Dictabelt, or face to face, into shorthand, but he'd rarely dictate anything of any great length. Apart from anything else I'd have protested. Very often, when I was typing something, it could easily go through two, three typed drafts. I'd present him with a typed draft from the cassette that he'd recorded, and he'd scribble all over it. I'm one of the very few people, probably, along with Henry Hardy, who can read Isaiah's handwriting, certainly as it became in later years when it got very small. But Henry and I can read it. And I would get drafts back absolutely *covered* – so that you would think nobody could decipher them; and then maybe there'd be another draft and then finally the copy that he was prepared to accept.

CARPENTER Of course this was in pre-word-processing days, so everything had to be retyped.

UTECHIN By the time word-processors were the thing, Isaiah wasn't doing enough work for it to be worth it, thank goodness. I'm very happy indeed with my semi-electric typewriter. We did get a photocopier, which was a big advance in technology for us.

CARPENTER Tell me the story about the Dictabelt you got on back to front.

UTECHIN That was ages ago. Isaiah often used to dictate on to cassette late at night, and I'd come in in the morning and find piles of cassettes. But way back in the early days in the 1960s we were still using red plastic Dictaphone belts. I came in one morning and there were a couple of belts in the tray, and I put one of them on to my machine the wrong way round, which simply meant that his voice came out backwards: and honestly, for a moment or two I really didn't notice that much difference, I just thought: Oh, Isaiah sounds a wee bit funny this morning.

CARPENTER Listening to *The Magus of the North* – the famous Dictabelts that Henry Hardy recovered from the basement at Headington House – I hadn't realised that, when dictating something like that, he would dictate some of the punctuation but not other bits.

UTECHIN He would dictate some of his punctuation. This was one of the very few subjects that he and I used to have long arguments about, because I regard myself as an *extremely* good punctuator and also speller, and he would dictate the word – the name 'Kant' for instance – and he'd say 'K-a-n-t'. He'd then dictate some literally impossible name, which even *I* couldn't begin to spell, and he wouldn't spell it. So I was continually remonstrating – I'd say, 'Isaiah, I *can* spell Kant, but when you produce a name like so-and-so, could you please spell it for me?'

CARPENTER We all know that he thought at high speed, and that he thought in parentheses and in subordinate clauses and so forth, but I hadn't realised that he could dictate all of that including the punctuation: he obviously had a very strong sense of where that enormous sentence was finally going to go.

UTECHIN He often liked dictating to me direct, and I'd take it down in short-hand, and that would be absolutely marvellous because very often it would turn into a series of stories and mini-anecdotes, mini-lectures: I'd say, 'Who was so-and-so, Isaiah?' or, 'What was it really like in Oxford in the 1930s?' And then he'd be away, and I'd listen and listen and I wish I'd written half of it down. But to get back to punctuation: I was madly going on with my pencil on my shorthand pad, and every now and then I did have to say, 'Isaiah, could we *please* have a full stop? *Is* this sentence going to come to an end?' Or I'd say, 'This sentence isn't going to work, Isaiah.' And he'd say, 'Read it back to me'; and indeed I was right, it wouldn't work because he'd got so many clauses.

CARPENTER Alfred Brendel mentioned last night that, when Isaiah went out, he would sometimes take a Walkman and listen to that?

UTECHIN Absolutely. There's a heavenly picture – an imaginative picture in one's mind. When he and Aline used to go to Italy in the summer, he would walk over the hills with his Walkman and a beret and in a pair of shorts, and the peasants would say, 'Buongiorno, Signor Professore.'

CARPENTER Striding the hills, listening to Schubert.

UTECHIN Yes, and the Schubert would be infinitely more important. Isaiah always used to say that nature meant absolutely nothing to him, which is interesting.

CARPENTER Really? Did he expand on that at all?

UTECHIN I used to say, 'But mountains, Isaiah, or sunsets, or ...' 'No, no, no. The works of man.'

CARPENTER He was still lecturing when you began to work for him?

UTECHIN Yes, he was still lecturing when I began to work for him, even when I came back from Glasgow in 1972. After all, he was then still President of Wolfson: he'd become President in 1966 when I was in Glasgow.

CARPENTER This famous lecturing method of preparing a lecture by writing the whole thing and then gradually boiling it down stage by stage to a post-card, and then not even taking the postcard on to the platform: is this how you remember it?

UTECHIN Not very clearly, but I think that when he talks about that, as he has often done, he's primarily referring to the regular lectures that he used to give in university courses. By the early seventies, when I came back from Glasgow, it was a matter of special lectures, and those – my memory is pretty firm – were dictated on to belt or cassette and then typed by me. He liked a script as fall-back.

CARPENTER Or was it that all the concentration that went into writing the script was actually putting it into his mind, like an actor learning his lines?

UTECHIN Very possibly.

CARPENTER And he used to say, didn't he, that he couldn't look either at a script or at anybody in the audience, because he'd be put off?

UTECHIN The top right-hand corner of the room, he always used to say.

CARPENTER That's where his eyes went. That's true, is it?

UTECHIN I think so, yes. The only *famous* lecture of his that I ever went to personally was in the Examination Schools; it was what came out in *Personal Impressions* as 'Meetings with Russian Writers' – Pasternak and Akhmatova. And it was absolutely true, he just stared straight up into the top right-hand corner of the room.

CARPENTER And yet, when one met him, there was no question of the eyes looking elsewhere. He was very good on eye contact.

UTECHIN Absolutely. He was just so nervous about lecturing. I know this because fifteen, twenty years ago, when one of his vocal cords became paralysed, and it didn't have any serious effect but it made his voice much huskier, it gave him an excellent excuse for refusing invitations to lecture. It was a genuine excuse, but it was one that he was very glad to have.

CARPENTER Was he capable of losing his temper?

UTECHIN Very occasionally – it was very quickly over, no question of sulking or anything like that. He could get irritated easily. He'd occasionally quite justifiably be irritated with me if he was really convinced I'd lost the bit of paper or something and I couldn't find a strong enough defence, but it would never last. This was rare, though.

CARPENTER And was there any sort of fluctuation in mood from day to day?

UTECHIN He wasn't noticeably any moodier than any of the rest of us. If he was worried about something or if there was some bad news, public news from Israel or somewhere, then perhaps. But he always regarded himself as a very contented, equable person, and I would say that's not far wrong.

CARPENTER And he kept saying, when asked, 'I've had a very happy life.' He did feel that?

UTECHIN Absolutely. He felt that it was most extraordinary how nothing major had ever really gone wrong for him; he wasn't proud or boasting about this, he didn't think it was due to any merit of his, it was just something he observed and was grateful for.

CARPENTER And it didn't make him complacent, did it?

UTECHIN Totally not. Nor did it stop him from being understanding about other people's worries, or when things went wrong for them. It didn't make him ignore that. He was very aware and good and kind, and did whatever seemed suitable, whether it was a matter of talking or practical help or whatever, if somebody was in a bad spot.

CARPENTER That's interesting, because it was a sheltered life in many ways after he'd arrived in this country: St Paul's, then Oxford – and that was it, really?

UTECHIN   Yes, people always say that about him. But everybody goes through personal difficulties: your parents die, or somebody doesn't fall in love with you, or whatever. You could say it's a sheltered life being an Inland Revenue clerk – or anything you like.

CARPENTER   He also liked to say, 'I'm a taxi, I only do things when I'm called upon.' Is that really true?

UTECHIN   It's true that he would usually wait to be asked to do something. A lot of people, excellent people, including scholars, will volunteer, put themselves forward, be a bit entrepreneurial. Isaiah would always wait to be invited to give a lecture, not in the least out of any kind of arrogance; he might even have said that he was a bit lazy by nature, and did need to be called or pushed.

CARPENTER   And when asked on *Desert Island Discs* what his luxury would be, he said 'A big armchair in which to read.' I presume he was at his happiest when he could do that?

UTECHIN   Well, don't forget music. A big armchair and reading, but also listening to music. I was terribly touched once – it was long, long before he was ill, five, six, seven, eight years ago – I'd been in the library at Headington House and there'd been a long discussion about concert tickets, and I must get these ones, and I said, 'But Isaiah, this is August. The concert's happening next April; they'll laugh at me if I ring up and try to reserve.' And he'd say, 'Well, it's advertised, try and get it anyway.' And as I went out of the room he said, three-quarters to himself probably, only one-quarter to me, 'I *do love* music', or 'I *do love* listening to music', and the fervour and the feeling – it was said in an undertone – were very touching.

CARPENTER   How formally did he listen to it? Did he ever have it on as background while he was working?

UTECHIN   Not to my knowledge. Certainly not when he and I were dictating and talking in the morning. However, a lot of his dictating on to cassettes used to be done, as I've said, late at night. He and Lady Berlin may have been in London or wherever, and when they were back he'd go up to his study, and he might dictate for an hour or more. Quite often I would find on the cassette the next morning, when I put it on to type back from it, some loud piece of music – he'd got the volume turned up high – and occasionally I said, 'Isaiah, if you've got music on when you're dictating, could you very kindly turn the volume down a little?' But he never used music as mere wallpaper. He went to concerts a very great deal and listened and listened and listened.

CARPENTER   His musical taste, as Alfred Brendel has said, and as is well known, was fairly conservative, wasn't it?

UTECHIN I wouldn't like to pronounce on that. He belonged to a society for the propagation of new music, but probably.

CARPENTER What about his involvement with Covent Garden? Were you with him then?

UTECHIN Yes indeed. I was working for him most of the time that he was on the Opera Sub-Committee – for a few years, if I remember rightly, as Chairman, after which he reverted to being an ordinary member. He was assiduous in his attendance at meetings. He loved it: he was devoted to opera, but he also put an enormous amount of work and thought into it.

CARPENTER How much did he respond to current events in the news? Was he a great newspaper reader?

UTECHIN Very much so: not just the daily newspaper but all the obvious journals that the intelligent middle classes take, the *New York Review of Books*, the *London Review of Books*, the *Spectator*, the *Listener* in the old days (alas no more), the *TLS*; and I used occasionally to get into trouble because I'd think he was going to be away, and I would 'borrow' the *TLS* or the *Spectator* which had just arrived, and he'd say: 'Where is the *Times Literary Supplement*?' I'd say, 'I'll bring it at once, Isaiah', and I'd rush down to my house and get it and bring it to him.

CARPENTER Which daily paper did he take?

UTECHIN Basically *The Times*. But there was quite a long time when they took the *Independent* as well.

CARPENTER My impression is that, though he had a bad last year physically, mentally there was no decline at the end. Is that right?

UTECHIN Absolutely none at all, except that since he was taken very seriously ill in July he was terribly tired all the time. The mental capacity was still absolutely there, but not the ability to concentrate for longer than five or ten minutes – simply because he was so tired, that was the only reason. I remember he used to play games with himself. I was in the room once, and he said, 'Can you think of a composer beginning with N?' So I said, 'No, Isaiah, not offhand.' He was going through the alphabet, a composer for each letter of the alphabet.

CARPENTER Just to keep his mind going, really? When was the last time you saw him?

UTECHIN I saw him on the Tuesday morning [4 November] and he died in the Acland on the Wednesday night.

CARPENTER And he was quite cheerful then?

UTECHIN He wasn't too cheerful because he was going off to have a minor procedure which they hoped would ease his eating problem – his swallowing mechanism had gone wrong. I think my last words to him were, 'Well, Isaiah, all you can do is grin and bear it'; and he said, 'I'm bearing it, but I'm not grinning.'

CARPENTER Was he frightened of death?

UTECHIN I don't think so. He's written about this in Anna Howard's book. I think he was frightened, like 99 out of 100 of us, of pain and indignity in dying, but not of death as such.

CARPENTER And then of course, almost at the very end, he sent this extraordinary letter to a friend in Israel. Were you surprised when that happened?

UTECHIN I suppose I was, a little, because it was so unlike him. The two great overseas countries that he was passionate about were Russia and Israel. In the old days he *never* pronounced on public matters in Russia because he had family there – that was clear-cut. And he never wanted to intervene publicly in Israeli politics, although everybody knew – both his friends there and his friends here – where his sympathies lay. So it was an unusual thing for him to do, and it makes one wonder a little that he should have suddenly decided to do it three weeks before he died – it's dated 16 October.

CARPENTER He then sent it by ordinary post.

UTECHIN Well, that may have been my fault. I still haven't quite got used to modern technology: it didn't occur to me to fax it, and he didn't tell me to. So I just posted it by airmail to Israel.

CARPENTER In fact it was beautifully timed, as it turned out, wasn't it?

UTECHIN Precisely. I gather that it lay in the postbox in the university for two weeks because of the Jewish religious holidays; so it was opened only the day before his death.

CARPENTER What was your personal relationship with him like?

UTECHIN I think he and I had an extremely good relationship. He was always very, very nice to me, and I was extremely fond of him.

CARPENTER What will you miss most about him?

UTECHIN That's an impossible question to ask so early. An old colleague and friend of his wrote me a personal note – I know him simply because I've had to ring him up endlessly and make appointments. He put it absolutely beautifully, and I can't at the moment get beyond what he said: 'The sheer sense of disappearance must be very disorientating for you.'

New York City, Autumn 1966

Samuel Guttenplan

ONE MIGHT THINK that what follows is more about Isaiah than it is about his thought, more anecdote than analysis. Moreover, since it deals with only a very short period in his life – his initial visit as Schweitzer Professor at the City University of New York (CUNY) – it might seem too restricted to be illuminating. I think both appearances are misleading.

I met Isaiah in 1966 on his first visit to the City University, and, though I had no way of knowing this at the time, I came to understand that Isaiah in New York was a very different character from the one familiar to his Oxford circle. It might have been that, away from Oxford and England, certain sides of his personality expanded, or that in its special way New York magnified them. Either way, I think he was more real, more himself, when he visited New York, and thus a snapshot of him there should be valuable in itself; it is also the best thing I can present as a tribute to a man so important to my own life.

Those who knew Isaiah and know his work will understand why I am unapologetic about focusing on aspects of his life and character. But it is perhaps worth being more explicit about this. His own writing about any philosopher, writer, musician or politician was never just about that person's thought. In a way few can match, Isaiah was somehow able to see into the mind and character of his subject, weaving a narrative that revealed why that particular person made that particular contribution to human thought and culture. Reading Isaiah, one gets a sense, not simply of ideas, but of their origin in individual human lives. Many of the thinkers Isaiah singled out were, to use his own word, 'monsters', and he never thought Kant's claim about the crooked timber of humanity a merely ornamental metaphor. But Isaiah's interest in human beings was not simply that of a historian of ideas, however gifted he was in this field, nor was it an interest only in monsters, fascinated as he was by them. He had an insatiable curiosity about human beings that was in no way limited to those we have come to regard as contributors to thought and culture. It is this feature of his character that was so forcefully brought home to me when I got to know him, and it was out of that curiosity that Isaiah's own thought grew. So, in the nicest possible way, I am turning the tables on him: he found a deep and seamless link between the thought and character of his subjects, and I have always found the same link between his intense and almost playful interest in everyday human behaviour and his own thought about morals and politics.

Isaiah shared the first Albert Schweitzer Professorships at the City University
with Arthur Schlesinger; but whereas the latter accepted a permanent full-time
appointment, Isaiah undertook his post on a visiting basis that involved his
giving a seminar during the first semester every other year. (This arrangement
ran from 1966 to 1971.) The City University Graduate Programme was a new
development: it offered PhD degrees, till then not available at its constituent
undergraduate colleges. With a level of funding that now seems lavish, a large
building at 33 West 42nd was acquired and rebuilt, floor by floor, to serve as the
Graduate Center. Three months before Isaiah was due to take up his professorship, I was asked whether I would be his research assistant. At the time I had
a heavy and poorly paid teaching load at City College (CCNY), and several
part-time jobs to make ends meet, so the honorarium of the assistantship, as
much as the honour, made the decision easy. However, as my philosophical
background was largely in logic and the philosophies of language and mind,
I was more than a little nervous at the prospect. (I suspect I was asked simply
because I had at least a reading knowledge of German and French and because
there weren't many postgraduates in philosophy on the books then at CUNY.)
Though I knew of Isaiah and his reputation – and who didn't? – I could only
just remember reading his *Two Concepts of Liberty* as an undergraduate. To
make matters worse, the Berlin vacation reading course I had set myself wasn't a
success; having to teach two intensive summer courses at CCNY made sure of
that.

Against this background, it should be easy to imagine how I felt about my
first meeting with Isaiah. Towards the end of September, negotiating the building works around the ground-floor entrance to the Graduate Centre, I took the
lift to the tenth floor. The floor with the Schweitzer Professorship offices wasn't
quite ready, so both Isaiah and Arthur Schlesinger were accommodated in
offices on an old floor in the building. Those with long memories will remember midtown office buildings whose corridors were lined with frosted glass
doors and gold-leaf signs attesting to the presence of attorneys, employment
agencies, import–export businesses and various medical professions. The effect
of the unremodelled tenth floor was thus doubly unnerving: not only did my
visit feel like a trip to the dentist, it looked like one.

The Schweitzer suite consisted of two pairs of offices that were linked
by a short hallway, and each pair gave out on to the corridor through one
of the frosted glass doors. As I was coming in – and this was straight out of
Hollywood – a signwriter was putting the finishing touches on the gold-leaf
names of the new, though temporary, occupants. That door gave directly into
a windowless office which, when he got one, would belong to Isaiah's secretary,
and the little hallway led to the similar office of Arthur Schlesinger's secretary,
Gretchen Stewart. Both of the professors occupied rear offices with windows

overlooking 42nd Street. Gretchen, seriously overburdened but always calmly cheerful, told me that Isaiah had himself just arrived, and was expecting me.

There is of course no need to describe Isaiah: any of the familiar photographs of him, whether taken in the 1940s or the 1990s, would give an accurate enough sense of how he looked in 1966. When I came in, he was sitting with his glasses above his eyebrows, thumbing through his diary and making a noise that sounded something like whistling, but was perhaps more accurately described as the sound of someone attempting to whistle and whisper at the same time. To say that the office was unlived-in would be an understatement: there were neither books nor any other signs of academic occupancy aside from the distinguished professor sitting not behind but off to one side of a nondescript desk. He stopped what he was doing, and without saying anything he managed by his look to ask me who I was and why I was here.

Introducing myself, I said that I had been appointed to be his research assistant, and that, to be honest, I had never been any such thing before. I had already prepared myself to go further, by admitting that I was perhaps the wrong research assistant for him, but before I could get this out, he said – or rather mumbled – that he had never had a research assistant, had no idea of what such a person did, and thought that the best thing for us to do was to go shopping. It would be misdescribing my feeling to say simply that I was relieved: it was more as if the dentist had announced that the anticipated painful work was not required.

Shopping, working with his secretaries (there were several), and smoothing the way for his trips to the New York Public Library – in roughly that order – these turned out to be a central part of my job over the next months. Nor was the shopping merely speculative: our first trip was to Macy's to see about his getting some wheels for his luggage, other trips took in stationers, especially those that sold all the latest gadgets for home and office (he once bought a radio that was also a clock, a torch and a cigarette-lighter), a wholesaler that sold his favourite little Villiger Kiel cigars (difficult to find – I did do actual research on that one), and Bloomingdale's, to see if we could find him 'one of those summer jackets Americans wear' (seersucker, he meant, and this proved a difficult thing to find in the autumn in New York City).

On these expeditions, which were as much about taking in the city as about shopping, he was the intrepid explorer, and I was the guide, required both for local knowledge, and for interpreting linguistic exchanges with the locals. Though it would have been understandable if I had had difficulty, I somehow found it easy to understand what Isaiah said. This was most emphatically not true in general of native New Yorkers. Nor did Isaiah always find it easy to understand them. On that first trip to Macy's, I had to translate everything he and the salesgirl tried to say to one another. Even then, when it came to pay for the luggage-wheels, things almost got out of hand: she wouldn't accept his cheque because he had signed it (just recognisably) 'Isaiah Berlin' and the chequebook provided by the university had 'Sir Isaiah Berlin' printed on it. I told him what she said – that she thought he had not signed his full name on the chequebook. 'You don't write "Sir" – it's like "Duke"; a title is not a part of a name,' he said. I repeated this to the uncomprehending salesgirl, and New Yorker that she was, there was no hesitation: 'What about Duke Ellington?' Unsure whether he had understood, or what he made of this, I suggested that it would be better all round if I paid for the wheels myself. Isaiah later made it clear to me that he had explicitly told the University not to use his title at any point, and he insisted that I accept what was to me a fairly large cash float to be used on future expeditions.

A week or two later, and having failed to find a seersucker jacket, we stopped at a coffee shop on Madison Avenue, one of those with both counter seating and booths. This was the first of many such stops that we made over the next months, since they afforded Isaiah a chance to exercise his favourite pastime: observing humanity from a close but safe distance. On that particular occasion, we ended up speaking about an 'argument' we witnessed between a male customer and the waitress behind the counter. What to me was simply typical of the friction one sees in New York City every day – and not even a serious case of it at that – was to Isaiah an occasion for speculation about the life of the customer ('definitely not a bank clerk, probably an administrator who has found out this morning that, just as last time, he would not be promoted ... lives with his parents') and the waitress ('too intelligent to work here ... lives alone but has several brothers'). There was of course no real conviction behind these speculations – they were light-hearted and the clichés intentional – but he really did look at these people, and would have been genuinely interested if someone could have provided further information about them. The fact that they were wholly ordinary was neither here nor there; he was simply riveted by their sharp, even witty, combativeness. This was mirrored in his choice of intellectual subjects: the very fact that some of them were monsters, that they were human beings who protested fiercely, often inappropriately, about perceived wrongs to themselves or their societies, that they were typically very difficult to live with, all of this was part of their attraction for Isaiah, even if he himself neither had that sort of character nor aspired to it.

When he was sitting opposite me in coffee shops, it was always evident when he became an observer. A certain look took over his features, a look that I came to think of as 'the Isaiah stare': head cocked a little to one side, eyes narrowly focused, eyebrows slightly raised, lips thrust forward and partly open. When turned on you it could be disconcerting: it had an intensity that could have been mistaken for ferocity, and though it was invariably benign, it wasn't always comfortable.

He often told me that while he loved trying to figure out what people were like – what they got up to – he was no good at what he called 'feelings in a room'. What he meant was that, when he was himself the object of attention – whether in a lecture hall, in a seminar room, or even in a social gathering – he felt unable to tell what others thought or expected of him, much less what they, there and then, were thinking of each other. From too close up, and when he was involved, he simply didn't trust his own judgement. Though I am sure he exaggerated what he saw as a deficiency here, I often witnessed the consequences of his view of himself: nervous and unsure how things were going, he substituted talk for observation. One example from years later in Oxford best captures what I mean. Peter Geach and Elizabeth Anscombe had been invited to tea in his office before Anscombe was to give her Wolfson College Lecture. (Geach's lecture was later in the series.) Before they arrived, he told me how unsettling they were, how little they thought of him, and how prone they were to ask all sorts of awkward questions. For all these reasons, he asked me to do what I could to deflect them. For obvious enough reasons, I doubted that there would be any such need, or, if there were, that I was up to fulfilling it. Still, I tried to reassure him by saying that, as the organiser of the lectures, there were certainly things I could discuss with them. What then happened was remarkable, but – and this is my point – typical: from the instant they came into the room until the time they left – with the possible exception of some talk about sugar, milk or biscuits – Isaiah was the only person who spoke. At a higher pitch than usual, and certainly at a greater rate, his own words smothered any imagined attack they might launch. They sat there obviously fascinated, and, it seemed to me, wholly well-disposed to him, but he didn't seem to recognise this. Though originally said of someone else, I have also heard it said of Isaiah: *Er schweigt nur wenn er selbst redet* ('He is silent only when he himself is speaking'). But I think that is wrong, as well as unfair. His talk was never self-promoting or exhibitionist. Remarkably, even when he was by and large the sole speaker, he had the ability to make you think you had just had a conversation with him; you came away believing that you were crucial to what he was saying – that you were contributing to some kind of joint project – whether or not you actually said anything at all. And he managed this not only when you and he were alone, or with one or two others, but even when he gave lectures to large audiences.

As noted earlier, I wasn't properly prepared to meet Isaiah: I didn't manage more than a re-reading of *Two Concepts*, and several chapters of his *Karl Marx*. I thoroughly enjoyed the first, though I remember thinking that it lacked the kind of sharp edge I was used to in more analytic philosophical articles (I have a very different view now), and I found the second less than gripping (no doubt because I simply lacked the relevant background). But I was even less prepared for the character of the man with whom I spent so many hours that autumn. I expected brilliance in conversation, but not of the kind that became so familiar. And most of all, I simply didn't expect the mixture of genuine humility, natural curiosity, good-natured humour, breathtaking indiscretion, a serious appreciation of what others might call gossip, and his special kind of warmth, one which seemed to radiate effortlessly in all directions.

The seminar that Isaiah gave that autumn gave evidence of all these characteristics. I don't recall it having any particular theme beyond 'thought about the nature of society', and it was built around the authors now familiar to Isaiah's readers, including Machiavelli, Vico, Hamann, Herder, Rousseau, Kant, Maistre, Saint-Simon, Hegel and Marx. However, most of his published work on these authors appeared after 1966, and though he had given many talks about them, we always had the sense that everything was being thought out as we went along. The length of the seminars reflected that sense of freedom: we started at 2 p.m. and almost never finished before 6 (p.m., that is, though none of us would have found it surprising if it had on occasion been 6 *a.m.*). Yet in spite of their length, no one seemed to notice the passage of time, least of all Isaiah, and only the approach of evening put an end to proceedings. (The Schweitzer programme had by this time moved to its futuristic 16th-floor home, and the seminar room had a floor-to-ceiling window overlooking Bryant Park.) There were twelve registered postgraduates in the seminar and though we did have the occasional visitor, Isaiah very much wanted the seminar to have the kind of intimacy and continuity that made him (and us) more comfortable.

Each meeting was started off by Isaiah, but in no sense did he give a paper, and he welcomed interruptions. In his remarks, he had frequent recourse to dozens of apparently haphazard notes on postcards – sometimes picture postcards – and sheets of hotel stationery. In many cases, these notes were citations from some primary source, though they rarely included any page references, and they were sometimes a mixture of the citation and Isaiah's own thought about it. (One of the things I did that came closer to the conventional role of research assistant was sorting these notes out – Isaiah discarded them rather haphazardly, one by one on the table or nearby chairs. Looking them over, I always marvelled that such a coherent flow of thought could be built from them.)

Any initial hesitation we might have had about interrupting his remarks was soon dissipated by the challenges he threw out. For example, I remember his asserting at one point early in the seminar, and without any qualification: 'Before 1830, sincerity was not valued.' What would follow would be a lively attempt to find claims in philosophers before 1830 that would undermine this bald statement. 'What about Socrates?' someone asked. 'No, what matters to him is that an agent knows what is right and decent – Socrates wouldn't have seen any intrinsic merit in an agent's sincerity.' Unsatisfied with this, and with the somewhat shifting ground on which he inevitably took his stand when other counter-examples were offered, the very notion of sincerity came under closer scrutiny, and I recall that most of the students in the seminar joined in at this point, even if they hadn't before. On another occasion, we were invited to say what profundity was – not some specific instance of it, but rather the notion itself. Here I am sure that Isaiah had no specific thesis, though I know that the idea of profundity held a special fascination for him. However ambivalent he was about the characters of those he wrote about, I am sure he thought that their importance lay in the profundity of their work and lives. But he was never satisfied that he had a grip on the notion; though often confident about instances, he wanted, in the familiar Socratic way, a general understanding, if not a definition, of this notion. So it was unsurprising to me that the question raised in the seminar came up time and again in other contexts.

Some weeks into the seminar, Isaiah asked all twelve of us to dinner in the dining room of his hotel. He was staying at the Blackstone on 58th Street, which was then more a temporary residence than a typical hotel. Not having the experience to understand this at the time, I came to see that he had somehow managed to recreate a combination of high table and senior common room in the small, elegant dining room of the Blackstone. The staff who arranged the meal and waited on us – and we were the only guests that night – seemed only too pleased to be involved, even though the dinner went on until after midnight. It was obvious that their pleasure was based on their respect and affection for him, rather than anything mercenary, and this was not something typical of staff in New York hotels and restaurants. The dinner was in some ways like an extra session of the seminar, though the approach to human nature and society was more light-hearted, anecdotal and did not call on the usual historical suspects. Many of us tried to use the occasion to find out more about Isaiah himself, but we were only partly successful in this. I simply don't think he found himself an interesting subject, and he was more interested in finding out about each of us. ('Now tell me,' the gentle interrogation would begin, accompanied by the Isaiah stare that made non-compliance impossible.) The only story of any length that we could get out of him turned out to be one to which he was not himself a witness. This was the now familiar story of Winston Churchill having lunch with the 'wrong I. Berlin' – Irving not Isaiah. 'There are many versions of this story, all true', a light-hearted qualification he often made, though in fact it goes to the heart of his own thought.

Perhaps because of the wine, my recollection of the dinner is only hazy. But another incident shortly afterwards stands out sharply. Not I think generally

known, it seems a fitting conclusion to a portrait of the remarkable man I came
to know in New York City that autumn. In late November, to be precise on
the 28th, Isaiah was working well into the evening, and, as often happened, I
was using the secretarial office to do some work of my own. Emerging from his
office, he announced, in a way that was as much an invitation as a statement,
that he felt like going for a walk. Packing our things took some time – it wasn't
yet particularly cold but he always wore an extremely heavy overcoat and filled
its pockets with notebooks, snacks, cigars and other things he deemed essential
for any walk, however short. When we got out of the lift and stood on 42nd
Street, he seemed unconcerned about the direction of the walk, but somehow
we found ourselves turning up Fifth Avenue. I assumed that he was making
for the Blackstone, and this direction suited me, as a convenient subway station wasn't far away. As we reached the open space and fountain in front of the
Plaza Hotel on 58th Street, there were police barriers and a sizeable and growing crowd. Though I hadn't remembered that it was happening that evening,
like all those in New York I had known of Truman Capote's Black and White
Ball at the Plaza. With the passage of time this event has become legendary, but
even then it was intriguing enough to fill page after page in the newspapers. We
all knew that Capote and his co-host Kay Graham had carefully selected 500
guests, and though the list was not made public at the time, it turned out to
include many from Hollywood (Greta Garbo, Marlene Dietrich, Henry Fonda,
Gregory Peck, Frank Sinatra and his new wife Mia Farrow, Lauren Bacall,
Vivien Leigh, Billy Wilder), from the theatre (Joan Fontaine, Noël Coward,
Jason Robards, Alan Jay Lerner), from the arts (Arthur Miller, Philip Roth,
Christopher Isherwood, Norman Mailer, Gloria Steinem, William Styron,
Tennessee Williams, Andy Warhol), from politics, publishing, finance and,
well, many of those with power of one sort or another (Robert Kennedy, Jackie
Kennedy, Robert McNamara, Lynda Bird Johnson, Alfred Knopf, William
Randolf Hearst, Paul Mellon, Arthur Sulzburger, Averell Harriman, Henry
Ford, Stavros Niarchos, the Baroness de Rothschild, McGeorge Bundy). One
guest, however, didn't quite make it. Though I found out later that he had the
invitation in his overcoat, Isaiah decided against going. None the less, standing
at the police barrier, he watched fascinated as the limousines deposited their
occupants for the short walk into the hotel. It was late and I was long overdue
at home, so I didn't stay long. But when we spoke about it the next day, he was
still full of wonder at the parade of the rich and famous – monsters among
them – that he had witnessed.

Lunching with Isaiah

Alan Montefiore in conversation with Nick Rankin

An interview for a BBC World Service Meridian feature on IB broadcast on 15 November 1997

RANKIN How did you meet Isaiah Berlin?

MONTEFIORE The answer comes in two stages. As a student I hardly ever went to lectures, because I used to fall asleep, however good the lecturer was; but I went to Isaiah's lectures, without falling asleep, not so much to hear what he was saying, but just to listen to him talking. It was a pure joy for an hour just to listen to this overflowing, continuous cascade of beautifully formed language, with Isaiah always staring at the upper corner of the room, because, as he explained to me later in life, he didn't like looking at his audience – he was always intimidated. So I knew him before I met him, if I can put it that way.

Then the man I was sharing rooms with at Balliol turned out to know him personally, and said to me, 'You must meet Isaiah.' So I met him through this friend, Robin Jessell, and at some point after that Isaiah and I somehow connived in persuading John Sparrow, then Warden of All Souls, that he must get his College to invite Leszek Kołakowski, who was then somewhat stranded in the United States, to become a Fellow of All Souls.

Later we formed a lunch club, of which there were at most only ever three members – Arnold Goodman being the third, which didn't really work very well because Arnold was too large to sit easily at the tables in the lunchtime dining room at All Souls – but most of the time it was just Isaiah and myself; typically we met once a month, alternately at his invitation and at mine, for over a quarter of a century.

RANKIN What did you talk about at these lunches?

MONTEFIORE It was mostly Isaiah talking, because (as anyone who knew Isaiah would know) you had really to interrupt to get a word in. I think he talked mostly about people that he knew or had known, or the affairs either of the intellectual community or of the Jewish community – of which, of course, we were both members.

RANKIN How would you place Berlin? I've heard him described as very important in the tradition of radical, liberal humanism. Is that fair? Can you give me a headline that would place him in intellectual life?

MONTEFIORE Isaiah was certainly in some sense a radical liberal. His main thought was that people's lives take very different forms, and that the different values that animate them are what he called 'incommensurable'. (I use this difficult word because it's one with which Isaiah's views are now closely associated.) By this he meant that there is no common currency by which you might measure the values off against each other. Compare this with a theory like Utilitarianism, according to which all values are measurable, ultimately, in terms of a common currency, namely happiness or pleasure. Isaiah thought that you couldn't reduce the different values that animate peoples' lives to the terms of a common currency in such a way that you could say that one was more important, or better, or worse than another, but that in a liberal society people should be free as far as possible to pursue their different lives, unless they clashed in absolutely impossible ways.

RANKIN Does this lead naturally to pluralism, with which he is associated?

MONTEFIORE Well, it is a pluralist doctrine – a doctrine of a plurality of values. So it isn't so much that it leads to pluralism, it is already at the heart of pluralism, or at least his particular kind of pluralism.

RANKIN How did he get to this position, in your view?

MONTEFIORE I suppose that the answer has to be in terms of his basic temperament, modified no doubt by his experiences as a child and as a young man – but to explain exactly how he arrived at it would involve too much psychological speculation. It was just a very, very deeply held conviction.

RANKIN In describing your lunch club with Berlin you referred to the intelligentsia or intellectual life, but also Jewish life. How important was Jewishness to Berlin?

MONTEFIORE Immensely important. But let me just say rapidly in brackets: You just used the word 'intelligentsia', I didn't. It would have made Isaiah laugh, because he thought that the British simply didn't have an intelligentsia, or didn't really know what the term 'intelligentsia' meant, in the way in which continentals think that they know.

RANKIN 'Intelligentsia' is originally a Russian word.[1]

MONTEFIORE Yes, I agree. But I don't think that Isaiah would have thought of himself in his English embodiment as a member of an intelligentsia, because for him there was no such thing in England, though there were of course English intellectuals, in some good sense of that word.

Isaiah was very English. This seems to me one of the most interesting paradoxes about him. He was very cosmopolitan and yet very English – English in the frameworks of his thought, and English, in some respects, in the way

[1] Strictly, Polish: see Andrzej Walicki, 'Berlin and the Russian Intelligentsia', OM 48–9.

in which he spoke. But his Jewish heritage and belonging were of immense importance to him. He was born in Riga (then part of the Russian Empire), lived from the age of six in Russia proper, and left Russia at the age of eleven, but was brought up in a Jewish family with a Hasidic background, though his parents were not that kind of orthodox, practising Jew. He became very closely involved with many of the founders of the Zionist movement, whom he knew, and respected greatly, and about whom he has written. It is fair to say that his background gave him a natural sympathy with the passions that drove the Jews towards a Zionist solution to their problems in Europe. At the same time, as a schoolboy at St Paul's he was aware of the pressures of 'genteel' or 'quasi-civilized' anti-Semitism in this country. When he was there, there was a *numerus clausus* for Jews at the school, which is to say that the number of Jewish boys admitted was limited, so that the proportion should never be higher than whatever the figure was, in an institution that then saw itself as – and was – a Christian foundation. This subsequently gave rise to some delicate problems, when Isaiah was asked to become a governor of St Paul's.

RANKIN As you say, he wrote about the intellectual roots and history of Zionism, but he did not write about the Holocaust in the Second World War – the Nazis' attempt to eliminate Jewish people in Europe.

MONTEFIORE That's an interesting and somewhat delicate question. Isaiah was very resistant to the idea that one should institute anything called 'Holocaust studies', which many of my friends who were survivors of the Holocaust were deeply and passionately attached to. Isaiah felt, rightly or wrongly, that this would lead to the Jews focusing the wrong sort of attention on themselves, not only in the eyes of the surrounding non-Jewish world, but even in their own eyes. He thought of the Holocaust as just one (I say 'just' – the Holocaust was, of course, what it was: an appalling event), perhaps the worst, among many other appalling events in the history of the Jewish people, and the history of other peoples. He didn't want to focus attention on the Holocaust in that particular way, which he took to be somewhat morbid.

RANKIN There's an essay that Berlin wrote about Marx and Disraeli – the founder of Communism and a Prime Minister of England – called 'Benjamin Disraeli, Karl Marx, and the Search for Identity'. They were both Jewish, but had very different attitudes to what they did. Do you think that essay was important?

MONTEFIORE Curiously, it's not one of the essays of Isaiah's that I remember with the greatest clarity. But I think the essay *was* important, and that Isaiah's sense of the need for identity was important. In some curious way Isaiah was never the kind of self-confident man that you would have thought he must have been, given his extraordinary eminence and the impact he had on so many different kinds of people. He was diffident, and always surprised to discover himself a celebrity. He enjoyed being a celebrity, undoubtedly, but was surprised. I think his concern for identity was a mixed concern: he had been a foreigner, a little Jewish boy from Russia, brought up in a strange land when at school, and so he was sensitive to all the uncertainties of somebody who didn't quite know whether he fitted in or not. In that sense we come back to Jewishness again: the Jewishness provided a central thread of identity for him in a land where he was both at home and not 100 per cent at home.

RANKIN In that essay he talks about how Karl Marx denied his own Jewish roots, and how his wounded feelings became identified with the predicament of the proletariat; Disraeli, on the other hand, identified with peers and Lords and became a kind of aristocrat; and there is another essay in the same book about Moses Hess, who said, 'No, you shouldn't deny your roots, but you should be proud of your identity' – and he, in his modest way, was also a founder of Zionism. It's those three examples that I thought were relevant to Isaiah Berlin.

MONTEFIORE Absolutely. You've put flesh on the bare bones of the answer I tried to give you before. What attracted him to Hess was the fact that he clung to the threads of identity with which he started, and wove the rest of his identity round them, rather than tearing them up or pretending that they weren't there; he tried to create a new identity out of what could be woven on to already existing threads. But if you have nothing to weave the new threads of identity on to, they are left somehow hanging in the air – rather artificial, unreal – and don't really ever convince anyone, yourself or anybody else; which was true of both Disraeli and Marx.

RANKIN It seems to me that identity, what group people feel they belong to, is a source of great hope and pride in people, but also a source of great danger, because your identity, your ethnic roots, your religion, your faith, your belief-system, may be in conflict with the belief-systems of others. Is it true to say that nowadays, where there are more ethnic and nationalist conflicts, Isaiah Berlin's ideas are still extremely important?

MONTEFIORE In some ways more important than ever. More important because Isaiah felt very strongly and believed very strongly and lived very strongly his belief that identities are not unitary, that one should think of one's own identity and other peoples' identity as made up of many different facets (threads is the metaphor I used earlier on), some of which may be more dominant at one period, and others of which may be more dominant at another period. But once you start trying to pull out one of these threads and pretend it's the whole of your identity, then you have to distinguish yourself from other people, and your identity becomes a matter of not being that man or that woman across the street or across the sea, or whatever it may be, who may be threatening you if he comes trespassing on your identity. So I think Isaiah's ideas of 'Live and let live' to the maximum possible, and the plurality of values, and the plurality not only of identities but the plurality of any one person's identity – the different threads that go to make it up – are of immense importance today in so far as ideas can really influence the way peoples behave when they are in the grip of this sort of madness.

RANKIN If Berlin is seen as a historian of ideas, in many of his essays he seems to me to be seeking the roots of his notion of pluralism. He looks, for example, at Giambattista Vico as one of the first people who understood that different cultures had their own different belief-systems, and that these might be just as valid as each other.

MONTEFIORE Yes, I would agree with that.

RANKIN You said that, for Berlin, out of pluralism comes the idea of 'Live and let live', that cultures should be tolerant of other cultures. How does this square with ethics – the ideas of right and wrong? And does it require compassion?

MONTEFIORE I should have stressed before that Isaiah certainly didn't think that, because there are a number of equally valid different ways of living – or, let's say, a number of equally valid but incommensurable values – that all values or all ways of living were acceptable. He was very clear that some were totally unacceptable. He had very strong ethical beliefs – in some ways, one might say, a pre-philosophical view of ethics. That's to say, he had a deep conviction that certain things were just wrong. On the other hand, he didn't think there was any one right. One side of his ethics would be a matter of fighting against what was wrong, and one of the things which would be wrong would be to attempt to render impossible the living out of another way of life which he might think not wrong but perfectly acceptable.

As for compassion, Isaiah was endlessly fascinated with people; on the whole he liked people, too, and liked being liked by people, and I think these things very frequently go together. One might even argue that they necessarily go together: you can't really like people properly unless you like being liked by them. Certainly he was quite conscious of this. He used often to say, self-deprecatingly, that he was too weak in many of his public stances because he didn't want people to dislike him. You can call that compassion; I think it's a liking for people.

RANKIN Curiously, many of the big ideas that his thought was opposed to were misanthropic. Their proponents wanted to crush people, or to make people better – or perfect. Very often, it seems to me, there is at the core of Isaiah Berlin's ideas a concern for ordinary people and their feelings.

MONTEFIORE Absolutely. I don't know why you're interviewing me: I should be interviewing you – you're giving me all the answers! I completely agree with that. He did have a feeling for ordinary people. But I should enter this one caveat: he specially enjoyed *extra*ordinary people. He enjoyed the peculiarities of people who were, not necessarily larger than life, not necessarily more important – but people who in some way or another stood out. He had a great taste for eccentricities.

RANKIN What sort of eccentrics did he enjoy?

MONTEFIORE He enjoyed people who stood out from the ordinary run of the mill. In that sense, while you're perfectly right in saying that he had a great deal of understanding of how ordinary people might feel, most of all he enjoyed less ordinary people, people who in some way or other were characters belonging, as it were, in a club. He himself was a member of a number of clubs, and he used to take me to lunch at the Garrick, when it was his turn, unless we were lunching at All Souls. If one wants examples, perhaps the best way to put it is to say, 'Look around a club like the Garrick, and you will see quite a lot of examples of the sorts of people Isaiah enjoyed.'

RANKIN How would you describe his sense of humour, or fun?

MONTEFIORE He had a tremendous sense of humour and fun. A lot of it was the sort of self-deprecation that you get, typically and classically, in Jewish humour, but also in a lot of English humour. He would laugh at people's foibles, at their oddities of behaviour; at people who did funny or incongruous things. It was a sort of humour which was partially mocking, but mocking in a way that was certainly never deliberately hurtful, and generally was not in fact hurtful; though everybody who knew Isaiah knew that he thoroughly enjoyed high-level high-table gossip.

Let me tell you an anecdote that would surely have amused him. I remember going to see my then supervisor Stuart Hampshire, who was a lifelong friend of Isaiah's, I think in May 1951, when Stuart was a don at New College, and Isaiah was also based there. As I went towards Stuart's staircase, I passed Isaiah's staircase – he had a room, I think, on the bottom floor – and I heard him talking about Rousseau in his typical Isaiah way. Then, to my somewhat disturbed, alarmed astonishment, I suddenly heard him break in on himself, saying, 'No, no, no, this won't do at all, we can't possibly have that.' This was in the days before anybody had become really familiar with tapes and playing back recordings. What Isaiah was doing was listening to a tape of a lecture he had just recorded for the BBC Third Programme (as it then was) on Rousseau, and checking it, and explaining that he couldn't possibly accept what he'd heard himself saying on the tape. But I was unaware of this. I thought he was talking to himself, in this particularly voluble, Isaiah-like way.

A Luminous Personality

Aileen Kelly

F EW TEACHERS will ever be as much loved and mourned as Isaiah. As a graduate student at Wolfson College, Oxford, whose first President he became in the late 1960s, I was constantly made aware of my great luck: my choice of college within the University had brought me into the daily orbit of what we all sensed was the most fascinating, the most remarkable person we would ever encounter. Soon after I joined the College, he sent me a note asking me to come and discuss my research on the Russian intelligentsia. Out of nervousness I delayed replying until one day he descended on me at lunch, commanding me to come back with him to his office. I emerged nearly three hours later after a dazzling tour of the landscape of Russian thought combined with a passionate vindication of the subject of my research, which others had frequently urged me to change. In the 1960s Western liberal academics tended to regard the Russian intelligentsia mainly as fanatical precursors of Communism. With a warmth that recreated them as persons, Isaiah defended them as worthy of admiration for their moral commitment to dispelling illusions about the world and our place in it.

Much of that afternoon we spent discussing Alexander Herzen, whom Isaiah described as his hero. Later that day I sought out his essays on Herzen and came upon a precise description of my own recent impressions:

> I was puzzled and overwhelmed, when I first came to know Herzen – by this extraordinary mind which darted from one topic to another with unbelievable swiftness, with inexhaustible wit and brilliance; which could see in the turn of somebody's talk, in some simple incident, in some abstract idea, that vivid feature which gives expression and life. He had [...] a kind of prodigal opulence of intellect which astonished his audience. [... His talk] demanded of those who were with him not only intense concentration, but also perpetual alertness, because you had always to be prepared to respond instantly. On the other hand, nothing cheap or tawdry could stand even half an hour of contact with him. All pretentiousness, all pompousness, all pedantic self-importance simply fled from him or melted like wax before a fire.[1]

[1] P. V. Annenkov, 'Zamechatel'noe desyatiletie' (1880), *Literaturnye vospominaniya* (Moscow, 1960), chapter 17, 218; P. V. Annenkov, *The Extraordinary Decade: Literary Memoirs*, ed. Arthur P. Mendel, trans. Irwin R. Titunik (Ann Arbor, 1968), 86; quoted by IB in the above (his own) translation at RT2 216.

Isaiah was citing a contemporary's portrait of Herzen. His own resemblance to that extraordinary figure was striking (many of us would echo, with regard to Isaiah, Tolstoy's comment on Herzen – that he had never met anyone with 'so rare a combination of scintillating depth and brilliance'),[1] but his sense of affinity with Herzen was based above all on a shared moral outlook. They both combined a deep respect for honesty and purity of motivation with an unerring ability to detect artificiality and self-deception in intellectual endeavour and everyday behaviour. Students sensed that with Isaiah they were not required to perform, amuse or entertain, but simply to give their best, and this paradoxically put us at ease with him, the more so as we soon found out that straining to impress him was counterproductive. (Once, hoping to be congratulated on the originality of an essay I had given him for comment, I was chagrined to find that he had read the footnotes just as closely as the text and had unearthed some errors of fact which I had overlooked in my haste to impress.)

Isaiah's personality and utterances were the subject of continual discussion by the students of his College. His Russian connections and his exotic past provided much food for inventive speculation: Had the unusual circular hole in his ancient felt hat been acquired during hostile action somewhere in the Baltic states? More than once he walked unexpectedly into a room where a passable imitation of his own unforgettable voice was in full flow.

I believe that his true voice can be found at its clearest in his essays on Herzen. More self-revealing than anything else he ever wrote, they shed light on the most enduring mystery about him: his combination of what many have seen as a tragic vision of the world with an inexhaustible curiosity and an irrepressible sense of fun.

Isaiah can be said to have rediscovered Herzen, who he believed had either been ignored or misrepresented for so long because he had revealed a truth too bleak for most people to bear: that faith in universally valid formulas and goals was an attempt to escape from the unpredictability of life into the false security of fantasy. His devotion to Herzen remained undiminished to the end of his life. Not long ago he wrote reproaching me for obscuring the uniqueness of Herzen's contribution by drawing parallels between him and thinkers such as Mikhail Bakhtin who had considered similar problems: 'I can think of none, but perhaps I am too fanatical an admirer.' He often cited Herzen's phrase 'history has no libretto':[2] all questions make sense and must be resolved

---

[1] Reported by P. A. Sergeenko in his book on Tolstoy, *Tolstoy i ego sovremenniki* (Moscow, 1911), 13; cited at AC 189, PSM 500.

[2] 'S togo berega', in A. I. Gertsen, *Sobranie sochinenii v tridsati tomakh* (Moscow, 1954–66), vi 36; Alexander Herzen, *From the Other Shore*, trans. Moura Budberg, and *The Russian People and Socialism*, trans. Richard Wollheim, with an introduction by Isaiah Berlin (London, 1956), 39. See also RT2 105.

in terms not of final goals but of the specific needs of actual persons at specific times and places. Herzen, he wrote, believed 'that the day and the hour were ends in themselves, not a means to another day or another experience'.[1]

Here we have the key to one of the central paradoxes of Isaiah. Although his diary was always full and he was scrupulous about keeping appointments, he never gave the impression of being in a hurry, of being distracted from a person or an issue by anticipation of the next person or problem in line. Young academics were often astonished (as I was in my first encounter with him) that so important and busy a man was prepared to give them so much of his time. An American Slavist whom I met recently at a conference recalled having sent him her first book, not expecting a reply. His warm and detailed response, she told me, had her walking on air for weeks. On the evening after his death I remembered him with a Russian colleague whom he had encouraged in the same way in Oxford many years ago. A *svetlaya lichnost'* (luminous personality), she said.

But we would diminish him if we did not appreciate that the instinctive goodness we loved was coupled with a carefully thought-through moral vision of whose validity he earnestly sought to persuade us. One of its distinctive characteristics, which he saw embodied in Herzen, was the total absence of a utilitarian approach to people and events, an 'unquenchable delight in the variety of life and the comedy of human character'.[2] This was also one of Isaiah's most entrancing qualities. I remember him as the only one of us to emerge unexasperated from an interminable and contentious College meeting, happily quoting Kant's statement that 'Out of the crooked timber of humanity no straight thing was ever made.'[3] He was convinced (again I quote him on Herzen) that there was value in the very irregularity of the structure of human beings, 'which is violated by attempts to force it into patterns or straitjackets'.[4]

Like Herzen (and Schiller) he believed profoundly in the seriousness of the play of life and human creativity, and was easily drawn into all kinds of frivolity. One night after dinner at Wolfson he joined a conversation in which a student was explaining the board game Diplomacy, where each player represented one of the Great Powers of pre-1914 Europe. He invited us to his house the following Sunday morning to initiate him into the game; he then gave an impressively illiberal performance as the Ottoman Empire. I have another memory of him sitting on a bale of hay in his three-piece suit, complete with watch chain and hat, holding forth to a group of fascinated students at a bonfire party held in a

[1] AC 211, PSM 523.
[2] AC 207, PSM 519.
[3] Immanuel Kant, 'Idee zu einer allgemeinen Geschichte in weltbürgerlicher Absicht' ['Idea for a Universal History with a Cosmopolitan Purpose', 1784], *Kant's gesammelte Schriften* (Berlin, 1900–), viii 23.
[4] RT2 234.

damp field on the bank of the Cherwell, where the building of the new College was to start the next day. It was late evening; a more typical college President, having put in the obligatory early appearance, would have been long gone.

All those who knew him well were asked over the years to persuade him to write more and not to squander his gifts in conversation. Yet his profligacy has not prevented him from being recognised as one of the major liberal thinkers of the twentieth century, and he belongs to an even more select group who achieved harmony between their moral vision and their life. He showed us virtue in action, not as obedience to a set of rules but as a generous responsiveness to the creative possibilities of the present moment. One always came away from a few hours in his company with a sense of living more intensely, with all one's perceptions heightened, although the topics of conversation were often far from exalted. He much enjoyed exchanging news about the latest academic scandals in Oxford and Cambridge, and expected the exchange to be on equal terms: his view of humanity required that Cambridge should be as fertile a source of stories about human frailty as Oxford, and he was never disappointed. We had an unfinished debate lasting several years over the precise difference between a cad and a bounder; he could always find fresh examples of each to offer from among our mutual acquaintances.

He loved to gossip about the concerns and quarrels of nineteenth-century Russian thinkers as though they were our common friends, but there was a serious side to this entertainment. He had the greatest respect for these thinkers' commitment to acting out their beliefs in their daily lives, and fiercely championed them against what he perceived as misjudgements of their motives; our one painful difference was over the question of how Turgenev would have behaved under particular pressures.

Isaiah saw no contradiction between recognising that moral ideals were not absolute and believing one's own ideals binding on oneself. Again, his model was Herzen, who, he tells us, for all his scepticism, had an unshakable belief in the sanctity of personal liberty and the noble instincts of the human soul, as well as a hatred of 'conformism, cowardice, submission to the tyranny of brute force or pressure of opinion, arbitrary violence, and anxious submissiveness; [...] the worship of power, blind reverence for the past, for institutions, for mysteries or myths; the humiliation of the weak by the strong, sectarianism, philistinism, the resentment and envy of majorities, the brutal arrogance of minorities'.[1] Here, albeit in the third person, is Isaiah's profession of faith, in his own cadences.

He admired Herzen more than Turgenev because while neither had any illusions about the permanence of human existence and human values, Turgenev

---

[1] RT2 99.

had achieved a cool detachment from the struggles and triumphs of contingent life, while Herzen 'cared far too violently';[1] his realism was therefore the more courageous. In his last years Isaiah confronted the tragic side of his own philosophy with the same unflinching directness as his hero. On arriving for dinner in Cambridge sixteen months ago, he told me that something 'very terrible' concerning him had just appeared in the press. He would say no more about it and I assumed it was some adverse review. The next day I found the interview, reprinted in the London *Times*, in which he reflects on his own death, declaring that, much though he would like it to be otherwise, the idea that there was some world in which there would be perfect truth, love, justice and happiness made no sense in any conceptual scheme he knew. It was just a comforting idea for people who could not face the possibility of total extinction. But, he adds, 'I wouldn't mind living on and on. [...] I am filled with curiosity and long to know, what next?'[2]

[1] RT2 232.
[2] In *Death: Breaking the Taboo*, interviews by Anna Howard (Evesham, 1996), 32, 33; extracted in *The Times*, 19 July 1996, 16.

In the President's Office

Serena Moore

I

'TELL ME, Miss Denholm-Young, are you flighty?'

This was 13 December 1971, in the large first-floor room at the front of 47 Banbury Road, the administrative half of the pair of houses in which Wolfson College was temporarily camping while its permanent buildings were going up at the bottom of Linton Road. Book-lined, over-furnished with chintz-covered armchairs and standard lamps, and over-heated by a sealed-in, tropical warmth, the place was quiet, its traditional comfort suggesting an exclusive club in Mayfair or Manhattan. Cigar smoke hung in the air, mixed with a suggestion of apple lofts. The President, leaning back in his chair behind a large desk, was asking questions. It was an interview.

Aged twenty-four, I had applied, from London, for the job of his secretary in College (he had another, private, one at his house). I had a degree in English from UCL, had done a graduate PA course, and was thinking of leaving my dizzy first job at Morgan Grenfell because I was concerned that I couldn't understand merchant banking and wanted something that I could actually be interested in. I knew little about Berlin (though I was much taken by the fact that he knew David Cecil and had known Elizabeth Bowen, two of my favourite writers), and not much more about Oxford, but hoped I could learn, and had a brother at Queen's and a cousin at St Benet's Hall. Downstairs, I had already had a session with the College Secretary, who had briskly outlined a busy diary, a voluminous correspondence, and rapid audiotape dictation.

The man behind the desk was sixty-two, acute of gaze, through large brown eyes, serious of expression, and, in spite of the Savile Row suit and Oxford accent, foreign. The sort of classic Englishness that I had been used to (and I am very English), illustrated in the men I had grown up among, was evinced by a certain debonairness, a lightness of touch. This man was made of darker, more complex material – an exotic from a different clime. And he did the talking. He described his College and said that he travelled a lot and was writing a book on Vico and Herder for the Hogarth Press and editing the text of his 1970 Romanes Lecture, *Fathers and Children: Turgenev and the Liberal Predicament*, for OUP.

'And are you any relation of Noel Denholm-Young, the medieval historian at Magdalen?' he wanted to know.

'Yes, I am.'

'*Very*, very fine academic,' he replied, adding, with a slight gleam, 'drank, you know.' (I did.) Sparing a thought for my poor cousin, thus written off, I wasn't sure how to take this: was it a sophisticated tease or a dig, or some kind of test – or all three? A man who loved to gossip was new to me.

In due course, having been taken on with flawless formality by the Vice-President, I accepted the College Secretary's generous hospitality of her spare room pro tem and moved down to Oxford on 31 January 1972. It was cold, the streets were icy, and that evening during dinner with my father and brother, with an increasing sense that something was wrong, I tried several times to telephone my mother in Norwich: finally learning that she had been in Casualty, having fallen and broken her wrist. The next morning I began work. The President's Secretary had the small room behind his, with a view of the back garden and its single tree. Two months later one looked straight into an airy mass of pink blossom. The rest of the building housed, on the ground floor, the General Office and the orderly engine-room, filled with files of minutes, occupied by the College Secretary, Sheila McMeekin; attic rooms, the domain of the Vice-President, Michael Brock, his secretary, Beryl Schweder, their assistant, Liz Scaramanga, and also the Buildings Officer, Paul Boddington, among all his drawings and plans; and a basement, containing the Domestic Bursar, Cecilia Dick, and her secretary, Sue Hales. The Catering Officer and the College Accountant were also about the place, though not based in this house. Twice a day everyone assembled in the General Office for coffee or tea and shop-talk. At lunchtime we crossed the Banbury Road to no. 60 and queued in the hall to collect food at the hatch, or went through the back gate to St Antony's by reciprocal arrangement.

During the next month Gillian Hylton-Potts shared her job with me. Never easy, this arrangement was complicated for her by an impending move of house and for me by hunting for somewhere permanent to live, but we managed, and the President must have been amused by his two-headed Moneypenny. When he buzzed, we went into his room together, as a double act, and he would hand over tapes and sign his letters and rattle off instructions, and gossip with Gilly, who was quick and confident with the work and with him, while I felt largely de trop, except when I could take things down, because I did shorthand. But mostly we were in that rear room, where Gilly at first did everything, and then, increasingly, withdrew and sat expertly retyping a corrected draft of *Vico and Herder: Two Studies in the History of Ideas*. On a separate table in the window sat the telephone and the diary. The former was of the kind then common in outer offices, with buttons to press for holding and transferring calls through to an extension. It took practice and, of course, I cut several callers off, with all the agony of doing this in front of Gilly. To complicate matters, the President also had a private line on his desk, and might well be talking on that when one needed to put a call through. Gilly had become adept at picking up his voice through the wall. The diary was one's bible and another minefield, for extra items might lurk in the tiny pages of the President's pocket version, causing, hey presto, unexpected visitors or sudden departures. The rest of the room consisted of the President's papers (his personal records being managed in Headington – from April, by Pat Utechin). In 1972, approximately eight years before word-processors became widespread, the only record of outgoing typewritten material was its carbon copy, and all text that might be recycled – such as the long, and invariably generous, academic references that the President supplied on request – had to be retyped each time. Fifteen years before universal email and fax, written communication still moved at the pace of the posts, though the President also used telegrams, friends and the Diplomatic Bags, for he was punctilious about answering letters promptly (and happy to sign, ahead, blank sheets of headed typing paper for use in his absences). He also never threw anything away ('I stuff all letters into huge sacks and they disappear into my mother's house in Hampstead')[1] and consequently left an extraordinary paper trail, a deep litter, at once ephemeral and enduring, in which Henry Hardy and I were later to spend literally years, up to our knees, roosting.

The work was partly the standard administration done by all secretaries (flighty and otherwise) to Oxbridge Heads of House – with glimpses of another, wider world the President also inhabited. While his base was always Oxford, he was up and down to London once or twice a week. Having a driver (the equable Casimiro at the wheel of a blue mini) and a set in Albany made for a rapid turnaround, and appointments could be crammed into every corner at either end. He could be attending Wolfson meetings, seeing graduate students and examining up until 4.30, talking to someone in the Ritz Lobby at 6.30, and in his seat at the opera or dining at the Athenaeum at 8. One domain in this wider sphere – and the most unfamiliar and opaque one to me – was the Jewish circle that began with his family and spread to a coterie of businessmen and politicians who dominated Jewish affairs and philanthropy; another was the musical world largely centred on Covent Garden; and a third was an older, Russian, set, peopled with characters who might have come out of Chekhov. Other ripples spread to America and beyond.

These glimpses came, for me, partly from the diary, but largely from the 'enormous personal correspondence' that had first caught my eye in the agency advertisement, and that lay at the heart of the job. It was an extraordinary privilege to work at first hand on this uniquely varied and colourful continuum, this huge and growing 'work in progress', and my return to it twenty-six years later completed a benign loop in my own life. The roll-call of correspondents

[1] 18 May 1972 to Cyril Connolly.

was terrific. To name but a few: there were American friends such as Joe Alsop
and Arthur Schlesinger, Jr; the fellow academics Noel Annan, Jean Floud,
Karl Popper and Bernard Williams; the Russians – Lidiya Chukovskaya, the
Nabokovs and Dimitri Obolensky; the Jewish tribe – the Montefiores and
Rothschilds and Sieffs and Weinstocks and Weizmanns and Weidenfelds –
including Mrs Dollie de Rothschild, the old lady to whom Berlin turned
about so many things; there were those from the world of music and the arts,
such as George Solti, Garrett Moore, Frederick Ashton and Marie Rambert
(always addressed as 'Dearest Dame'); the writers and critics Angus Wilson, Iris
Murdoch and Cyril Connolly; the editors and publishers Hamish Hamilton
and Ham Armstrong; the BBC; and the rest – for instance, Penelope
Betjeman, James Billington, Richard Crossman, Mary McCarthy, Jacqueline
Onassis, Freya Stark and Margaret Thatcher. One might come upon anything
in this treasure chest: delightful self-mockery on the subject of attending meetings ('So, creaking and groaning, I shall turn out'),[1] and on ageing ('I regard
that [75] as a splendid age: I certainly propose to live to it and beyond, and
continue to go on talking until the end');[2] an impromptu pen-portrait of Igor
Stravinsky who 'knew he was immortal, and was happy in the thought';[3] gossip ('I see that Bob Silvers's lady was intimately connected with the Duke of
Windsor's funeral');[4] an evocative letter of condolence about Edmund Wilson
('I was very sorry about, & terribly touched by, the inner thrashing about, the
agony, the cost to him of living & the suffering that things, people, circumstances, works of art, caused him');[5] and an air of events in which even the small
change is writ large – in remarks about General Dayan, Anthony Eden, Henry
Kissinger and W. H. Auden (whose crumpled tortoise face I subsequently
passed one morning in St Aldate's). And always there is no stopping this voice.
The subtleties of English reserve and understatement were not Berlin's style,
and prolixity reigns. Time and again, he says 'I must not go on ...' – and then
does.

When the President was in, we went up several gears. The telephone was
constantly busy (once it was Alexander Solzhenitsyn, talking in Russian, from
London and wanting to meet), and there were lots of visitors – *inter alios*,
graduate students he was either supervising or talking to generally: Naheed
Ahmad, Sam Guttenplan, Roger Hausheer, Aileen Kelly, Ruth Moshinsky,
Guy Parkhurst, Robert Wokler – and the rather formidable Henry Hardy;
other members of the College such as Michael Argyle and David Robey and

[1] 12 April 1972 to Bernard Williams.
[2] 19 January 1972 to Arthur Schlesinger, Jr.
[3] 25 April 1972 to Chimen Abramsky.
[4] 8 June 1972 to Joseph Alsop.
[5] 19 June 1972 to Elena Wilson.

Cecilia Dick; other Heads of House, such as his old friend Stuart Hampshire, or Raymond Carr; or family – his youngest stepson, reading biochemistry at Univ., used to drop in. They might well be kept waiting, so one got to know them all.

This was also the winter of the Miners' Strike with its three-day week and power cuts across the national grid. People boxed and coxed, moving from home to office according to where the electricity was on. The colleges organised what they could, and in our case it was decided that for part of the time Gilly and I would work at the President's house; so the whole of my third week, 14–18 February, was spent this way. On the Monday morning we put our (ton-weight) typewriters and papers into the back of Gilly's mini and sped up Headington Hill to the imposing eighteenth-century house secluded within its trees and high walls. The façade looked so English, and had beguiling associations (the elegant spare bedroom conjured for me Elizabeth Bowen sitting, in the late 1950s, writing letters in her firm, stylish hand, raising her head now and then to gaze thoughtfully down the garden). Yet there were subtle other factors: the foreign domestics, the European taste in pictures and furnishings, the high heat, and a lack of that airy, out-of-doors element and love of animals that the truly English bring into their houses (and that once caused them to quarter their horses in buildings as fine as their own). We lugged all our equipment up the stairs to two empty bedrooms, and got down to work. At some point IB would appear, to sign things on his way out somewhere. Once, we heard music coming from his library and, on going in with the post, discovered him, sitting at his table, Balzac-like in an enormous dressing-gown, listening to one of his recordings of Maria Callas.

On 3 March, Gilly left and I was on my own. One of my anxieties was a month's worth of accumulated filing. I stayed on that evening, wrestling with it, and the President found me: 'Too late, too late, you must go home!' But I was also lucky, because on 5 March the Berlins flew to India, where he gave the first Humayun Kabir Memorial Lecture in New Delhi, as guest of the Indian Council for Cultural Relations, after which they toured the major sites, and then, on the return leg, visited 'Persia' as guests of the British Ambassador in Teheran, to see Isfahan, Persepolis and Shiraz – and were away nearly three weeks, allowing me time to catch up and take stock. And although, often, after work, I went up to London to sit in the amphitheatre at Covent Garden and watch the ballet, I also worked hard to establish a new life in Oxford, and on 8 March moved into a room of my own behind St Aldate's with a view over a jumble of gardens just breaking into new leaf. The Berlins had to be back by 23 March 'to see Mr Leonard Wolfson receive an honorary degree and lunch at which all the client kings greet the emperor's son – twelve colleges in all. I am not very good at beating the ground with my forehead, but shall practise it in India':[1] on the 28th the College office closed for Easter, and in mid April, having booked it months earlier, I took my twenty-two-year-old sister (artistic, slow, old-fashioned and affectionate), who was becoming worryingly withdrawn, to Sorrento for a week – and memories ever after associated with the scent of lemon-groves.

Trinity Term opened – with blossom, then swaying masses of lilac, spilling over college walls at every corner – and after a busy month in the office with Collections and committees, the President's summer circuit got under way. It included: dinner at Downing College on 30 April before speaking on Weizmann to the Cambridge University Israel Society (who sent a car specially); lecturing in Dublin on 5 May; dinner at Trinity Hall on 8 May before speaking on 'The Origins of Cultural History' to the History Society; speaking on Turgenev at Marlborough College on 11 May; meetings of a Jewish educational charity in Zurich on 15 May; dinner at Merton before talking about Vico to the Stubbs Society on 22 May – and I went to listen to that; dinner with David and Rachel Cecil on 23 May; then a week's leave in Italy; to Tel Aviv on 3 June to receive an Honorary Doctorate; hosting the annual Wolfson Garden Party at Headington House on 17 June, followed by Encaenia on the 21st, to which we all went, because the honorands included Leonard Wolfson (again); down to Forest Mere Health Spa in Hants on 25 June, returning, a stone lighter, in time for his youngest stepson's wedding on 8 July; to Italy again on 17 July, reappearing on the 30th for performances at Glyndebourne two nights running, then finally back to Italy on 1 August. In the shadow of all this lay for me the learning curve of how to judge what was important in his absence and how to deal with it; plus family preoccupations: on 27 June my father had thyroid surgery, and on 19 July my sister, by now seriously anorexic, was admitted to a psychiatric hospital.

II

Several sizes larger than life he might be, but as someone to work for, Berlin was even-tempered and reasonable. Rooted from childhood in the immense emotional security of being the only surviving offspring of adoring parents, he had a stable and hopeful nature, alight with humour and a sparkling *joie de vivre*. He seemed, as I look back, to occupy a kind of Berlin bubble, a spaceship, that flew happily about between Oxford and London, Jerusalem and Princeton, Paris and Milan, visiting the world's lecture theatres and opera houses. Oxford life, familiar and congenial in short, concentrated bursts, was interspersed with a wider scene in London, America and Israel, the whole rounded off with the summers in Italy. He was, when I knew him, exceptionally busy. Yet apart from

[1] 28 January 1972 to George Backer.

the odd superficial flurry, he got to meetings on time, with the right papers, and seldom lost things. Possessed of a phenomenally retentive and accurate memory, and the habit of steady, daily application to work (even if he did, all his life, keep extravagant hours), he was in fact organised, efficient and effective. His travel schedule was punishing, and he took little exercise. Yet he was invariably well, rarely tired, and his humour was seldom far from the surface. This took the form of verbal gaiety and mischief, resulting in *jeux d'esprit*, effervescing like beads of champagne on the page, or a torrent of gossip tumbling out with such relish that, laughing and talking and breathing all at once, he would literally swallow words and air, in an ecstasy of gulping. I soon learnt that music was his great passion, and that he was an enormously knowledgeable member of the Covent Garden Opera Sub-Committee. When, two years later, I went to one of the first performances of Ashton's ballet *A Month in the Country* (adapted from Turgenev's play) it was fascinating to discover in the programme that Berlin had been responsible for the score. Literally. For Ashton, unable to decide what music to use, had consulted IB, who, after requesting half an hour's pause for thought, had come back and said 'Chopin', an inspired choice. His visual sensitivity, however, was weak: he frequently admitted to being blind to the beauties of landscape, and (hilariously) was deeply bored and depressed by the English Lake District.

III

A major challenge for me initially was, of course, the famous dictation. The job seldom called for shorthand, for Berlin had years ago grown used to the dictaphone with the freedom it brought to work after hours. He was at his best late in the day, and all his life filled his diary with a glittering succession of evening engagements – dinner in college halls, in restaurants, or in clubs; seats (often a box) at the opera or ballet; recitals (Brendel was a friend and Menuhin a cousin) and lectures. After which he would come back to his room in College, or to his library at home, and resume work, dictating for an hour or two, while nibbling on the nuts and raisins he carried about in little tins in his pockets, or munching Granny Smith apples that he kept in the drawers of his desks, where they rolled about or subsided into brown and mouldy softness. The results – tapes of dictation, messages and instructions, signed off with the endearing formality of: 'That's all. Thank you *very*, very much. Yours' – would be there on my desk in the morning, or would shortly arrive. He accepted the technology, but his handling of it could lack imagination, and was sometimes plain dotty, for he would take up the handset and switch it on at the same time as starting to speak, often while also eating an apple: so either the first few words of the deep-throated, fruity, convoluted, tumbling Oxford English were not registered, or they were obscured by sounds of heavy munching. After rattling off a passage or two, he would switch off the machine and pause for thought (in that order), and then begin again. These stops and starts were not helpful and hence the habit, among all his secretaries, of simply leaving gaps, for him to fill in. I described this in a letter to my mother, who replied on 14 February, typing with her left hand only (as difficult as one-handed clapping): 'I shouldn't think Sir I. would mind at all if you have to leave words out; he sounds exceedingly nice, and rather like Bertrand Russell, who used to type letters to Grandfather himself on odd scraps of paper and using an ancient and rickety portable, with many letters missing altogether ...'.

In contrast to the opacity of his recorded words, Berlin's handwriting was a joy to work with – and I still find it so today. Here is a clear, plain, stable, harmonious and at times (in graphology terms) 'painted' hand, with a very high form level (or general quality). A 'painted' script has a printed, unlinked look, often indicating deep thought and a sense of word order and flow; and a light overall pressure is commonly seen in the writing of those who dislike physical force. In what is not a fast, driving hand but a considered and polite one, is also seen a tiny, but unmistakable, sign of high originality – the letter 's' always written upwards. I used to watch him doing it. His friend Igor Stravinsky had a similar singularity: the tiny notebook of musical sketches for *Pulcinella* shows that he used to form his bass clefs with a unique dive and roll stroke, written from the far left, quite unlike the norm. Equally interesting and pleasurable to work with was IB's writing style – the sphere of reference wide as the sky (how useful the Internet would have been then), the delightfully funny jokes, and the massive Miltonic paragraphs – portmanteau structures full of accumulating subclauses and parentheses – that meandered about exploring down tangential avenues, eventually to return, all in good time, miraculously spot-on, to the main verb and come finally to a halt. Working with language had always pleased me, and here was wonderful scope. But it was not typical English: far from it: it was very much its own man. Like Anita Brookner, whose novels are so often and so wrongly likened to Jane Austen's, Berlin was essentially European, and his prose, like hers, is studded with French and German words and phrases, and sprung with un-English rhythms.

Looking back, it seems to me now that, though so cosmopolitan, so experienced, and so sophisticated, though so pre-eminently social, and possessed of so many friends, Berlin was subtly handicapped by a somewhat undeveloped response to women. He had not grown up with sisters, had married late, and had no daughters. The women he surrounded himself with tended to be of one mould: confident, clever, decisive and in no way intimidated. So, for example, his contemporary women friends were in distinguished positions, the women he had so expertly selected to join the Wolfson team were admirably able, and the graduate students he taught were of the intellectual élite. This was the type that he seemed happiest with, and it presumably sprang from the pattern set by a dominant mother. Marie Berlin – demanding and assertive – had been, and still was, perhaps the strongest influence in his life, always there, at the other end of a huge umbilical hawser stretching all the way to Hampstead. Ever since childhood he had been the centre of her attention, a sensation he had learnt to like in general. By the same token, he seemed less able to manage unassertive women who were diffident and quiet. Being one such myself, I suffered greatly for a long time from feelings of inadequacy and anxiety, worried about the work and whether I was measuring up: but if he perceived this, I am not sure he knew how to cope with it.

Nor, I came to see, was he as adept at dealing with subordinates as he was with his peers. In his own circle of senior academics, gifted students and prominent figures in many arenas, he was entirely at home – animated, a star turn, talking non-stop like a train. With the rest of the world, with those simply getting on with ordinary jobs, he seemed to be rather at a loss, and tended to ignore them. Brenda Tripp was probably right when she suspected shyness in the thirty-six-year-old in Leningrad in 1945, but in an eminent man of sixty-two it was less easy to explain. Although from modest, lower-middle-class origins, all his life he had been encouraged to maintain a certain level, had lived and travelled in a grand manner, always with a background of supporting staff – but how to behave towards such staff was, it seemed, something he had never thought to learn. I witnessed several occasions on which he demonstrated, in dealings with others, that he was quite unaware of that fine definition of the 'gentleman' as 'someone who never speaks harshly or contemptuously to a person who is in no position to answer back on an equal footing'.[1]

Berlin in early 1972 was, I think, a near-perfect example of a human being in his element. Established, famous, respected in many fields, free and able to influence the spheres that most interested him, and personally content, he was his own benign circle, being and doing what suited him best, and hence being and doing it well. Michael Ignatieff's *Life* maintains that the benignity was indeed lifelong. At any rate, the cloud that appeared on the horizon in mid-1972, and stood over Hampstead, where Marie Berlin was finally failing, was a rare one. As long as her son could remember, there had been the habit of visits to her, and the rain of dutiful postcards sent to her whenever he was abroad. Now he had to watch as this most basic structure of his life crumbled, and his reaction was an acute anxiety ('This distracts me utterly – I cannot get anything written or said in a coherent fashion').[2] Apart from the death of his father in 1953, his existence had been unusually free thus far from the conundrums of trauma and

---

[1] Richard Davenport-Hines, 'Time, Gentlemen' (reviewing Peregrine Worsthorne, *In Defence of Aristocracy*), *The Times Literary Supplement*, 23 July 2004, 36.

[2] 13 June 1972 to Hamilton Fish Armstrong.

suffering, something he himself readily acknowledged. Perhaps he realised that a life unshadowed by pain, unstretched, untested, is itself a loss. He may have done. It is certainly true that in 1974, after I had left him for a job that was less lonely, and nearer to my family (and to the sister who was to improve, marry and then die in a road accident in 1981), when I wrote to him on the death of his mother, he replied in the most appreciative and sensitive terms.

Tea at the Athenaeum

Joseph Brodsky

This impression is taken from an essay that first appeared in the issue of the *New York Review of Books* dated 17 August 1989. After some more general reflections that fall outside the scope of this volume, Brodsky recounts that he first saw Isaiah Berlin when Berlin was 63 and Brodsky 32. 'I had just left the country where I'd spent those thirty-two years and it was my third day in London, where I knew nobody.'

I WAS STAYING in St John's Wood, in the house of Stephen Spender, whose wife had come to the airport three days before to fetch W. H. Auden, who had flown in from Vienna to participate in the annual Poetry International Festival in Queen Elizabeth Hall. I was on the same flight, for the same reason. As I had no place to stay in London, the Spenders offered to put me up.

On the third day in that house in the city where I knew nobody the phone rang and Natasha Spender cried, 'Joseph, it's for you.' Naturally, I was puzzled. My puzzlement hadn't subsided when I heard in the receiver my mother tongue, spoken with the most extraordinary clarity and velocity, unparalleled in my experience. The speed of sound, one felt, was courting the speed of light. That was Isaiah Berlin, suggesting tea at his club, the Athenaeum.

I accepted, although of all my foggy notions about English life, that of a club was the foggiest. (The last reference I had seen to one was in Pushkin's *Eugene Onegin*.) Mrs Spender gave me a lift to Pall Mall and before she deposited me in front of an imposing Regency edifice with a gilded Athena and Wedgewoodlike cornice, I, being unsure of my English, asked her whether she wouldn't mind accompanying me inside. She said that she wouldn't, except that women were not allowed. I found this puzzling, again, opened the door, and announced myself to the doorman.

'I'd like to see Sir Isaiah Berlin,' I said, and attributed the look of controlled disbelief in his eyes to my accent rather than to my Russian clothes. Two minutes later, however, climbing the majestic staircases and glancing at the huge oil portraits of Gladstones, Spencers, Actons, Darwins *et alii* that patterned the club's walls like wallpaper, I knew that the matter with me was neither my accent nor my turtleneck but my age. At thirty-two I was as much out of sync here as if I were a woman.

Presently I was standing in the huge, mahogany-cum-leather shell of the club's library. Through high windows the afternoon sun was pouring its rays on to the parquet as though testing its resolve to refract light. In various corners two or three rather ancient members were sunk deep in their tall armchairs, in various stages of newspaper-induced reverie. From across the room, a man in a baggy three-piece suit was waving to me. Against the sunlight, the silhouette looked Chaplinesque, or penguinish.

I walked toward him and we shook hands. Apart from the Russian language, the only other thing we had in common was that we both knew that language's best poet, Anna Akhmatova, who dedicated to Sir Isaiah a magnificent cycle of poems, *A Sweetbriar in Blossom*. The cycle was occasioned by a visit Isaiah Berlin, then a First Secretary in the British Embassy in Moscow, paid to Akhmatova in 1945. Aside from the poems, that encounter provoked Stalin's wrath, the dark shadow of which completely enveloped Akhmatova's life for the next decade and a half.

Since in one of the poems from that cycle[1] – spanning in its own turn a decade – the poet assumed the persona of Dido, addressing her visitor as Aeneas, I wasn't altogether surprised by the opening remark of that bespectacled man: 'What has she done to me? Aeneas! Aeneas! What sort of Aeneas am I really?' Indeed, he didn't look like one, and the mixture of embarrassment and pride in his voice was genuine.

Years later, on the other hand, in his own memoirs about visiting Pasternak and Akhmatova in 1945, 'When the world's strength was all spent [...] And only graves were fresh',[2] Sir Isaiah himself compares his Russian hosts to victims of a shipwreck on a desert island, enquiring about the civilisation which they've been cut off from for decades. For one thing, the essence of this simile echoes somewhat the circumstances of Aeneas's appearance before the queen of Carthage; for another, if not participants themselves, then the context of their meeting was epic enough to endure subsequent disclaimers.

But that was years later. Now I was staring at a face I saw for the first time. The paperback edition of *The Hedgehog and the Fox* that Akhmatova had once given to me to pass on to Nadezhda Mandel'shtam lacked a picture of its author; as for a copy of *Four Essays on Liberty*, it came to me from a book shark with its cover torn off – out of caution, given the book's subject. It was a wonderful face, a cross, I thought, between a wood grouse and a spaniel, with large brown eyes ready at once for flight and for hunting.

I felt comfortable with this face being old because the finality of its features alone excluded all pretension. Also, in this foreign realm where I had suddenly found myself, it was the first face that looked familiar. A traveller always clings to a recognisable object, be it a telephone or a statue. In the parts I was from that kind of face would belong to a physician, a schoolteacher, a musician, a

[1] 'Don't be startled', *A Sweetbriar in Blossom*, 11.
[2] 'You invented me', *A Sweetbriar in Blossom*, 8.

watchmaker, a scholar – to someone from whom you vaguely expect help. It was also the face of a potential victim, and so I suddenly felt comfortable.

Besides, we spoke Russian – to the great bewilderment of the uniformed personnel. The conversation naturally ran to Akhmatova until I asked Sir Isaiah how he had found me in London. The answer made me recall the front page of that mutilated edition of *Four Essays on Liberty*, and I felt ashamed. I should have remembered that that book, which for three years served me as an antidote to all sorts of demagoguery in which my native realm was virtually awash, was dedicated to the man under whose roof I now stayed.

It turned out that Stephen Spender was Sir Isaiah's friend from their days at Oxford. It turned out that so, though a bit later, was Wystan Auden, whose 'Letter to Lord Byron' had once been, like those *Four Essays*, my daily pocket companion. In a flash I realised that I owed a great deal of my sanity to men of a single generation, to the Oxford class, as it were, of *circa* 1930; that I was, in fact, also an unwitting product of their friendship; that they wandered through each other's books the way they did through their rooms at Corpus Christi or University College; that those rooms had, in the end, shrunk to the paperbacks in my possession.

On top of that, they were sheltering me now. Of course, I wanted to know everything about each one of them, and immediately. The two most interesting things in this world, as E. M. Cioran has remarked somewhere, are gossip and metaphysics. One could add, they have a similar structure: one can easily be taken for the other. That's what the remainder of the afternoon turned into, owing to the nature of the lives of those I was asking about, and owing to my host's tenacious memory.

The latter of course made me think again about Akhmatova, who also had this astonishing ability to retain everything: dates, details of topography, names and personal data of individuals, their family circumstances, their cousins, nephews, nieces, second and third marriages, where their husbands or wives were from, their party affiliations, when and by whom their books were published, and, had they come to a sorry end, the identities of those who had denounced them. She, too, could spin this vast, weblike, palpable fabric on a minute's notice, and even the timbre of her low monotone was similar to the voice I was listening to now in the Athenaeum's library.

No, the man before me was not Aeneas, because Aeneas, I think, remembered nothing. Nor was Akhmatova a Dido to be destroyed by one tragedy, to die in flames. Had she permitted herself to do so, who could describe their tongues? On the other hand, there is indeed something Vergilian about the ability to retain lives other than your own, about the intensity of attention to others' fates, and it is not necessarily the property of a poet.

But, then again, I couldn't apply to Sir Isaiah the label 'philosopher', because that mutilated copy of *Four Essays on Liberty* was more the product of a gut reaction against an atrocious century than a philosophical tract. For the same reason, I couldn't call him a historian of ideas. To me, his words always were a cry from the bowels of the monster, a call not so much for help as *of* help – a normal response of the mind singed and scarred by the present, and wishing it upon nobody as the future.

Besides, in the realm I was from, 'philosophy' was by and large a foul word and entailed the notion of a system. What was good about *Four Essays on Liberty* was that it advanced none, since 'liberty' and 'system' are antonyms. As to the smart-alecky retort that the absence of a system in itself is a system, I was pretty confident that I could live with this syllogism, not to mention in this sort of system.

And I remember that as I was making my way through that book without a cover I'd often pause, exclaiming to myself: How Russian this is! And by that I meant not only the author's arguments, but also the way that they were presented: his piling up of subordinate clauses, his digressions and questions, the cadences of his prose, which resembled the sardonic eloquence of the best of nineteenth-century Russian fiction.

Of course I knew that the man entertaining me now in the Athenaeum was born in Riga – I think Akhmatova told me so. She also thought that he was a personal friend of Churchill's, whose favorite wartime reading had been Berlin's dispatches from Washington. She was also absolutely sure that it was Berlin who arranged for her to receive an honorary degree from Oxford and the Etna Taormina Prize for Poetry in Italy in 1963. (Having seen something of Oxford dons years later, I think that making these arrangements was a good deal rockier than she could have imagined.) 'His great hero is Herzen,' she would add with a shrug and turn her face to the window.

Yet for all that, what I was reading wasn't 'Russian'. Nor was it Western rationalism marrying Eastern soulfulness, or Russian syntax burdening English clarity with its inflections. It appeared to me to be the fullest articulation of a unique human psyche, aware of the limitations imposed upon it by either language, and cognisant of those limitations' perils. Where I had cried 'Russian!' I should have said 'human'. The same goes for the passages where one might have sighed 'How English!'

The fusion of two cultures? Reconciliation of their conflicting values? If so, it would reflect only the human psyche's appetite for and ability to fuse and reconcile a lot more. Perhaps what could have been perceived here as faintly Eastern was the notion that reason doesn't deserve to have such a high premium put on it, the sense that reason is but an articulated emotion. That's why the defense of rational ideas turns out sometimes to be a highly emotional affair.

I remarked that the place looked positively English, very Victorian, to be precise. 'Indeed so,' replied my host with a smile. 'This is an island within an island. This is what's left of England, an idea of it, if you will.' And, as though not sure of my fully grasping the nuance, he added, 'a Herzen idea of London. All it lacks is fog.' And that was itself a glance at oneself from the outside, from afar, from a vantage point which was the psychological equivalent of the mid-Atlantic. It sounded like Auden's 'Look, stranger, on this island now [...].'[1]

No, neither a philosopher nor a historian of ideas, not a literary critic or social utopian, but an autonomous mind in the grip of an outward gravity, whose pull extends its perspective on this life in so far as this mind cares to send back signals. The word, perhaps, would be 'penseur', were it not for the muscular and crouching associations so much at odds with this civilised, alert figure comfortably reclining in the bottle-green leather armchair at the Athenaeum – the West and the East of it mentally at the same time.

[...] The sad irony of all this is of course that, so far as I know, not a line of Berlin's writings has been translated into the language of the country which needs that intellect the most, and which could profit from those writings enormously.[2] If anything, that country could learn from him a lot more about its intellectual history – and by the same token about its present choices – than it seems capable of thus far. His syntax, to say the least, wouldn't be an obstacle. Nor should they be perturbed by Herzen's shadow, for while Herzen indeed was appalled by and sought to change the mental climate of Russia, Berlin seems to take on the entire world's weather.

Short of being able to alter it, he still helps one to endure it. One cloud less – if only a cloud in one's mind – is improvement enough, like removing from a brow its 'tactile fever'. An improvement far greater is the idea that it is the ability to choose that defines a being as human; that, hence, choice is the species's recognised necessity – which flies into the moronic face of the reduction of the human adventure to the exclusively moral dimensions of right and wrong.

Of course, one says all this with the benefit of hindsight, sharpened by what one could have read of Berlin since. I think, however, that seventeen years ago, with only *The Hedgehog and the Fox* and *Four Essays on Liberty* on my mind, I could not have reacted to their author differently. Before our tea at the Athenaeum was over I knew that others' lives are this man's forte, for what other reason could there be for a sixty-three-year-old knight of England to talk to a thirty-two-year-old Russian poet? What could I possibly tell him that he didn't already know, one way or the other?

---

[1] The opening line of a poem in Auden's *Look, Stranger!* (London, 1936), 19; the 1937 New York edition was entitled *On This Island*.

[2] Even when this essay was published, *Four Essays on Liberty* and a number of other essays had in fact appeared in Russian translation. Ed.

Still, I think I was sitting in front of him on that sunny July afternoon not only because his work is the life of the mind, the life of ideas. Ideas of course reside in people, but they can also be gleaned from clouds, water, trees; indeed, from a fallen apple. And at best I could qualify as an apple fallen from Akhmatova's tree. I believe he wanted to see me not for what I knew but for what I didn't – a role in which, I suppose, he quite frequently finds himself vis-à-vis most of the world.

To put it somewhat less stridently, if not less autobiographically, with Berlin the world gets one more choice. This choice consists not so much of following his precepts as of adopting his mental patterns. In the final analysis, Berlin's notion of pluralism is not a blueprint but rather a reflection of the omniscience of his own unique mind, which indeed appears to be both older and more generous than what it observes. This omniscience in other words is very man-like and therefore can and should be emulated, not just applauded or envied.

Later the same evening, as we sat for supper in Stephen Spender's basement, Wystan said, 'Well, how did it go today with Isaiah?' And Stephen immediately asked, 'Yes, is his Russian really good?' I began, in my tortured English, a long story about the nobility of old Petersburg pronunciation, about its similarity to Stephen's own Oxonian, and how Isaiah's vocabulary was free of unpalatable accretions of the Soviet period and how his idiom was so much his own, when Natasha Spender interrupted me and said, 'Yes, but does he speak Russian as fast as he speaks English?' I looked at the faces of those three people who had known Isaiah Berlin for much longer than I had lived and wondered whether I should carry on with my exegesis. Then I thought better of it.

'Faster,' I said.

Some Musical Encounters

Alfred Brendel

I WAS FIRST INTRODUCED to Isaiah Berlin in the green room of the Queen Elizabeth Hall after one of my Beethoven recitals – in 1975, I think. Dana Scott, the American mathematician and logician, and his wife, the pianist Irene Schreier, had brought him along from Oxford, where Dana was lecturing at that time. With Irene as a four-hand partner, Dana sometimes played pieces of his own composition, which sounded roughly like the Viennese waltzes of Lanner.

A few days later I saw Isaiah again at Lord Drogheda's. His voice, still strong and firm, was booming across the dinner table with great incisiveness and speed. A friendship soon developed, and my wife Reni and I would often spend time with Isaiah and Aline, either at Headington House, the Berlins' lovely Oxford residence, or at our London home, or in their Ligurian refuge at Paraggi, or at Plush Manor in Dorset, where we entertained Isaiah and his friends on his eightieth birthday.

Before the birthday dinner, I gave a concert in the adjacent church, a recital that included Schubert's B flat Sonata, whose Andante sostenuto I was to perform again at Isaiah's memorial service in Hampstead Synagogue in January 1998 – the movement had become one of Isaiah's favourites. A few years previously, he had listened to a programme of Schubert's last three sonatas that I gave at Stowe School, and it seemed to have persuaded him of the greatness of this triad. He must have heard Artur Schnabel, the revered pianist of his younger years, play some Schubert; but the cumulative impact of the three works seemed new to him. It was as though part of his enthusiasm for Rossini and Verdi (Isaiah was a regular patron of the Pesaro Festival) had gradually been transferred to Beethoven and Schubert. There was something childlike about Isaiah's appreciation of music. When a piece stayed strictly in time, as in some Italian opera, he delighted in beating the rhythm on his thigh. (Isaiah greatly valued Toscanini.) But his nostalgia for musical naivety, memorably expressed in his essay on 'naive' and 'sentimental' music (in Schiller's sense), did not mean that he was unable to enjoy the different, more complex rewards of the great 'German' composers.

Isaiah's special interest, however, was opera. To please him, it needed opera producers who served the composer, not themselves. His knowledge of obscure Russian operas was astonishing – and he loved to hum the tunes. As a member of the Covent Garden Board, he attended virtually every new opera production in London, including – with a bit of pleading from me – the first night of Birtwistle's phenomenal *Mask of Orpheus* at the English National Opera, and also Busoni's *Doktor Faust*, the music of which he credited with having 'moral charm' – an elusive quality that Isaiah otherwise granted only to human beings. Among contemporary composers, it was George Benjamin whom he befriended.

Wagner presented a bigger obstacle. For Isaiah, the notion that a great composer could be an odious person, and that this odiousness was not necessarily reflected in the music, seemed difficult to accept. With Rossini or Verdi he could readily identify on purely human grounds. Wagner's personality, however, he was bound to find abhorrent. Nevertheless, Isaiah made gallant attempts to deal with a composer whom he recognised as a musical and dramatic genius. I can recall him, during an interval of *Parsifal* at Covent Garden, telling me in his characteristically staccato delivery: 'The idea of redemption I do *not* understand.'

Armed with manuals on Baroque architecture and commentaries on Wagner's *Ring*, including George Bernard Shaw's still brilliantly readable essay, the Berlin and Brendel families went to Bayreuth for Boulez's and Chéreau's final *Ring* in 1979. One of our aims was to scrutinise Wagner's libretti – a task I had till then strenuously avoided – in order to penetrate the surface of their off-puttingly artificial language and arrive at the wider and hardly anti-Semitic or narrowly nationalistic implications of Wagner's plot. Though Isaiah never quite conquered his aversion, he seemed in the end to gain a more acute awareness of Wagner's musical power and theatrical vision – due in no small measure to the Boulez/Chéreau team, as well as the unforgettable Bayreuth acoustics.

Another joint excursion triggered by musical events was our trip to Moscow and Leningrad in 1988. This was the first time I had performed in the Soviet Union, and I was joined by Isaiah and a number of friends from the US and Germany. The Gorbachev era had started, and this was only Isaiah's second visit to Russia since his famous encounter with Akhmatova. We were privileged to stay at the British Embassy, which overlooks the domes of the Kremlin from the other side of the Moskva River. My recital in Moscow took place in a strange venue normally used for chess championships and funerals for Heroes of the Soviet Union. Isaiah seemed thoroughly relaxed, talking in fluent Russian to passers-by on the street.

In Leningrad, the hotel we all stayed in faced the concert hall, whose architectural style betrayed its former use as the stock exchange. During breakfast one of my friends, the former film actress Marianne Koch, started a conversation with a bearded Muscovite and his twelve-year-old daughter Polina, a rather tall and sturdy piano *Wunderkind*. On discovering my presence, they invited us all to join them in their hotel room that night for a drink. Curious to meet Russians unconnected with Goskonzert, the rather unsavoury official concert agency, we decided to accept. At their apartment, Polina's father was joined by a language teacher who taught businessmen basic English, by a tall, ironic Jewish actor who introduced himself as Paul Schofield, and by the well-groomed director of the local television station. Our host, a figure straight out of Dostoevsky, delivered rambling monologues about his musical idols, who included Haydn and Horowitz (pronounced 'Gaydn' and 'Gorowitz'), while armfuls of wine bottles were carried in through the door. Then Polina, who had been busy rehearsing, stormed into the room, sat down at the appalling upright (brand 'Red October'), and played the beginning of every piece her father cared to mention. Next day, we were told, Polina would be rehearsing three Bach concertos with a chamber orchestra – wouldn't we like to attend? Some of us, including Isaiah, duly did, and watched the girl negotiate all the notes with firm fingers while, for no obvious reason, the conductorless string ensemble played standing up. Polina's father walked up and down the middle aisle with huge strides and wild gestures; when he arrived next to the girl he shouted some advice which she registered by turning her head towards him without interrupting the performance. As we realised later, this man was not a musician at all but a sportsman. His fractured nose bore evidence of his true vocation: he had trained his son to become a boxer.

The conclusion to this story occurred when Isaiah and Aline had already left for London. After my final recital, which Polina's party had promised to attend, none of them showed up backstage. I returned to my hotel and was packing my bags when someone knocked at the door. As I opened it, I saw Polina standing there, dressed – hard to believe – in a tutu, flanked by her surrogate mother of the moment and the nice English teacher, each of whom carried one single flower and begged me to come over. It was like returning to a play: the same people had reassembled, and a fairly drunk Mr Dostoevsky informed me that, having heard my recital, he had revised his sceptical opinion of Schubert. As Polina's tutu brushed against my thigh, I detected a man with a camera in the corner. The whole thing was being filmed for a documentary on Polina's career.

Isaiah enjoyed listening to people no less than to opera. Of course, he preferred conversation to writing. But no one ever wrote obituaries like Isaiah. Unlike some of those printed in British papers, they appraised mainly by praising. Isaiah knew a vast amount about an amazing number of people. Never full of himself, he was full of others. His curiosity was insatiable, his criticism playful rather than malicious. The first person to be critical about was himself. Since he never seemed to take himself too seriously, he intimidated no one. Always keen to take in new information, his memory seized on it, and retained it precisely. A lot of gossip was sifted through and put to higher use. No matter how animatedly Isaiah spoke, he always managed to remain clear and to the point.

His virtuosity in summing up any book he had ever read seemed to me unique. As in his torrential lectures, he never left any – even the longest – sentence unfinished.

Watching Woody Allen's *Zelig*, Isaiah revelled in the sight of orthodox Jews performing *A Midsummer Night's Dream*. He adored humour. Stories, anecdotes or jokes that he told were never too long. Like this one. When Stravinsky, at his teacher Rimsky-Korsakov's funeral, was visibly moved, the composer's widow turned to him and said: 'Pull yourself together, young man, we've still got Glazunov.'

To Isaiah, wit and profundity were not mutually exclusive; a combination of both was appreciated, and indeed demonstrated by himself. Consequently, the notion of 'funny' music did not appear alien to him, as it still does to some philosophers and musicians. (Isaiah relished quasi-oxymorons: I've already mentioned 'moral charm', and he used to call a prominent academic a 'genuine charlatan'.) He took a keen interest in my 1984 Darwin lecture, which discussed the comic possibilities of absolute music, and actually suggested the lecture's title: 'Does Classical Music Have To Be Entirely Serious?'

At home with friends he delighted in playing games. One of them involved selecting personalities we all knew and awarding them marks from 1 to 10 in various categories, made up on the spot, such as intelligence, talent, imagination, decency etc. (In the case of a well-known cultural administrator, we settled for an intellect that fluctuated between 2 and 9.) He also enjoyed being sounded out about matters of intellectual interest. When I asked him whether, within all the plurality surrounding us, he could name a single human virtue that would be equally valued in many different cultures, Isaiah, after a pause, said: 'reliability'.

During his frequent walks, he would often stop to explain something or make a point, whether about Truth and Truths, the impact of Genius, his own propensity to hero-worship, or the meaning of life ('I believe it has none'). At the seaside, he would stand in the water – Isaiah didn't swim – and talk cheerfully to anyone who came along. It was on an hour-long walk in Paraggi that he explained to me the reasons for his Zionist sympathies and the need for the Jewish people to have a place where they belonged, a country to feel at home in. I deeply sympathise with the Jewish predicament, and shall never forget the sight of Jews being forced to wear yellow stars under Nazi and Ustashi rule. However, such nationalist fanaticism also inoculated me against the concept of 'soil', and turned me into a self-styled Central European in diaspora, a permanent paying guest. Nevertheless, I felt most honoured to have been one of the first musicians from former Nazi countries invited to play with the Israel Philharmonic. Isaiah was kind enough to join me there, introducing me in Jerusalem to Avishai and Edna Margalit, who became friends. For a number

of years I returned to Israel to share, as soloist, the orchestra's harrowing schedule, unique in the whole world, of six consecutive concerts each week. (Thank
heaven for the Shabbat.) Then Netanyahu, to the consternation of anyone I
came to know in Israel, won the election. It may have been around this time
that Isaiah discontinued his visits to a country resembling less and less the Israel
he had hoped for.

Besides the Margalits, there were several delightful friends of the Berlins
whom Reni and I got to know. There was Stephen Spender with his ever-
youthful radiance, and his pianist wife Natasha. There was Bernard Williams,
whose superior eloquence once made Harold Pinter, uncharacteristically, yield
during an argument at our dinner table and say: 'I take your point.' There were
Noel and Gaby Annan, as well as Ronald Dworkin, composed yet witty, one
of the few people able to match Philip Roth in conversation. And there was
Robert Silvers, the widely admired editor of the *New York Review of Books*, who
invited me to contribute. Certainly, the intellectuals around Isaiah were the
most stimulating dinner guests one could wish for, with Aline as the perfect
hostess. These are memories that continue to warm my heart.

Editing Berlin, Interpreting Berlin

Henry Hardy in Conversation with Kei Hiruta

An interview conducted for this volume at Wolfson College, Oxford, on 8 August 2008

EDITING BERLIN

HIRUTA It has been more than three decades since you started editing the work of Isaiah Berlin in 1974. How did you come to know him and his work in the first place?

HARDY As a result of coming here to Wolfson College as a philosophy graduate student in 1972. As soon as I arrived, I became involved in conversations with Isaiah, usually in the common room, where he would sit and talk for hours to all comers, mainly after lunch. Since I was a philosopher, I naturally took an interest in what he'd written, although I didn't know anything about him or his work when I first came here. I asked people who were already here and knew more about him what I should read. They recommended *Four Essays on Liberty*, which had been published only three years before, in 1969. I read it on holiday one vacation and found it absolutely enthralling, and moving in many ways, and became a Berlinophile (though not an uncritical one) from that point onward, quite apart from already liking him as a person and finding his conversation absorbingly interesting. It is hard to exaggerate the transforming effect of talking to him. He said of geniuses that he had met personally that they made his mind race. If this is a criterion of genius, he was a genius. He made the world of the intellect intensely alive, important, exhilarating – and fun – in a way that was quite new to me, and made me glad in a way I could not have anticipated that I had returned to Oxford to do graduate work. He defined an intellectual as someone who wants ideas to be as interesting as possible, and that definition provides part of the answer to those who ask why he was so celebrated. I would defy anyone to name someone who better exemplified what Madame de Staël said of Rousseau: 'He said nothing new, but set everything on fire.'[1] Except that Isaiah did say new things, which puts him ahead of Rousseau on that count, if de Staël is right.

---

[1] *De la littérature considérée dans ses rapports avec les institutions sociales*, ed. Paul van Tieghem (Geneva, 1959), ii 280–1.

HIRUTA   Your work as Berlin's editor has a prehistory: you constructed a bibliography of his work.[1] He did not keep a record of his publications, did he?

HARDY   This is the moment to quote yet again the famous remark by Maurice Bowra, made in a letter to Noel Annan when Isaiah won the Order of Merit in 1971. He wrote, 'Though like Our Lord and Socrates he does not publish much, he thinks and says a great deal and has had an enormous influence on our times.'[2] The general reputation and image of Berlin at that point was of a man who talked enormously, a terrific conversationalist, famous for his intellectual powers, but who, people thought, had published only a few occasional pieces, underperforming in comparison with his potential by quite a wide margin. However, I started to investigate what he really had published when friends of mine who knew that I enjoyed editing of various kinds suggested that here was a much more important and rewarding object of my editorial propensities than I had previously found. I asked Isaiah if I could have a look at what he had written and try to compile a list, with a view, possibly, to publishing a collection of it. He agreed. So I examined various sources – chiefly a cupboard full of off-prints and drawers full of press-cuttings in his house. There was a press-cuttings agency called Durrants which you could sign up with, and they would send you clippings of any mention of you in the newspapers and certain journals. These provided a good deal of information about what Isaiah had written, as did various files of notes and drafts that were in his house. I was greatly helped in this exploration by his private secretary, Pat Utechin, who had been involved for many years in sending his work to publishers. It turned out that he'd written not just more than people thought, but enormously much more than people thought. And it became clear very soon that there was the potential not just for a single volume but for a number of volumes, perhaps organised thematically, which is how it turned out in the end.

HIRUTA   The first set of volumes that you edited was *Russian Thinkers* (co-edited with Aileen Kelly), *Concepts and Categories*, *Against the Current* and *Personal Impressions*. These are collections of Berlin's published essays that had not been previously made available in a collected form. What was it like to edit these volumes? It is often said that Berlin was a reluctant publisher. How reluctant was he?

HARDY   His reluctance was more marked in some cases than others. In par-ticular, in the case of *Concepts and Categories*, he was very hard to persuade that his philosophical writings were worth collecting and republishing. In the

---

[1] 'A Bibliography of Isaiah Berlin', *Lycidas* 3 (1974–5), 41–5; now online in the IBVL, as are all of Hardy's writings cited in the notes.

[2] Maurice Bowra to Noel Annan, 1971, quoted in Noel Annan, 'A Man I Loved', in Hugh Lloyd-Jones (ed.), *Maurice Bowra: A Celebration* (London, 1974), 53.

end, we had to get Bernard Williams, who was a close friend of his, and whose opinion he respected, to read the essays that I wanted to put into that volume. It was only because Williams was in favour of publishing all but one of them that Isaiah eventually agreed to the volume. As for the rest, he was in general fairly reluctant because he thought that the activity of collecting essays and publishing them together was something that normally and properly happened after somebody had died. So he referred to these volumes as 'my posthumous writings'. He also felt that he ought to publish a solid, continuous book, possibly on Romanticism, before it would be decent to start gathering up old essays. Nevertheless, partly because we suggested that the royalties from the collections could go to Wolfson College, he did eventually agree.

HIRUTA In 1990 you published another volume of Berlin's collected essays – *The Crooked Timber of Humanity* – and soon after that you left your job as a Senior Editor at Oxford University Press and became a full-time editor of Berlin's work and a Fellow of Wolfson. I guess that was a big step for you to take. What made you do that? Did you imagine in 1990 that you might be editing Berlin's work in 2009?

HARDY I suppose I hoped that I should be. But I should not have dared predict it. I knew that there was enough work to be done to keep me going until then – above all the enormous task of editing his scintillating correspondence, which some think will be his greatest legacy. Thousands upon thousands of letters survive, and their range is forbidding. To edit them satisfactorily one has to delve into a series of radically different worlds: Oxford, London, Israel, America, Russia. I thank providence for the co-editor of the second and third volumes of the letters, Jennifer Holmes, who has a genius for historical research without which our current rate of progress, not to mention the standard of the finished product, would be inconceivable.

As for the reasons why I switched jobs, there were two. One was that I had been forcibly moved at OUP from work that I enjoyed to an area that didn't suit me, so I was looking for an alternative occupation. Secondly, in the late 1980s Berlin decided to rewrite his Will, and he asked me if I would be one of no fewer than four literary executors.[1] In agreeing to that, I also said that I'd naturally be keen to see what it was I would have to be dealing with when the time came. So I asked him if I could do a full survey of the papers in his house, which he agreed to. I discovered, to my delight and astonishment, that there was a very great deal of finished but unpublished work. From the attics to the cellars, there were suitcases, boxes, folders, shelves stuffed with unimaginable riches of which I had no inkling until I saw them. He evidently never threw

---

[1] This arrangment was superseded in 1996, when Berlin set up a Literary Trust, of which Hardy was appointed one of the three initial Trustees.

anything away. I was amazed that he could have generated so much wonderful work and simply put it aside, often enough forgetting it entirely. I remember showing him the typescript of his lecture on 'The Sense of Reality', corrected in his own hand, which I had found in an old brown envelope on which he had written 'Historical realism'. 'Are you sure this is by me?' he asked. This was not an affectation, believe me.

So I said to him, 'It would be much better if I began work now, when you're available to answer questions.' That's how I came to leave OUP and begin this task.

HIRUTA Then you embarked on a different kind of project, that is, to edit Berlin's unpublished work. *The Magus of the North* and *The Sense of Reality* appeared in 1993 and 1996 respectively, followed by the posthumously published volumes *The Roots of Romanticism, Freedom and Its Betrayal* and *Political Ideas in the Romantic Age*. What was the main difference between editing a collection of Berlin's published essays and editing his unpublished work?

HARDY Editing his published essays was largely a matter of normal copy-editing, in particular tracking down, with the help of experts, the many quotations that he had used, checking and correcting them, and providing references where they were missing. His quotations are, notoriously, often inaccurate – creative reconstructions of what their authors might have said if they had been as eloquent as he. Kant wrote that 'Out of timber as crooked as that from which man is made, nothing entirely straight can be constructed.' Would we remember this if Isaiah had not transformed it into 'Out of the crooked timber of humanity no straight thing was ever made'? Also, he had frequently not kept careful records of his sources – many in foreign languages, which created an extra barrier. And all this was going on in the days before the Internet, which has since made work of this kind somewhat easier.

As for his unpublished work, the answer to your question depends on what kind of material one is confronted with. In the case of *Freedom and Its Betrayal*, there were very rough transcripts of the lectures he'd given on the radio, but no recording, except in one case – the lecture on Rousseau. So I was dealing with transcripts made by people who knew nothing about the subject matter – stenographers at the BBC – and the transcripts were riddled with nonsensical inaccuracies (such as 'Sir Seymour' for 'Saint-Simon'), and sometimes entirely incoherent. The first task was to recover his meaning, which was luckily rarely in real doubt. But for *The Roots of Romanticism* we had not only transcripts but a complete tape-recording; so there weren't the same problems of establishing a text, although I still had to convert extempore spoken sentences into publishable ones, which means changing almost every sentence slightly. Finally, in the case of *The Magus of the North*, the essays that comprise *The Sense of Reality*, and *Political Ideas in the Romantic Age*, there were draft typescripts, mostly dictated. The texts essentially existed, but still needed considerable tidying up. An exception was a long section of *The Magus of the North* that survived only on an obsolete type of recording carrier called Dictabelts: the recovery of this from the now brittle plastic belts, which had to be warmed in an oven before they would yield up their secret, was undoubtedly the most enthralling episode of the whole project.[1]

HIRUTA Among the posthumous publications of Berlin's that you have edited are *Liberty* and *Three Critics of the Enlightenment*. They incorporate respectively *Four Essays on Liberty* and *Vico and Herder*, books that Berlin published in his lifetime without an editor. What made you intervene and produce a refined version?

HARDY In the case of *Four Essays on Liberty*, I was aware that it had various editorial deficiencies. I also knew that Berlin had originally wanted it to be *Five Essays on Liberty*, but had tried to insert the fifth essay only at the last moment, and therefore it hadn't been done. This was a book that was prescribed on many political studies courses, and it seemed to me that it ought to be brought up to standard and expanded to include other things that he had written in the same area. In the case of *Vico and Herder*, the book had gone out of print, as had *The Magus of the North*, which is the other component of *Three Critics*. One of my guiding principles is to keep as much of Berlin in print as I can, and I thought that the publisher might be more prepared to reprint those essays if they were put together into a single volume, which, indeed, corresponded to a volume that Berlin himself had been planning to produce at some point in his life, but which had fallen by the wayside.

HIRUTA Berlin's surviving papers are enormous; he called them 'a huge unsorted heap'. When the major part of them was transferred to the Bodleian Library in Oxford, it occupied over 250 archive boxes; and many more papers are stored in the Wolfson College Archives.[2] In addition, a number of audio (and some video) recordings are kept in the British Library Sound Archive, the BBC Sound Archives and elsewhere. Apart from his letters, whose third volume is currently in preparation, is there anything in those 'heaps' that deserves publication but has not been published so far?

HARDY I believe so, yes. There are three main categories of material to mention here. First of all, there's early philosophical material, which often takes the

---

[1] For more details see 'Confessions of an Editor', *Australian Financial Review*, 30 June 2000, Review Section, 4–5.

[2] Henry Hardy, 'A Huge Unsorted Heap', *Oxford Today* 14 no. 2 (Trinity 2002), 51. Berlin's papers were donated to the Bodleian Library in 1999. For more about the papers, see Michael Hughes, 'The Papers of Sir Isaiah Berlin at the Bodleian Library', *Twentieth Century British History* 16 (2005), 193–205, repr. in this volume.

form of lecture notes or drafts of papers rather than the finished essays which we know from *Concepts and Categories*. I think this is of the greatest interest in showing, even more clearly, the continuity between his early philosophical work and his later work in the history of ideas, which are often supposed to be discontinuous; and there is a growing interest in this link on the part of various scholars. So I think that more of this material should be made available – probably on the Berlin website rather than in printed form. Next, he wrote a number of pieces on the cultural history of the twentieth century, in particular three long articles for volumes of the *Britannica Book of the Year* published in the early 1950s. These are extremely interesting both for what they tell us about the twentieth century and for what they show about the range of Berlin's understanding and reading at the time. Finally, there are several still uncollected essays which Berlin himself didn't publish, but which I've managed to bring to publishable standard and publish here and there over the years. There are plenty of those to make at least one more volume.

INTERPRETING BERLIN

HIRUTA You contributed an obituary of Isaiah Berlin to the *Independent* when he died in 1997.[1] That was the first time you published something substantial about Berlin, not only as his editor but as somebody who knew him well and so was able to give a reliable description of his life and work. Have you received more requests to write or talk about Berlin in recent years, as he comes to be seen as a historic figure?

HARDY Yes, from time to time I have. But I remember something Berlin once said to me when he published his essay 'Giambattista Vico and Cultural History', now included in *The Crooked Timber of Humanity*. He said, 'As far as Vico goes, I have now put all my cards on the table.' I feel similarly that, as far as Berlin goes, I have now put all my cards on the table; I have little more that I want or feel able to say about him. Nevertheless, I have been invited to give talks of various kinds in connection with the centenary of his birth in 2009, and I'm planning to use the images from an exhibition that I'm curating at Wolfson, and also some clips of him talking, as a basis for a couple of new talks, which simply use these images and clips as occasions for looking at Berlin and his work from a fresh angle.

HIRUTA You once said, in an article published in the *Australian Financial Review*, that an editor like you – one whose task is 'bringing into existence books that would otherwise not have appeared' – is 'someone who feels more comfortable saying "Look at what this person thinks" than saying "Here is what

---

[1] Henry Hardy, 'Isaiah Berlin', *Independent*, 7 November 1997, repr. as 'A Personal Impression of Isaiah Berlin' in L1.

I think." ' Interpretation is a different matter; when you interpret somebody's work, you say 'Look, here is what I think this person thinks.' Having been Berlin's editor, how do you find yourself acting as Berlin's interpreter?

HARDY I always feel slightly shifty about interpreting Berlin, because, in order to interpret an intellectual figure reliably and fully, you need to be able to see him in terms of the historical position that he occupies, and in the context of his contemporaries and other figures in the field in which he is active. As I explained in my preface to the first volume of his letters, because I concern myself pretty exclusively with Berlin and his own work, I have rather blink-ered vision, like that of a butler who is aware of the household in which he operates but not of other households elsewhere. My view of Berlin's work is very much constrained in that way, and I'm anxious not to trespass beyond my competence.

HIRUTA You have been quite explicit that you are interested in one particu-lar issue in Berlin's work, namely, the implications of his value pluralism for religion.² Your argument, to put it in an oversimplified form, is that if value pluralism is true, all monisms are false, and since many religions – 'especially mainstream variants of Christianity and Islam' ³ – aspire to monistic status, tak-ing pluralism seriously entails a hope that they will wither away. This is certainly a highly controversial claim; but the issue is of pressing concern to many of us today. Was it a central issue for Berlin himself? Or is it something that you find interesting but which did not particularly attract Berlin's attention?

HARDY It wasn't as central for Berlin as I should have liked it to be. I do rec-ognise that I must not foist on him a concern that's mine and not his. His own central preoccupations were set to some degree by the political events through which he lived – in particular, by his reaction to Communism and Nazism, and especially by Stalin and the Cold War. So he was preoccupied by totalitarian-ism and oppression whose origin was political. Certainly, what he said about these phenomena can be seen as applicable to religion. But he himself wasn't so exercised by that aspect of his views, probably because religion hadn't been an instrument of oppression in his own life, as it has in mine; and I'm obviously reacting against certain manifestations of religion to which I take exception. However, there are two reasons why I feel that what I'm trying to say about this issue are in the spirit of Berlin. One is that, when I wrote an article about it, he read it and said he agreed with it, in terms which made me believe that he meant what he said and wasn't simply being polite. Secondly, he wrote a piece

¹ 'Confessions of an Editor', op. cit. (139 above, note 1).
² See 'The Compatibility of Incompatibles', *Independent*, 20 February 1993, 33; 'Taking Pluralism Seriously', in OM; 'Isaiah Berlin's *Four Essays on Liberty*', 'Speaking Volumes' series, *Times Higher Education Supplement*, 21 November 1997, 21.
³ OM 281.

for a friend who wanted his help with a lecture, a moving document headed 'Notes on Prejudice'.[1] I think you can see from that, very clearly, that what he said applied to religion, even from his own point of view, though this was something he didn't usually stress.

HIRUTA Is there anything about which you strongly disagree with Berlin?

HARDY Two things come to mind. The first is his apparent reluctance to attribute human behaviour to malevolence or evil. He held, quite properly, that one should always try to understand before one condemned. But it seems to me that plenty of what human beings do can't be understood as resulting from, let us say, a mistake about the facts – which is one of the explanations he gave of Nazism – but simply stems from that element in human nature which makes us prone to do bad things for their own sake. The other disagreement connects with what I was saying about religion. That is, his own attitude to religious practice seems to have been that this is a valuable vehicle of cultural identity. For him the ceremonies and practices of Judaism kept the collective identity of the Jews alive. And he was perfectly happy, indeed anxious, to join in with them on this basis without subscribing to any of the doctrinal, metaphysical claims that they entailed. This seems to me an intellectually and morally unacceptable conjunction of views. However, it's one he held.

HIRUTA Why do you think that it's unacceptable?

HARDY Because it means, in effect, wishing for the preservation of a religious tradition based on beliefs you do not share, beliefs that have a life-forming effect on many people, just so that one of its side-effects that you value can continue in play. I remember Mary Warnock saying once on the radio something to the effect that she believed none of the theological propositions in the Prayer Book, but wanted the Church of England to continue in being so that the beauty of Evensong could be preserved. More seriously, if you believe, as I do, that religious belief at least has the potential to become oppressive and destructive, then anything which encourages religion to exist and to thrive seems to me regrettable.

Berlin once wrote that a new dimension of horror was opened up when the Nazis loaded people 'into trains bound for gas chambers, telling them that they were going to emigrate to some happier place'.[2] Well, the logic of that situation seems to me comparable to that of Berlin's attitude to religion. It's too close for comfort to Marx's characterisation of religion as the opium of the people. And opium is an enslaver, not a liberator.

HIRUTA We already have several interpretations of Berlin – John Gray's

[1] Published in L.
[2] L 339.

Berlin, George Crowder's Berlin, and so on. Do you think of contributing one by yourself – Henry Hardy's Berlin?

HARDY No, for the reasons given before. I do think of writing some account, at some stage, of my work on and with Berlin – perhaps expanding on some of the things I've been saying in this interview. But I'm simply not competent, and could not become competent in the remaining time available to me in this life, to write a book of that kind.

HIRUTA I understand that there is a large collection of letters between you and Berlin in which you ask him questions that touch upon philosophically interesting issues. Do you think of publishing those letters?

HARDY Yes, that too is something I might do. I have already dipped into those letters for a talk I gave in Spain.[1] It would be possible to publish an edition of those letters with linking commentary, which would go some way to providing an account of my view of Berlin. But it would touch only on those particular issues which I raised with him, which constitute a very small proportion of the whole of his thought.

HIRUTA A final question: you have worked on Isaiah Berlin, principally as his editor and occasionally as his interpreter, for more than three decades. Has it been always rewarding?

HARDY Overall, absolutely, if not absolutely always. I couldn't have asked for a more interesting way to spend my life. I'm extremely fortunate to have stumbled across this opportunity, and to have been able to exploit it. Admittedly, the rewards have been interspersed with frustrations. Although he was in general extremely kind and generous to me, as his family have been after him, Berlin was in many ways a difficult person to work with. He was very prone to change his mind, sometimes at the last minute, apparently inconsiderately (he was after all the indulged only surviving child of doting parents), so that one could spend a lot of time working on something only to find that it was not going to happen. There have been times, too, when I have found my self-imposed narrowness of focus claustrophobic, and the sheer scale of the material to be processed frighteningly daunting, partly because I have unfortunately become prone to serious bouts of clinical depression. Also, I've had perpetual problems with raising the necessary funding to keep the project going. People assume that Wolfson College pays my salary and research expenses – well, it does (so far!), but only with money that I raise myself or that is raised for me. I live in permanent fear that the project will have to be aborted, or slowed to a crawl, because of lack of funds, and this is deeply dispiriting. But the work

---

[1] 'Dear Isaiah', published as 'Querido Isaiah' in Mira Milosevich and Julio Crespo (eds), *Isaiah Berlin: un liberal en perspectiva* (Madrid, 2008), 61–91.

in itself couldn't be more rewarding to somebody of my rather peculiar, in some ways defectively obsessional, disposition; and so I don't regret that this task, for better or worse, has become my vocation, so long as I can keep at it. If I have helped people to experience the special magic of Berlin's mind, I am content.

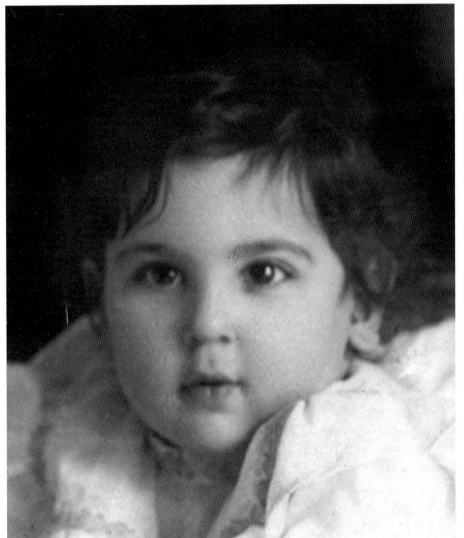

The first known photograph: in Riga, 1910

Identification of these unlabelled photographs from family albums can only be speculative, but **2** and/or **3** might be Isaiah Berlin senior, and **4** IB's paternal grandfather Ber Berlin, né Zuckerman; **5** is probably his maternal grandfather Salmon Izchok Volshonok before he succumbed to the blindness evident in **22**.

6

7

Marie Volshonok, IB's mother, from an identity card bearing the stamp of the Institute of the Riga section of the Imperial Russian Musical Society

Mendel Berlin, IB's father, in 1904

8

9

Marie Berlin is second from left; the others may be Mendel's sisters Maria and Evgenia, and his mother Shifra

Marie and Mendel Berlin, with (probably) Mendel's sister Evgenia

10

11

12

13

Childhood in Russia: **10** and (probably) **11**, in Riga; **12**, in Petrograd in 1917 (aged 8);
13, between then and the family's departure for England in 1921

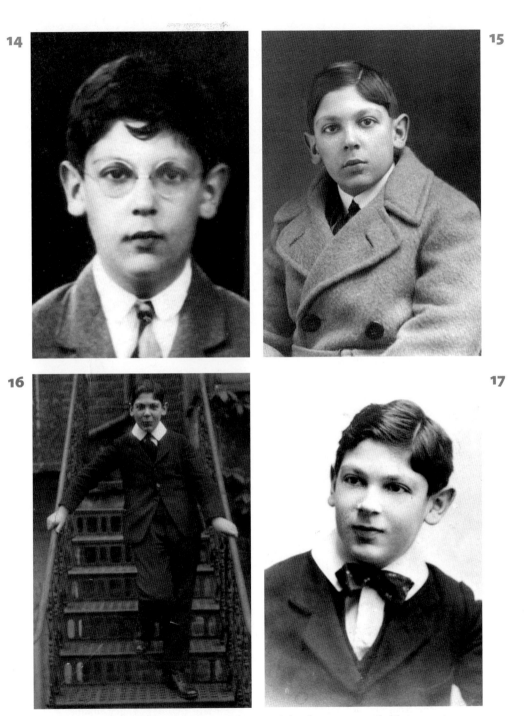

Boyhood in London: **14**, at Arundel House School, 1921; **15**, probably in 1921/2;
16, at home at the rear of 33 Upper Addison Gardens, London, in 1923 (aged 14);
17, in 1924

18

Marie and Mendel Berlin

19

20

IB's maternal aunt, Ida Samunov,
née Volshonok. She and her husband
Yitzhak moved to London in 1922
before settling in Palestine in 1934.

Marie Berlin's youngest siblings,
Berta and Alexander Siskind Volshonok,
who remained in Riga and were
murdered by the Nazis in 1941

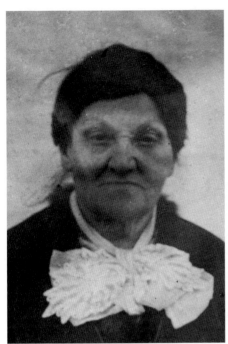

Probably Rodsia-Freude Volshonok, née Zuckerman, IB's maternal grandmother

'My maternal grandfather [Salman Izchok Volshonok] shortly before his murder by the Gestapo' (IB)

Ida and Yitzhak Samunov with the family of her (and Marie Berlin's) uncle Victor Volshonok in Riga in the early 1920s: Chasia (Victor's wife), Sofia, Yitzhak Samunov, Ida, Ida Samunov, Yosef, Victor, Zinaida. The Samunovs and Yosef settled in Palestine and survived the war; one of the Volshonok daughters died of natural causes; the others in this photograph were killed in 1941.

Adolescence: **24**, on 25 August 1924, signed I[saiah] M[endelevich] Berlin;
26, at Corpus Christi College, *c.*1930; dates of other photos unknown

In the 1930s

In the 1940s

With Natasha Spender in Geneva, August 1946

Mendel Berlin

With Stuart Hampshire

Mendel and Marie Berlin, probably not long before Mendel's death in 1953

In a radio studio, 1959: still from a documentary film about the BBC

35

At the time of his appointment as Professor of Social and Political Theory, 1957

In 1964

Topping out the new Wolfson College
buildings, 15 December 1972

Entertaining Wolfsonians with Aline
at Headington House, 1975

Several of this volume's authors appear in this photograph of contributors to *The Idea of Freedom*, the first Festschrift in IB's honour, taken at Wolfson College in June 1979: *(back)* Patricia Utechin, H. L. A. Hart, G. A. Cohen, Henry Hardy, Charles Taylor, Bernard Williams, Richard Wollheim, Stuart Hampshire; *(front)* Robert Wokler, Alan Ryan, IB, Robin Milner-Gulland, Patrick Gardiner, Larry Siedentop

With Arthur Schlesinger, Jr, and Robert Silvers, New York City, 1982

At the launch of the Bodleian Library
Campaign, Oxford, 5 July 1988

On 18 November 1996

In the last year of his life: on 3 February 1997

One of the Giants of the Twentieth Century

Beata Połanowska-Sygulska

WHEN ONE OF MY Oxford friends called me on a November night to pass on the mournful news of Sir Isaiah Berlin's death, I only half believed. Next morning the Polish newspapers brought the same sad information. While going over the headlines announcing the passing away of 'one of the giants of our century',[1] I could not help thinking how exceptionally privileged I had been, having corresponded with Sir Isaiah for years and having met him many times during my stays on scholarships in Oxford. I also reflected upon the peculiarity of official obituaries, which hardly ever reveal the deepest truth about the deceased. Though I am fully aware of the intellectual range of Sir Isaiah's achievement, I shall remember him as one of the most generous and warmest persons I have ever met. Just imagine the intellectual 'giant of our century' writing the following words to an unknown Polish graduate student (at the end of a six-page letter):

> Let me now say how grateful I am to you for taking my work seriously and for writing to me the letter that you have. I should love to talk to you about these things, which I am sure would be very useful to me and may be of some use to you. I enclose, therefore, a kind of annexe to this letter, which explains the machinery whereby you might be able to come to Oxford for a month or longer, in which case I could talk to you 'freely' (in the negative sense) from time to time, and you could also meet other philosophers who might be of even greater interest and profit to you.[2]

I needed only to show the letter to Dr Zbigniew Pełczyński, then visiting Poland, to be accepted for a two-month stay at St John's under the Oxford Colleges Hospitality Scheme. I can still recollect in detail the first meeting at All Souls. How could I expect then that there were going to be over twenty of them? I introduced myself (in a trembling voice) to the porter, who made a short phone call and told me to wait. In a moment an elderly gentleman in a brown three-piece suit and a brown hat rushed towards the lodge especially to meet me. I kept glancing at the face so familiar to me from the books' covers and suddenly felt completely unreal. He greeted me as if he had known me for

---

[1] This phrase was used by Leszek Kołakowski: see 'Jeden z olbrzymów stulecia' ['One of the Giants of Our Century'], *Gazeta Wyborcza*, 7 November 1997, 1.

[2] Letter of 24 February 1986.

years and bombarded me with questions. It was hardly possible to keep up with the answers. We climbed up the stairs; large black letters over my host's door, forming the label 'Isaiah Berlin', made me feel still less real.

What happened next surpassed my highest expectations. I had sent Sir Isaiah my first article,[1] published in Poland two years before my arrival in Oxford. The offprint was supposed to be, as I wrote in the dedication, an exotic gift never to be made use of. What I saw in my host's hands was, to my horror, an English translation of that text! A thought crossed my mind that Sir Isaiah, like myself, had prepared for our first meeting. I was so stunned that I could not utter a word. After so many years I still find it difficult to confess what followed. Sir Isaiah, as a master of empathetic understanding, instantly deciphered my state of mind. 'Why have you lost your voice?' he asked. 'This is one of the most intelligent texts on my concept of liberty I have ever read!' What he said had much less to do with the merit of my humble paper than with his own generosity. I did not delude myself for a moment into thinking that he was serious; and yet the 'opinion' I heard helped me to find my voice, at that meeting and all the following ones, when one of the greatest of contemporary intellectuals, with characteristic subtlety, did his best to create the impression that he was talking – it feels ridiculous to write these words – to his equal.

I was eventually able to ask Berlin hundreds of questions that had tormented me while reading his writings. Our conversations during my first stay in Oxford mostly concerned the questions that I posed. Following the good Oxford habit, I made the effort to prepare essays in advance of each appointment. My hosts at St John's were astonished – how very demanding Professor Berlin was! – but writing essays was my own idea. I conceived them as a way to bridle the incredible intellectual vivacity of my interlocutor: to steer the monologues, articulated at breathtaking speed, towards topics that I thought important for the doctoral thesis I was working on at that time. Two years later, after the defence of my PhD, I was privileged to have more meetings at All Souls. During my second stay in Oxford I gave up tormenting Sir Isaiah with my essays; I just listened. Some threads from our earlier conversations kept coming back. This was unbelievable – he remembered problems I had posed two years before.

Sometimes our conversations developed in completely unforeseeable directions. I once happened to admit having spent a sleepless night devouring Nabokov's *Lolita* in Wolfson College library. To make things worse, I sat within the range of vision of a large portrait of Sir Isaiah, hanging on the back wall. 'One of the giants of our century' shook his finger at me and then spoke

---

[1] Beata Połanowska-Sygulska, 'Krytyka koncepcji wolności pozytywnej w ujęciu Isaiaha Berlina' ['Isaiah Berlin's Critique of the Positive Concept of Freedom'], *Studia Nauk Politycznych* 3 (1984), 49–65.

for nearly two hours about his fascination with Russian literature – about Turgenev, Herzen, Akhmatova, Pasternak. Another time I communicated my great anxiety after having heard from home that my father was seriously ill. Sir Isaiah showed deep understanding and subtlety. He told me he had had a similar experience when he was staying in America – his father also fell seriously ill. We then talked about death for over an hour. I remember that he invoked the ancient argument – there is no death as long as I am here; when there is death, there is no me. He told me he was not at all afraid of his own death. Some of the things I heard I shall keep only to myself. The reflections I remember best are those which their author would probably never agree to publish.

Fragments of conversations, utterances of import and valuable reflections intertwine in my recollections with funny episodes, which I retain in my memory equally scrupulously. After our meetings at All Souls the Berlins' driver usually came to take Sir Isaiah home. He used to offer me a lift to Wolfson College, completely out of his way. I was embarrassed by such kindness. 'I can go by bus,' I protested. 'I can go by bus, too,' with a twinkle in his eye and with great seriousness Sir Isaiah would reply.

He always insisted that I should treat him in an informal way. I found it too difficult to overcome my reservations; for instance I never dared just telephone him, so I used to write letters, during my first scholarship and the following ones. Sir Isaiah commented playfully on this inhibition of mine: 'I am delighted you are here, and wish to inform you that I think it absurd that you do not telephone me! Still, if you would rather not I shall accept that – what else can I do?'

I visited Oxford four times altogether. Sir Isaiah was always willing to spare me his time. Our last meeting took place at Headington at the end of May 1995. We continued our unfinished conversation in a taxi, driving in the rain. Sir Isaiah was going to a reception and, true to his habit, was giving me a lift, that time to St John's again. We were talking about Max Weber and his famous differentiation between the ethics of responsibility and the ethics of conscience. Suddenly a well-known feeling of utter unreality overwhelmed me. 'What am I doing here?' I thought. A typical English taxi, typical English weather, Max Weber and this great intellectual, thoroughly unreasonably regarded by me as a close person. Unexpectedly I heard him say: 'This is all real, this is actually going on. And we'll meet again. You'll come back here one day.' And yet it was to be a farewell.

What is left is correspondence. The first letter was written on 3 May 1983 and the last on 17 July 1997. So much generosity, warmth and personal interest that it is difficult to quote certain passages without embarrassment. Like the letters of 20 May 1989 and 29 May 1990, in which Sir Isaiah referred to my articles, published in succession in *Political Studies* and in *Reports on Philosophy*:

Dear Beata,

I received your article with great pleasure, thank you for defending me against all those terrible people [...]. I fear that being about to reach the age of 80 (thank you very much for your congratulations, by which I am deeply touched), I doubt if I shall ever turn into a communitarian. I don't think I am an isolated island, but I think that relationships in an archipelago are more human and morally and politically preferable to coral reefs with little organisms squeezed all together. [...]

Best wishes to you and your youngest daughter, I am not at all sure about the world she will live in. [...][1]

Dear Beata (if I may?),

You cannot imagine how delighted I was to receive from Claude Galipeau your article, but above all your letter. I read the article with pleasure and pride. [...] Your letter was deeply touching and went to my heart. If you ever feel inclined to write to me again, do – I wish to assure you that your letters mean a good deal to me, more, perhaps, than mine mean to you. As I am getting on in years, as you know, now almost 81, do not leave it too long – do write to me again whenever you feel you have something to say to me, I should be delighted to receive and shall certainly reply.[2]

As far as I can remember this second letter was a reply to my description of the process of transformation in Poland. These matters deeply interested my correspondent and he often referred to them:

[L]et me tell you that I never predicted the recent events any more than anyone else succeeded in doing: whatever may happen to Gorbachev in the Soviet Union, there is no doubt that statues should be put up to him in Poland, Czechoslovakia, even Romania – without him, the collapse of the old system could, in my opinion, not have occurred so soon. I realise only too well what you mean by saying that you and others are 'too tired' to glory in the fruits of this situation, welcome as it must be, with all its dangers and deficiencies.[3]

Poland of the early 1990s provided a perfect experimental plot for those engaged in social studies. Certain developments infused new life into long-lasting theoretical discussions. One of the totally new phenomena was a sudden invasion of advertisements, mostly on TV. These were almost unknown under Communism, because of the permanent scarcity of goods. What made me

[1] Letter of 20 May 1989.
[2] Letter of 29 May 1990.
[3] ibid.

think about the impact of persuasive techniques upon individual liberty was the reaction of my five-and-a-half-year-old daughter to virtually the first professional advertisement she had seen in Poland for a washing powder. The poor child literally begged me for the advertised article and, at the same time, not being able to make head or tail of her own behaviour, she did her best to analyse the unexpected desire. 'I have no idea *why* on earth I want this washing powder; the only thing I know is that I terribly need it and just *must* have it,' she used to say. I instantly associated this purely artificial desire I had to cope with in my own home with Charles Taylor's polemics against *Two Concepts of Liberty* and the reflections of other authors, mainly S. I. Benn and W. L. Weinstein. I could not help sharing my observations and thoughts with Sir Isaiah; his reply was characteristic of his style – seemingly light, playful, and yet weighty and important for understanding his liberal theory: 'Your daughter seems to me to be gifted with an exceptional sensibility and imagination, and I do not wonder that this is so – genes are important, we are told, and she has obviously inherited excellent ones. I am glad you gave her that washing powder – once one's imagination fixes on something it is right to increase people's happiness as you have done.'[1]

In spring 1997 our correspondence became more frequent. I was intensively working on a book on Berlin's liberal doctrine and some new doubts occurred to me. His invaluable reply to my interpretations, in a letter of 19 April 1997, made me both happy and a bit confused. The last paragraph read as follows: 'If you still have questions, please address them to me: I was very stimulated by your letter – I have never expressed myself so clearly before, I believe, so do write to me again if you feel inclined. I fully realise the central importance of the problem you put.'[2]

The issue concerned the mutual relation between ethical pluralism and liberalism. The question had originally been posed by John Gray – I tried to find answers to Gray's objections.

The typewritten part of the letter ended here – below there remained about two-thirds of the page, covered with handwriting, unfortunately absolutely unintelligible to me. The only two words that I managed to decipher were a hardly readable signature, winding towards the top of the page. Dr Henry Hardy, the editor of Berlin's writings, very kindly sent me a typewritten version of that note.

I did not manage to hand my book over to Sir Isaiah. The night call from Oxford found me working on footnotes. Several weeks later I received a moving line from Dr Hardy:

[1] ibid.
[2] Letter of 19 April 1997.

Dear Beata,

I am sure you are as desolated as I am at Isaiah's death. It is very hard to bear. I thought you would like to know that his letter to you of 17 July was the last serious intellectual letter he wrote. Five days later his final illness began, and he was not able to deal with correspondence of this level thereafter.[1]

[1] Letter of 18 November 1997.

The Day After

G. A. Cohen

An interview for the Canadian Broadcasting Corporation programme *As It Happens*, broadcast on 6 November 1997, the day after IB died

CBC What was the most remarkable thing about Isaiah Berlin?

COHEN I have never known anyone who was so alive as he was, nor anyone who even came close. He celebrated life throughout all his waking moments, and he attracted everybody around him because he exuded life. He was a prism through which people's ideas, conceptions, motivations took on enormous brilliance and sparkle in the exposition that he was able to give of them, whether they were ordinary people that he happened to know, and about whom he would relate entertaining anecdotes, or great thinkers of the past, whose ideas he expounded by impersonating the thinkers whose ideas they were, so that what we got was not a Dryasdust description of a logical structure, but a presentation of the great personality as a human being whose ideas reflected his preoccupations, anxieties, hopes and fears.

When he lectured, and he was most famous as a lecturer – he was, what very few people are, a *great* lecturer – he wouldn't use notes. He'd bring notes because he was anxious that maybe he wouldn't succeed in carrying off the lecture spontaneously without them, but he invariably didn't look at the notes; instead, he spoke to you in the first person, as though he were Voltaire, or Rousseau or Marx, or Mill, and he didn't say 'He thought this, he thought that, he said this' (and so forth) but 'I look around me and what do I see? I see men struggling, striving, enjoying etc., and here is what I think about all that.' So, in that fashion, he could get you to understand why people whose ideas might be very different from your own thought the way they did, and he could render those ideas attractive. He could render even very repugnant ideas attractive, he could show you why fascists, or crazed terrorists, thought the way they did. It didn't mean he was sympathetic to those ideas, but he showed you how it was conceivable for a human being to think in that way. And so he was a great, you could say, animator.

CBC He was interested in knowing how people thought, and why?

COHEN Yes, he was ceaselessly curious, and to walk with him in the streets was a marvellous experience, because you could see that he was endlessly fed by all the sights and sounds around him, that he was puzzled and curious about the parade of people before him. If he saw people wearing strange clothing, he would want to know what kind of ideology that represented. You'd have to explain to him what a Rastafarian was, what a follower of the Baghwan Shree Rajneesh – you know, the people who wear orange clothing and believe in a kind of Hinduism – what they were. He was always, as it were, abreast of what was going on now, because he could not turn off his curiosity, and he insisted on answers. And so he attracted many people who fed that curiosity and who were nourished by the wonderful things that he had to say about everything that was going on.

CBC   Did he have special concerns about the modern world?

COHEN   One of his central ideas in political philosophy related very closely to struggles in the real world: he discerned within the traditional rhetoric of liberty what he called 'two concepts of liberty'. One concept was the idea of a person being free from other people's direction, just going his or her own way, even if that way led to perdition and to the destruction of the person in question – the idea of freedom as simply being free from the interference of other people. And he said that there was an equally important idea of freedom which was rather different, the idea of a person realising his deepest potentialities, developing his personality. And he plausibly associated the first idea of freedom with the capitalist West, and the second idea of freedom, the idea of the realisation of everything in the self, with the Communist East. He thought that there was a great distortion of that idea in the actual institutions of the Communist East, but he thought that what nevertheless gave strength to that civilisation was not just its regiments and guns and bombs, but also the fact that there was a central idea that could be affirmed, with some plausibility, and which was not an idea that capitalism was able to cater to.

CBC   What did he think about the rampaging capitalism we now see in globalisation?

COHEN   Well, he hated it. He absolutely hated it. Just a few days before his death, he encouraged me (I don't know why he thought I had this kind of influence, but he was perhaps harking back to a day when this College, All Souls, was influential in the real world) – he encouraged me to encourage the present Labour Government to imitate his great political hero, Franklin Roosevelt, and to institute a grand programme of public works which would enthuse young people, which would reduce unemployment. He could not see why there was this turn away, in our time, from the use of the State for progressive purposes, even by a Labour government.

He was entirely hostile to total State control, he thought the idea of socialist planning was an illusion, but he was passionately against Thatcherism and the unrestricted role of the free market. He knew that it destroyed people's lives.

If we return to the two concepts of liberty that I distinguished a moment or two ago, he thought that what we have in the world today is a blind commitment to the idea of liberty as freedom from interference, at the expense of nourishing the potentialities of people, so many of whom go to the wall under a system which recognises only lack of interference as valuable.

CBC What about his effect on you personally?

COHEN Well, it's difficult for me to talk about that today without becoming very emotional, because he died last night, and I just feel personally that something that was an enormous part of the background to my life and thought is gone.

We quarrelled an enormous amount, intellectually, because he was extremely anti-Soviet and anti-Communist and I was anti-anti-Soviet, if you see what I mean. He was widely regarded, and not unjustly, as an intellectual cold-warrior, but that was because he cared so much about the pretensions of the Bolsheviks and about how incorrect they were. As a socialist person myself, I knew that the standards that my thinking as a socialist had to meet were extremely high ones, because they had to face the objections to socialism which he elaborated and which he felt deeply and which he was so good at deploying.

He had no disciples. He often said 'I have no disciples, and I am glad I have no disciples.' He had nobody who worked in his shadow and continued his thought. Nobody could. Nobody could work in the particular way that he did. But hundreds of people did their work, as it were, in the light of his work, and admired him and drew sustenance from his interest in them.

CBC You not only worked together, but you played together, I gather?

COHEN Yes, this happened very late. About eighteen months ago I discovered, on an All Souls College shelf, a nineteenth-century board game called *L'Attaque*, in which there are two warring sides, British soldiers and French, of various ranks, from General all the way down to Private, painted on cardboard, and each one set upon a little metal frame to facilitate their movement.

He loved playing that game, and I enjoyed playing it with him. We were pretty evenly matched. I wasn't desperate to win, but I certainly wanted to, I preferred winning to losing. But he didn't care about winning, he just hugely enjoyed the game. And he similarly didn't care about all the worldly honours that were showered on him, but he certainly enjoyed them, and the life that brought them to him. The same vitality, the same effervescence that he brought to intellectual work was present in the way he played this game.

I saw him quite a lot over the last three or four months, when he was very ill. He was a diminished figure physically, and there wasn't much energy, but there was still delight in life. He wanted me constantly to report to him what was happening in the College. He loved All Souls. He was very devoted to it. He thought it was a very important centre of learning and excellence. He talked about it with great warmth, and he continued to radiate ideas and vitality, even though the physical embodiment of the person that was doing it was diminished.

CBC You said the players in the game were England and France. Did he always insist on playing England?

COHEN He didn't care.

CBC But he loved England, didn't he?

COHEN Yes, he loved England. He famously regarded England as more true to the values of liberty that meant so much to him than any other country in the world, and also he admired the tolerance of Britain. Indeed, he once said to me, with respect to the issue of tolerance, and anti-Semitism, which was a very important one for him, because he was very Jewish and strongly committed to the safety and flourishing of the Jewish people – he said that if you meet an Englishman, you have to assume he is not an anti-Semite until something shows otherwise, whereas with people from other European countries you couldn't begin with such a sanguine hypothesis.

CBC You said you were with him right up until the end?

COHEN I guess I saw him a week before he died, yes.

CBC How was he dealing with his approaching death?

COHEN It's very difficult to convey the combination of dejection and ebullience that I witnessed. I mean, he retained his vitality and he was constantly thrusting up with new ideas and new insights. He *said* that life had lost its taste for him, but you couldn't see that.

CBC Obviously you're going to miss him a great deal.

COHEN I keep on thinking that it's a desert, now. The image that his death makes me have is of a place that was a flourishing garden, and now some great wind has gone through it and everything has been torn up by the roots, and now it's just a desert. I'm sure I won't continue to feel this way, but it's very difficult to feel otherwise right now. It's such a great loss, an absolutely massive loss, for so many people.

Fast Talker

Alistair Cooke

From *Letter from America* no. 2545, BBC Radio 4, 21 and 23 November 1997[1]

I SHALL TRY TO SAY something vivid and worthy about a great man who has died, who was also a friend to whom I was writing when the sad word came in. The *New York Times* in a splendid obituary last Friday said a great deal in its first sentence. 'Sir Isaiah Berlin, the philosopher and historian of ideas, revered for his intellect and cherished for his wit and his gift for friendship, has died in Oxford, England, following a long illness.'

You have to picture a middle-sized but large shambling man, a swarthy face, bird's-nest eyebrows, a large firm mouth, and, behind a pair of horn-rimmed glasses, dark, glaring eyes. The expression is that of a glorious Russian clown pretending to be a stern headmaster, and when his eyes twinkled and he opened that large generous mouth it was as if a two-minute silence had been proclaimed. All other human traffic stopped; he began to pour out a cascade of ideas, a Niagara of thoughts and images that never paused in its down-rushing volume and eloquence. It was no surprise to learn that he wrote his essays, his books, that way, by torrential dictation. I assume he'd discovered a short-hand typist who could take down from a machine enormous, perfectly parsed and structured sentences, spoken at the rate of about seven hundred words a minute, in a rolling operatic baritone with still the echo of mother Russia. For that's where he was brought up, the son of a timber merchant who, being a prospering Jew, quickly departed from Petrograd on the arrival of Lenin, and took his eleven-year-old son to London, where he went to school – and then on to Oxford, where for the rest of his life he lived (he wrote) 'in my eyrie, far removed from the bustle of real politics and the movers and shakers you spend your life reporting'.[2]

Once he was a guest with my wife and me in the house of my oldest American friend, Dean of the Yale Law School. Along that evening too was the late Denis Brogan, the astonishingly erudite Scot who knew more about American history than Americans, and French history than the French. He spoke with a marked Scottish brogue (well named) at only *six* hundred words a minute. There came a moment when Berlin and Brogan began to discuss a very knotty problem (I recall sharply): Had Napoleon ever read Maccihab Macciavellia, and if so could

---

[1] The third paragraph appears in Cooke's typescript but was not broadcast.
[2] Letter not found.

it have been through Napoleon's confessor, the abbé Poussin, or some other cleric? They got steamed up, and in no time they were both teeming with eloquence in unison. We onlookers fell about in helpless laughter – they thought, because of their wit. It was at the sheer thundering flood of talk coming at us in two wildly different accents – at such a rate that none of us could understand a syllable of it.

What has this to do with America or *Letter from America*? Well, true, his gift for friendship was so generous and sustained that just to talk about him, for no particular reason, is a delight. There's just one thing I want to say about him and America. European exiles who become Englishmen very often become also, in one matter or another, more English than the English, and there's one embarrassing trait in particular they're likely to pick up more than another: the gift which every sort of Englishman has by instinct and has to learn to conquer, the gift of condescending to America and Americans. Isaiah Berlin had no trace of it. He talked to everybody, to Duke Ellington and the Duke of Devonshire and a dustman, in exactly the same way. He lectured to American students as he did to British, or Italian, or Russian students. He once told me, after judicious thought, that the most intellectually curious, inquisitive students he ever lectured to were not at Oxford, or Harvard or Cambridge, but at the University of Chicago. He had the deepest and sharpest knowledge of American government, and was an almost prophetic observer of American politics. In 1952 he came over here briefly for the Eisenhower–Stevenson presidential campaign. He was not greatly impressed by the Stevenson effort because he feared, way back then, that in embracing the beloved Adlai the Democrats were betraying their radical roots, planted by Roosevelt. Stevenson he called 'A Republican for Stevenson': it was about as acid as he could ever be. He was a very rare type, if indeed there is such a type, a man of enormous learning, a brilliant man, who was at the same time, and always, warm and kindly.

He was six months younger than me, and I used to josh him about his comparative youth and ask him, whenever his birthday came around, when and where we next should meet. The last letter I had from him ended, that wherever we were next to meet, 'Arm in arm, we march into the future.'[1] I'd hoped to have a photograph showing the starting moment of that march. Of course, it is not to be. But I see him slumping smartly off into the Elysian fields ready to enlighten the angels, *if* they can keep up with, and understand, a newcomer who talks seven hundred words to the minute.

[1] Letter of 11 June 1990.

Isaiah the Jew

Shlomo Avineri in conversation with Alan Ryan

An edited transcript of a discussion that took place at Jewish Book Week in London on 25 February 2008

RYAN In his article in the volume of essays on Isaiah called *The One and the Many* Shlomo Avineri reflected on the fact that, although it was absolutely clear to everybody that Isaiah was Jewish – his loyalty to Israel was unflinching, and he had never made any secret of his origins or attachments – in some curious way those attachments don't come out very visibly or prominently, or in the way you'd expect them to come out, in the essays and books for which we remember him. The Russianness comes out, the liberalism comes out, but there are aspects of the Jewishness that don't.

AVINERI When one addresses this issue in Isaiah's work, I think there is a certain paradox. On the one hand, as you said, it's very clear – and Isaiah said it several times in short autobiographical notes or statements – how much he owed to the Russian intelligentsia, how much he owed in his liberal thinking to the British tradition; but there's very little in which he admits he has a specific debt to the Judaic tradition, be it the biblical or the talmudic or the modern Hebrew enlightenment tradition. And there's also very little which *shows* this influence. However, when you look at some of the subjects which he chose to discuss, especially in his essays in the 1950s and 1960s, you will find that it's no accident that some of the most fascinating essays deal with, I wouldn't say 'borderline' Jews, because not all of them were such, but people who were on the one hand Jewish, or of Jewish origin – and Isaiah tried to analyse what this component of their origin was – but, on the other hand, whose impact was not necessarily in the Jewish community or in the Jewish world of letters, but on world history. So: Karl Marx, Benjamin Disraeli and Moses Hess (though the latter is much more of a Jewish writer, and much better known in a Jewish context). And what Isaiah says about both Disraeli and Marx is very indicative. I don't think it's at all autobiographical, because both Marx and Disraeli converted, and were not active in any way in Jewish affairs. But in the intellectual context out of which Isaiah came, and in which he worked, there is an understanding of the kind of peculiarity he saw in both Marx and Disraeli. (It's very unusual to have Marx and Disraeli discussed in the same essay: one the symbol of the world revolution and the other a founder of modern conservatism.) Isaiah says something very significant, which brings out his understanding – what in Germany you would call *Fingerspitzengefühl* – his immediate, intuitive understanding, not always mediated through intellectual analysis, but very deeply rooted, when he says the following: When Disraeli, Lord Beaconsfield, in developing the idea of British conservatism, sings the praises of aristocracy (and most of his writings were a paean to the idea of aristocracy), and says that all world history is the history of aristocracies, and then adds, 'and the Jews are really the aristocrats of history', he's really saying that you British aristocrats are newcomers. I am a scion of the *old* aristocracy, of the *real* aristocracy. When you were still climbing up trees and painting yourselves blue, my ancestors were already prophets and kings.

RYAN That's rather a trope in quite a lot of nineteenth-century novels. You get it in Disraeli's novels, but you also get it a certain amount in Walter Scott.

AVINERI In Walter Scott as well, but when it comes in Walter Scott it's written from the *inside*, whilst in Disraeli it's written from the outside: he is really praising *himself* in this very sly way, by praising the British aristocracy. In a contrapuntal way this is also what's happening in Marx, as Isaiah read him (and I think he read him correctly). When Marx speaks about the travails of the proletariat, when he speaks on behalf of the oppressed, he's not speaking just of the real-life proletarians, he's speaking on behalf of a downtrodden race that has been oppressed for generations. So in a way he's not identifying with the real proletarians. (We know that Marx didn't usually like real proletarians. He saw that they didn't understand *Das Kapital*. A lot of academics don't understand it to this very day. Chapter 1 of *Das Kapital* is very tough reading, even for us.) There is an idealised proletariat in Marx, an idealised aristocracy in Disraeli, and these were the totally unrealistic social classes with whom these two very contradictory people could identify, because both of them felt alienated from the bourgeois world into which their parents – Jews who converted – brought them. To understand this you need to have some understanding of the role of Jews, and the ambivalence and power of being Jewish, in a non-Jewish society, and feeling torn between these two poles. Isaiah brought this out very well, despite the fact that he didn't really treat Jewish tropes as such.

RYAN So what's missing? Is it curiosity about Jewish mysticism? Was he unwilling to explore the idea that there might be some particular Jewish take on kinds of freedom that don't fit comfortably into the standard liberal picture? He used to make a joke about Stuart Hampshire. He would smile good-naturedly and say, 'Of course you've enjoyed reading Stuart – Spinoza, Marx, Freud, the three great Jewish liberators, and Stuart, their humble Aryan interpreter.' But he himself, oddly, wasn't much attracted by any of the three, by curiosity about deep spiritual forms of emancipation, whereas a lot of people writing about Jewish thinkers in the late twentieth century have precisely gone down that track. Do you have any thoughts on why he resolutely *didn't*?

AVINERI I don't. Just as Isaiah didn't have much sympathy for Freud, neither do I; so I'm in a very bad position to analyse his response. But I think there is something complex going on here. I think Isaiah – and not just because he wrote his path-breaking little book on Marx in the 1930s, which was such an intellectual achievement – had, I wouldn't say an affinity, but an understanding of and an empathy with Marx. Not Marx as a person: he says some pretty nasty things about Marx as a person. He also says some very critical things about Marx's philosophy. There's a direct line in Isaiah's thinking, not between Marx and Stalin, but certainly between Marx and Lenin. Marxism leads to some sort of authoritarian if not totalitarian regime. But there's an empathy with the intellectual situation in which Marx found himself, and in which he was working.

This great sympathy which he had came out in some of the smaller writings – on Chaim Weizmann, whom he knew well personally, on Albert Einstein, on Jacob Herzog. There are people, like George Steiner, for whom all Jews are Moses, Spinoza, Einstein and Freud. But Jewish thieves and Jewish crooks and Jewish financiers and Jewish exploiters never figure in their thinking or writings: for them, everybody was a Freud and a Spinoza in his time. Isaiah knew better. There is no idealisation of the Jewish people as a people, there is no idealisation even of those Jewish people whom he admired. When you look very carefully at what he said about Weizmann and Einstein there are critical remarks, but there is also *understanding* of how, out of this unusual situation in which on the one hand you have oppression, on the other hand you have a call to excellence, something unique emerges. In this sense Isaiah is very Jewish: not in the sense that he's quoting Jewish writers – on this score there is a deficit that I tried to bring out in my essay – but there is an understanding of real-life Jews, some more famous than others, working in a complex world – not necessarily an alien world or an inimical world – and how out of that complexity they produce uniqueness. We all know this quote by Isaiah, 'The Jews are like everybody else only more so.' So yes, they are more so, but they're also like everybody else.

RYAN But are *you* puzzled? Your essay has slight overtones of something which I once asked Isaiah about, that the specifically religious tradition seems not to bite at all. I once said to him: Was he curious about the revival of an interest in mystical Jewish philosophers? And he said to me that he was tone-deaf (which was certainly not true in music): this was a way of looking at the world that he simply couldn't get on the same wavelength with; what people were trying to say didn't resonate at all. My mind doesn't go there. Do you have the sense that that's an accurate account?

AVINERI Very much so. In this respect Isaiah was a true Enlightenment person, not in the Voltairean sense, in which the Enlightenment still fights religion,
but in the sense that you are a little bit indifferent to religion. There are good
things and bad things in it, but it doesn't really touch me, and you can lead a
perfectly normal and moral life without it. About this Isaiah was very consistent. This is not a criticism of other people, or other Jews, but there are Jewish
thinkers who are all for the Enlightenment when it comes to the Gentiles, but
when it comes to *us*, we have to keep a little bit of the God and a little bit of the
divinity and a little bit of the mysticism because this is *ours* and we shouldn't
really give it up. When the Gentiles are religious and fanatical, this is very bad;
but we have a secular dispensation from God to keep it. Isaiah didn't take any
of this nonsense. For him, if you are an enlightened person you have to be – he
said 'tone-deaf' to religion; I think the idea was 'indifferent': this is not part of
my discourse, whether it is Catholic or Protestant or Jewish; it's *passé*. And this
was my impression when he came to Israel: he was, as you've said, always loyal
to his very deep love of Israel, but not necessarily to everything that happens in
Israel, and as such he behaved as a citizen, even if an honorary citizen – as Isaiah
was – who is entitled and even enjoined to be critical as part of his responsibility as a citizen. And one of the things which bothered him in Israel was
this combination of nationalism and religiosity. Nationalism is problematic as
such – extreme nationalism, chauvinism – but when it gets legitimacy from
religion, it is very combustible. He was very much aware of that.

RYAN That brings me on to the other issue which your essay raises, and the
wonderful essay on Moses Hess brings out so well. Isaiah was very curious
about nationalism, especially about the fact that nineteenth-century Europe
after the Enlightenment, the dawn of universalism, sees a break-up into com-
peting national identities, the growth of the notion that cultures need nations
to shelter them. And that goes straight back to his ambivalence about Israel –
the aspects that he was deeply attached to and those he was pretty frightened
about. I wonder whether you have a clear sense of how the argument works
about people needing shelters for their cultural identity, and places where they
get respect without having to ask for it, and that as providing a base for nationalism, while all the other things, the chauvinism, the militarism, the telling
spectacular untruths about the racial and genetic qualities of your own people –
all that gets pushed off to one side. One gets sympathy for the one thing, and
fear, hostility, anxiety about the other, though John Gray, for example, tries to
recruit Isaiah as an enemy of the Enlightenment by assuming that all cultural
particularists are going to be anti-Enlightenment, irrationalist defenders of
identity. Isaiah's way of trying to negotiate his way through this seems to be one
of the things that you've been always interested in, and is certainly one of the

things I've always found fascinating, though never absolutely sure that I know where Isaiah's feet are actually planted.

AVINERI Well, for Isaiah, the key person in the intersection between the Enlightenment and nationalism was Herder. On the one hand, Herder was the typical enlightened person, who in the name of enlightenment and universalism argued that all people, and all peoples or nations, have a right to view themselves in terms of their own culture, history, language, religion if they so wish, because this is what today we would call self-determination (not, of course, a term used by Herder). This is a matter of human autonomy, part of which is also to be a member of a nation, if one so chooses. This starts as a universalistic argument, but is in great danger of switching to something else. In an early essay on nationalism Isaiah, on the one hand, strongly defends the universalistic underpinning of the quest for national belonging – being at home, belonging to one's own culture, belonging to one's own society, choosing the group of which one would like to be a member; but on the other hand he is very much aware how this can very easily skip over into something which is very xenophobic, nationalistic, chauvinistic and aggressive. And although Isaiah never (as far as I remember) drew this analogy, one can say the same kind of thing about religion. On the one hand religion is about redemption, salvation, giving you a moral compass; but on the other hand it can become xenophobic, nationalistic, chauvinistic and aggressive. And just as religion is Janus-faced, so is nationalism. Because of the terrible things done in the name of nationalistic ideologies, we sometimes overlook their emancipatory element. It is because of this universalist insight that Isaiah was a Zionist, because he believed that the Jews, like everybody else, have a right to a place in the sun, to determine their own ways of thinking and walking and talking and eating, if they so wish; and that Jewish emancipation in Europe after the Holocaust was a failure (the situation is perhaps a little different today, but this was certainly a well-justified claim after the Second World War). And for him the great tragic figures in modern Jewish history were precisely the German Jews, who, more than any other Jewish community, identified with the German nation of which they thought they were a part. But the Gentiles didn't really feel like this: this was a love that was not reciprocated, which was such a great tragedy for so many German Jews. For Isaiah the role of Jews in modern society will be determined not by emancipation but by *auto*-emancipation (he didn't use the term, but one of the proto-Zionist thinkers did). You have to emancipate yourself. Emancipation given or granted by the *other*, by somebody who has power over you and says 'Now you can do this and that' is not true freedom. Isaiah's nationalism, Zionism and liberalism share this common element, which leads us back to this unique moment in the Enlightenment – namely Herder.

RYAN Another issue which worries a lot of people is the notion of assimilation – even if the society into which you wish to be assimilated were more receptive than it often turns out to be. Do you have the sense that part of the argument is that the world is just very much better if there's not too much assimilation, so that there isn't a uniform soup of human cultures, but something distinctive, kaleidoscopic, interactive?

AVINERI Precisely. I think this is also part of Isaiah's liberalism. His liberalism is not an ontological, metaphysical liberalism that starts with Kantian or Rawlsian generalities, but it comes out of the variety of human experience. Liberalism is a respect for otherness, for difference; and out of this, too, comes the view that a world in which everybody behaved according to the same universalistic norms, as Rousseau probably wanted (I may be misrepresenting Rousseau here), would be an impoverished world, because it would be one-dimensional, it would have no depth, it would have no internal tension. Isaiah believed that liberalism is not just a do-good universalism, it is based on tensions, out of which comes the kind of freedom he valued. In this respect he draws on John Stuart Mill, and on some of the British tradition of liberalism, which is non-abstract, non-a-priori, much more pragmatic, and relates to people as they behave in reality.

RYAN We've spent half our time on what we both agreed we think is Isaiah not saying enough about what he thought he'd drawn from his Jewishness. I wonder if I can chase you round the other two components of what you quote him about? I'll start by ten seconds' autobiography and then lob the question at you. I think the moment I first thought that life was going to be interesting was when I read Bertrand Russell and was told off by my housemaster on the grounds that a man who'd had four wives clearly had nothing that he could possibly have to say to the world, and that if I went on reading this stuff, then expulsion was too good for me. So I then turned to John Stuart Mill, and I was taught by a man called Michael Cherniavsky, whose father was a great cellist,[1] whose family were of course both Russian and Jewish, and who at one point said, 'Had I come across ...?' – and of course what I was asked to come across was 'A Marvellous Decade'. I could make absolutely no sense of any of this, because I was fifteen years old or thereabouts, and quite a lot of other things had to happen before I could begin to see the point. But once I began to see the point, it seemed to me that one of the great things that Isaiah contributed, like Disraeli doing good to the clumping English aristocracy – this is Isaiah doing good to the otherwise rather clumping home-grown English liberal – was this vision of a world oppressed by tsarism, by the Orthodox Church, by a kind of superstitious populism, which then fell upon, slightly strangely,

[1] Mischel Cherniavsky (1893–1982).

Hegel, Schelling, Fichte, all manner of ill-assimilated German philosophers, and suddenly had this passion to join a modern, liberal, Western, free-thinking, free-acting world. And it always struck me that there were *we*, who of course would tend to say, 'Oh yes, they were about to discover John Stuart Mill, icon of Victorian liberalism, very good', but in our own politics would lumber on taking altogether too much for granted. What 'A Marvellous Decade' did was to say: Here are people being liberated in ways that you slow, friendly, complacent English don't really have a grip on. It was romantic and wilder and much more alarming; the question of whether it was art, politics or the exploration of personal relationships that was going to *do* it all for us was deeply mysterious (great Tom Stoppard themes); it was utopian, risk-taking, all kinds of things of that sort. I always thought that that was a fantastic gift to Isaiah's adopted country. None the less, it was never clear to me whether, when one said 'But why does this matter so much?' and he reminded one of the lost opportunities for a liberal, non-totalitarian Russia that had been extinguished after 1917, the focus was on the extraordinary contrast between the oppressive background out of which Belinsky, Herzen and Turgenev sprang and the vividness of their reaction to it, or whether he wanted to make a more philosophical point about their having put forward a culturally richer, deeper, livelier sort of liberalism than even Mill.

AVINERI   I don't really know, but I think you have put your finger on something very crucial in Isaiah's mental make-up. Isaiah was a historian of ideas: he was not a social historian, but he was always aware of the social context of ideas, and Russia and Britain to him were two very different entities, and he related to both of them in very different ways. The Russian intelligentsia – this wonderful decade which was so extremely enriching – was basically a tragic phenomenon. It was exhilarating, it was wonderful, it was humanely astonishing. But it failed. Russian society produced those wonderful people who were open to the West, adopted Western philosophies (in many cases derived from German Idealist philosophy, but also others) – and yet they failed. Tsarism didn't liberalise. The Kadets, which would have been Isaiah's party if he had stayed in Russia – the liberals – didn't succeed. And then you had a revolution which produced this terrible Leninism and Stalinism and the Gulag. You had a shining city on the hill, but only in the realm of ideas.

And then you had Britain. Isaiah didn't have much respect for traditional British philosophy – John Stuart Mill is a different story – but he had this wonderful understanding that Britain is liberal not because of the thinkers but because of the doers, because of the institutions, because of the culture, because of the liberal civilisation. This may not boast great names – no Jean-Jacques Rousseau but, yes, Locke – but you have liberal practice. To bring the two together, the Russian dream and the British reality, gave Isaiah this unusual power: he was speaking, not exactly like a prophet, but from the depths of the Russian experience, yet also with the experience of Britain, which generally, and also to him and his family, and to many other Jews, was a haven at the time when Russia, despite all these big ideas, was not a haven but a prison. So being able to combine the Russian utopia with British down-to-earth pragmatism was something entirely unique. Isaiah more than anybody else was able to bring out this combination – without being too systematic about it, because the idea was not to build another system but to provide insight into the Russian dream in relation to the much more down-to-earth, pragmatic, perhaps boring, but very liberal and free British experience.

In one interesting passage when Isaiah is trying to identify the roots of the Israeli experience, he traces it to the Russian intelligentsia. He saw in Israel a realisation of sorts of Russian ideas: this was part of his deep sympathy for Israel. Perhaps Israel today is different, but I mean the founding fathers and mothers of Israel, its social democratic and libertarian tradition. What ended up as a Gulag in Russia ended up as a kibbutz – I am oversimplifying – in Israel. The kibbutz is not a Jewish idea. You can't quote the Bible or the Talmud about the kibbutz – there's nothing in it about that, not in Isaiah I or Isaiah II – but you can quote Bakunin, Chernyshevsky, Herzen and so forth. So on the Mediterranean something succeeded which failed on the Volga; and for Isaiah this was a great achievement.

RYAN Yet another instance of how useful it is not to start with a feudal culture behind you.

This reminds me of a kite I'd like to fly. One of the things that people always had trouble with when they tried to describe exactly what it was that Isaiah did, was that they always thought that he really *had* to be a historian of ideas. This was because he himself had misguidedly said that that's what he was. And when asked why, he said: Well, philosophy had got rather boring and the trouble with philosophy was that you never knew whether you'd actually known anything, and he felt he'd rather like to end his life knowing slightly more than when he'd started; and the one thing about history was that at least there was *information*. It's a very un-Isaiah-like argument, that. It never seemed to me that it really did justice to what actually happened. Instead I'd like to offer you something to bring us back from this thought to Isaiah's Jewishness.

If you ask 'What is so wonderful about reading Isaiah?' my response is that it's the sensation that there you are, doing nothing very much, the door opens. In comes this ebullient figure saying, 'I'd like you meet Machiavelli.' You say, 'Who's he?' 'He's a wild Italian, found him in the garden, brought him in for tea. He thinks this, this, this. What have *you* got to say?' The whole Isaiah mode, it seems to me, works entirely like this: you pick up the hero of the argument for the moment, and you drag them on to the carpet, and you prompt them slightly so that they then utter – well, in the case of Machiavelli it's, say, the twenty-seventh theory; there are twenty-six theories about Machiavelli, all of which are wrong, and here comes Isaiah's, which is the twenty-seventh. It's very much Isaiah saying he thinks this and this and this, and you reel back, the torrent of ideas pours over you, and it's as though Isaiah then says, 'Well?' And you say, 'What do you mean, well?' 'Well, what have you got to say for yourself?' So it's very much *they* turn up, and you are supposed to use your own resources to react.

It always seems to me when I'm in nit-picking mode that this isn't really history, but a sort of biographical re-enactment. And one thinks: Why does Isaiah pick up Vico? No doubt he'd come across him and got hooked, but ... Anyway, there's Vico. What does Vico say? 'The characteristic human mode of apprehending other human beings is *fantasia*. It's the imaginative reconstruction of what it is that must be going on in the minds of somebody else.' There's always a danger with this as a method, and the danger is that if you have Isaiah's temperament, everyone who turns up takes on his semblance. Alan Montefiore once said to me, when I'd been going to Isaiah's lectures, 'Do you realise that when you read your essays out you sound just like Isaiah?' 'No,' I said. 'Well anyway,' he says, 'in a person your age it's quite ridiculous.' So I tried to stop. There *is* a danger. The danger is ventriloquism, because you pick up the people you feel affinity with, you credit them with your own ideas, you bring them back into the room and then ... *But* when it's people who are sufficiently at a distance, then it's likely to work astonishingly well. And I've always thought that the non-systematic quality, the passion for sheer quirk of perspective, the reason why the *éloge* was so wonderful, is that it's the recapturing of personality, intellectual style, so that the nuts and bolts argument is perhaps less crucial than the cast of mind and the argumentative mode of whoever you're picking up.

It always occurred to me that one reason why Isaiah was so good at this might well have been two things simultaneously. A very clever small boy arrives from Russia, is Russian in an English prep school, is Jewish in a rock-ribbed Anglican school environment, is therefore always – and however much he becomes part of the establishment – *watching*, as if to say, 'Who are these curious people?' And the story about wanting something to which you absolutely belong, though it's true, leaves out the other thing that made the whole thing work so well, which was the sense that he *didn't* wholly belong, because he was looking at English society from various angles, and hadn't simply swum in it since the age of three. And I've thought that one of the ways in which one always has the sense that everything he did was of a piece is because *that's* the intellectual temperament that permeates the whole thing.

AVINERI OK. I'm not going to say 'No.' There are two things that come out of what you've said. The description of Isaiah you just gave, which is so true and so plastic, is a description of a typical Jewish *maskil* (enlightener) of Eastern Europe, somebody who wants to burst into and conquer the world of ideas which is out there, to make it his and to share it with his people, and feels always that, yes, those are ideas from outside, but we can make them our own. This is what the Jewish *Haskalah* was. It wasn't just an enlightenment; it was of course part of the spirit of the Enlightenment, but it was very specific – people coming from a Jewish background wanting to integrate the world into their Jewish heritage, into their Jewish existence. This is precisely what you have just said, and it makes for a very exciting voyage.

Isaiah was able to make ideas exciting. We've been teaching for years and we know that sometimes when you teach ideas, theories, the eyes of the students glaze over. It probably didn't happen to you but it happened to me. Why is this? Because there is an abstraction there, there are systems there, and for every system there can be a counter-system, and this is really boring. Isaiah, by focusing on personalities and almost having a dialogue, as you said, with the person, be it Machiavelli or Herder or Marx, be it Chernyshevsky or Herzen, was cross-examining them, not in a KGB way but in a high table way: 'Now you tell me ... Now you explain to me ...'. It made things exciting because he was relating it to people, to their vicissitudes, to their problems, to the way they were looking at the world and the way in which the world was responding to them or slapping them on the face. And it is not history in the sense of the history of kings, or just abstract movements, but history that is made up of so many biographies, of great people, small people, *popolo minuto*, who are also part of history. Isaiah was able in this way to redeem Vico, because before he started to work on Vico, very few people knew about him. There was Edmund Wilson; Vico was mentioned. But Isaiah made Vico, not exactly a household word, but part of modernity. He was pre-modern, very much in a scholastic mode, living not in one of the capital cities of modernity but somewhere out in Naples, and who cared about Naples at that time? But he was the transition from pre-modern to modern; he brought with him all the classical education and all the classical background, but was opening windows to a new world. So the *New Science* was not just a new science in a scientific way, it was a new world. And when Vico opened up this new world to Isaiah, the Eastern European Jewish *maskil* spoke to him, because this is exactly the window on the world through which Isaiah was looking; and not only did he *open* the window, but he became *himself* the window for many of us who were his students, and many others who were his listeners.

RYAN The other thing that always struck me was the extraordinary egalitarianism that permeated everything that he wrote. I don't of course mean egalitarianism in the economic sense, because although earlier on, like most people I daresay, he was more prepared to sacrifice a certain amount of economic and other freedoms for the sake of greater equality, later on he became rather less enthusiastic about this. I mean intellectual egalitarianism. Nobody ever shows up in his pages as an authority. They're more or less interesting, or deep, or vivid, but the notion of a sentence that begins 'As Kant demonstrated ...' is on the whole very un-Isaiah-ish. This is why it's so wonderful for students.

AVINERI He was never speaking *ex cathedra*, neither to his students nor to the figures he was analysing. Here I should like to add a personal tribute to Isaiah. When I was doing my work on Karl Marx, one of the books I read, obviously, was Isaiah's short and wonderful biography. I was a PhD student at that time, and I knew Isaiah from his visits to Israel. My wife Dvora and I were here in London at the LSE. I started reading about Marx, and this was the time when Marx's 1844 economic-philosophical manuscripts were discovered and discussed for the first time. All of a sudden I discovered a facet of Marx which was unknown to me, and unknown to Isaiah, and this altered the picture of Marx that Isaiah offered. I read much more philosophical, humanitarian elements into Marx than he did. From time to time, because he knew me through my teacher Jacob Talmon, Isaiah checked with me: 'How is your work going?' I was very timid – this was Isaiah Berlin, I was a graduate student – but I said, 'The more I read, the more I think that some things look different from how they appear in your book.' He said, 'Tell me.' I told him, and he said, 'That's OK, go ahead, you're probably right; I'm wrong.' To hear this as a graduate student from the great Isaiah Berlin – 'You're probably right; I'm wrong' – that's not what you hear from many teachers. This was to me an example – I'm not sure I always lived up to it – of how you should behave in the republic of letters. There should be egalitarianism, no *ex cathedra*, no *authority* – not just because you have to challenge authority as a matter of principle, but because we are all equal, we are all working in the same salt mines. Isaiah gave you this exhilarating and emancipating feeling.

RYAN I think that went with his fascination with the personalities of the thinkers, because his own ego was very rarely at stake. It amounted to saying, 'Karl, I'd like you to meet this bright young man, Shlomo, who has questions he'd like to ask you.' It was as though he was running this amazing round-table dinner party at which guests from vast numbers of places, times, would all come streaming in; and the price of lunch, dinner, was having something to say, having interesting questions. It's getting on for fifty years ago that I said – as a very pushy second-year undergraduate – 'Are you *quite* sure that what you've just said about Saint-Simon was right?' 'Very probably not, very probably not. Come and have lunch.' So there was I, dragged across the road from the Examination Schools into All Souls, plonked down, fed lunch and addressed as though I might actually *understand* what I was being told. That was the exhilarating thing: you were treated as if you were not just allowed to ask questions, but might understand some of the answers.

AVINERI In this sense Isaiah was a rabbi for many of us without being rabbinical; and it takes some intellectual stature to be able to do this.

RYAN Right. Fire and flood have descended. One of Isaiah's essays has survived. Which one would you like it to be?

AVINERI I think the one on Disraeli and Marx, because it encapsulates so many facets of his writings. What do *you* think?

RYAN I think the essay on Herzen in 'A Marvellous Decade'. Isaiah was impressed by the conversation between Dostoevsky and Herzen that Dostoevsky quotes in *A Writer's Diary*. Dostoevsky told Herzen that what impressed him about *From the Other Shore* was that his opponent was not a man of straw but a formidable controversialist who drove him into akward corners. To which Herzen replied, 'Yes, but of course that is the whole point.'[1] Isaiah picked up on that: the great thing was that you had to be passionate about the project. If I lost everything else I'd want to be able to re-read that from time to time as an inspiration – as it were, this is why we mind and it's what we mind about.

AVINERI I agree.

---

[1] *Dnevnik pisatelya*, Introduction: F. M. Dostoevsky, *Polnoe sobranie sochinenii v tridtsati tomakh* (Leningrad, 1972–90), xxi 8; F. M. Dostoievsky, *The Diary of a Writer*, trans. Boris Brasol (London etc., 1949), i 4.

All Ears

Robert Wokler

A commemorative lecture delivered at the Harvard Club in New York on 2 June 1998

I N TELEVISION PARLANCE, Isaiah Berlin was what is called a talking head. Not only that inimitable voice but his whole face was continually animated, his eyes sparkling – and they were beautiful eyes, as Greta Garbo once had occasion to remark. Those eyes had witnessed much calamity, particularly to Russians and Jews whose communal identity Isaiah shared, and they moistened as well at the loss of lifelong friends, like Stephen Spender, about whom Isaiah spoke with tender affection when we met two summers ago, by chance just a few days after Spender's death. But it was more generally the vitality of his enthusiasms – social, intellectual, perhaps above all musical – which his eyes displayed. He was continually bemused at his own good fortune, at the excess of the esteem in which he was held over his actual achievement, which he would not have failed to stress this very evening if he could speak for himself. 'What have I done in my life?' he used to ask when such honours as the Order of Merit or the Presidency of the British Academy were bestowed on him, even before Henry Hardy had begun so assiduously to assemble and edit his occasional publications and broadcasts for a wider audience. 'A little book on Marx and a handful of essays,' he would reply to his own question. 'Grossly overrated. Long may it last!'

It was of course his voice that we remember most of all – its richness, its humour, its velocity. If he completed a lecture in less than the allotted time, he might apologise for having arrived a fraction late by leaving early: 'Goodbye.' In virtually every one of his public lectures in Oxford, New York and elsewhere, his was the face that launched a thousand quips. I recall his hurtling through the twenty-eight alternative readings of Machiavelli which were to become a chapter of *Against the Current*, as entranced students listened while the insecure stenographers among them hopelessly failed to get it all down. Isaiah himself, of course, had not brought along a text at all. He spoke from memory, without props, apart perhaps from a crumpled sheet of paper at the lectern or even in his pocket, which he seldom consulted. His voice alone was the overhead projector; from his mouth cascaded proper names and nouns and especially adjectives, layered one upon another like coats of varnish, each of a subtly nuanced, ever so slightly different, shade. I know of no academic figure who could intelligibly articulate more words in a shorter space of time. To his critics, there seemed occasionally to be too many words, insufficiently distinguished. In a close comparison of the different editions of *Two Concepts of Liberty*, Anthony Arblaster detected that Hobbes had replaced Aquinas in a particular passage, as if, for Isaiah, he remarked churlishly, any doubting Thomas would suffice.[1] But when Michael Oakeshott once introduced him as 'a Paganini of ideas',[2] there was a hint of envy as well as malice in that false compliment.

By way especially of the filmed interview with Göran Rosenberg, we have heard Isaiah's voice ourselves this evening. For more than thirty years after the war, it was the most widely mimicked voice not only in Oxford but perhaps in intellectual circles throughout the whole of the English-speaking world. In these very brief reflections, I should like to concentrate most of all, however, on Isaiah's ears. They had a refinement about them which I believe was central to his character. It was through them that he heard the voices around him, enabling him, while still a young man, to entertain his colleagues with stylish imitations of Maurice Bowra, for instance, or David Cecil, as well as many others among the most resonant voices of the Oxford he knew.

One of the reasons why a meeting with him proved so exhilarating was that Isaiah listened to his interlocutors so attentively. Even when it was difficult to get a word in edgeways, he somehow seemed to be all ears, warm, sooth-ing, intimate. For all its brilliance, his talk was always conversational, never rhetorical or declamatory. It perpetually bore the trace of those exchanges he had had with his philosophically minded friends at Oxford – J. L. Austin and Freddie Ayer chief among them – which could turn for hours around verbal and conceptual subtleties anchored in nothing particular because they sprang from no settled doctrines. Isaiah's voice in Oxford became progressively that of a historian of ideas among philosophers, but when he addressed the history of ideas, it was not contextually in the fashion of John Pocock or Quentin Skinner, but still philosophically quizzical or puzzled in the manner of Austin. In order to interpret the meaning of other thinkers, he interrogated them, undeterred by the methodological strictures which would confine what they had said to their own time and place. He gave them a hearing – he interviewed them, as it were – and, through his own voice, attuned to their arguments, he attempted to let them speak for themselves.

I stress that aspect of his personality because it bears most directly upon

---

[1] A. Arblaster, 'Vision and Revision: A Note on the Text of Isaiah Berlin's *Four Essays on Liberty*', *Political Studies* 19 (1971), 81–6, at 85. Wokler improves on Arblaster, who observes merely that the replacement was made 'almost as if it had to be Thomas somebody'.

[2] The phrase in Oakeshott's notes for his introduction of IB as the first Auguste Comte Memorial Lecturer at the London School of Economics on 12 May 1953. The lecture, 'History as an Alibi', was later published as *Historical Inevitability*. LSE Archives, Oakeshott 1/3.

the subjects we discussed at length at our meetings for over thirty years, and around which his current reputation as an intellectual and cultural pluralist turns. It was Isaiah who put the expression 'the Counter-Enlightenment' into general circulation. By way of his essays on Vico, Hamann, Herder and Maistre, he contributed much to our understanding of those distinctive thinkers of the eighteenth and early nineteenth century who did not subscribe to the dictates of what, through Alasdair MacIntyre, has come to be termed the Enlightenment Project, which for Isaiah, as witnessed in the film we have just seen, was nothing other than a modern formulation of the central intellectual tradition of the West, with its familiar underlying presuppositions. This crucial element of his philosophy has endeared him to many contemporary critics of Enlightenment thought, who have blamed much of modernity's failures, including the Holocaust, on that philosophical movement's notions of universal truth, on its allegedly monolithic treatments of human nature and excessively zealous commitments – because too prone to abuse – to science and reason. In his attachment to the Counter-Enlightenment, Berlin has of late come to be portrayed as if he had been a postmodernist before his time, a precursor of Michel Foucault or Jacques Derrida who had needed no inspiration from Martin Heidegger to celebrate the difference between cultures and the incompatibility and incommensurability of their values.

This had not always been the case. In the 1950s and 1960s, by way of his *Two Concepts of Liberty* in particular, he had instead been esteemed, or sometimes reviled, for articulating the philosophy of modern liberalism in what was taken to be its quintessentially English voice. His *The Hedgehog and the Fox* and his essay on *Historical Inevitability* had made his critique of determinism almost as conspicuous a feature of the then fashionable philosophy of history as were Karl Popper's *The Open Society and its Enemies* or his *The Poverty of Historicism*. At All Souls or Wolfson College Isaiah had many pupils who were writing dissertations on such themes; I almost never discussed them with him. We instead talked at length about the Enlightenment and about the philosophy of Rousseau, for which, in each case, he displayed less enthusiasm than I did myself and, despite protests to the contrary, less than I had hoped he might share with me, if only by contagion.

Since Rousseau was himself the eighteenth century's most formidable critic of the Enlightenment Project, I sometimes found it difficult to understand why Isaiah himself, in apparently distancing himself from the one, did not feel specially drawn to the other. His view of Rousseau seemed to me somewhat tinged by those interpretations of modern German or Russian totalitarianism, already fashionable in the period between the two World Wars, which traced their conceptual underpinnings to Rousseau's ideals of popular sovereignty. In that regard, Jacob Talmon's *The Origins of Totalitarian Democracy* owes him a great, and acknowledged, debt. Isaiah's conception of a uniformitarian Enlightenment Project, committed to the creation of an ideal society through the implementation of scientifically attested laws of human nature, struck me as cast in much the same mould. We argued at length about the Enlightenment and modernity, and about Rousseau's connection with both of these concepts together and with each of them separately. I told him that the Counter-Enlightenment was, to my mind, just another face of the Enlightenment; that Herder, who followed Montesquieu and Ferguson, was one of its pre-eminent spokesmen; and that notions of cultural pluralism lay at the heart of its critique of a monolithic Christian civilisation and its commitment to religious toleration.

If Isaiah was ever persuaded by any objection I put to his own views, he never showed me any sign of it. And yet I invariably felt, in his company, that however much he disagreed with me, he wanted my case to have a hearing even more than that the error of my ways should be corrected. In his rooms at All Souls, confronted by that beguiling smile and perpetual curiosity as to what I might have to say in defence of my misguided eighteenth-century friends, I felt myself in the presence of Voltaire. While he insisted that he was no genuine Englishman himself, as an Anglophile Jew he surpassed even Lewis Namier in the depth and profundity of his devotion to the country in which his career flourished, and whose intellectual classes, even whose Queen, adopted him as their favourite expatriate of all. In England, surrounded by otherness and difference, he was perfectly at home and at ease.

It is just that point about the sensitivity of Isaiah's ears that I wish to stress here, because to my mind it was the feature of his character that drew him towards the Enlightenment much more than it did away from it, that made this most urbane of all the polyglot figures of the international republic of letters that I ever knew an eighteenth-century *philosophe malgré lui*. In that regard I hold John Gray's virtual canonisation of Isaiah as a fundamentally anti-Enlightenment figure to be grievously mistaken, though Isaiah himself of course never much minded that his greatest admirers were so much at odds as to what it was in his philosophy that most merited their praise. Unlike so many postmodernist critics of eighteenth-century philosophy, Isaiah almost always displayed interpretive charity, even magnanimity, towards doctrines he found uncongenial. No pluralism of the Counter-Enlightenment ever won his esteem more than did Montesquieu, at the very heart of the so-called Enlightenment Project itself. No political thinker of the nineteenth century commanded his admiration more than did Alexander Herzen, that ebullient Westerniser among dour Slavophils, that cosmopolitan Russian abroad, that generous spirit of enlightenment in a still benighted age.

Berlin's writings on Herzen are, I believe, his finest of all, but if pride of place had to be contested, I think his tributes to Namier and to Austin in his collection of *Personal Impressions* must count as among the best alternatives. His oldest surviving friend, Stuart Hampshire, has rightly remarked upon Isaiah's comprehensive mastery of that most enlightened form of discourse, the *oraison funèbre* or funeral oration, in the manner of Fontenelle or Condorcet. More than any of his contemporaries, Berlin could make the ideas and personalities of both past and contemporary thinkers vivid and compelling because in his fashion he came close to entering their own minds and to conveying their own thoughts. Such transitivity of ideas, such clairvoyance, is quite alien to the prevailing critiques of the Enlightenment Project. In his ideals, his enthusiasms, his conversation; in his manner of speaking most distinctively in his own voice when conveying the ideas of other thinkers; most particularly, perhaps, in his reluctance to see his essentially oral contribution to literary and philosophical issues somewhat dulled by appearing in print, and especially books, Isaiah could make me feel that I was also in the company of our civilisation's Diderot. That was not always a comfortable position for a student of Rousseau. But our friendship lasted longer than did that of Diderot and Rousseau, and I sometimes regret that in addition to receiving his knighthood and the Order of Merit Isaiah was not also made a corresponding fellow of the Académie française, because then, as was his due, he could join the ranks of the immortals, as members of that august society are rightly called, which would have enabled us this evening to hear his own voice rather than merely overhear it, as it were, by way of our collective reflections.

A Philosopher's Stroll

Nicholas Henderson

'WHEN PEOPLE ASK ME what I do, I reply, "Nothing",' Isaiah said, apropos of no particular subject when we were putting on our coats before walking back from the Garrick where we had been lunching together.

I said: 'I saw your step-grandson the other day in Paris – young Strauss – and he asked me about your sex-life: ' "Lurid," I hope you answered.' To which I replied, 'I told him I'd known you for a long time.' Isaiah then asked me how and when we had first met – which in fact was at Oxford in the mid-1930s.

He looked along the clothes-hooks for his hat. He chose the wrong one, and, as we descended the steps into Garrick Street, he discovered his error and, in some anxiety, returned to the hooks as if in search of a lost child.

As we sauntered towards St Martin's Lane I commented on the elaborate and alluring elevations of the tall Victorian buildings, and, more generally, on the charms of this part of London. 'Yes, yes,' Isaiah bumbled, not dismissively, but as if it were self-evident.

'I suppose we could go via Chinatown,' I said. Isaiah gave a grunt of approval and we set off towards Charing Cross Road, which we agreed, as we crossed it, was not what it was when it enjoyed the reputation of a book-browsers' paradise. Isaiah is a keen browser, not just of books. Someone once told me of an hour or two he had spent with Isaiah browsing amongst the medicines in John Bell & Croyden in Wigmore Street, a passion that may reflect his tendency to hypochondria; but also his love of shopping.

He alluded to this love later in our walk when we came to an ironmonger's shop whose windows were full of paints, coils of string and hand-tools. Isaiah stared at the window with rapt attention as if he were contemplating a display in some oriental souk. I suggested we should enter. He replied that he wanted to buy a rubber tip for the end of his umbrella, which he then lifted up to show me. We entered the shop and he was immediately taken by the array of little wooden drawers behind the counter, each bearing a label. He seemed to be in no hurry to indicate his intended purchase. Nor did the shopkeeper show any impatience. Nevertheless, I thought that between us we ought to show some purchasing spirit, so I decided to buy a small oil-can. Isaiah then gave an eloquent description of what he wanted to buy, upon which drawer upon drawer was laid on the counter, each opened in turn, and the contents rummaged in an effort to find an umbrella-tip of exactly the right size. It was not to be found; but Isaiah, enchanted by the drawers, was determined to buy something, so he explained that he had a walking stick at home and that he would like to find a rubber tip for that. The shopkeeper enquired about the size, which was obviously difficult to determine, so he held out for selection handfuls of different tips. Isaiah said that he would buy six of them so as to be sure of having one at any rate that fitted. As they were being wrapped up, Isaiah produced his wallet, which was bulging with new, crisp notes.

While this transaction, which was far from hurried, was taking place, I asked him whether he had enjoyed his lunch, to which he replied emphatically: 'Yes, very much, especially the walk; and I love shopping.'

He seemed to take a fancy to Chinatown, and, catching sight of some porcelain in a shop window, he scurried over to it, saying 'I'd like to buy something.' But on closer inspection he changed his mind. We passed boxes of strange-looking prickly fruits, piled high on the pavement, and I suggested that Aline, his wife, might be pleased if he bought one for her. He thought not. On reflection, I had to agree. He was right.

On the other side of Shaftesbury Avenue we entered Soho. He appeared to be delighted by the mountains of fruits on the wooden barrows that lined the narrow streets, and by the glittering lights that could be seen above, proclaiming Raymond's Revue Bar. He walked very slowly, apparently taking it all in. We stopped opposite a shop selling old newspapers and film and jazz posters. Commenting on the busts in the window, he said 'There's always one of Beethoven.' We passed a shop that specialised in goods for left-handed people, which excited some curiosity in him. Then, we came to a double window sporting ladies' underwear, much of it of leather and all of it black and shining. This also absorbed Isaiah's attention, but, uncharacteristically, he appeared lost for words.

Strolling on, we started a conversation on the subject of intelligence. 'You know,' he said, 'Keith Joseph didn't understand anything about people.' To which I retorted tritely that I thought some very clever people were like that. From which he went on to say something that would have surprised all those, and they are many, who regard him as the cleverest person they have ever met. 'You know, I was never top of my form at school. Sometimes second. Never top.'

Very slowly, as if reluctant to reach the end of our journey, we crossed Regent Street and made our way to the back door of Albany. Isaiah reached in his pocket for his keys, making sure that his purchases were still there, and let himself in through the secret entrance.

Berlin in Autumn: The Philosopher in Old Age
Michael Ignatieff

BY COMMON CONSENT Isaiah Berlin enjoyed a happy old age. The autumn of his life was a time of serenity. But serenity in old age is a philosophical puzzle. Why did he manage to avoid the shipwreck which is the more common fate of us all? The obvious answer is that he was exceedingly fortunate. He married happily, late in life, and he enjoyed good health, good fortune and a growing reputation. His life between 1975, when he retired from the Presidency of Wolfson College, Oxford, and his death in 1997, were years both of ease and increasing public recognition. Berlin's editor, Henry Hardy, began editing and republishing his previously unpublished essays and lectures, and this transformed Berlin's reputation, giving the lie to Maurice Bowra's joke that like our Lord and Socrates, Berlin talked much but published little.[1] He lived long enough to see his reputation, which had been in relative eclipse, blossom into what he referred to as a 'posthumous fame'.

Certainly, Berlin's serenity in his final years owed a great deal to good fortune. But there are temperaments which frown even when fortune shines, and even those with sunny temperaments find mortal decline a depressing experience. So Berlin's serenity is worth trying to explain, both for what it tells us about him and for what it tells us about how to face our own ageing. I want to ask whether his serenity was a matter of temperament or a result of conviction, whether it was a capacity he inherited or a goal he achieved, and in particular whether his convictions – liberal, sceptical, agnostic and moderate – helped to fortify him against the ordeals of later life.

Being philosophical about old age implies being reconciled or being resigned or some combination of the two. I want to ask whether Isaiah was resigned or reconciled and in what sense philosophy helped him to be philosophical in either of these senses.

From Socrates onwards, philosophy – especially the Stoic tradition – has made the question of how to die well one of its central preoccupations. Indeed until philosophers became academic specialists devoted to instruction of the young and maintenance of that walled garden known as professional philosophy – in other words until the second half of the nineteenth century – one of the central tests of a philosophy was whether it helped its adherents to live and die in an instructively rational and inspirational fashion. The great modern

---

[1] See 136 above, note 2.

example of the philosophical death is David Hume, whose even-tempered scepticism made him one of Isaiah's favorite philosophers. The story of Hume's death, told in James Boswell's *Journals* and in Adam Smith's memoir, became a *cause célèbre* for the Enlightenment.[1] In the summer of 1776, Boswell returned repeatedly to Hume's house in the final days, awaiting some wavering which would indicate that the philosopher had recanted and embraced the Christian faith. No such wavering occurred. Hume went to his death with all the good humour of Socrates, joking with Boswell about what he might say to Charon the boatman when they met at the banks of the Styx. The jokes sent a shiver through every fibre of Boswell's errant but Christian soul. After visiting Hume for the last time, he found a whore in the streets of Edinburgh and coupled with her within sight of Hume's bedroom, as if wishing to embrace the carnal in order to drive the tormenting fear of death out of his mind. So a philosophical death was both a noble spectacle and a metaphysical puzzle. Hume's death placed him securely in this grand philosophical tradition going back to Socrates. But his philosophical positions broke with the assumption that philosophy should teach men how to live and die well. His philosophical writings maintained – and his own experience of life deepened this into a settled conviction – that while philosophy could clarify the terms of mental and moral debate, it could not generate meaningful reasons to live or die.[2] In particular, it was not a substitute source for the consolations provided by religion. Indeed, the search for metaphysical consolations was bound to be insatiable and profoundly unsettling. If men were seeking for serenity in their final hours, they should not seek it in philosophy. Hume himself had little to say about the sources of his own serenity, but they seem to have owed more to temperament than to conviction, more to the sense of a life fully lived and enjoyed than to any received or formulated set of stoic opinions.

The same proved true of Isaiah Berlin. He was a Humean from the time he came up to Oxford in 1928, an unbeliever and philosophical sceptic. As it happened, a modern twentieth-century form of Humean scepticism – 'logical positivism' – was soon to come into the ascendant in Oxford (while Berlin, still in his twenties, was becoming one of the founding fathers of the form of linguistic analysis known as 'Oxford philosophy'). While the immediate originators of this view were the Vienna School – Carnap, Schlick and Waismann – Hume remains the grandfather of this view of philosophy and its most characteristic

[1] I have discussed Hume's death in my *The Needs of Strangers* (London, 1984), chapter 3. See also James Boswell, *Boswell in Extremes, 1776–1778*, ed. Charles McC. Weis and Frederick A. Pottle (London and New York, 1971), 11–15; *The Correspondence of Adam Smith*, ed. Ernest Campbell Mossner and Ian Simpson Ross (Oxford, 1977), 203–21.

[2] David Hume, *A Treatise of Human Nature*, ed. L. A. Selby-Bigge, 2nd ed., ed. P. H. Nidditch (Oxford, 1978), 264.

Anglo-Saxon exponent.[1] Logical positivism strengthened Berlin's Humean distrust of metaphysics and what the Germans called *Lebensphilosophie*. Philosophy, as the logical positivists conceived it, had to emancipate itself from the Socratic heritage of asking questions about the meaning of life and the manner of a good death. It would never achieve results, it would never make progress as a discipline unless it rigorously excluded unanswerable questions from its research programme. This view of philosophy was in turn a view of life. It was central to this view that if you persisted in asking questions about the meaning of life, you had not understood life in any degree. Life was life and its plausibility was a matter of sentiment not a matter of argument. Philosophical propositions were of no use at all in living or dying and to ask philosophy to console was to mistake what it was. Although Berlin always rejected the scientistic and reductive style of logical positivism, he was deeply marked by its anti-metaphysical bent. Philosophy's function was to clarify common terms of argument, to elucidate the nature of moral choices, and to interpret certain puzzles in the relation between the mind and the world. It was not a substitute for religion and had nothing to say about death or how we should face it. Like most of the analytical philosophers of his generation, Berlin felt that unless philosophy kept the demarcation line with metaphysics clear, it would lose all claim to rigour, seriousness and self-respect.

These views, developed in late adolescence, made him deeply sceptical, by the time he reached his eighties, about the very possibility that philosophy could assist one to be philosophical about old age. He was not scornful of those who sought comforting systems of belief but he did not stand in need of one himself. He thought of ageing and death in consistently materialist terms and believed, accordingly, that death held no terrors since, logically speaking, it was not an event in life. This formulation, taken from Wittgenstein's *Tractatus*, implied both that death was not to be feared, since it could not be experienced, and also that death was only the end, not the defining property, of life.[2] Yet we cannot leave the matter there. Berlin the anti-metaphysical philosopher may have been sceptical of the very idea that philosophical propositions can shape the encounter with death, but when it came to deciding upon his own funeral, he chose the Jewish Orthodox form of service rather than the Reform or non-denominational service his agnostic beliefs might have logically entailed. This reflected a choice of allegiance and belonging, rather than a commitment of faith. He could subscribe to the rituals of Judaism without subscribing to their content. He did so serenely, refusing to see any contradiction. The faith of his fathers had disposed of these matters of burial and mourning very well for centuries. Why should he quarrel with any of it? His scepticism

[1] See Ben Rogers, *A. J. Ayer: A Life* (London, 1999), esp. 69; MI 81–90.
[2] MI 83.

about matters religious was more respectful than many of his more bone-dry sceptical friends – A. J. Ayer or Stuart Hampshire, for example. Why this is so is not easy to explain. As a refugee and exile, he perhaps needed the reassurance of religious ritual more than his English colleagues; just possibly, he thought that there was a sort of arid presumption in the modernist dismissal of ritual as superstition. He also differed from his colleagues, ultimately, in his view of the relation between philosophical propositions and life. Like the logical positivists, he was sceptical about the very attempt to justify life philosophically. But he turned away from philosophy proper in his late twenties in part because he had become fascinated precisely by the ways in which men did use ideas to justify, explain and even modify their lives. As a historian of ideas, he was keenly aware that men do live and die by their ideas. Few philosophers had such a keen sense of the intense interaction between propositions, convictions and temperament. If we are going to look at the impact of Berlin's thought on the manner of his own ageing we shall have to look beyond the impact of logical positivism itself.

All of his thinking associated serenity with belonging, and belonging with self-knowledge. If he was serene in old age it was because he knew who he was and where he belonged. This personal sense of the necessity of roots informed all of his writing on nationalism. He always located the origins of nationalist feeling in the passion to be understood. People need to live in communities where they are understood – and not merely for what they say, but for what they mean. To have a national home was to live in a world of such shared meanings.[1] He attached more importance to belonging than any other modern liberal philosopher. He had a clear sense of his own origins, as the son of a Baltic timber merchant born in the Jewish community of Riga in the twilight of the Tsarist Empire. Despite going into exile he kept a strong sense of connection to these roots throughout his adult life. This organic connection was possible because his mother remained alive until he was well into his sixties. When he tried to speak about losing her, he used the German verb *zerreißen*, meaning 'to tear in pieces'. In the letters he wrote in the week after her death in 1974, he went on to say that without such living links to his past he felt accidental, contingent, directionless.[2] Life briefly lost its momentum and point. In time, he recovered it again: his organic capacities for repair and recovery were formidable. It is doubtful that he had more than several months' experience of genuine depression in his whole life, and if his mother's death brought about one such occasion, it was brief. His equanimity in old age had a great deal to do with the degree to which he made his own life – its needs and cravings – the

---

[1] See 'Nationalism: Past Neglect and Present Power' and 'The Apotheosis of the Romantic Will', both in PSM.

[2] MI 272.

tacit subject of his work, and through apparently abstract writings about nationalism explored the need for belonging which was central to his own identity. If this produced equanimity it was because it was done tacitly, with a minimum of self-disclosure, so that his work both revealed his inner preoccupations and helped him to resolve them, without exposing him to ridicule or shame.

Among expatriates like Berlin, identities soldered together in exile often come apart in old age. In retirement and old age, people are brought up short with the realisation of how far they have come from their beginnings. Often their past is now in another country and in another time. When this realisation dawns, identity comes under strain. They begin to go to church or synagogue more often, they begin to dream in their languages of origin in an attempt to recover past connections; more often than not, they begin to have a sense of inner fragmentation. They are not able to pull past, present and future together. The span of life is simply too long. There are too many twists and turns in the road. This did not happen to Berlin. In fact, old age represented a coming together of the Russian, Jewish and English skeins of his identity. During his years as a schoolboy and then as a young Oxford don, he assimilated thoroughly. His accent, for example, impersonated the upper-middle-class Oxford dons of his acquaintance. But with old age, the Russian and Jewish parts of his identity began to return. His voice became less English with time and more Russian in its vowel sounds. He himself was aware of this. It cannot be accidental that his most extended excursion into autobiography, the Jerusalem prize speech, was delivered as he turned seventy.[1] In it he made a point of saying that his identity consisted of three elements, English, Russian and Jewish, all braided together into one skein. The philosophical equanimity of his old age owed a great deal to this recovery of all the elements of his past, this braiding of the skein of self-hood. It made him an exceedingly economical persona: no energy was wasted in repression or denial of the origins which made him up.

There was no question of a return to Judaism in old age, because he had never left. While he did not keep a kosher table, he observed the major Jewish festivals and liked to joke that the Orthodox synagogue was the synagogue he did not attend. He had no time for reformed Judaism because he thought it was incoherent to combine religion and rationalism, to reduce an ancient faith to nothing more than an agreeable and modern ethical content. He respected the claims of the ancient Jewish tradition precisely because of their irrational and inhuman content. Igor Stravinsky came to lunch in 1963 and asked Isaiah to suggest a religious subject for a composition he had been commissioned to write for the Jerusalem Festival. Berlin went upstairs, returned with his Bible

[1] 'The Three Strands in My Life', in PI2.

and read Stravinsky the passage in Hebrew describing Abraham's binding of Isaac. Stravinsky took Berlin's advice and went on to compose a cantata on the theme. The Abraham and Isaac story was a parable for Berlin about the inscrutability both of God's commands and of human life itself. Unlike many of his fellow unbelievers, Berlin had a healthy respect for the religious dimension in human consciousness. It also helped to sustain his ultimately metaphysical view that there were a lot of things about the shape of human life which we cannot know.[1] Because he was a famous man, he would be asked, sometimes by complete strangers, to pronounce on the meaning of life. He found this very comic, but his replies were terse and matter of fact. When he was seventy-five, he replied to one such questioner, 'As for the Meaning of Life, I do not believe it has any: I do not at all ask what it is, for I suspect it has none, and this is a source of great comfort to me – we make of it what we can and that is all there is about it. Those who seek for some deep, cosmic, all embracing teleologically arguable libretto or goal are, believe me, pathetically mistaken.'[2]

These then were the metaphysical sources of his serenity: a deep and abiding sense of who he was and where he came from, coupled with a cool and sceptical refusal to entertain questions about the meaning of life which he thought were beyond the reach of reason.

This is about as far as doctrine and mature conviction will take us in explaining his autumnal serenity and they do not take us very far. We need to look at his temperament, at the attitudes to self and habits of mind which made it easy for him to greet old age with relative calm.

As his biographer I had expected that when he left Wolfson College, when he was no longer President of the British Academy, no longer Chichele Professor of Social and Political Theory, no longer a Fellow of All Souls, he might have felt bereft and denuded, as professional men often do at the end of their careers. Retirement can initiate a period of lonely inner questioning. This did not happen for Berlin. This is because he was never heavily invested in these roles in the first place. He did not lack ambition, he liked to be taken seriously, he could be prickly if he felt his dignity or reputation were attacked – but he also stood outside himself and mocked his own desire for recognition. When T. S. Eliot wrote to congratulate him on his knighthood in 1957, Isaiah replied that he felt as silly as if he were wearing a paper hat at a children's party.[3] He liked recognition – the knighthood mattered deeply – but he held some part of himself back. Irony and a sense of the ridiculous, therefore, were important components of the serenity his friends admired in the autumn of his life.

Of course irony and a sense of humour about the scramble for honour and

[1] MI 237–8.
[2] Letter to Irving Singer, 20 November 1984; cf. MI 279.
[3] MI 222.

fame are easier if you've had your share of both. He always said his success had been based on a systematic overestimation of his abilities. 'Long may this continue,' he would say. He had very little to be bitter about, very little to regret. Yet even those who have known a success equivalent to his are often bitter and depressed in old age. He was not. He always insisted that he was not an essentially introspective man; he was an observer, certainly, but fundamentally directed outwards rather than inwards. He never kept a diary and his most characteristic forms of self-revelation were addressed outwards in letters and conversation. He thought more about what other people made of him than he thought about himself. He found it easy to take a distance from his own life, to be ironical about himself, because he wasn't imprisoned in his own self to begin with.

He had a particular talent for imagining other lives, and that gave him a vantage point from which to see his own. He loved reading in order to lose himself in some other person, often someone radically alien to his own temperament. He had a fascination with ideas and temperaments opposite to his own: figures like Joseph de Maistre, the counter-revolutionary theorist and fanatical hater of bourgeois liberal reformism.[1] In entering into Maistre's inner world, he could see himself as Maistre might have seen him, and this capacity for self-distancing freed him from excessive or burdening investment in his own roles. Keeping himself apart from his roles followed, I think, from being a Jew and an exile. His belonging in England was both secure and conditional. Irony, self-distancing and self-deprecation had survival value for any Jewish exile in England. This is one of the reasons that he remained, even in secure old age, a watchful character, acutely aware that he was a sojourner and a stranger even in the Establishment which took him to its heart.

He also refused to vest his own commitments, ideas and values with existential or historical importance. After the fall of Communism, he was constantly asked whether he felt vindicated, and his replies always challenged the premise of the question itself. Why, he asked, should any liberal feel vindicated? History, he always said, had no libretto. To claim that it vindicated him or his liberalism seemed an absurd inflation of both himself and the doctrines with which he was associated. He was also self-knowing enough to realise that he had never risked anything decisive in the struggle against Communist tyranny, as Koestler, Orwell, Miłosz or Akhmatova had. Since that was the case, it was unbecoming to make a show of rejoicing at its fall. He did take quiet pleasure in the fact that Communism ended as his own life came to a close. He could look back across the century and feel that the intellectuals with whom he felt the closest spiritual kinship, the anti-Bolshevik writers and artists of Russia's Silver Age,

---

[1] 'Joseph de Maistre and the Origins of Fascism', in CTH.

1896–1917 – chiefly Pasternak and Akhmatova – would have rejoiced to have lived the hours he had been lucky enough to see. In this sense, history did shine on him in his final years.

He was distanced from his roles, from his own ideas and from his own posterity. He was fond of saying, 'Après moi le déluge.' Of course, there was an element of pose in this, a very Oxford style of appearing not to care about reputation. In fact, of course, he was a careful custodian of his reputation – worrying whether he should accept such and such an honour, sit at such and such a table, with such and such a person, give his name to such and such an appeal. All of this indicates a concern to husband the coinage of his fame. But as to what came after, he always purported to be indifferent.

His attitude to my work on his biography, for example, was complex. Initially, he thought it was a ludicrous idea. 'Why would I want to do such a thing?' I can remember him asking me. It was only after three years of oral interviewing – in which I would ask him a question at the beginning of the hour and get to ask him another one at the end – that he broached the issue of what would become of the tapes. The idea of a biography grew upon him as he came to trust me and grow comfortable in my company. As the years passed, he engaged with the project, checking with me about this or that detail, retelling certain stories with a new twist or nuance in order that I would appreciate its significance. But he took a fundamentally passive approach to my project, waiting for the right question before proffering the answer, and I had to wait for years for him to disclose what he took to be the essential elements of his life and thought. He seemed to have little anxiety about posterity. When I asked him how he thought he would be remembered, his replies were always of the form 'How can we possibly know?' and 'Why should it matter?'

This attitude towards posterity was reinforced by the fact that he had no children of his own. He was quite content to be a stepfather to his wife's children, but he never wanted any of his own. The patriarchal and paternal instincts – all of which usually go with a desire to shape and mould posterity – were absent in him.

He also never had disciples. There were many former students, friends and associates who liked to say 'Ich bin ein Berliner', but he never sought to create a circle of followers who would propagate his ideas and safeguard his reputation. There was no Berlin school, tendency or faction. He disliked the idea of having to take responsibility for a Berlinian doctrine, with orthodoxy to defend and disciples to promote it.

He watched Henry Hardy, a young graduate student in philosophy, attach himself to his work; he supported Hardy's editions of his works and greatly enjoyed the revival of his reputation which Hardy's work achieved, but never took any initiative in the relationship beyond benign approval. The same genial detachment characterised his relationship to my biography. Neither Hardy nor I ever thought of ourselves as surrogate sons, disciples or acolytes. Isaiah simply did not want this kind of entourage around him – did not want the responsibility.

The final source of his equanimity, I believe, was in relation to ageing itself. Almost all of us have a quarrel with how old we actually are, and present ourselves as younger or older than our biological age. Biological and phenomenological age are never exactly the same. Isaiah was a complex instance of this. All the people who remember him from his early youth always said that he was the oldest person in any room. When he was twenty he was already behaving as if he were a middle-aged man. Stephen Spender, one of his oldest friends, once said to me that he had trouble thinking of Isaiah as having aged at all. He was always 'a baby elephant, always the same baby elephant'.[1] In early pictures of him, he is wearing the same kind of three-piece suit that he wore to the end of his life. He valued continuity in the details: the same kind of polished shoes, the same look of cautious bourgeois sobriety as his father. He dressed like his father all his life, and he did so from adolescence onwards. The paradox of his extraordinary youthfulness and vitality, therefore, was that he always thought of himself as a middle-aged man. He always seemed older than he was and he always remained younger than he seemed.

Age did him many favours. He was not a prepossessing twenty- or thirty- or even forty-year-old. It wasn't until he was in his sixties that he looked fully at ease with what he had become. He thinned down, his whole face acquired a certain nobility, as if he were finally growing into the age at which he was most himself.

His vernacular of odd behavior – going to parties with crispbread in a matchbox in his pocket so that he could have his own little snacks – belonged more to the personality of an indulged child than of a sage. In a restaurant he would suddenly begin humming some little Yiddish ditty that he had heard in Hebrew school in 1915. That ability to recover his childhood and be a child again was one of the reasons that he was much loved and that he was never weighed down by life.

The other element of his ageing – which he noticed himself – was that it rendered him more – not less – susceptible to pity. In a letter written late in life, he said, 'The proposition that the longer one lives the more indifferent one becomes to the ills that beset one or one's dearest is totally false; I suffer much more from this than I used to, and I now realise that there must have been a long period of my life when I was, comparatively speaking, too little sensitive to the misfortunes of others, however close – certainly of my friends.'[2] In 1993,

[1] MI 3.
[2] MI 288.

one year before his death, Stephen Spender sent Isaiah the following poem, written in China in AD 835. It commemorated their sixty years of friendship:

> We are growing old together, you and I;
> Let us ask ourselves, what is age like?
> The dull eye is closed ere night comes;
> The idle head, still uncombed at noon.
> Propped on a staff, sometimes a walk abroad;
> Or all day sitting with closed doors.
> One dares not look in the mirror's polished face;
> One cannot read small-letter books.
> Deeper and deeper, one's love of old friends;
> Fewer and fewer, one's dealings with young men.
> One thing only, the pleasure of idle talk,
> Is great as ever, when you and I meet.[1]

That does catch perhaps the final element of what kept both of them young: the pleasure of idle talk, and the idler the better. Memory, word games and puns, the sheer pleasure of orality, which connected him to the pleasures of infancy all his life. There was nothing that meant more to him than the pleasure of talk. He died tragically of esophageal constriction, literally unable to get words out of his throat. The condition was terrible to him, and it was the only time I ever saw him depressed, because it made it difficult for him to speak to other human beings and that was what made life worth living.

What he seemed to vindicate by his life was life itself. Life could not be philosophically justified; it could only be lived. He trusted life and certainly helped those who loved him to trust it more themselves.

---

[1] This poem by Po Chü-i is addressed to Liu Yü-hsi, who was born in the same year (772), and this translation by Arthur Waley appeared as 'Old Age' in *More Translations from the Chinese* (London, 1919), 55. Cf. MI 287–8.

When a Sage Dies, All Are His Kin

Leon Wieseltier

I

'WHEN A SAGE DIES,' says the Talmud, 'all are his kin.'[1]
The rabbis were speaking practically, not philosophically. They were ruling that, when a sage dies, everyone must observe some of the practices of mourning. When a sage dies, for example, all must rend their garments. 'But do you really think that all are his kin?' the text asks itself, incredulously. For all are obviously not his kin. It is a big world. The injunction seems sentimental, onerous. 'So say, rather, that all are like his kin.' A distinction! But it is not enough of a distinction to release anybody from the duty to mourn.

And if you never knew the man, if you never sat in the dust at his feet, if you never heard him teach? Still he is not a stranger. The Talmud proceeds to the story of the death of Rabbi Safra, a scholar and a merchant of the fourth century. 'When Rabbi Safra died, the rabbis did not rend their garments, because they said: "We did not study with him ourselves." But Abbaye said to them: "Does it say 'when your master dies'? No, it says 'when a sage dies'! Besides, every day in the house of study we consider his views."' If you know the teaching, you know the teacher. You are required to rend.

In Oxford, last week, a sage died. And every day in the house of study we consider his views. Who are Isaiah Berlin's kin, who must mourn?

II

The pluralists are his kin, and they must mourn.

Isaiah Berlin was the most original, the most lucid, the most erudite, and the most relentless enemy of the idea of totality in his age, which was an age of totality. More precisely, an age of failed totality; and it owed that failure, which was the late and saving glory of an inglorious modernity, not least to the notions of this professor and his crowded, benevolent mind. 'It seems to me,' he wrote, 'that the belief that some single formula can in principle be found whereby all the diverse ends of men can be harmoniously realised is demonstrably false.'[2] The geniality of the statement should not obscure the scale of the claim. It is the language of a don, but it is the conception of a world-historical thinker. What made him a world-historical thinker was his assault on the idea of the world-historical.

[1] Moed Qatan 25a.
[2] L 214.

From Parmenides to Marx, philosophers dreamed of the single principle, the single method, the single being, metaphysical or anti-metaphysical, sacred or profane, that would account for everything that exists, and bring everything that exists under a single description. Berlin set out to awaken Western thought from that dream. His lifelong analysis of the ideal of wholeness exposed it as a dangerous illusion. But he did not repudiate it only on moral and political grounds. He carried the criticism of totality beyond the criticism of totalitarianism, back to the elementary consideration of its philosophical sense. He showed that it had no philosophical sense.

'In the house of history,' he wrote, 'there are many mansions.'[1] But the force of Berlin's attack on holism in all its forms was owed to the fact that it was not only a historical attack, it was also a logical attack. It is commonly assumed that his defence of pluralism was the work of his years as a political thinker and a historian of ideas, but in fact Berlin's quarrel with totality originated in his early papers, in the Oxford-style exercises in analytical philosophy that he later liked to disavow. 'I could not bring myself to re-read them,'[2] he said about these writings; but it was in his animadversions against logical positivism that he began to suggest what is preposterous about 'the infallible knowledge of incorrigible propositions',[3] and 'the Ionian fallacy of asking what everything is made of',[4] and 'the privileged class of basic propositions [...] and [...] the desire to translate all other propositions into them or combinations of them'.[5] It was logic that made Berlin a liberal.

For Berlin, pluralism was not a conclusion drawn prudently from experience, a kind and expedient concession to the obstacles that life puts in the way of the right and the good. Rather, pluralism was a conclusion drawn from a proper analysis of concepts, from a strict reflection about the nature of human values and human goods, which are essentially incompatible, not just empirically incompatible, with one another. 'The notion of a total human fulfillment is a formal contradiction.'[6] A formal contradiction: is there a greater curse upon an idea? But this was the curse that Berlin cast upon the idea of totality, and may the idea never escape the curse. It was Berlin who demonstrated that the illiberal view of the world was not only an evil, it was also an error; that the liberal view of the world is not only a practical necessity, it is also a theoretical necessity. If society must be pluralist, it is because reality is plural; because pluralism is what there is.

[1] CTH 79.
[2] CC xi.
[3] CC 77.
[4] CC 76.
[5] CC 79.
[6] L 213.

Berlin was one of liberalism's great foundationalists, and his writings will stand as a permanent embarrassment to those who believe that justice can dispense with philosophy. The pluralism that he preached was not a gospel of relaxation. 'If, as I believe, the ends of men are many, and not all of them are in principle compatible with each other, then the possibility of conflict – and of tragedy – can never be wholly eliminated from human life, either personal or social.'[1] The strife and the sorrow of which Berlin warned might wrack the same society, the same culture, the same individual. Pluralism promises peace, not serenity. But Berlin kindled to the friction. He prized the shadows of the Many over the darkness of the One; for it is darkness, and not light, that the One generally vouchsafes. He had an almost aesthetic relationship to the heterogeneity that he championed. In his work and in his person, he demonstrated that the world of the Many is a more enchanted world, not a less enchanted world, than the world of the One. In this way, Berlin made a fruitful contribution to the idea of happiness.

III

The rationalists are his kin, and they must mourn.

The rationalists? Surely not the rationalists. For it was Berlin, was it not, who shook the confidence of reason, and denied that reason was immune to time and to place, and denounced the rationalism of the Enlightenment as an indefensible absolutism? Yes, it was Berlin. But something has gone a little awry in the appreciation of his work in recent years. Some people think that they have detected in 'value pluralism' and the 'incommensurability thesis' endorsements of the miserable flight from reason that characterises so much of contemporary intellectual life. Thus, one reads that 'There is in Berlin's idea of radical choice arising from conflicts among incommensurables a decisionist, voluntarist, or existentialist element.'[2] Berlin's attack on absolutes has been taken to imply relativism, or subjectivism, or perspectivism, or even a quaint postmodernism.

This is all exaggerated and imprecise. There is not a whiff of *fumisme* in Berlin, not a touch of Fichte or Sartre. 'We seek to adjust the unadjustable, we do the best we can',[3] but we do not do so gratuitously, or helplessly, or in the service only of our interests. The hero of Berlin's epic of the collision of ends is a deliberative hero, whose choices are rational, or at least reasonable, and merit praise or blame. He does not despair of coherence or truth. Berlin's point is not that reason has been retired by irony or by will; it is that reason dictates many things, and comes with costs. It was not against reason that Berlin inveighed, it was against the Church of Rationalism (or the Temple of Sarastro, as he liked to

[1] L 214.
[2] John Gray, *Isaiah Berlin* (London, 1995), 71.
[3] L 47.

call it); and it was reason, not unreason, that he pitted against rationalism's dogmas. When 'Herder and the Enlightenment', his extraordinary essay of 1965, was reprinted last year in a new collection of his writings,[1] Berlin added a note in which he described Herder's standpoint, which was also his own standpoint, as 'objective pluralism'.[2] It was not one of his magical formulations, but it suffices to establish that he offers no comfort to the cheerful obscurers.

What is 'objective pluralism'? It is the view that a pluralist world is a porous world, that societies and cultures and minds are not so shut up within themselves that meaningful communication among them, or meaningful comparison between them, is impossible ('it is idle to tell men to learn to see other worlds through the eyes of those whom they seek to understand, if they are prevented by the walls of their own culture from doing so');[3] and also the view that each of these societies and cultures and minds may be evaluated by logical and moral categories that apply across them all. About relativism, Berlin wrote that 'I take it to mean a doctrine according to which the judgement of a man or a group, since it is the expression or statement of a taste, or emotional attitude or outlook, is simply what it is, with no objective correlate that determines its truth or falsehood.'[4] And this he rejected. He would not countenance the ideal of an islanded existence. It made the study of different forms of life and ancient forms of life and primitive forms of life impossible. Is 'objectivity', then, another term for universalism? Berlin did not speak keenly of universalism, and in his writings he often identified it with what a historian once called 'uniformitarianism'. But really he abhorred only a coercive universalism (and its incarnation on earth, Communism). He was a universalist of the multiformitarian kind.

What bothered Berlin about rationalism was its insulation. This was especially true of rationalism in Oxford, as he recalled it in an elegiac but devastating memoir of J. L. Austin. For nothing was more vivid to Berlin than the reality of an idea; the external reality as well as the internal reality. A particular idea occurred in a particular time and a particular place. This did not mean that the idea was contingent, or nothing more than an expression of the individual who thought it. It might be a necessary idea; but even necessary ideas do not think themselves. An abstract conception is voluptuously actual. A thought is an experience. Berlin did not become a historian of ideas because he believed that ideas are nothing but history. His historicism was a way of making reason worldly; or of acting on the rude and marvellous discovery that reason already was worldly, even when it pretended otherwise.

It was not only for its more various picture of the human that Berlin kept

[1] PSM. The essay also appears in TCE.
[2] PSM 390 note 1, TCE 198 note 1.
[3] CTH 85–6.
[4] CTH 80.

returning to what he called the Counter-Enlightenment. He was on a mission. He was a spy for reason in the house of unreason. (His studies in the history of Romanticism and reaction were the most important cables that he ever wrote.) He needed all the dark and complicating information, if he was to get on with the unapologetically progressive task of understanding the conditions for the development of personality and decency. He belongs in the small and valorous company of rationalists who did not flinch before the facticity of unreason, who knew that reason cripples itself when it regards only itself, who taught reason sympathy.

IV

The democrats are his kin, and they must mourn.

Berlin criticised classical rationalism as much for some of its effects as for some of its assumptions. He showed that, even in its nobler versions, it often culminated in a sanctimonious and sometimes murderous authoritarianism.

> One belief, more than any other, is responsible for the slaughter of individuals on the altars of the great historical ideals – justice or progress or the happiness of future generations, or the sacred mission or emancipation of a nation or race or class, or even liberty itself, which demands the sacrifice of individuals for the freedom of society. This is the belief that somewhere, in the past or in the future, in divine revelation or in the mind of an individual thinker, in the pronouncements of history or science, or in the simple heart of an uncorrupted good man, there is a final solution.[1]

A final solution: the phrase recurs often in Berlin's studies of Western thought, and he saw no need to remark upon its chill.

Was it really a surfeit of reason from which this century suffered? Of course not. But this was not Berlin's claim. He was warning, rather, of the perversion of reason. He admired the power of the mind to understand, but he feared the power of the mind to unify; and he was adamant that unifying was not the same as understanding. It was plain to him that the crimes of his century were the crimes of monism, and he toiled to make this plain to others. In political theory, monism took the form of what he called 'positive liberty'. He was against it; it was a fancy invitation to compulsion, a theory of authority disguised as a theory of freedom. Freedom for, freedom to: this kind of freedom was a demand for a prescription for a way to live, and it defined freedom as conformity to such a prescription, as obedience. Berlin maintained, against Lenin but also against

---

[1] L 212, PSM 237.

Kant, that freedom was not obedience, that it was the obstreperous antithesis of conformity.

Freedom was not general, it was individual. In his appraisal of political ideas and political systems, Berlin never took his eyes off 'the empirical spatio-temporal existence of the finite individual'.[1] For this reason, he became the unvatic prophet of 'negative liberty'. This he defined as 'a maximum degree of non-interference compatible with the minimum demands of social life'.[2] In Berlin's hands, the homely ideal of non-interference was homely no more. It was transformed into philosophy's powerful weapon against despotism. Berlin gave it grandeur: 'It seems unlikely that this extreme demand for liberty has ever been made by any but a small company of highly civilised and self-conscious human beings.'[3] Or, a little morbidly, it may be that the objective of the struggle for freedom, of the longest and bloodiest struggle in human history, was nothing more magnificent than the right to be left alone.

Berlin was himself one of those highly civilised and self-conscious human beings. He, too, imagined the reign of respect, the paradise of no paradise. He was the heir in his time of Mill and Constant. He simply and truly detested determinisms. He did not deny that power was legitimate (though he discussed anarchism with glee, and took a wicked pleasure in contrasting Marx unfavourably to Bakunin); but he demanded that power be legitimate, and he propounded an exceedingly stringent criterion for its legitimacy. He was not a libertarian, and he criticised 'the evils of unrestricted laissez-faire, and of the social and legal systems that permitted and encouraged it, that led to brutal violations of "negative" liberty';[4] but he criticised collectivism more. (In 1917, as a boy in Petrograd, he watched the Russian Revolution.) 'Genuine belief in the inviolability of a minimum extent of individual liberty', he wrote, 'entails [an] absolute stand.'[5] This, from the master anti-absolutist! But there was nothing paradoxical about this stand. It was the corollary of his consecration.

Berlin's writings display in abundance the natural democracy of the contrapuntal mind. He was not a party man or a fisher of souls. With his friend Lionel Trilling, he believed that 'a criticism which has at heart the interests of liberalism might find its most useful work not in confirming liberalism in its sense of general rightness but rather in putting under some degree of pressure the liberal ideas and assumptions of the present time'.[6] Berlin did not exempt liberals and democrats from the fairness and the candour of his judgement. The conflation

---

[1] L 37.
[2] L 207, PSM 232.
[3] ibid.
[4] L 38.
[5] L 210, PSM 236.
[6] Lionel Trilling, *The Liberal Imagination* (New York, 1953), viii.

of freedom with power by modern revolutionaries, he observed, 'has, perhaps, blinded some contemporary liberals to the world in which they live. Their plea is clear, their cause is just. But they do not allow for the variety of human needs. Nor yet for the ingenuity with which men can prove to their satisfaction that the road to one ideal also leads to its contrary.'[1] He was wise in part because he was not ingenious.

v

The nationalists are his kin, and they must mourn.

Not all the nationalists, no. Berlin was withering about the low side of belonging, about 'the pathological developments of nationalism in our own times', about 'modern national narcissism: the self-adoration of peoples, of their conviction of their own immeasurable superiority to others and consequent right to dominate them'.[2] He carefully delineated the debt that fascism and other outrages of collective will owed to Romanticism. He was alienated by the celebration of the organic and the mythological that characterises, and inflames, nationalist thinking and nationalist feeling. And yet he was not prepared to follow his faith in individualism all the way to an internationalist conclusion. He was sharply critical of liberals and socialists for having scanted the reality, and the validity, and the durability, of group feeling.

Berlin had two reasons for lingering over nationalism. The first was his indignation at injustice. In his view, nationalism almost always originated as an effort at redress, as an attempt to right a wrong. 'It usually seems to be caused by wounds.'[3] In response to oppression and exploitation, a people desires recognition and independence. Not to understand such desires, and the solidarity out of which they arise, is to be morally obtuse, or worse. 'The consciousness that although all oppression is hateful, yet to be ordered about by a man of my own community or nation, or class or culture or religion, humiliates me less than if it is done by strangers [...] that sentiment is surely intelligible enough.'[4] Nationalism, in Berlin's wonderful phrase, is 'the straightening of bent backs'.[5]

But this is a purely reactive account of nationalism, and a purely political one; and for Berlin it did not suffice. The second reason for his interest in nationalism was his interest in the world as it is. For there are nations, formed or forming, Stateless or in States, with languages, traditions, customs, institutions and beliefs of their own. Regardless of what theory has to say about it, the human world is already so constituted and so diversified. Berlin's nationalism was an

[1] L 208, PSM 233.
[2] SR 248.
[3] CTH 245.
[4] SR 258.
[5] CTH 261.

expression of his humanism. As a matter of principle, he dignified human needs and human aspirations. And the past was philosophically significant for him. The sphere of freedom that Berlin described was not a stripped and empty shell, and he did not seek to secure it for the purpose of Nietzschean melodrama. He did not require people to create themselves and their meanings. Identities are not only invented, they are also inherited; and they are invented out of what is inherited. Berlin never recoiled from the involuntary dimensions of life. This supremely unmystical man warmly invoked 'the nation as a society of the living, the dead and those yet unborn (sinister as this could prove to be when driven to a point of pathological exacerbation)'.[1]

He was the great teacher of liberal nationalism, which is surely one of the urgent teachings of our time. Berlin revered Mazzini: 'true internationalism must be based on mutual regard and respect between nations. To have internationalism you must have individual nations.'[2] And those nations must be held to common standards of right and wrong. Is this universalism? It is. 'No culture that we know lacks the notions of good and bad [...] There are universal values.'[3] The ethical trumps the ethnic. But Berlin's liberal nationalism was not only a brake upon the thraldom of the group to the nation. It was also a brake upon the thraldom of the individual to the nation. Berlin did not agree that nationalism required the immersion of the individual in the group. 'Total harmony with others is incompatible with self-identity.'[4] There is dignity in membership; but in partial membership. Partial membership is still profound. The part is precious, but it must not be mistaken for the whole. The participation in shared traditions is an important element in the cultivation of personality, until it becomes its only element, and then it leads to the degradation of personality. Berlin prized authenticity, except ideologically.

The most deeply felt essay in the history of ideas that he wrote, I think, was his essay on Moses Hess, and these are the most deeply felt words in the essay:

> [...] through his most extreme and radical beliefs there persists a conviction that there is never any duty to maim or impoverish oneself for the sake of an abstract ideal; that nobody can, or should, be required to vivisect himself, to throw away that which affords him the deepest spiritual satisfaction known to human beings – the right to self-expression, to personal relationships, to the love of familiar places or forms of life, of beautiful things, or the roots and symbols of one's own, or one's family's, or one's nation's past. He believed that nobody should be made to sacrifice

[1] AC 352–3, PSM 602.
[2] CIB 121.
[3] CIB 37.
[4] L 36.

his own individual pattern of the unanalysable relationships – the central emotional or intellectual experiences – of which human lives are compounded, to offer them up, even as a temporary expedient, for the sake of some tidy solution, deduced from abstract and impersonal premises, some form of life derived from an alien source, imposed upon men by artificial means, and felt to be the mechanical application of some general rule to a concrete situation for which it was not made. All that Hess, towards the end of his life, wrote or said rests on the assumption that to deny what inwardly one knows to be true, to do violence to the facts for whatever tactical or doctrinal motive, is at once degrading and doomed to futility.[1]

Berlin was a creature of loyalties, and he expounded a critical philosophy of loyalty. He lived a dutiful, polycentric, generous and unidolatrous life. 'I remain totally loyal to Britain, to Oxford, to liberalism, to Israel,'[2] he remarked. He was, you might say, a rootful Jewish cosmopolitan, and so the most blessed of men.

VI

The Jews were his kin, and they must mourn.

He was a happy Zionist. 'The origins of Zionism were very civilised and Herderian,'[3] he observed, meaning that his own nationalism had the same philosophical ground as the nationalism of others. It was owed also to his understanding of history, to his awareness of an emergency, to 'the realisation (it seems destined to come, late or soon, to almost every Jewish social thinker, whatever his views) that the Jewish problem is something *sui generis*, and seems to need a specific solution of its own, since it resists the solvent of even the most powerful universal panaceas'.[4] But Berlin's Zionism was not just an intellectual's Zionism. It was a bias of his heart. The sensation of peoplehood never deserted him. He vibrated to his patrimony.

Not to all of it, though. He was rather indifferent to Judaism as a religion, and rather ignorant about it, even if he liked to remind you that he was a cousin of the Lubavitcher Rebbe. (The Messiah would have profited from his cousin's thoughts about messianism in history.) He never quite overcame the Zionist condescension toward Yiddish. And in Jewish politics there was much that he would not accept. He condemned the chauvinists and the jingoists in the Zionist movement and in the Jewish State. (When asked about the Arabs who oppose Israel, he replied that 'Understanding people who oppose us is what Herder taught us.'[5] Consider that first 'us', and then that second 'us', and you

[1] AC 250–1.
[2] CIB 87.
[3] CIB 103.
[4] AC 242.
[5] CIB 88.

will have the whole man.) And yet, as a Jew, Berlin was free, glad, open, busy, grateful and utterly without anxiety. His past made him feel princely, as it should have. There was our exilarch, in Oxford; and there he is buried.

And those for whom he was not only a sage but also a master, those who sat in the dust at his feet – they, too, must mourn, for they are the mourners who will remember the teacher and not just the teaching. They will remember him in all his gentleness and all his gaiety, in his uncanny ability to see through them, and with sweetness and severity to explain them to themselves. They will remember him at the big white door, how delighted he was to see them, and how delighted they were that he was delighted to see them. They will remember him slouched in his chair by the fire, telling tales of what he had seen and what he had heard, singing 'Rachel, quand du Seigneur' or 'A un dottor della mia sorte',[1] imparting to them all that he had satisfied himself was true, until they were emboldened to think that they, too, might become a link in the chain. (He was indeed an unforgettable talker; but it was what he said that was unforgettable.) They will remember him

> [...] unvexed, unwarped
> By partial bondage. In his steady course,
> No piteous revolutions had he felt,
> No wild varieties of joy and grief.
> Unoccupied by sorrow of its own,
> His heart lay open; and, by nature tuned
> And constant disposition of his thoughts
> To sympathy with man, he was alive
> To all that was enjoyed where'er he went,
> And all that was endured; for, in himself
> Happy, and quiet in his cheerfulness,
> He had no painful pressure from within
> That made him turn aside from wretchedness
> With coward fears. He could afford to suffer
> With those whom he saw suffer. Hence it came
> That in our best experience he was rich,
> And in the wisdom of our daily life.[2]

They will remember him, and their mourning will rend them.

'When a sage dies, all are his kin.' A dispute is recorded[3] between the last great rabbis of Germany in the Middle Ages, Meir ben Baruch of Rothenberg

---

[1] Arias sung by Éléazar in Halévy's *La Juive* and by Bartolo in Rossini's *The Barber of Seville*.
[2] William Wordsworth, *The Excursion*, lines 353–73.
[3] Asher ben Yehiel, commentary on Moed Qatan 3:59.

and his student Asher ben Yehiel. Meir leniently ruled that you mourn for a sage 'if you know the ideas that he introduced, but if you know none of the ideas that he introduced, and he was not your master, then you are not required to rend when you hear the news after the funeral, since you do not, as Abbaye said, consider his views in the house of study every day'. Asher stringently demurred, likewise in the name of Abbaye: 'Does it say "when your master dies"? No, it says "when a sage dies"!' And so there is no reprieve from mourning. In 1286, when the Hapsburg emperor acted on the official view of the Jews as 'serfs of our chamber', and promulgated capricious and punitive policies of taxation, Meir and his family attempted to leave Germany, but he was informed upon and imprisoned, and he died in the dungeon seven years later. In 1303, to avoid the fate of his teacher, Asher left Germany for Spain. About the mourning for a sage, they disagreed; but they agreed, certainly, that unreason was impending and wisdom was escaping.

The Last Englishman

Ian Buruma

RARELY, IF EVER, had so many British grandees gathered under the domed roof of the Hampstead Synagogue as on the occasion of Sir Isaiah Berlin's memorial service on a blustery morning in January 1998. The grandees were mostly of a liberal, secular kind, as Berlin had been himself. But this was an Orthodox synagogue. The men were seated separately from the women. There was Lord Jenkins of Hillhead, and there Lord Annan, looking faintly Russian in a black astrakhan coat, and there Lord Carrington, and Lord Gowrie, whose splendid hair resembled a powdered wig, and, as a touch of peculiar grandeur, Lord Menuhin as 'representative of Her Majesty the Queen'. There they all were, the great and the good, in electric-blue yarmulkes, Garrick Club ties and trilby hats, standing up as the Kaddish was read for a man born in Riga who had always insisted that he was not an Englishman but an Anglophile Jew.

The service was Sir Isaiah's posthumous way of asserting tradition, of paying ceremonial deference to faith and continuity, without which he believed liberalism could not be sustained. Reason is reason, faith is faith, and in Berlin's mind it made no sense to reconcile the two in some wishy-washy attempt at religious reform. My great-grandfather had worshipped at this synagogue. But it was too late for me to feel unselfconscious there. Whatever sense of ancestral continuity I might have felt, it didn't run through the synagogue, let alone an Orthodox synagogue. On this Anglo-Jewish occasion, I felt neither Anglo nor Jewish.

Lord Annan, that consummate English grandee, recalled his long friendship with Isaiah Berlin. He spoke with tears in his eyes and a dramatic vibrato. The delivery owed something to the style of John Gielgud in the 1950s Old Vic. The sentiments were of that same generation. Lord Annan remembered how, at he beginning of the war, the continuity of Britain itself was in the balance, and the State of Israel still a distant dream. It was a moving speech, because what was being mourned was the passing not just of a great man, but of an idea of England, of Berlin's England.

A synagogue was a good place for such an act of mourning. For the memorial service brought to mind that other synagogue, built in 1700 by a Quaker in the City of London. Bevis Marks, the Sephardic temple held together by beams donated by Queen Anne, symbolised the tolerant society that had attracted the French *philosophes*. Berlin's Anglophilia was not so different from Montesquieu's or Voltaire's. It too was centred round an eighteenth-century ideal of reason, tolerance and stylish free-thinking, an ideal linked to a potent myth of British exceptionalism, of a free Britain standing alone against Continental tyranny.

No one was more English and yet less English at the same time. That was how the novelist Chaim Raphael described a fictional character based on Isaiah Berlin. In the four years before he died, I used to meet Berlin for lunch at regular intervals, always at the same Italian restaurant near his Albany flat. He would arrive, a shrunken but always dapper figure in his eighties, wearing a chocolate fedora and a dark grey three-piece suit which looked a little too big for him. Every time, he made a point of studying the menu closely, always to end up ordering – in serviceable Italian – the same simple risotto. He then launched into his famous torrent of talk, while slowly crunching his bread into tiny bits, which he would scoop into his mouth. His voice was a soft basso and he spoke so fast that I couldn't always follow him. I would fix my face in an expression of amusement, hoping it was appropriate. It usually was.

Berlin had cultivated the mannerisms of a pre-war Oxford don: the stuttering delivery, the anecdotes, the relish for gossip, the absolute refusal to be too obviously serious. There was something studied about this, as if he were behaving as an Eastern European Anglophile believed an Oxford don should. But there were twists and angles to his conversation which were idiosyncratic. Not only did he produce gossip from the 1930s, breathing life into the sepia snaps imprinted on his voluminous memory, but he would tell sharp little anecdotes about obscure nineteenth-century German thinkers, preferably anti-Semites, as though they were people he had just observed at some dinner party. Like so many others, I was captivated by Berlin's talk. In a way he was his own greatest creation. Out of his Russian, Jewish and English materials, he had forged his eccentric version of the perfect Englishman.

Like all forms of Anglophilia, Berlin's was an ideal, a flattering portrait in the émigré's mind, gratefully and sometimes complacently received by those it portrayed. But Berlin's England, although idealised, was recognisable in his own lifetime. It was Arthur Koestler's 'Davos for internally bruised veterans of the totalitarian age', the burial ground of utopian dreams and ideologies, the fabled land of common sense, fairness and good manners, the revered country governed by decent gentlemen with grand titles and liberal views, that half-mythical place where liberty, humour and respect for the law always prevailed over the radical search for human perfection. I looked around me, inside the freezing Hampstead Synagogue, at the old men who had come to pay tribute in this oddly Orthodox setting, and wondered what was left of Berlin's England now.

The Chief Rabbi, Dr Jonathan Sacks, spoke about the end of an era. He meant the demise of a particular generation of mostly Jewish immigrants who fled to the island Davos from various forms of State terror. Many, including

Berlin's father Mendel, a prosperous timber merchant in Riga, had admired England as a 'civilised' place long before they made their move. In fact, however, many of them did a great deal to civilise Britain themselves. Publishing, art history, philosophy and the writing of British history were transformed by European immigrants. The idea of England as the uniquely stable society in Europe owes much to the historical works of Sir Lewis Namier, a Jew from Poland whom Isaiah Berlin knew well. Listening to the Chief Rabbi, I wondered who would supply the cosmopolitan oxygen now that Berlin's generation had largely gone. Those known collectively and rather too vaguely as Asians? Or would it be 'Europe', or at least the young Europeans who still come to London for its popular culture and its air of freedom?

Of course the European civilising mission of the British Isles did not start with twentieth-century refugees. It had been going on since Julius Caesar's expedition in 55 BC. The image of England as an island of freedom battling European tyranny goes back at least to Tudor times. But the liberties which Anglophiles (and the English themselves) have praised were often inspired by Greek, Roman, Italian, French and Dutch examples. Britain was neither uniquely democratic nor necessarily always the most democratic European nation. Theodor Fontane, in England during the 1850s, thought, rather wildly: 'No country – its civil liberties notwithstanding – is further removed from democracy than England, and more eager to curry favour with the aristocracy, or mimic its flash and dazzle.' [1] Tocqueville marvelled at the political survival of the aristocracy. And many an Austrian refugee in the 1930s saw the last decades of the British Empire through a rosy haze of Habsburgian nostalgia.

The Empire, however, is gone, and the last vestiges of aristocratic privilege are disappearing. And not because of 'Europe'. Only months before Isaiah Berlin's death, the British government was planning to abolish hereditary peerage in the House of Lords. I don't think Berlin would have minded particularly. He thought of himself as a man of the moderate left. But his idea of England still contained a great deal of the *ancien régime*. He arrived in England as a small boy in 1921, when Britain's domination over its Empire was taken for granted. And although he often said, and no doubt believed, that Britain paid too high a price for its public schools in terms of social inequality, Berlin's England was governed mostly by former public schoolboys.

His England would have been recognised by Hippolyte Taine and baron de Coubertin. It was a country of clubs and coteries, societies and ancient universities, a place where the trappings and rituals of old hierarchies were still observed, not least by Berlin himself, even as he kept the outsider's eye for their absurdities. Like Alexander Herzen, a writer whom he loved above all others,

---

[1] Theodor Fontane, *Ein Sommer in London* (Dessau, 1854), 'Parallelen', 268.

Berlin appreciated the stability of British institutions and even saw merit in a kind of English philistinism, or at least a lack of intellectual recklessness. He once said he was not an imaginative man, but then nor, in his view, were the English, which was why he felt at home with them. Like most Anglophiles, he was also a snob. He shared Theodor Herzl's weakness for liberal goyim with aristocratic manners.

Berlin's England was, however, not just about the United Kingdom. At one of our Italian lunches, the subject of 'Europe' came up, somewhere between an anecdote about Stephen Spender and an exposition on the arrogance of German Jews. He asked me whether I thought a European federation would ever come about. I answered that I rather thought it would. After a rare moment of silence, he said he rather thought so too and immediately launched into a story about Verdi attending a Wagner opera in Paris – and hating it. It was impossible to tell whether the prospect of a federal Europe pleased or alarmed Berlin. I don't think the problem exercised him much one way or the other. He wouldn't live to see it and his England survived in his own mind, if only as an ideal.

BERLIN ON PAPER

You have unquestionably the greatest critical mind of this generation – warmed with a charity that might well be the envy of 99 out of 100 Christians, and enriched with an ordering power so extraordinary that its mere operation is itself a creative act, affecting that which it touches & even changing it – just as scientific experimentation is said to alter, by its own action, the substance it is supposed to illuminate.

George Kennan to Isaiah Berlin, 16 June 1958

I have not the slightest faith in anything I write myself. It is exactly like money – if you make it yourself it seems a forgery. I still belong to a world where what comes from outside, even if it is printed in the newspapers, appears to carry great authority simply by virtue of the fact that it does come from outside, and anything made up by oneself, with however much blood, sweat, tears, seems fake, simply because it is made up by oneself – and the more professional it seems, the closer the fake to reality, the deeper the degree of the forgery. This is no doubt a most neurotic attitude towards one's work, and certainly absurd objectively speaking. Yet I have felt it all my life. Hence total lack of confidence in anything I do.

Isaiah Berlin to Jack Stephenson, 21 January 1963

The Value of the Personal

Joshua Cherniss

> All central beliefs on human matters spring from a personal predicament.
> Isaiah Berlin to Jean Floud, 5 July 1968

I HAVE PROBABLY spent more time in Isaiah Berlin's 'company' than in that of any other thinker; most of my own work has been concerned, directly or indirectly, with his thought and with themes central to it. I began reading his work when young; the elements of his thought – his arguments and beliefs, his basic categories and terms – have shaped my own. It is therefore difficult for me to take stock of his achievement and its legacy. In trying to do so, I shall simultaneously follow two paths, which intertwine, but involve different perspectives. One is autobiographical; the other seeks to assess the qualities of Berlin's work which I think particularly distinctive and valuable. The latter, no less than the former, will be a personal view. This is appropriate: for one of Berlin's great contributions is to enrich our appreciation of the role of the personal in intellectual activity, making the intellect's approach to life more appreciative of the value of personality.

I first came across Berlin's name and, shortly thereafter, his work when I was thirteen. I had been interested in history from a young age. Bookish by nature, as I grew more self-aware and introspective – or, perhaps, more self-involved and narcissistic – my interests shifted increasingly away from war and high politics to the history of intellectuals and the practice and philosophy of history. I was also an Anglophile; so my interests tended to British intellectual life and, for reasons I cannot remember, to Oxford. This led me to Ved Mehta's chronicle of disputes amongst British historians and philosophers in the late 1950s and early 1960s, *Fly and the Fly-Bottle*. Berlin was not one of those vividly evoked therein; but Mehta did recount, at length, Berlin's polemical exchanges with E. H. Carr about determinism and the role of the individual in history. These questions interested, indeed gripped, me; and I found myself siding with Berlin. I was already resistant to claims that history resembled science, either in the regularity and predictability of its subject matter, or in the degree of certainty achievable by its practitioners. This resistance reflected not only scepticism, but moral anxiety, an unwillingness to see individuals devalued, their freedom of action and stature as actors diminished by grand, impersonal theories. Berlin gave voice to this intellectual scepticism and moral aversion: he expressed not

only what I tended to believe, but why I believed it, and why it was so important to me. I decided to look up his work.

Fortunately, the first book of his I picked up was *Personal Impressions*. I doubt
that I would have fully appreciated (or made it through) his more intellectually substantial writings; this, the most accessible, vividly evocative of Berlin's
works, was perfectly calibrated to my intellectual character at that point. Above
all, these portraits exhibited the psychological insight, the feeling for and
appreciation of human character, and the ability vividly to convey it, which
were among Berlin's most characteristic and most attractive gifts. Through his
éloges to the friends and heroes of his own day, I encountered Berlin the person
before I encountered his theories and arguments. I found his personal background, interests, perspective and habits of thought similar to my own – and,
at the same time, representative of what I aspired to. Here was a Russian Jew –
like my own ancestors – who had become the epitome of British academia,
yet continued to feel himself an outsider, and sympathise with the condition
of outsiders and dissenters. (I too often felt an outsider, despite never having
undergone anything like Berlin's experience of uprooting.) Here was a liberal,
committed to freedom, appreciative of variety and individuality, opposed to
paternalism and pressures towards conformity. Much of Berlin's work speaks
on behalf of the individual, and especially the little person – which seemed
at once a very Jewish, a very British, and a very liberal thing to do. This was all
sympathetic. Furthermore, Berlin was a most historically minded thinker; and
one particularly concerned with the Enlightenment and Romanticism – which
at that time also preoccupied me.

Indeed, I had, before I encountered Berlin, fallen under the spell of the *philosophes*. Not that I knew much about them. But I did know that they were critics of religion, custom, received opinion and tribal allegiances – all of which I
had begun to rebel against. Berlin was himself fundamentally an adherent of
the Enlightenment. He nevertheless protested against its scientism, its disdain
for what did not fit into its lucid and impatient philosophy. Since I too chafed
at the more severe strictures of rationalism, and found progressive optimism
unbelievable, Berlin's rejection of these made me question the assumptions I
had begun to accept. Beyond this, his work drew me towards the history of
ideas, and especially of political thought. This determined my intellectual path,
my sense of scholarly identity.

Berlin further provided what was, in some respects, a model of how to practise the history of ideas. Its hallmarks are imaginative richness; ethical engagement; and a focus on and feel for individuals, which draws upon historical
knowledge and psychological perception to understand arguments as reflecting personal visions and preoccupations. These visions, in turn, are revealed as
responses to social, cultural, political and intellectual problems.

Berlin's work in the history of ideas has been much criticised. It is true that few of his interpretations of individual thinkers can be accepted without qualifications, and in some cases deep misgivings. Yet to seek in his work an authoritative, perfectly accurate account of either individual thinkers or the larger history of European thought is to miss the point. Berlin's accounts of the history of ideas are remarkable, and valuable, not for the conclusions they yield, but for the questions they raise. They are excellent works to think about, and think with; they open up vistas for consideration and avenues of enquiry – not just by introducing the reader to obscure figures and neglected moments in the history of ideas, but by presenting significant problems in a captivating way, so that the reader feels their import and urgency. For all their faults, Berlin's historical writings have a value that sounder, less sweeping, less stirring scholarly works lack.

For example, many have objected to Berlin's account of Romanticism. Yet this account raises questions which are worth asking – What, exactly, was Romanticism? How did it affect Western thought? Why did it intoxicate so many, and infuriate and disturb others? What intellectual lacks or needs did it meet? – and provides provocative suggestions for thinking about them. As for individual thinkers, in addition to doing much to revive interest in neglected figures such as Vico, Hamann, Herder and Herzen, Berlin's work cast beneficial light on such familiar thinkers as Machiavelli and Mill. His depiction of Mill helped to blow the Victorian and Utilitarian cobwebs from this venerated thinker, emphasising Mill's passionate commitment to individual variety, self-creation and flourishing – and provoking a reconsideration of how these commitments could be squared with Utilitarianism. And his depiction of Machiavelli as a moralist who recognised the incompatibility between Christian and classical-pagan moralities, and sought to bring his readers to understand this incompatibility (and to embrace the classical-pagan, or civic republican, side of the divide), seems to me broadly correct – and not so distant from some of the distinguished readings of Machiavelli that have enriched our understanding of that thinker in the years since Berlin's essay was published.

Even Berlin's most flawed portrayals contain significant insights. Let us take two of the hardest cases: those of Rousseau and Hegel. Berlin's depictions of these thinkers are not merely deeply hostile, and often over-broad, simplified and even sloppy in their treatment of complicated, ambiguous texts; with a few exceptions they fail to convey the impact of reading these great, difficult, often mesmerising giants. Yet they do capture something about the experience of encountering Rousseau and, particularly, Hegel – or, at least, the experience of a certain kind of reader.

Berlin's depiction of Rousseau is not a fair portrait. Banished to the margins of his account are Rousseau's profound insights into human psychology, and the appalled protest at humiliation so eloquently advanced by this 'Homer of the losers'.[1] But Berlin picks up on those aspects of Rousseau's philosophical temperament that made his work so dangerous to individual liberty: his insistence that liberty must be compatible with virtue, his idea of a single common good – in short, his extremism of thought, his faith in harmony, and his attempt to overcome all obstacles to it. Berlin's Rousseau is a 'rationalist metaphysician', wedded to the ideal of a 'final harmony in which all riddles are solved, all contradictions reconciled'.[2] There is much more to Rousseau than this. But it does play a role in Rousseau's thought, as a spur to his impassioned questionings, and the root of his more dangerous conclusions.

Berlin similarly puts his finger on what disturbs some of us in Hegel's thought. Part of Berlin's aversion to Hegel has to do with the latter's essentially anti-empirical and anti-individualist outlook. But what most antagonised Berlin in Hegel was world-historical ruthlessness, the 'worship of power, of the movement of force for its own sake'. For Berlin, Hegel's philosophy of history was 'a sinister mythology which authorises the indefinite sacrifice of individuals to [...] abstractions';[3] an 'alibi' [4] for ruthlessness and a justification of contempt for those who resist or condemn it: 'Whatever is on the side of victorious reason is just and wise; whatever is on the other side, on the side of the world that is doomed to destruction by the working of the forces of reason, is rightly called foolish, ignorant, subjective, arbitrary, blind.' [5]

Berlin's perception of Hegel can't be fully understood outside its Cold War context.[6] Yet its significance and value transcend these political circumstances. Berlin's pointing to the connection between theories of historical inevitability, moral relativism and political ruthlessness – and the more basic tendency to worship power and bow before success – applies widely. And his contention that the future is always unpredictable undercuts visions celebrating the 'end of history' in global capitalism just as much as Marxist prophecies of the coming of true Communism. His attacks on the political tendency to sacrifice living human beings to distant goals and visions of utopia still have bite – as does his recognition that many calls for 'toughness' and the remorseless, morally unfettered assertion of strength are often justifications for simple cruelty, or masks for inner moral bankruptcy or confusion.

Berlin's attacks on these tendencies reflected a commitment to moral

---

[1] Judith N. Shklar, 'Jean-Jacques Rousseau and Equality', in her *Political Thought and Political Thinkers*, ed. Stanley Hoffmann (Chicago, 1998), 290.
[2] L 213.
[3] FIB 95, 94.
[4] L 154, 164.
[5] L 114.
[6] See 'Democracy, Communism and the Individual', in the IBVL at http://berlin.wolf. ox.ac.uk/lists/nachlass/demcomind.pdf.

individualism and egalitarianism, a belief in the equal and primary moral worth of individual human beings. This was the basis of Berlin's rejection of theories which subordinated individual judgement and aspirations to abstractions, or disregarded them in their name:

> [to the armed prophet] the millions slaughtered in wars or revolutions [...] are the price men must pay for the felicity of future generations. If your desire to save mankind is serious, you must harden your heart, and not reckon the cost. [...] The one thing that we may be sure of is the reality of the sacrifice, the dying and the dead. But the ideal for the sake of which they die remains unrealised. The eggs are broken, and the habit of breaking them grows, but the omelette remains invisible. Sacrifices for short-term goals, coercion, if men's plight is desperate enough and truly requires such measures, may be justified. But holocausts for the sake of distant goals, that is a cruel mockery of all that men hold dear, now and at all times.[1]

While Berlin's work rebukes ruthlessness and hard-heartedness, it is also a warning against the temptation of self-righteousness and the blinding power of beautiful ideals. Berlin attacked the idea of perfection itself, and the longing for harmony, certainty and security.[2] Indeed, he wrote that 'the entire burden' and unifying theme of his essays was 'distrust of all claims to the possession of incorrigible knowledge about issues of fact or principle in any sphere of human behaviour'.[3] This involved both scepticism, and opposition to the morally deleterious consequences of dogmatism: 'To force people into the neat uniforms demanded by dogmatically believed-in schemes is almost always the road to inhumanity.' Dogmatism was culpably inhumane not only when it led to acts of violence, but also in causing the atrophy of human understanding – the ability to appreciate human existence, and human beings themselves: 'those who rest on [...] comfortable beds of dogma are victims of self-induced myopia, blinkers which may make for contentment, but not for understanding of what it is to be human'.[4] Berlin provided an eloquent, far-reaching restatement of the liberal tradition's commitment to tolerance, by focusing on the errors and evils of intolerance, which have rarely been described better:

> Few things have done more harm than the belief on the part of individuals or groups [...] that he or she or they are in *sole* possession of the truth [...] – & that those who differ from them are not merely mistaken, but wicked

[1] CTH 16.
[2] See e.g. CTH 13, 18.
[3] RT2 x.
[4] CTH 19, 14.

or mad: & need restraining or suppressing. It is a terrible and dangerous arrogance to believe that you alone are right: have a magical eye which sees *the* truth: & that others cannot be right if they disagree. This makes one certain that there is *one* goal & one only [...], & that it is worth any amount of suffering (particularly on the part of other people) if only the goal is attained [...][1]

This brings us to Berlin's pluralism. Pluralism was central to Berlin's outlook and his work; he himself regarded it as perhaps his most important insight. It has rightly been extensively discussed by others; I will say little about it here. On my first encounter with it, Berlin's pluralism struck me as a wholly convincing account of human moral experience. I have been some sort of pluralist ever since (even as I, like many others, have worried over pluralism's implications, and the many questions about moral experience and thought that Berlin failed to ask or answer).

Pluralism powerfully reinforces Berlin's plea for the value of variety. Most of us (including many liberals committed to toleration in principle) tend toward intolerance, in part because we tend to discount the value of ideals, virtues and ways of life which differ greatly from our own. Berlin points out what a dismal world it would be if everyone were like us, if there were no serious disagreement about matters of value: such a world would be one 'in which the inner life of man, the moral and spiritual and aesthetic imagination, no longer speaks at all.'[2] Perfection, harmony, certainty, security were all to be disavowed as goals not only because they were impossible – or because the pursuit of these goals often led to bloodshed – but because, even if they *could* be achieved, they would pose dangers to the individual liberty and plurality that made human life human. Such a condition would not be true 'perfection'; it would be – like most theoretical visions of perfection – the imposition of one person's or group's one-sided, incomplete vision of perfection on others.

One of the foremost lessons of Berlin's work is the importance of modesty. Such modesty conduces to political moderation. It need not promote conservatism – a resistance to change as such – nor (immoderate) pessimism, nor passivity. Berlin did not intend his writings to foster any of these things. Rather, he called his readers to modest, difficult and necessary action: 'The first public obligation is to avoid extremes of suffering. [...] promoting and preserving an uneasy equilibrium, which is constantly threatened and in constant need of repair – that alone [...] is the precondition for decent societies and morally acceptable behaviour.'[3]

[1] L 345.
[2] CTH 15.
[3] CTH 17, 19.

Berlin's work represents an attempt to reconcile the impulses of scepticism and moral idealism. His rejection of utopia and perfection, and of ruthlessness and moral relativism, did not make him prey to cynicism, or quietism, or a puristic refusal to engage in the pragmatic, compromising, often dirty business of political action. All of these would have been opposed to the moral idealism, clear-eyed and hard-headed (but not hard-hearted) realism, and sense of the tragic inescapability of loss, which together characterised his outlook.

When I first encountered it, I was both sympathetic and resistant to Berlin's counsel that we must accept limitation and loss. I was a dreamy and cautious child, and became an idealistic but sceptical adolescent; my tendency toward pessimism did not make me immune to high hopes and lofty aspirations, or invulnerable to disappointment. I have always longed for security and certainty, and lamented their absence; like all people, I find loss – and the idea that loss is inescapable – painful. Berlin's message was not easy to accept fully. But coming to terms with it was liberating and heartening.

Despite these difficulties, I was receptive to the outlook embodied in Berlin's work. This was a matter partly of personal temperament, partly of inheritance. My political outlook owes a great deal to my parents. Berlin's emphasis on limitation, the dangers of abstract theory, the importance of attending to particulars, and his consequent advocacy of a pragmatic, flexible approach to political and social problems (and to the unanticipated further problems likely to grow out of the solutions to the initial problems)[1] was also characteristic of my father's outlook. This, in turn, reflected the influence of his mentor, the psychologist Seymour Sarason – who had, when he taught my father in the early 1970s, been much influenced by Berlin, whom he admired and urged my father to read. I was unaware of all of this at the time; but Berlin was as much a background, indirect influence in my formation as a discovery of my own.

In addition (and related) to his embrace of variety and his opposition to intolerance and dogmatism, Berlin's commitment to liberty entailed opposition to oppression and a particular sympathy for individuals who were marginal, unpopular and vulnerable. In this, he harked back to earlier liberals such as Mill. But his own version of liberalism was more resolutely 'negative' than those of many liberal writers preceding him (if less so than, say, that of his near-contemporary Judith Shklar).

Part of this 'negativity' centred on Berlin's account of liberty as primarily a matter of individuals being *protected* from interference. Yet he did not neglect liberty's positive value, which he saw as deriving from the importance of choice and selfhood – living a life that is one's own, that expresses and suits one's self.

---

[1] See e.g. CTH 14: 'We cannot legislate for the unknown consequences of consequences of consequences.'

As for the experience of liberty, Berlin has always seemed to me to express it as well as anyone:

> There can be no liberty where obedience to the pattern is the only true self-expression, where what you call liberty is not the possibility of acting within some kind of vacuum, however small, which is left for your own personal choice, in which you are not interfered with by others. [...] The essence of liberty has always lain in the ability to choose as you wish to choose, because you wish so to choose, uncoerced, unbullied, not swallowed up in some vast system; and in the right to resist, to be unpopular, to stand up for your convictions merely because they are your convictions. That is true freedom, and without it there is neither freedom of any kind, nor even the illusion of it.[1]

This emphasis on freedom as the ability to make one's own choices, and on coercion and bullying as the antitheses of freedom, are related to Berlin's deep aversion to paternalism. This, too, was an element in Berlin's work that appealed to me, and of which I have become increasingly aware and appreciative over time. Paternalism, Berlin explained, was premised on the belief that 'Human beings are children. We must first herd them together, create certain institutions, make them obey orders.' Such an attitude could be honourable and benevolent; but 'it always leads to bad consequences in the end'.[2] His opposition to paternalism was connected to his more general warning against subjugating individuals to lofty visions. But it went beyond this: paternalism was always dangerous, and an affront to human dignity, even when it aimed at relatively mild, and unquestionably positive, goals, and was not cruel or violent. It was wrong because it was arrogant, because it was humiliating, because it was infantilising, because it failed to recognise the liberal principle that 'problems, social and personal, must be decided ideally by each person asking himself, in accordance with his own lights, what he should do and how he should live and how he should behave to his fellows'.[3]

Paternalism was one, particularly insidious, motive for 'the deliberate act of tampering with human beings so as to make them behave in a way which, if they knew what they were doing, or what its consequences were likely to be, would make them recoil with horror and disgust'. Berlin passionately protested against such

> use of human beings as mere means – the doctoring of them until they are made to do what they do, not for the sake of the purposes which are their

---

[1] FIB 103–4.

[2] 'Conversations for Tomorrow', BBC Television, 25 April 1964, transcript in IBVL at http://berlin.wolf.ox.ac.uk/lists/nachlass/conversa.pdf, 14.

[3] op. cit. (205 above, note 6), 4.

purposes, [...] but for reasons which only we, the manipulators, who freely twist them for our purposes, can understand. What horrifies one about Soviet or Nazi practice is not merely the suffering and the cruelty [...]; what turns one inside out, and is indescribable, is the spectacle of one set of persons who so tamper and 'get at' others that the others do their will without knowing what they are doing; and in this lose their status as free human beings, indeed as human beings at all.[1]

The evil of manipulation was not (merely) a matter of human suffering: as Berlin acknowledged, such deception often diminished the suffering of the victims, who did not know their fates. Rather, it had to do with the destruction of human personality by 'creating unequal moral terms between the gaoler and the victim, whereby the gaoler knows what he is doing, and why, and plays upon the victim, i.e. treats him as a mere object and not as a subject whose motives, views, intentions have any intrinsic weight whatever'. This deprived the victims of independence, and the distinctively human capacity for choice; and with the desire for choice broken, 'what men do thereby loses all moral value, and actions lose all significance (in terms of good and evil) in their own eyes; that is what is meant by destroying people's self-respect, by turning them [...] into rags'.[2]

Berlin's opposition to paternalism and manipulation was related to another aspect of his outlook that appealed to me. This was his special feeling for outsiders, dissenters, eccentrics (few thinkers have used the term 'eccentricity' so often and so positively), to 'the toad beneath the harrow',[3] those who are crushed in the process of progress and enlightenment, even where these dislocations are truly improvements, justified and indeed demanded by humanitarianism. It is sometimes necessary to disregard, to overcome, such people, for the greater good of more numerous others. But one must never forget or deafen oneself to the cries of those who suffer in such cases. Humanitarian reforms undermine themselves and betray the principles by which they are justified when they ignore human suffering, when they deny the genuine losses involved in justified action, when they (selectively) cut themselves off from human

---

[1] L 337, 339.

[2] L 339–40. This phrase about turning people into rags echoes the indelible scene in Primo Levi's *If This Is a Man* (1958), in which Levi describes a *Kapo* [a prisoner acting as an overseer in a concentration camp] wiping his hand on Levi's shoulder, using Levi as a rag to clean his hand: 'on the basis of this action, I judge him [...] and the innumerable others like him, big and small, in Auschwitz and everywhere'. Primo Levi, *Survival in Auschwitz* [a retitled edition of *If This Is a Man*], trans. Stuart Woolf (New York, 1996), 107–8.

[3] TCE 350. [The epigraph to Rudyard Kipling's poem 'Pagett, M.P.', in *Departmental Ditties and Other Verses* (Calcutta, 1886), 43, begins 'The Toad beneath the Harrow knows / Exactly where each tooth-point goes.' Ed.]

feeling, when they fail to respect the aspirations and dignity of those they frustrate.

My sympathy with Berlin on this point no doubt owes much to the mixture of progressivist rationalism and romantic nostalgia in my make-up. It is also related to my own sense of being an outsider – a sense that has never fully left me. I have never been a toad beneath a harrow; but I can readily imagine being one. Those who lack this sense (and are immune to acquiring it) will remain deaf to the most poignant, moving music in Berlin's prose; and therefore, perhaps, also to the attractions of his thought.

This consciousness of outsiderhood is, I suspect, related to the Jewishness that I share with Berlin (though growing up Jewish must have been far easier for me than it was in the world of Berlin's childhood – or indeed adulthood). When I discovered Berlin's work I was rebelling against the Jewish religion, and my own Jewish upbringing and identity. This prompted, or was prompted by, a more general rejection of communal solidarity – or, as I thought of it then (and still do, sometimes), tribalism. Yet (like many Jews) I still felt a deep residual attachment to my roots; and some appreciation of the importance of rooted-ness to human beings. In the years-long process of trying to sort all this out, Berlin was of immense help. He provided an example of how to be rational, liberal, assimilated, (more or less) at peace with oneself and one's surround-ings – but still Jewish; and of how to acknowledge and give voice to one's own ambivalence about Jewishness: one's dislike of and pain at certain aspects of Jewish culture, the Jewish community, Jewish experience, as well as one's (not wholly rational) affection for all of these. He also provided a model of how to regard Jews and Jewishness: not as a creed or nation or morality or even cul-ture, but as a family – and as exasperating and loved and inescapable as one's family.[1]

I am still, I think, more of an individualist and cosmopolitan, less comfort-able with nationalism and communitarianism, than Berlin was. Yet I also took from Berlin the belief that the worth of community lies solely in its value to individuals. Berlin is sometimes identified as some sort of communitarian or nationalist. This contradicts the moral individualism and wariness of 'holism' clearly set out in his early work, and never abandoned or disavowed thereafter. Berlin held that the world was ultimately made up of 'things and persons'. States and societies – and communities generally – were not things or persons, but ways in which things and persons came to be arranged; the components are separate from the wholes, which exist, ultimately, only by their action and for their sakes. The merit of such supra-personal entities depends on how well they serve the individuals who make them up, and who give these entities whatever

[1] On this see Avishai Margalit, 'The Philosopher of Sympathy: Isaiah Berlin and the Fate of Humanism', *New Republic*, 20 February 1995, 31–7.

value they may have.[1] It is important for individuals to be able to define their own identities – and to have conditions of choice in which to do so. These conditions include the resources of community, as well as the ability to escape and overcome them. The ties of language, religion and nation may be, in Stephen Daedalus's term, 'nets' through which one must fly in order to achieve full self-hood. But they are also nets which might save one if, like the son of Daedalus, one flies too high. Community, family, belonging are valuable if they conduce to individuals' ability to live as they choose, to be and do what they decide to be and do; to the extent that they impede this, they should be questioned – and in some cases rejected, abandoned and fought.

Concerning nationalism, Berlin teaches us – particularly those liberals who are inclined to agree with him on matters of basic political principle – to understand the aspirations and experiences of those with whom we disagree. The importance of such empathy – and the imaginative insight which it requires – was a central thread connecting Berlin's political and moral thought, his writings on the human sciences, and his practice of the history of ideas. As a historian, Berlin teaches us to read and interpret the works of past thinkers sympathetically (as opposed to 'charitably' – a term which betrays the assumption that the interpreter is clearer about the truth than the author being interpreted, who requires indulgence and help). As a political theorist, he insists on the importance of listening to others – and (where it does not involve their harming others) allowing them to go their own way, even if this means going 'to the dogs'.[2] In his application of empathetic understanding to politics as well as to the human sciences, Berlin blended empiricism and epistemological modesty with 'Kantian humanism' and pluralism. This combination promoted a liberalism of modesty, best summed up in his own words:

> All we can know for certain is what men actually want. Let us at least have the courage of our admitted ignorance, of our doubts and uncertainties. At least we can try to discover what others [...] require, by taking off the spectacles of tradition, prejudice, dogma, and making it possible for ourselves to know men as they truly are, by listening to them carefully and sympathetically, and understanding them and their lives and their needs, one by one individually. Let us at least try to provide them with what they ask for, and leave them as free as possible.[3]

This emphasis on the need to listen to others, to study their beliefs and situations, reminds us that a capacity for imaginative empathy is not in itself enough. It must be grounded in and disciplined by knowledge: 'intuitive certainty is no

---

[1] FIB 95; cf. PIRA 203–7.
[2] Letter to Alan Dudley received 17 March 1948, L2 45.
[3] RT2 296.

substitute for carefully tested empirical knowledge based on observation and experiment and free discussion between men'. Knowledge 'opens the windows of the mind (and soul) and makes people wiser, nicer, & more civilized'.[1] But it was not only as a means for promoting other valuable ends that Berlin praised knowledge. He championed 'disinterested curiosity' (or even 'idle curiosity') against more utilitarian, socially conscious understandings of knowledge's value.[2] However, knowledge did have political significance. Because enlarged knowledge combined with deeper, critical contemplation and the play of imagination tended to shake up settled opinions and orthodoxies, they were, if not necessarily conducive to liberalism, at least antithetical to tyranny.

The knowledge with which Berlin was most concerned was knowledge of the particular outlooks, characters and actions of individuals. His work as a historian of ideas was deeply 'personal', both in the sense that it was indelibly imprinted with his own personal concerns, and in its engagement with the personalities and personal visions of past thinkers. So, too, Berlin's work as a theorist of history, ethics and politics was also 'personal' in a double sense: directed by personal moral commitments, and dedicated to vindicating the importance and value of individual character, consciousness and agency. He was always ready to remind his interlocutors that intellectual convictions spring from personal predicaments. In place of the radical motto that the personal is political, Berlin suggested that the political is, in part and among other things, personal, wrapped up with questions of what one should, as an individual, be and do – and, at best, guided by a concern for the consequences of political action for individual lives.

This may seem trite. Yet Berlin detected a cold impersonality in much social science, and a deep hostility to the claims of personal experience and consciousness in the works of philosophers such as Hegel (and his many followers). Berlin believed that he and his contemporaries had witnessed a 'degradation of human personality',[3] which was the consequence of a devaluation of human persons. Every aspect of his work reflected resistance to this. All of this affected my own outlook significantly.

Berlin's impact on me was 'personal' in a further sense. I was influenced not only by his ideas, but by his personality, as reflected in his work, and as described by those who knew him. I devoured not only Berlin's writings, but personal reminiscences about him.

Was there any intellectual value in this? I think there was some; there was certainly personal value. Berlin's generosity and sensitivity to others, his liveliness and enthusiasm, his benevolence, his blend of scepticism, irony, wit,

[1] L 346, 345.
[2] L 81, 92.
[3] CTH 205.

light-heartedness and moral seriousness, his range of curiosity and sympathy were an inspiration – a model of how humane intellectual life could be, and how beneficial it could be to human existence.

Although much of Berlin's thought is critical, his personality was life-affirming – and this personality comes across in his writings. The very combination of insistence on loss and tragedy, and celebration of human diversity, liberty and possibility, teaches us how to accept life; in fact, how to live.[1] Berlin once remarked that men could be divided into those who are in favour of life and those who are against it. He was unquestionably of the former camp, and devoted much of his work to attacking the assumptions and intellectual habits (the hatred of disorder and uncertainty, the fastidious rejection of that which falls short of the ideal, the stifling of spontaneous human sympathy in the name of doctrine) that make for opposition to life. Yet he also, characteristically, recognised that there were 'sensitive and wise and penetrating people' among those who were 'against life':[2] and he sought to learn from them, too.

I recognise such life-denying fastidiousness in myself. And Berlin's work and example acted on me as a tonic, working against the more wintry elements in my nature – anxiety and timidity, priggishness, melancholia – on behalf of other, more life-affirming, impulses. Yet I also responded to Berlin because I detected, in his own outlook, a more sombre and anxious disposition (indeed, how could a thoughtful, intellectually serious, morally sensitive person living in the twentieth century – particularly if he were a Russian Jew – fail to be sombre and anxious?).

There are, of course, limitations to what we should admire and emulate in Berlin. At crucial places his work suffers from conceptual confusion, or ducks difficult issues. His scholarship was often based on secondary sources which were sometimes outdated (even in his own day), biased or exaggerated. Despite his counsels of tolerance, he could be unfair to views of which he was critical or which he associated with historical evils. On a more biographical level he was sometimes a bit too comfortable with the 'Establishment' of his own day. We should aim for greater rigour, a more sharply critical and empirically grounded approach to social questions, and greater political courage than Berlin was sometimes able to muster. But in doing so – provided that we remain humble, moderate, generous, cautious, imaginative and humane – we will be acting very much within the spirit of his work and the values to which he was devoted, even if he (like all of us) imperfectly fulfilled them.

---

[1] This is reflected in the testaments to his impact on them provided by Berlin's friends. Thus, Stuart Hampshire called Berlin 'life-creating', while Noel Annan declared that Berlin had taught him 'to think more clearly, to feel more deeply, to hope, and to put my trust in life' (18, 15 above).

[2] FIB 154.

I conclude with a return to autobiography. Within a year or so of discovering Berlin's work, I wrote him a juvenile fan-letter, to which he kindly replied. He concluded his letter by predicting 'an intellectually honourable and successful career' for me. These were intoxicating words indeed. And the notion of intellectual honour has been a watchword, an aspiration, to which I have tried to adhere ever since. In doing so, I have continued to be guided by Berlin's example, with its reminder that intellectual honour is a matter not only of integrity, honesty and rigour (vital though these are); but also of intellectual humility, moral decency and human feeling.

A Berlinian Education

George Crowder

I NEVER MET Isaiah Berlin. I might have done so when I was a graduate student at Oxford in the 1980s, but meeting Berlin never occurred to me then as either possible or especially desirable. At that time I regarded him as a rather distant critical target belonging to an earlier generation of political theorists whose work had been largely superseded. Later, when Berlin's thought became a central interest for me, I was no longer living in Britain and he seemed remote geographically. Eventually it was too late. In 1997 I finally wrote to see if I could get an interview, only to receive a reply from Berlin's secretary that Isaiah Berlin had died soon after I sent my letter. Unkind colleagues suggested that the prospect of seeing me had been too much for him. At any rate, a personal meeting was not to be.

Never having spoken to Berlin face to face is something I greatly regret. Everyone who knew him reports what a remarkable person he was, and especially what a mesmerising conversationalist. One of the favourite party pieces of many of his former students and colleagues is an impersonation of the characteristic Berlinian monologue, which is like a Joycean stream of consciousness with history of ideas content delivered by someone who has to race off to catch a bus. These performances are often very funny and always affectionate.

But not having been subjected to the famous charm may have its compensations. Critics of those who defend Berlin's ideas, or of those who are inspired by them, sometimes complain that the name of the great man is invoked as if it were an argument in itself: 'Berlin agrees, therefore it must be so.' I think that this kind of criticism is often exaggerated, but also that there's sometimes an element of truth in it. The reason, I suspect, has something to do with the extraordinary personal loyalty that Berlin seems to have inspired in so many of his students and friends. Berlin does appear to have cast a spell on people, making it hard for them to take him to task even when they want to. Those who have not been under the personal spell may be better placed to be independent critics.

In my case, at any rate, engagement with Berlin has been with the work rather than the man – although the point should be acknowledged that so much of his personality comes through the work that the two can't be separated entirely. The rest of what I have to say here will consist of a narrative of my experience of encountering, enjoying and struggling with Berlin's ideas, and a general, rather impressionistic assessment of his political thought as a whole.

I can make no strong claim for why anyone other than myself should find this interesting, except to say that I have studied Berlin's thought for many years, and perhaps my experience with it can help to bring out some of its attractions and difficulties.

I don't remember when I first read Berlin. It may have been as early as the late 1970s, when I first studied philosophy and political theory. I do remember beginning to think seriously about 'Two Concepts of Liberty' in the mid-1980s, when I was a DPhil candidate at University College, Oxford. I was studying the anarchist thinkers of the nineteenth century. My argument was that writers like Godwin, Proudhon, Bakunin and Kropotkin constituted a more coherent tradition of thought, and that their arguments, when placed in context, made more sense, than was generally supposed. The key, I believed, was their understanding of freedom.[1]

To explore this, I went to the classic starting point for analysing freedom – namely, Berlin's account of the negative–positive distinction in 'Two Concepts'. In these terms, it might be supposed that the anarchists, with their emphasis on rejecting the State and other sources of authority, held a negative conception of freedom: absence of coercion. However, what I usually found in the texts were variations on the positive idea of freedom as self-mastery: self-direction in accordance with the will of the 'true' or authentic part of the personality.

One curious thing about this discovery was that it didn't seem to fit with Berlin's central thesis in 'Two Concepts', which tends to associate positive liberty with political authoritarianism. If Berlin was right about the tendency of positive liberty to slide into 'forcing to be free' arguments, then how could the anarchists be libertarians?

A possible response to this apparent conflict is to argue that Berlin's thesis is wrong, or at least overstated – that he's too hostile to positive liberty overall. This was my own conclusion in the 1980s, and it still seems to me to be basically right, though it needs qualification. I have a stronger sense now of the extent to which Berlin actually accepts the positive idea as a genuine, and genuinely valuable, kind of freedom (and also of the extent to which he concedes that the negative idea can also be abused).

But it remains true that Berlin's emphasis in 'Two Concepts' is on the greater corruptibility of positive compared with negative liberty, a difference he attributes to the core notion of the true or authentic self that is essential to, and distinctive of, all forms of the positive idea. When the authentic self is distinguished from people's 'actual will and wishes', the door is opened to the oppression of real people in the name of ideals that are supposed to express their better selves. Since this idea of a divided self is definitive of the whole

---

[1] I later published a revised version of this thesis as *Classical Anarchism: The Political Thought of Godwin, Proudhon, Bakunin and Kropotkin* (Oxford, 1991).

family of positive conceptions of freedom, that whole family is infected by its potential for abuse. The infection may be dormant in some cases, but it's always there. Hence Berlin's broad preference for negative liberty as the safer ideal in the context of politics.

The trouble with this view, it still seems to me, is that it doesn't do justice to the importance of positive liberty from a liberal point of view. Not all forms of the positive idea are equally vulnerable to the slippery slope that Berlin alleges. Modern conceptions of individual autonomy as involving independent thought and action through personal critical reflection – conceptions of freedom found in such liberal thinkers as J. S. Mill and Joseph Raz – seem to me to be an essential part of an adequate liberal vision of politics. Although Berlin half-recognises this point in some passages, I don't think it emerges clearly enough from his writing.[1]

In the 1990s there was a significant change of focus in the study of Berlin's work: away from the analysis of freedom towards the opposition between pluralism and monism in morality. It may be no accident that this shift coincided with the end of the Cold War, which had provided much of the backdrop for the debate over negative and positive liberty, and the emergence of a rather more complicated, not to say confused, political world. In this emergent world, initial hubristic claims about 'the end of history' and the inauguration of a 'new world order' soon gave way to a fresh set of divisions and conflicts, often generated by particular national and cultural loyalties. In this context, Berlin's ideas about freedom suddenly seemed less urgent than his work on nationalism, on the 'recognition' of cultural belonging, and on value pluralism.

In the case of pluralism in particular, it was the work of John Gray that, for me and I suspect many others, really opened up the hitherto unrealised potential of Berlin's writing.[2] It seems odd in retrospect, but while people wrangled for thirty years over the negative–positive issues, virtually no notice was taken of the last section of 'Two Concepts', 'The One and the Many', in which the pluralism–monism distinction was broached and some political inferences drawn. Gray deserves much of the credit for raising the deep questions that Berlin's pluralism invites but, strangely, never received before.

Gray's view was that Berlin's notion of value pluralism – the multiplicity and incommensurability of fundamental human values – ought to be accepted as a true account of the nature of morality, but that the political implications of pluralism were more radical, in particular far less favourable to liberalism, than Berlin seemed to believe. If values are plural and incommensurable, then it's

---

[1] For a more detailed assessment of Berlin's treatment of freedom, see my *Isaiah Berlin: Liberty and Pluralism* (Cambridge, 2004), chapter 4.

[2] See, e.g., Gray's books *Liberalisms: Essays in Political Philosophy* (London, 1989); *Post-Liberalism: Studies in Political Thought* (London, 1993); *Isaiah Berlin* (London, 1995).

not clear how we should, or can, choose among them when they conflict – that much Berlin had said. But if that's so, Gray added, then it's unclear why, in the political context, we should privilege those values that are characteristic of liberalism – equality, toleration and Berlin's negative liberty – rather than those values stressed by other ideologies – socialist solidarity, conservative tradition and so forth. Gray was happy to conclude that, indeed, canonical liberal theorists had no convincing reason to privilege liberal values, consistently with pluralism, at any rate universally. Further, no such reasons could be produced.

My first response to Gray's thesis was one of 'shock and awe', as the Pentagon strategists would say. Surely he couldn't be right? I went back to 'Two Concepts' and other liberal-pluralist texts to look for myself. To my surprise, I found myself agreeing with Gray: no one, Berlin included, had produced a convincing argument for liberal values in the face of pluralism. A common pattern of reasoning moved from pluralism to some intermediate value that was said to follow from pluralism, and then to a broader liberal order in which the value was emphasised. A persistent problem with this sequence, it seemed to me, was that in each case the privileging of the intermediate value flew in the face of the pluralist injunction against overriding values. From this I concluded, with Gray, that no existing justification of liberalism was compatible with pluralism, and (more tentatively) that no such justification *could* succeed. Among other things, this meant that there was a huge gap in Berlin's thought between its liberal and pluralist components.

When my article along these lines was accepted, I was astonished and delighted to hear that Berlin and Bernard Williams wanted to reply to it.[1] The general tone of their response was that of the inhabitants of Olympus addressing a donkey grazing in the foothills. However, they made the good point that a distinction should be made between ranking incommensurables in the abstract and ranking incommensurables in particular cases. While there is no good reason to rank liberty ahead of equality (or vice versa) in the abstract (i.e. in every case), there may be good reason to rank one value ahead of the other in a particular case. This reopened the door to rational choice under pluralism, and got me thinking again. If some rankings could be rationally justified under pluralism, then might a reasoned case for liberalism still be possible?

Searching for such a case, I felt that the contextualism proposed by Berlin and Williams gets us so far but no further. Is liberalism to be justified in some cases but not others? Gray accepted this line readily, since it meant that the most that could be legitimately claimed for liberalism was that there may be

---

[1] See my 'Pluralism and Liberalism', *Political Studies* 42 (1994), 293–305, and Berlin and Williams, 'Pluralism and Liberalism: A Reply', ibid. 306–9). Henry Hardy has since told me that the response was the work more of Williams than of Berlin. But it seems to me that, to adapt Colin Powell's phrase, 'If you sign it, you own it.'

reason to foreground liberal goods within some particular, appropriate cultural context where such goods were accepted. This position fell, deliberately for Gray, far short of the traditionally universalist ambitions of liberalism – and presumably of the Cold War liberalism of Berlin, for whom negative liberty was an ideal that was appropriate not only for those who already possessed it but also for the subject peoples of the Soviet Empire.

But might there be some other line of argument, still compatible with pluralism, that would ground a wider case? It occurred to me that Berlin himself provides a clue in 'Two Concepts'. There he argues briefly that the concept of pluralism implies the necessity of making choices among conflicting values, hence the value of freedom of choice – presumably best promoted by a liberal order in which negative liberty is emphasised. As it stands, this argument doesn't work, because it slides too quickly from the necessity of choice to the value of the freedom to choose. But I was struck by the general strategy Berlin employed, arguing for value commitments on the basis of the concept of pluralism itself. It seemed to me that if such a link could be carried through, then we would have a case for liberalism that was more than merely contingent on pre-existing cultural commitments. Can such a case be made out? I would say yes, but I've developed my view about this elsewhere, and won't rehearse it here.[1]

I want now to say a few words about Berlin's overall status as a political philosopher. I believe that Berlin is a very important political thinker. But how important? In this connection a striking claim is made by Jerry Cohen, the distinguished Marxist theorist and Berlin's former student, who couples Berlin with John Rawls as 'the most celebrated twentieth-century Anglophone political philosophers'.[2] While Rawls showed the way in the field of justice, Berlin did the same for the idea of freedom. Is this an accurate assessment? Most political theorists would say that Rawls's pre-eminence is secure, but many would doubt that the same can be said for Berlin.

Rawls possessed an immense moral authority that was in part personal, and an unrivalled capacity for original philosophical thought sustained over decades. It's a commonplace to say that he set most of the agenda for Anglo-American political theory from the 1970s onwards. Moreover, he remained a leading voice in the conversation he initiated, tirelessly extending and revising, sometimes changing direction significantly, to the very end of his life.

Some of these points could be made on behalf of Berlin too, but not all. Like Rawls, he possessed great moral gravitas, although nicely leavened by his

---

[1] See my *Liberalism and Value Pluralism* (London and New York, 2002) and *Isaiah Berlin* (218 above, note 1).

[2] G. A. Cohen, 'Freedom and Money', http://www.utdt.edu/Upload/_11563475311 4776100.pdf (accessed 28 September 2008), 6, quoted in my *Isaiah Berlin* (218 above, note 1), 189.

entertaining personal style. Like Rawls, he was an original thinker, his originality consisting mainly in his political deployment of the negative–positive distinction and, especially, his bringing to public prominence of the idea of pluralism. Unlike Rawls, however, he never published the sustained, book-length
statement that his ideas required; his reputation continues to rest mainly on
'Two Concepts'. He never really pursued and developed the major insights into
pluralism that were tantalisingly outlined in that essay.

It would not be too much to say that Berlin made very little *philosophical*
progress after 'Two Concepts'. In the 1960s and 1970s his principal work consisted of discussing the thinkers of the Counter-Enlightenment, especially Vico
and Herder, and the Romantics.[1] The result was some marvellous accounts of
these thinkers' world-views, accounts that contained further hints of the pluralist theme but little more about the precise nature of pluralism or its implications for Berlin's own political commitments. In his last essays Berlin generally
summarises his previous work without adding much, or even showing much
appreciation of the central tension between his pluralism and his liberalism. In
'The Pursuit of the Ideal', for example, he raises the question of how reasoned
choice is possible under pluralism, but does little to answer it. He throws out
a number of suggestions in quick succession, all pertinent and interesting, but
none developed or interrogated.[2]

Another entry that I think must be made on the negative side of the ledger is
Berlin's extraordinary lack of sustained critical attention to two major concerns
of contemporary political theory, namely distributive justice and multicultural-
ism. These topics are respectively addressed by Rawls's major books, *A Theory of
Justice* and *Political Liberalism*. Berlin, by contrast, although expressing private
dismay at the assault on the Welfare State by the Thatcher government, said
and wrote nothing in public.[3] Nor did he have much to say about minority
cultural rights, despite having promoted the idea of cultural recognition that
animates so much of the debate concerning these rights. Finally, it's revealing
that while Rawls was evidently influenced by Berlin, Berlin seemed to know
little of Rawls's work and to regard what little he knew of it with ill-informed
scepticism.[4]

And yet, Berlin's thought is in important respects no less persuasive and fruitful than that of Rawls. Fundamental to Rawls's view is his notion of 'reasonable
pluralism', the idea that in modern societies there is widespread and reasonable

---

[1] See the works collected in TCE; and RR.
[2] 'The Pursuit of the Ideal', in CTH.
[3] Berlin's private remarks about Thatcherism are reported by Cohen, 'Freedom and
Money' (220 above, note 2).
[4] Compare Rawls, *Political Liberalism* (New York, 1993), 57, with Berlin's comments on
Rawls in 'Isaiah Berlin in Conversation with Steven Lukes' (30 above, note 3), 112–15.

disagreement over the nature of the human good. Important as this is, Berlin's concept of value pluralism arguably captures something deeper: the thought that it is not only our beliefs about the good but also goods themselves that are multiple, conflicting and distinct. This stronger sense of pluralism is gaining ground in the field of distributive justice, for example, where the increasingly influential 'human capabilities' theorists (such as Amartya Sen and Martha Nussbaum) are closer to Berlin in their understanding of the multiplicity and distinctness of human goods than they are to Rawls's more generic 'resource'-based approach.[1] On the issue of the justificatory foundations of liberalism, Rawls claims that liberal commitments rest on a neutral or purely 'political' settlement. Here it can be argued that Berlinian pluralists are better placed to come clean about the extent to which liberalism is really based on a general (although not overriding) ranking of values that expresses a 'comprehensive' account of the human good. The jury is still out on these debates, but ideas and arguments of a Berlinian stripe may yet prove more resilient than those of Rawls (where they differ) in the long run.

Berlin has another advantage over Rawls: he is readable. With the exception of a few notable passages, Rawls is a rather wooden writer. That can never be said of Berlin – although his writing sometimes suffers from other problems, as when his penchant for synonyms, cognates and list-making runs away with him. Berlin's accessibility, to the general reader as well as to professional philosophers, coupled with the rich suggestiveness of his fundamental insights, are, for me, his greatest strengths. They are not, to my mind, quite sufficient to make Berlin the equal of Rawls as a political philosopher, all things considered, but they are more than enough to make him a very significant thinker indeed.

As a final verdict, I can't do better than the judgement of a distinguished Oxford political theorist who knew Berlin well: he is terrific at getting people started on a subject. He makes thinkers and their ideas comprehensible, exciting, intriguing. He paints us pictures, tells us stories, and sets us puzzles. He doesn't fill in the details of the picture, or finish the story, or solve the puzzle. He doesn't follow through on his themes the way Rawls does, but his insights are no less profound, perhaps more so. Although I've often found his work frustrating as well as inspirational, I find myself drawn back to it again and again. That's why I think of him as one of my principal teachers, even though we never met.

---

[1] See Amartya Sen, *Inequality Reexamined* (Oxford, 1992); Martha Nussbaum, *Women and Human Development* (Cambridge, 2000); Jonathan Wolff and Avner De-Shalit, *Disadvantage* (Oxford, 2007).

The Legacy of Open Thought

Steffen W. Groß

E VEN DURING HIS LIFETIME Isaiah Berlin was a controversial thinker. The orthodox view was that he owed his fame to his personal qualities – above all his remarkable gift for conversation, his exemplary liberal temperament and his unusual capacity for empathy – rather than to his academic achievements;[1] that it was his sparkling, inspirational gift as a speaker that made him 'Britain's most celebrated public intellectual' and an 'iconic figure'.[2] Even before his death the accusation was made that, although he was able to enter the minds of even the most obscure figures of European intellectual history, he was not an original theorist, but a brilliant narrator of modern political history and its philosophical background. On this view, however, this talent, tied as it was to his idiosyncratic personality and experiences, died with him, and cannot be artificially reactivated or imitated. And his unique liberal sensibility cannot be passed on to succeeding generations, being impossible to teach or to learn. As far as straight philosophy and political theory are concerned, others have done much better than him; so there is no lasting Berlinian legacy.

I

I was born too late to have met Isaiah Berlin in person. I know him only from his writings, from his letters, and from many conversations with people who have had the good fortune to meet him and to study with him. So I am not best placed to assess the claim that it is primarily his personality that explains his fame.[3] However, it should be borne in mind that his kind of conversation – intense debate about human beings and their activities – ought in any case to play a central role in the humanities, which are after all the study of mankind. Conversation is one of the most important didactic tools in the study of human culture; from my own experience as a university lecturer I know that open debate in seminars is indispensable in encouraging students

---

[1] See Mark Lilla, Ronald Dworkin and Robert Silvers (eds), *The Legacy of Isaiah Berlin* (New York, 2002).

[2] Timothy Garton Ash, 'A Genius for Friendship', *New York Review of Books*, 23 September 2004, 20–5, at 20.

[3] His conversational disposition apparently also cost him at least one interesting job. He was excluded from the British delegation to the Potsdam Conference in 1945 because he talked too much. As Anthony Eden put it, 'I can't have Isaiah chattering round the place.' L1 583. See also Peter Clarke, *The Last Thousand Days of the British Empire: The Demise of a Superpower 1944–1947* (London, 2008), 369.

to think independently, to question comfortable received opinion, and to find a justified standpoint of their own instead of merely parroting what they have heard in lectures. I always tell my students that the most important form of instruction at university is not the lecture, to which they merely listen, but the seminar, which is a structured form of conversation. The humanities are essentially a matter of dialogue. For just that reason Isaiah Berlin, as an exponent of a 'declining art',[1] is for me a lasting example.

On the basis of his writings, I regard Berlin as an original and coherent thinker, partly because of his highly individual liberal sensibility and temperament. For me his particular form of liberalism and his tolerance of human weaknesses, his exceptional capacity for intellectual empathy combined with the healthy scepticism about perfectibility which permeated his own life, is able to bridge some of the formal gaps in his political philosophy – is perhaps bound to do so, because theories, particularly in the humanities, quickly reach their limits. Berlin's awareness of this was not reached just by sitting at his desk and ratiocinating, but directly intuited. It is the manifest authenticity and wisdom of his instinct for the limits of ideas and theories that attracts me again and again.

Obviously Berlin's personal intellectual qualities do not by themselves constitute a sufficient response to the clashes posited by value pluralism. But in combination they yielded, in Berlin's case, a lived example of a disposition that makes the plurality of human values and goals, and the conflicts between them, acceptable and politically manageable. To live successfully in contradictory cultural and political conditions we must cultivate relaxed attentiveness and, most of all, political judgement. We cannot expect liberty to be secured and guaranteed for all time on firm philosophical or political foundations, because in human life nothing is fixed and everlasting. So for me Berlinian liberalism is a form of political culture, a mode of life characterised by liberal passions and temperaments, not a systematic, closed, teachable and learnable corpus of theory.

After his abandonment of the analytical philosophy of his Oxford friends and colleagues and his turn to the history of ideas, Berlin was sometimes called an enemy of theory. This is too stark. But he did fail to give theoretical form even to his principal politico-philosophical thesis, that there is an objective plurality of human values. Was this perhaps because this is simply impossible? Instead, he repeatedly asserted that some human values and aims, despite being widely regarded as worthwhile, cannot be combined with each other without serious tensions. One of his best-known statements of this principle is his image of the wolves and the sheep: 'You cannot combine full liberty with full

[1] Stephen Miller, *Conversation: A History of a Declining Art* (New Haven and London, 2006).

equality – full liberty for the wolves cannot be combined with full liberty for the sheep.'[1] Often enough, different values cannot even be compared with each other intelligibly, since they are qualitatively different: there is no common standard to measure them against, no lowest common denominator in terms of which to judge them. This is a fact, incidentally, which modern mainstream economics with its central idea of a clear transitive order of preferences has almost completely ignored, perhaps deliberately.

II

Berlin never argued directly in a systematic philosophical treatise for his central thesis of the plurality of, and conflict between, human values and goals. Rather he gives the impression that he found this view in other thinkers, in Herder, for example, or in Hamann. In his studies of the history of ideas he supported this claim in subtle ways – he wrote a good deal between the lines – and made it his own. However, none of his attempts to separate his pluralism of values clearly from mere relativism was completely successful, and the distinction remains blurred.

His way of presenting ideas, his portrayals and interpretations of other thinkers, strike me as the work of an artist rather than a hard-core academic scholar – they are full of imaginative and suggestive power. I am strongly sympathetic to this approach, since I regard the humanities, and also at least parts of the so-called hard sciences, as a form of art, of *poiesis*. We do not simply discover or investigate our objects of thought, but to a considerable extent let them emerge and develop within our minds. The razor-sharp divide between the arts and the sciences has never convinced me – and Berlin, as I understand him, must have felt the same. He paints large, though often very detailed, pictures with words and sentences. There are no long, abstract, theoretical demonstrations in his works. This clearly makes sense. For Berlin, the appropriate format in which to address problems of human culture is the essay. The essay is tentative, cautious, provisional, incomplete. This leaves it open to a variety of further connections, like an electric socket into which different appliances can be plugged.

The main difference between the academic treatise and the essay is that the treatise aims to settle a question finally. It is a monologue that leaves nothing unresolved, so that the reader has only two options: total agreement or wholesale rejection. The treatise aspires to excite deep awe in its reader, silencing all questions. The essay, the attempt, is completely different: it elucidates a problematic issue without claiming to have solved the problems it raises. The essay searches, asks questions, makes the reader aware of an issue by circling round it. It urges the reader to join in, to discuss, to dispute. It forces, inspires, the reader

[1] CIB 142.

to think for himself. The essay does not want to give final answers, it leaves questions open and encourages further questions. Thinking and reasoning in the study of mankind are thus principally a dialogue, a conversation either with living persons or with texts. This is something I have learnt from Berlin's style and method.

The open essay that avoids foreclosing formulations seems the right tool for Berlin's investigations. The anthropological foundation both for Berlin's political thought and for his liberal temperament is the idea of man he found in Immanuel Kant (who wrote of 'the crooked timber of humanity'), and in the German Romantics of the early nineteenth century: man as a partly self-creating being, able (and compelled by his nature) to express his inner self in a dramatic and astonishing variety of ways. This leads Berlin to the conclusion that a perfect society, a body politic without contradictions and tragic losses, cannot be constructed, even from an ideal blueprint, which cannot be conceived. Culture and society are complicated, fragile systems that do not work like a machine and should not be approached mechanically in search of secure, unambiguous answers.

This is why Berlin was always hostile to any social technology that promised a bright future. Stalin's idea of the 'engineer of human souls'[1] expresses, for Berlin, the paradigmatic evil of the twentieth century. Therefore it is modesty, moderation and restraint, and what Berlin called 'the sense of reality', not eternal answers from textbooks, that must guide political action in a world that is unavoidably diverse and internally contradictory. We must tolerate the decisions of others even if they cannot be conclusively rationally justified, and we must develop an awareness of the fact that all life-forming decisions, even the best of them, inevitably entail tragic losses. In the sphere of human action only second-best solutions are possible. It is one of Berlin's deepest insights that to be human means to be forced into 'tragic choices'.[2] A corollary of this is that every attempt to deny the complexity, heterogeneity and profound conflicts of modern society, or, even worse, to abolish them, must end in political and moral catastrophe. This is the lesson of a twentieth-century life.

The alternative is liberalism, in politics and society more generally. But it is impossible to construct a theory of liberal political action that can guide us by reference to scientific laws. This is the kind of theoretical gap we often find in the humanities, and it can be bridged only by life itself and by one's temperament. This is the source of Berlin's aversion to attempts by the 'social sciences', particularly economics, to imitate the methods of the natural sciences; to a

---

[1] POI 17–18.

[2] For a good introduction to this problematic field I strongly recommend Guido Calabresi and Philipp Bobbitt, *Tragic Choices*, The Fels Lectures on Public Policy Analysis (New York, 1978).

positivism that wants to find scientific laws of human life that do not change over time, space and culture. Rather we should reflect on the 'false dawns'[1] of the social sciences, not least of social engineering, as Berlin did in the development of his own understanding of social practice.

So are there any lasting effects of Isaiah Berlin's thought? There is no doubt that he was an ambivalent, if not melancholic, thinker about modern culture and the culture of modernity. This ambivalence in particular, related to his ability to empathise even with his intellectual enemies, accounts for the astonishing moral and psychological depth of his thought and of his personality. His complex moral psychology has an enduring, deep-seated explanatory power. This is exemplified by his treatment of modern nationalism. He tries to understand this phenomenon, but without accepting all its elements. Here his own personal experiences become important. He was an immigrant forced to fit into an unknown and sometimes hostile environment that spoke a foreign language. National structures of feeling and membership of a cultural community are for him not in the least illegitimate, but – here he follows Herder – basic human needs, just like food and shelter. Berlin calls them the need to belong. Only those who have a home can feel free and express themselves spontaneously. His own experience taught Berlin that the homeless were in constant danger of unjustified humiliation. Nationalism was a legitimate reaction to emotional wounds, or to the permanent liability to humiliation.

Berlin left us an enriched form of liberalism, coloured by Romanticism, and based above all on his positive response to cultural diversity and the ineradicable complexity of life. On this basis we might object to the so-called neo-liberalism that praises the commercialisation and privatisation of almost all human activities. Neo-liberalism must be attacked from a properly liberal point of view. Berlin saw this when he said: 'Something has collapsed. There is a world shift to the Right. I wish it were not so. I am a liberal.'[2]

For Berlin the most important thing is not the search for the ideal life, but the avoidance of evil. This stems from a kind of negative empathy. His main political question has always been, 'Which political and moral evils must be avoided under all circumstances if people are to lead a life which is minimally decent?' This question works against all theories that tell us how to construct the ideal society. It is not personal autonomy or individualism that forms the normative core of a liberalism in search of a minimal *modus vivendi* for plural and contradictory forms of life, but decency. When Berlin is asked what he means by decency he becomes brusquely untheoretical: 'Don't ask me what I mean by decent. By decent I mean decent – we all know what that is.'[3]

---

[1] See John Gray, *False Dawn: The Delusions of Global Capitalism* (London, 2002).
[2] CIB 128.
[3] CIB 114.

He is right: life does not occur at the level of theory, but in actual practice. We must fill the holes in our theories with responsible, creative, self-conscious, sensitive life, with engagement and passion. The decisive factors here are openness to and curiosity about different experiments in living and different collective modes of life.

III

The same openness strikes us when we read Berlin's essays in the history of ideas. For Berlin, the history of ideas asks where certain concepts, ideas, theories and methods come from, and what their lasting influence is. It is not an antiquarian activity. It is interested less in the past than in the present, in our contemporary situation, and it seeks to understand the origins of today's problems. Further, for him the history of ideas is not a purely academic endeavour, but a very practical activity. It aims to show how ideas and concepts shape our culture. Ideas do influence action; often enough, indeed, they determine the way we act. Intellectual history, then, is located at the intersection of theory and practice. When we try to understand the emergence and development of ideas, we gain an understanding of our actions and of our current predicament.

This is what really interests me – the interpenetration of theory and practice. In his 1895 Cambridge inaugural lecture, Lord Acton left no doubt about the necessity of historical studies and their practical value for the present and the shaping of the future: 'the knowledge of the past, the record of truths revealed by experience, is eminently practical, as an instrument of action and a power that goes to the making of the future'.[1] This expresses what historians are really interested in: not so much the past, let alone the glorification of allegedly better times, but the present and the future. Berlin is one of the few who have shown true inspiration in the implementation of Acton's programme.

His aim was to bring to our attention the connections and influences which might otherwise have escaped our notice. For example, the history of ideas throws valuable light on two topics of particular importance to Berlin as a person: totalitarianism and political violence. It is to his lasting credit that, as part of his work on the ideas of thinkers who are not often discussed, such as Joseph de Maistre, he made these four points:

1. Totalitarian, fascist and anti-liberal thinking is not a product of the twentieth century. Of course, openly fascist regimes arose only in that century, but they were based on concepts and ideas developed much earlier, or used earlier thinkers as a source of ideological support.

---

[1] John Edward Emerich, 1st Baron Acton [sc. John Emerich Edward Dalberg-Acton], 'Inaugural Lecture on the Study of History' (June 1895), in his *Lectures on Modern History* (London, 1952), 2.

2. This is one demonstration of the fact that ideas often travel by indirect routes, only rarely providing a direct, immediate guide to action. At first glance it can be unclear where social developments come from. Ideas and concepts change over time, acquire new meanings, and infiltrate other concepts. The task of the history of ideas is to follow these developments and make them intelligible.

3. We tend to associate the term 'Enlightenment' with an optimistic epoch of cultural and scientific advance, rapid educational expansion, the development and implementation of human and civil rights, of personal and democratic liberties, and radical questioning of the legitimacy of the ruling authorities. Light must displace darkness, clear-sightedness must be achieved. This is a central element in the meaning of 'Enlightenment', a term that refers directly to casting light, as its German counterpart, 'Aufklärung', does to clarification. But it is an everyday experience that where there is much light there are also dark shadows. Light and shade are inseparable, and the darkest shadow is thrown alongside the brightest light. This is why there emerged within the Enlightenment a kind of thinking directly opposed to its aims – glorification of merciless authority, power, illiberality and intolerance. Berlin makes it clear in his essays that we must also examine this dark side of human thought and action.

4. Berlin shows that a thinker's intellectual development cannot be understood unless it is viewed against his particular cultural background. The development of ideas is rarely clear, consistent and logical. Breaks, shifts and discontinuities are not the exception but the rule. If we want to understand a thinker's ideas, we must imaginatively identify with his biography. This is the task bequeathed to us by Berlin's studies in the history of ideas.

IV

Here is another connection between Berlin the theorist of liberty and Berlin the historian of ideas. Engagement with the dark side of the Enlightenment shows vividly that liberty cannot be a static condition, but is a permanent (and demanding) task or duty. Because we must never forget this, engagement with the avowed enemies of the Enlightenment is important. On one central point the anti-Enlightenment thinkers are right: the light of reason cannot reach everywhere and everything. This was the great illusion of the Enlightenment's rationalistic mainstream, most prominent in eighteenth-century France. If we are not to allow the dark shadows to overwhelm us, we have to remember that light and shade are inseparable.

The legacy of Isaiah Berlin's life and work, then, is the understanding that the Enlightenment is not a past epoch, but a continuing task that always lies before us. Berlin's 100th birthday should be an occasion for us not only to look back on a lived life, but to perceive and accept the lasting power of his ideas, his methods and, most of all, his vivid presentation of the past. This will help us to understand our current predicament more fully, and strengthen our ability to plan the future.

This article was initially written in German, and has been translated and edited by the author, Josephine von Zitzewitz and the editor

The Fox Is Still Running

James Chappel

IT HAS SOMETIMES been said of Isaiah Berlin that his aura and influence will dissipate once those who knew him cease proselytising for the cause. This has clearly not begun to happen, as can be seen, for instance, in the current excitement surrounding the centenary of his birth. This book is only one manifestation of a global celebration. But, one might respond, this represents merely the end of an era, a final conflagration that will be followed by a general recognition of the failure of Berlin's idiosyncratic liberalism, or indeed any kind of liberalism, to make sense of the new global situation. The Cold War is over, this argument runs, and we must thus leave Berlin and his ilk behind in a quest for new theories, capable of assimilating the variegated global practices of capitalism and terrorism. It is this judgement, perhaps more widespread in my native America than in Britain, that I hope to question here through an account of Berlin's influence on my decision to become, and my development as, a historian of ideas: an influence exercised entirely after his death.

The personal impression is a genre of which Berlin was an undisputed master. Perhaps it was, in the end, the only one in which he attained fluency. In saying this, I don't seek to question his brilliant and influential essays on Vico, Herder and others. Rather, I'm claiming that Berlin at his best, even and especially in these scholarly essays, never strayed far from the personal impression. This was a consequence of his method. He never engaged in the self-effacing scholarship of his Cambridge School successors. Instead, he claimed that to interpret a text – that is, to interpret another human being's unique vision of life – requires us to call on the resources of our humanity first, and those of scholarship only second. Berlin was never excessively concerned with the concrete doctrines espoused by a thinker, or by contributions to the philosophical canon as such. Rather, he felt that his duty as a historian was to enter, as far as possible, into the sometimes alien and frightening value system of his subject. There is, then, a grain of truth in the claim that Berlin's influence will not outlast his personality. Indeed this criticism, paradoxically, grasps an important part of Berlin's project. But his personality did not die when his heart stopped beating. Rather, it survives in his texts. This claim was fundamental to Berlin's own work, as it is to the apparently impossible task that I will attempt here: to write a personal impression of a man that I have never met.

The title is the last sentence of Michael Walzer's review of John Gray's *Isaiah Berlin* (London, 1995), 'Are There Limits to Liberalism?', *New York Review of Books*, 19 October 1995, 28–31.

I have been influenced far more by the vision of life expressed throughout Berlin's corpus than by the concrete doctrines that obliquely intersect the complex 'sense of reality' evinced in the texts themselves. I must admit that I have never been an enthusiastic proponent of Berlin's political theory. Like others, I am dubious about the attempt to extract a coherent set of theories from Berlin's work. He snakes his way in and around various liberal ideals without ever quite embracing them, somehow inhabiting the impossible space, the hair's breadth, between world-weary scepticism and fiery dogmatism. In terms of the famous dichotomy between the fox, who knows many things, and the hedgehog, who knows one big thing, Berlin was a fox.

This has some unsettling consequences, however, that are sometimes overlooked. If he were an unambiguous liberal, and all his writings were expressions of this one idea, he would be a hedgehog. If, however, he wished to throw his hands in the air and declare the impossibility of moral or political knowledge, he would be neither a hedgehog nor a fox – although a complete sceptic might be represented as a hedgehog turned inside out. It is more difficult to be a true fox than one might realise, but Berlin perhaps came as close as humanly possible. It is, then, the foxiness of Berlin's mind, which presents an incredible intellectual challenge, and not his liberal-pluralist theory, that has proven most influential for me as a budding historian (although the two are intimately related, they are not identical).

Like Berlin, I study primarily illiberal thinkers. My reasons for this are best expressed by Berlin himself: 'I am bored by reading people who are allies, people of roughly the same views. What is interesting is to read the enemy, because the enemy penetrates the defences.'[1] His use of the martial metaphor, here as elsewhere, is telling. The 'fortress' or 'citadel' is probably the most common description of a philosophical system to be found in Berlin's writing, and one that illuminates a crucial aspect of Berlin's relationship with ideas, including his own. True life is not to be found in the grey stone of the castle walls, but rather in the teeming multiplicity of human lives within. The walls exist for our convenience alone. We don't live to build fortresses, we build fortresses in order to live. But in philosophy as in warfare one cannot be complacent about one's defences. Berlin studied the figures he did because he was willing to invite attack, to renovate continually, and to point out the weak points in our own liberal *Weltanschauungen*. It seems to me that this aspect of Berlin's thought, seldom stated yet implicitly present in much of his work, can become outdated only at great peril to ourselves and our fortresses.

My own impression of Berlin's continuing relevance is perhaps a consequence of my introduction to his thought. I originally approached him as a historian,

---

[1] 'Isaiah Berlin in Conversation with Steven Lukes' (30 above, note 3), 90.

and not as a political theorist. The first essay of his that I encountered, in an undergraduate course on Russian literature, was 'Fathers and Children: Turgenev and the Liberal Predicament'. When announcing the assignment, the professor informed an uncomprehending class that it represented 'Berlin at his finest'. We had never heard of Berlin, but we had also never heard of Turgenev, so we acquiesced in the assignment with the shrugging acceptance that is both the virtue and the vice of American college students. We were immediately blown away by the essay's erudition and rhetorical force, although it was clear to me even then that the essay was about Berlin as much, if not more, than it was about Turgenev. The affinity between Berlin and his subject are obvious: Turgenev, Berlin writes, 'was not a preacher and did not wish to thunder at his generation. He was concerned, above all, to enter into, understand, views, ideals, temperaments, both those which he found sympathetic and those by which he was puzzled or repelled.'[1] Turgenev, like Berlin himself, was converted to the cause of liberalism and decency through personal childhood experience of injustice. In neither case did this take the form of conversion to a new and more just system. Instead, both Turgenev and Berlin rejected system altogether: 'All that was general, abstract, absolute, repelled him: his vision remained delicate, sharp, concrete and incurably realistic.'[2]

This did not, however, commit Turgenev, any more than it did Berlin, to a sniffing condescension towards dogmatic political activists. Indeed, one of the major purposes of Berlin's essay is to show that Turgenev did not, despite the prevailing caricature, simply ascend the ivory tower of aesthetics and declare himself a partisan of *l'art pour l'art*. Instead, he attempted truly to understand the novelty, source and possible value of the horrifying forces unleashed around him. After his falling out with Chernyshevsky and Dobrolyubov – the so-called 'new men' – Turgenev attempted to sympathise with these intriguing creatures instead of rejecting them outright. The result, of course, was the unforgettable Bazarov, the central character of *Fathers and Children*. The novel pleased no one, precisely because it was hopelessly unclear where Turgenev stood. 'He shook and shivered under the ceaseless criticisms to which he had exposed himself, but, in his own apologetic way, refused to "simplify" himself. He went on believing – perhaps this was a relic of his Hegelian youth – that no issue was closed for ever, that every thesis must be weighed against its antithesis.'[3]

Turgenev maintained his critical distance despite his knowledge that 'the Russian reader wanted to be told what to believe and how to live, expected to be provided with clearly contrasted values, clearly distinguishable heroes and

[1] RT2 301.
[2] RT2 308.
[3] RT2 341.

villains'.[1] He could not provide this, as his mind, like Berlin's, was far too supple for the required binaries. Paradoxically, Turgenev could not take a principled stand without betraying his principles, which committed him to a distanced and all too human stance of observation and description. Like Berlin, Turgenev was a fox. What's more, Berlin saw Turgenev as one of the first to inhabit the impossible space that he tried to occupy himself: 'The ambivalence of such moderates, who are not prepared to break their principles or betray the cause in which they believe, has become a common feature of political life.' Turgenev was one of the first to pay the price of ambivalence, later to be paid by Berlin himself: 'The middle ground is a notoriously exposed, dangerous and ungrateful position.'[2] To point out the weaknesses in the fortress walls, one must view them from the outside.

Many readers of Berlin tend to forget the danger of his ideas, imagining that he simply held uncontroversial or bland positions. He has been criticised for spinelessness and for refusing to take the principled stands necessary in a harsh world. What could be easier than to reject the extremes in favour of the ambivalent 'middle ground'? Doesn't Berlin exaggerate the danger of this most common and uninteresting of positions? These criticisms, however, perfectly demonstrate Berlin's own description of the middle ground as a peculiarly perilous place. While Berlin recognised the necessity and desirability of the principled 'Hier stehe ich'[3] – and anyone familiar with his biography would know that he took these stands more often than he is given credit for – this was always tempered by a humanist desire, in the mould of Turgenev, to understand his opponents deeply and intuitively.

As most readers of Berlin would attest, his most breathtaking work concerned the most illiberal of thinkers: the ones whose worlds we never imagined that we would be able to inhabit, and whose sensibilities were furthest from Berlin's own. He did not follow other Cold War liberals in rejecting the horrors of his century as the work of ignorant fanatics, or even as the lamentable but understandable result of economic depression. Rather, he gathered all of his considerable powers of human sympathy in an attempt to understand his opponents, as Turgenev had done with Bazarov. This can be seen in many of his essays, but I will focus here on 'Joseph de Maistre and the Origins of Fascism'. This is, in fact, the essay that made me a true convert to the Berlin cause (if such a thing exists), and pointed me towards the more or less uncharted waters of Catholicism's intellectual history, about which I am preparing a dissertation. What's more, it almost certainly determined me to become a historian in the first place.

[1] RT2 311.
[2] RT2 343.
[3] 'Here I stand' (attributed to Martin Luther).

Maistre is, on many levels, a deeply unattractive thinker. In this essay, however, Berlin is able to make him seem not only insightful and interesting, but also relevant (one of the great merits of his work is that he dissolves the barrier between 'attractive' and 'relevant'). He begins by showing that Maistre had usually been considered a simple and perfectly clear author: a Catholic reactionary born in the wrong century. While Berlin agreed with this assessment, he flipped it on its head, arguing that Maistre truly belonged in the twentieth century, not the seventeenth. That is to say, he was a precursor of fascism, and not a relic of absolutism. A conventional liberal would feel obliged, then, either to ignore him altogether, or to pen a facile essay condemning the monstrous evil he propounds, or smugly harping on the desirability of keeping religion and politics distinct. Berlin, of course, did neither of these things, believing not only that Maistre was historically important, but also, more controversially, that contemporary liberals have much to learn from this vicious obscurantist.

Maistre's critique of Enlightenment rationalism was also, to a certain extent, Berlin's own; in fact, Berlin couches Maistre's ultramontanism in nearly the same language he uses in his own theoretical essays. The *philosophes*, Berlin and Maistre together argued, erred in that they 'believed that all good and desirable things were necessarily compatible'.[1] Maistre violently rejected this and all the putatively shallow wisdom of the benevolent *lumières*, setting up instead his own 'famous, terrible vision of life'.[2] Despite Berlin's belief that this vision was a precursor to the fascism that murdered much of his family, he evocatively inhabits this world-view and, what's more, finds much in it to admire. Maistre, we are told, is 'bold', 'brilliant' and 'realistic'. He 'held very penetrating and remarkably modern views on the dangers (largely ignored by the French *lumières*) of general principles and their application. Both in theory and in practice he was exceptionally sensitive to differences of context'[3] – a virtue which leads Berlin to compare Maistre with Vico, one of his heroes.

Berlin does not, of course, unambiguously support Maistre's beliefs. His goal was always to renovate liberalism, not to raze it to the ground. 'Maistre is a dogmatic thinker whose ultimate principles and premises nothing can shake, whose considerable ingenuity and intellectual power is devoted to making the facts fit his preconceived notions.'[4] There is, for Berlin, no greater intellectual crime than this (it is also the crime, he believed, of Marx and Stalin). He elsewhere praises Voltaire, one of Maistre's *bêtes noires*, who, despite his flawed view of reason and human nature, 'probably did more for the triumph of

---

[1] CTH 108.
[2] CTH 112.
[3] CTH 102, 166, 155, 131.
[4] CTH 162.

civilised values than any writer who ever lived.'[1] Berlin was always clear that the violence and darkness at the heart of Maistre's vision had to be fought, but he was equally clear that this could not be done with the philosophical naivety of Voltaire, who refused to investigate the weaknesses of his own fortress.

I vividly recall the effect that this essay had on me. I was at the time travelling with a deeply conservative friend of mine, whose views I had spent years rejecting as foolish and outdated. I had, on a whim, purchased *The Crooked Timber of Humanity* as in-flight reading in order to see whether Berlin could sustain the rhetorical and intellectual fireworks of his Turgenev essay. I was, at first, surprised to find him writing about such an illiberal figure. By the time the plane landed, however, I had become deeply embarrassed at my former knee-jerk liberalism, and over the following weeks I tried, for the first time, truly to engage with the ideas of my evangelical friend.

This does not mean that I became a convert, any more than Berlin did. I simply realised that, however much I might dismiss views different from my own as wrong-headed or backward, I cannot pretend that they are completely incomprehensible to me. As Berlin wrote elsewhere, 'We are free to criticise the values of other cultures, to condemn them, but we cannot pretend not to understand them at all.'[2] In so far as different value systems – including fascism – are expressive of forms of life distinct from our own, we should be able to understand them, at least in part, since they are marked by the human hands that made them. Once this task is abandoned, our adversaries seem inhuman to us, with all the consequences with which we are unfortunately familiar. Moreover, it is not the sort of interpersonal, reflective activity that is inspired by more traditional liberal thought: I would be surprised if anyone became more open to apparently incomprehensible beliefs after reading Hayek or Rawls. Berlin's continuing relevance, then, lies hidden within the coils of the paradox which provides the famous *dénouement* to 'Two Concepts of Liberty': 'To realise the relative validity of one's convictions and yet stand for them unflinchingly is what distinguishes a civilised man from a barbarian.'[3]

Berlin's essay on Maistre was published in 1990, and can perhaps be read as his message to a post-Cold-War era, one of liberalism triumphant across the globe and the putative 'end of history'. Had he been a textbook liberal, he might have sighed in relief that liberalism had at last vanquished its enemies. Instead, he resuscitated a lengthy, iconoclastic article heaping praise upon one of the greatest critics of liberalism who ever wrote. Berlin had, of course, been working on Maistre for decades, and he did not conceive of this essay as a coded message to the 1990s; however, he surely felt the attack on liberal complacency to be

[1] AC 88.
[2] CTH 11.
[3] See 30 above, note 5.

especially relevant in the wake of the Cold War. In his eloquent ventriloquism of Maistre, he voices sentiments that were very much his own: 'What angered [Maistre] most was the bland, naturalistic optimism, the validity of which the fashionable philosophers of the age [...] seemed to take wholly for granted.'[1] Two years before Fukuyama described the 'last man' of neo-liberalism, Berlin published an essay that displayed great intuitive sympathy for a reactionary Catholic who claimed, in a passage quoted by Berlin, that 'The Constitution of 1795, just like its predecessors, was made for *man*. But there is no such thing as *man* in the world.'[2] It is this willingness endlessly to question our own truisms, and not merely those of our enemies, that has most influenced my intellectual ideal. Living in the times that we do, when our fortress is beginning to show signs of wear, this aspect of Berlin's life and work remains of enormous significance.

Berlin recounts that when Turgenev died, the workers, the intelligentsia and the imperial government all gathered to bid farewell to their complex countryman: 'perhaps the first and last occasion on which these groups peacefully met in Russia.'[3] It is possible, of course, that they all simply interpreted Turgenev according to their own lights and viewed this master of ambiguity as one of their own. More charitably, we might suppose that they were able to lay aside their differences in honour of someone who had laid aside his own in an effort truly to describe and understand each of them to the best of his abilities. The capacity to inspire this kind of non-partisan devotion is rare, and not often afforded to those whose names fill the history books. As Berlin wrote in a different essay on Turgenev, 'It is the fate of gentle and yielding characters to be overshadowed by more formidable contemporaries.'[4] This has not yet happened with Berlin, any more than it has with Turgenev. Let us hope, for our own sake, that it never does.

[1] CTH 106.
[2] *Œuvres complètes de J. de Maistre* (Lyons/Paris, 1884–7), i 74; cited at CTH 100.
[3] RT2 300.
[4] 'The Gentle Genius', review of *Turgenev's Letters*, selected, trans. and ed. A. V. Knowles, *New York Review of Books*, 27 October 1983, 23–33, at 23.

Isaiah Berlin on Himself

Jennifer Holmes

W HEN THE IDEA of an autobiography was suggested to Isaiah Berlin, he reacted with horror, rejecting the idea as a 'terrible thought [...] like walking naked in public' and adding that 'I take no interest in myself whatever.'[1] Apart from 'My Intellectual Path' and various passages in *Personal Impressions* (notably 'The Three Strands in My Life'), Berlin wrote little about himself for public consumption. But even if he had responded to requests for autobiographical pieces, his habit of reworking texts again and again before finally approving them for publication might have led to the creation of a quite new persona. As it is, the best source of information on how Berlin really viewed himself (and on the accuracy of that view) is the constant stream of letters which poured from him throughout his life, and which Henry Hardy and I are editing. Whether handwritten or dictated into a machine for his secretary to type, Berlin's letters to friends, acquaintances, professional contacts and total strangers have the unrestrained spontaneity of his conversation. And as they were frequently despatched without re-reading by their author, what he says about himself has the freshness of first thoughts.

Many of Berlin's letters can be seen as precursors of his academic pieces, as he tries out on friends the philosophical, intellectual and moral positions for which he later argues in public. His dismissal of overriding principles in favour of more pragmatic solutions is a frequent theme; in the mid-1930s he commends Macaulay for a scale of values 'not consisting in rules i.e. moralistic and irrational & ugly'[2] and by 1949 is ready to argue the position at length: 'Once principles are applied rigorously absurdities follow from the non-generalizability of the situations which originally suggested the principles. [...] one must judge each situation, so far as possible, on its own merits & not commit oneself to campaigns for general principles.'[3] Sometimes the letters expose the genesis of his intellectual preoccupations. Berlin's diatribes in his letters about the malign influence of sociology and the growing demand for education to be socially useful throw new light on the argument of 'Political Ideas in the Twentieth Century'. And a few months before his first public exploration of the theory of pluralism in 'Two Concepts of Liberty', Berlin spells out his distinctly pluralistic

---

[1] To Margot de Gunzbourg, 1 June 1960.
[2] To Stuart Hampshire, 1935?, L1 145.
[3] To Myron Gilmore, 26 December 1949, L2 151.

recognition of conflicting and irreconcilable goals within Israel in a letter to a pro-Arab friend:

> That Arab rights have been trodden on – that a wrong to them has been committed – it seems to be morally shameful to deny. If you then ask me why I am pro-Zionist, it is because I think that where right clashes with right – or rather misery with misery – one must not think about rights, which always exist [...] but of some calm utilitarian solution which produces on the whole the best or happiest solution in the end.[1]

In contrast with this intellectual consistency between Berlin's public and private faces, there is a startling disparity between the emotional self-portrait in his letters and the perception others had of him. This may be a question of age. Whereas the letters which have so far been examined for publication are those which survive from the first half of his life (until 1960), most of the friends and colleagues whose memories of Berlin appear elsewhere in this volume belong, inevitably, to his later years. Perhaps the letters from those years will demonstrate a sea-change in Berlin's character and self-perception. But the frequency with which friends comment on how little he changed during his life suggests otherwise.

Berlin is remembered as a happy person, either ebulliently cheerful or serenely contented, and it is possible (just) to see the self-pity and complaint he at times pours out to friends in his letters as the letting off of steam necessary to achieve a state of equanimity. The sparkle of his youthful letters gives way after the war to repeated and lengthy laments about his health, workload, treatment by critics and lack of solid achievement. Illness in others seems to bring out Berlin's competitive spirit: no one can be suffering as much as he is. (A long screed about the plight of overworked Oxford dons, for example, is unlikely to have done much to aid Sibyl Colefax's recovery from a broken hip.) He does not seem to have considered himself a happy person. Writing in 1932 about Tolstoy, Berlin comments 'It is extremely important to note the descriptions of (1) how he always found his face very ugly & (2) the speculation on what would be said after his suicide. Both are very considerable chunks of my early life.'[2] Twenty years later, cheerfulness has still not broken in: 'my quest for gaiety & cosiness is a perpetual defence against the extreme sense of the abyss by which I have been affected ever since I can remember myself'.[3] Brenda Tripp, his British Council colleague in Leningrad in 1945, confided to her diary that 'it is difficult to make any real contact with him. [...] There is not much warmth about him. He never [...] seems to be completely natural and friendly. [...] I think he is

---

[1] To Johanna Lambert, 20 May 1958, L2 630.
[2] To Shiela Grant Duff, 8 December 1932, L1 45.
[3] To Marion Frankfurter, 23 February 1952, L2 291.

really very shy and covers it up with too much talking.'[1] This is a far cry from the usual picture but it tallies with the Berlin who emerges from his letters.

Notoriously indifferent to the natural world, Berlin often claims that people are his landscape; once he revealingly adds 'I am a fancier of them as others of birds.'[2] The comparison is a curious one, suggesting a scientist examining a specimen under a microscope, or perhaps Gulliver observing the fallings out of the Big Endians and Little Endians. What it does not suggest is that for Berlin other people are of the same species as himself, with the same hopes, fears, joys and sorrows. Berlin's reputation for empathy in his lectures and essays derives from his skill in bringing the long-dead to life, in his words: 'I do try to paint the anschauung of these men: & delight in the colours themselves: & try to find out & say what their worlds looked like to them.'[3] The same skill is evident in the lively portraits of friends and acquaintances in his letters; but recreating an intellectual and social milieu is very different from penetrating an individual's psychology and identifying (or even sharing) his emotional responses. Berlin reveals himself in his letters as a fascinated and acute observer of people, but while his sympathy for the human condition in the abstract is readily apparent, sympathy for individuals – even his closest friends – is in fairly short supply, and empathy almost non-existent.

For all his skills in analysing the springs of human behaviour in general, when it comes to individuals Berlin often seems more comfortable with externals. After Berlin meets Albert Einstein in 1952, Einstein perceptively comments that Berlin seems to be 'a kind of spectator in God's big but mostly not very attractive theatre'.[4] (Berlin makes equally barbed comments about Einstein.) In his correspondence Berlin's descriptions of people, places and events often read as if written by an outside observer rather than a participant. His description to Elizabeth Bowen of breaking off contact with the besotted and mentally fragile 'Tips' Walker, the account he gives Jenifer Williams a few years later of dictating *Karl Marx* to an unimpressed Home Office typist, his letter of apology to a Brazilian diplomat for his failure to appear at a Washington dinner party, and his report to Edmund Wilson on lunch with the Queen all bring to mind characters acting on a stage; indeed Berlin admits that 'I romanticize every place I come to, I find: Moscow, Oxford, Ditchley, Harvard, Washington: each is a kind of legendary world framed within its own conventions in which the characters, suffused with unnatural brightness, perform with terrific responsiveness.'[5] Even the past is transformed into a stage set for nostalgic re-enactments;

[1] L1 600–1.

[2] To Marion Frankfurter, 13 August 1954, L2 451.

[3] To Noel Annan, 13 January 1954, L2 422.

[4] Albert Einstein to Felix Frankfurter, 12 April 1952, L2 300, note 1.

[5] To Marietta Tree, 7 July 1949, L2 103.

Georgetown, where he had lived during the war, is, on a return visit in 1949, 'exactly like an old battlefield with all the action over and the ancient inhabitants once again established in the towns and villages and the old commanders of regiments and battalions not far away, only too anxious to take over the lurid past'.[1]

In many letters the scene-setting and dramatic recreation of events have an ulterior motive: to obtain forgiveness for his own inconsiderate behaviour. In one highly amusing letter to Hamilton Fish Armstrong Berlin dramatises himself as a fictional friend of his pseudonym, O. Utis, blaming the non-existent Utis for the inconvenience to which Berlin is likely to (and does) subject the long-suffering publisher. Elsewhere fantastic excuses of varying plausibility are paraded to excuse failures to fulfil social and professional commitments. The letters often reveal Berlin bending the truth – or perhaps just indifferent to it; woe betide the editor who relies on him for factual accuracy. Berlin depends on correspondents to conceal his frequent breaches of confidence and acknowledges that he makes regular use of his minor illnesses (themselves the result of an erratic life-style and exaggerated by hypochondria) to evade social and professional pressures and to provide an excuse for not meeting deadlines. A persistent pattern emerges of a refusal to accept responsibility (which Berlin admits he hates).

One of the most attractive characteristics of the letters is Berlin's unfailing capacity for reaction. He is never apathetic, always responsive, and values this characteristic in others: 'I find it easier to exist in a medium filled with other persons filled with their own purposes, bubbling with vitality, who never don't react & smile & frown perpetually & don't sink under their own weight or get blown about because of lack of it.'[2] The letters also demonstrate his willingness to put considerable effort into advising those who solicit his advice (often on their children's education) and to answer a letter from a total stranger in the Midwest of America with as much care and consideration as if a Regius Professor had sought his views.

A less pleasant trait is the snobbery Berlin sometimes displays, particularly towards other Jews, such as the 'Jews with colossal noses, who hate Zionism, make jolly Jewish jokes, but ultimately *are* ashamed and aggressive',[3] whose vulgarity he despises. The descriptions he sends to his parents of Jewish fellow passengers on various sea voyages are at times positively vicious and provoke the same feeling of unease as his attempts in later life to rid his father's memoir of any taint of Yiddish influence. In contrast with this, his socialising with the British Establishment, also well recorded in his letters, seems quite harmless.

[1] To Ursula Niebuhr, 5 March 1949, L2 79.
[2] To Aline Halban, 24 August 1954, L2 452.
[3] To Marie Berlin, 20 November 1955, L2 508.

Writing to Ben Nicolson in 1937, Berlin nails his colours firmly to the mast: 'I approve of gangs.'[1] Never a loner – indeed a self-confessed 'hater of solitude & an almost neurotic avoider of it'[2] – Berlin recognises that he needs a stable social and cultural background in his own life and that 'I only feel happy when I feel the solidarity of the majority of people I respect with and behind me.'[3] He persistently prefers the familiar to the new, hates change and, for all his social skills, is slow to feel at ease in a new environment. But the past, no matter how painful at the time, is now part of the known, hence a continuing source of pleasure: 'I am delighted to look at *anything* provided it is past.'[4] Berlin's fascination with those who hold very different views from his – whether Joseph de Maistre or Alice Roosevelt Longworth – can be seen as an experiment in exploring other identities, finding out what another 'gang' feels like from the inside. 'I adore having relations with the enemy and crossing the lines [...] Nevertheless, the whole pleasure of doing even that derives from the fact that one does know where the lines are drawn and what one is doing.'[5] The essential point is to know which gang you belong to first.

The need to preserve an unbroken social unit around him frequently turns Berlin into what he describes as a 'self-appointed shock absorber'[6] between others, the pourer of oil on troubled waters. But where he is personally involved, the desire to avoid socially disruptive confrontation leads to less admirable results. 'I like liking and being liked very much, perhaps too much'[7] he admits, and his 'excessive anxiety to please'[8] at times produces letters nauseating in their insincerity. To A. L. Rowse, one of his least favourite All Souls colleagues, whose election as Warden of that College he successfully opposes, Berlin nevertheless writes 'whatever happens I shall always be genuinely & deeply fond of you, & happy about your affection for me in which I believe: goodness me! One cannot live for twenty years on & off with someone as wonderful & unique as, if you'll let me say so, you are & and not develop a strong & permanent bond.'[9] (Rowse never realised the depths of Berlin's dislike of him, so the flattery must have worked.)

Berlin's reputation for over-sensitivity to slights is confirmed in his letters. He concedes that he is 'dreadfully sensitive – much too much – to opinion'[10]

[1] To Ben Nicolson, late September? 1947, L1 258.
[2] To Alice James, 22 February 1952, L2 290.
[3] To Marion Frankfurter, 23 August 1940, L1 342.
[4] To Alice James, 7 August 1952, L2 311.
[5] To Morton White, 22 March 1954, L2 438.
[6] To Alice James, 7 August 1952, L2 308.
[7] To Alice James, 31 December 1949.
[8] To Kay Graham, 11 January 1950, L2 167.
[9] To A. L. Rowse, 20 January 1952, L2 273.
[10] To John Sparrow, 21 November 1953, L2 405.

and suffers from a 'a fatal self consciousness'.[1] When a series of magazine articles brings him criticism from all sides, Berlin tries to explain his predicament:

I can never actually stop myself from saying what I want to say either about or to people – if I do life immediately loses all possible savour and I see no point in carrying on at all; on the other hand I invariably cause a certain amount of discomfort not to say pain by these means, and for this I am only too anxious to make amends, all my anxiety to please leaps forward, reckless of any justification of what I may have said, and then some degree of pride and defence of the truth intervenes and I oscillate unhappily between the desire to retract what is wounding while not withdrawing what is true. This is plainly unmanageable and I therefore spin helplessly.[2]

He is particularly sensitive to being regarded as a licensed clown, 'a mere jolly & garrulous *vulgarisiteur*'.[3] When the BBC intends to televise a film about its activities, Berlin insists that four short clips in which he appears, totalling 11 seconds, be removed at considerable cost and inconvenience, since his appearance alongside light entertainers 'would humiliate me, and be degrading to my profession [...] I think there is a limit to the extent to which dons should be allowed to appear as clowns for the benefit of the public.' [4]

This sensitivity is plainly the reflection of his own self-doubt. Although Berlin is firm and consistent in his intellectual beliefs, the letters overflow with expressions of his low opinion of his own abilities, variations on the theme of 'I have never in my life thought anything that I ever said, wrote, did etc. of the slightest importance.' [5] His written work is the main focus of doubt. For Berlin writing (like lecturing) is torture both in prospect and in progress. But publication is even worse:

I suffer from the deepest contempt for everything I have ever written – no sooner does it appear in print that it seems hollow, false, vulgar, glib, clumsy, at once too smooth and too awkward, but above all it has long since ceased to convey anything I wish to say; and if I defend it, it is out of pure pique – it always seems to me that everything my detractors say is *always* profoundly true and unanswerable.[6]

And publication involves taking responsibility:

[1] To Chaim Weizmann, 15 September 1947.
[2] To Marion Frankfurter, 5 January 1950, L2 163.
[3] To Anna Kallin, 26 October 1952, L2 325.
[4] To P. H. Newby, 18 March 1960, L2 729.
[5] To Maire Gaster, 27 May 1960.
[6] To Arthur Schlesinger, Jr., 21 December 1949, L2 140.

I talk & talk, as you know, heedlessly & too much because, however falsely, one thinks that spoken words vanish, & no responsibility lingers, & one is freed from these embarrassing witnesses of one's momentary states – if ever I see a letter or any other handwriting of mine anywhere, I am possessed by a furious desire to destroy it – but to write – above all to write books, seems to me a terrible prospect.[1]

Berlin regularly paints his life as filled with shame and guilt about his own actions (or lack of them): 'I am as always, ashamed. Ashamed of broadcasting too much, too popularly. Ashamed of not writing enough – too much rubbish, & avoiding the real sour apple.'[2] He even goes so far as to link his intellectual interests with what he regards as personal failings:

I have owed you a letter for I don't know how long: & feel, as I nearly always do, a feeling of obscure guilt, shame, inability to face moral & intellectual & personal obligations [...]: indeed I am beginning to wonder uneasily whether my perpetual protests against preoccupation with morality and the elimination of spontaneous pursuits of truth, pleasure etc. in favour of some puritan or sentimental or Hegelian pattern of social duty, doesn't spring from obsession with something wrong in the region within myself.[3]

Berlin's heroes – particularly Toscanini, Weizmann and Churchill – are those who are free from this crippling self-doubt, 'monolithic characters with a clear conception of right and wrong' who go 'steadily forward regardless of things, persons and ever-present possibilities of error [...] – total unlikeness has great attractions'.[4]

A constant *leitmotiv* of Berlin's letters is his lack of self-discipline in organising his life (and the self-contempt this engenders). 'I cannot plan, order, distribute my time neatly & sensibly between occupations,'[5] he laments, and 'as always in my life, the most difficult, roundabout, precarious, complex methods are employed to bring about the most obvious results'.[6] The consequences of this (even allowing for some comic exaggeration) are dire:

There is something which must be deeply wrong in the whole conduct of my life and has been for two score years or more, since I never seem to get anything done quite in time: nothing that I do seems to be properly done;

[1] To Alice James, 3 September 1950, L2 195.
[2] To Marion Frankfurter, 28 December 1952, L2 347.
[3] To Myron Gilmore, 26 December 1949, L2 147.
[4] To Rowland Burdon-Muller, 12 February 1953, L2 362.
[5] To Vera Weizmann, 1 June 1950, L2 181.
[6] To Avis Bohlen, 24 April 1950, L2 177.

a little more time, a little more care, a little more patience and planning and it would have been so much better. I always have too much to do, I always go to bed too late: nothing ever lasts long enough before I must interrupt it in order to avoid some disaster, some breaking of the elaborate texture which seems to me at the time of supreme value and importance, and so I go careering from pillar to post like an American student perpetually harassed by examinations, perpetually judging and being judged, unable to achieve even a moment of the large calm, the minimum of tranquillity which all tolerable lives require.[1]

This 'melancholy chaos'[2] is self-induced and Berlin occasionally drops hints as to the reasons for it. He admits to 'an almost morbid inability to say no, plus a feeling that unless I obligate myself to do rather more than I can I should never do anything at all, but just spend time happily in armchairs and talking with friends'.[3] He knows that his obligations to All Souls, Bryn Mawr and several publishers require him to produce at least one major book, but 'I seek for every possible avenue of escape, and all these articles, introductions etc. are so many straws at which I clutch in order not to be drowned in real writing. Every time I promise to do one of these smaller things I feel shame and relief'.[4] The victim of natural indolence ('I detest lecturing, I detest writing, in fact I have decided that I detest all work and have to make myself do it by the most appalling efforts'),[5] he contrives structural inducements to produce the works which his own motivation and self-discipline have notably failed to deliver. In 1950 he returns to All Souls: 'lacking the means – the will power – to do it without an external sanction, I have had to contrive to place myself in a situation where I cannot escape this duty: & voluntarily, with eyes open, accepted the yoke of an All Souls research Fellowship (how ungrateful this sounds!) which obliges one to produce or be condemned by one's peers'.[6] But only three years later, one of the attractions of becoming Warden of Nuffield College is the escape route administrative responsibilities would offer from 'being a goose expected to lay if not a golden at least leaden or copper eggs'.[7] Ironically, the prophet of liberty persistently seeks constraints in his own life and admits 'I preach the virtues of liberty, choice, action, and flee from them myself, & always always shall.'[8]

I never knew Isaiah Berlin, and indeed had little idea of his life and work

[1] To Alice James, 14 August 1951, L2 238.
[2] To Marion Frankfurter, 4 January 1956, L2 517.
[3] To Alice James, 16 July 1949, L2 104.
[4] To Peter Calvocoressi, 11 March 1960 L2 727, note 4.
[5] To Alice James, 7 December 1954, L2 462.
[6] To Alice James, 3 September 1950, L2 195.
[7] To John Sparrow, 21 November 1953, L2 405.
[8] To Rowland Burdon-Muller, 25 December 1952, L2 345.

before becoming part of the team working on his letters. (I do have a faint memory of surprise at discovering as an undergraduate that someone I had heard of as a media celebrity was also a Professor.) Over the last few years the task of preparing a selection of his letters for publication has dominated my life, so it has been impossible not to form strong, though often contradictory, views about the man and his correspondence. What strikes me most is his self-absorption. He is fascinated by himself and tends to assume that his correspondents will be too (as indeed they often are). The habit appears to be lifelong and clearly recognised by Berlin himself, from the schoolboy's admission in 1928 that 'As usual I write about myself, because to tell the truth I cannot find a more interesting topic'[1] to the grown man's recognition in 1952 of how friends view him: '"You must not think about *yourself* so *much*" I hear Rowland sharply observing.'[2] Such egotism is unsurprising in an insecure only child of doting parents, but its relentlessness can be wearing.

In many ways Berlin emerges most attractively in those letters (about the progress of the war or the future of All Souls, for example) where personal comments have no place. Perhaps, despite his considerable self-knowledge, he was wise to eschew autobiography. For all his vitality, generosity and wisdom, Isaiah Berlin the letter-writer appears all too often as a gifted, spoiled infant prodigy, charming but irresponsible. (I look forward to discovering from later letters whether the role of father-figure of Wolfson College leads to greater maturity.) But the letters themselves are a different matter. Even after countless re-readings (and poring over every word of the passages we have selected for publication), Berlin's letters still delight me with their variety, colour, life, humour, gossip, perceptive vignettes of and anecdotes about well-known people, indiscreet revelations of the background to current events, political understanding, intellectual stimulation and inimitable style. And they are very, very revealing.

---

[1] To Ida Samunov, June 1928, L1 10–11.
[2] To Alice James, 2 April 1952, L2 297.

The Berlin Papers in the Bodleian Library

Michael Hughes

INTRODUCTION

U PON BEING AWARDED the Jerusalem Prize in 1979, Sir Isaiah Berlin wrote a short article, 'The Three Strands of My Life', in which he gave a considered response to a question asked at the time by an interviewer, about whether it was true to say that Berlin had been formed by three traditions: Russian, British and Jewish. To his Russian origins Berlin ascribed his lifelong interest in ideas, leading to the development of his work on liberalism and pluralism. The British tradition he described as a sense of civilised human reality and 'a quality of life founded on compromise and toleration as these have been developed in the British world', with which he identified strongly, having lived in Britain for sixty years. His Jewish identity he felt to be so deeply rooted that it was impossible for him to analyse it, though he described his sharing of a common past, feelings and language with the Jewish community, and related this to a wider sense of fraternity in other cultures as well as his own.[1]

Evidence of these three strands is to be found, in different guises, intertwined throughout the extensive body of personal papers left behind by Berlin after his death. Wherever one looks, it is possible to detect one or more of them acting on his thought or deeds and in his relations with others, whether in correspondence about his views on Zionism, in papers relating to his academic activities in Oxford and elsewhere, or in notes made in researching his works on the history of ideas. It is impossible to separate from each other these deep-rooted and personal themes in describing such an archive, but it is hoped that this report will indicate and illustrate the full breadth and interest of Berlin's papers, now in the Bodleian Library, Oxford, for researchers in several fields.

BERLIN AND HIS ARCHIVE

Isaiah Berlin was born in Riga, in what is now Latvia, of Russian Jewish parents. After spending his early years mainly in Riga and in Petrograd, Russia, he moved with his parents to London in 1921. Thereafter he was educated at St

---

[1] 'The Three Strands in My Life', bib. 172; MS. Berlin 522, folios 257–90; repr. in PI2 (quotation at 257). Bibliographical ('bib.') references are to the entries in Henry Hardy's bibliography of Berlin's works in the IBVL, http://berlin.wolf.ox.ac.uk/lists/bibliography/index.html; those to manuscript material (hereafter abbreviated thus: MSB 522/257–90) are to the Berlin papers at the Bodleian Library, Oxford.

Paul's School and at Corpus Christi College, Oxford, the beginning of a life-long association with the University.

Between 1932 and 1938 Berlin was a Fellow of All Souls College, where he studied and taught philosophy, and wrote a biography of Karl Marx.[1] In 1938 he moved to New College, where he remained until 1950, with the exception of the war years: the period 1940–6 was spent working for British Information Services in New York and Washington, reporting on the state of US opinion on the war. In late 1945, he spent three months in Moscow and Leningrad on official business. During this period he met the poets Anna Akhmatova and Boris Pasternak: his conversations with Akhmatova in particular he considered one of the most significant and moving experiences in his life.

Following his return to academic life after the war, Berlin gradually created his own niche in the history of ideas, while also developing original ideas in political thought: especially in the fields of liberalism and pluralism. He returned to All Souls College in 1950, became Chichele Professor of Social and Political Theory in 1957, and was knighted that same year. From 1949 he lectured regularly in the United States, establishing close links with many American academics and finding great intellectual stimulus from those among them interested in the history of ideas. In 1966 Berlin accepted the Presidency of Wolfson College (initially known as Iffley College), and was instrumental in its creation as a building and institution. He retired from the University in 1975 but in 1974 had already become President of the British Academy, a position he retained until 1978. Thereafter he continued to pursue his academic and social interests, and was to see the publication of numerous uncollected and unpublished writings through the efforts of his editor, Henry Hardy.

Berlin had many interests beyond his professional work. He was involved in many aspects of Israeli political, cultural and academic affairs, and was a committed Zionist. He had a lifelong passion for music and the arts, and became a Director of the Royal Opera House. On both professional and social levels Berlin maintained a hectic round of engagements, his capacity for brilliant talk making him a guest eagerly sought after by countless friends and acquaintances at home and abroad. Throughout his life he developed close friendships with people from many walks of life. In 1956 Berlin married Aline Halban (née de Gunzbourg). Thereafter they enjoyed many years of happily married life, until Berlin's death in 1997.[2]

Berlin's surviving papers provide a rich source for further information on and research into nearly all aspects of his life, career and interests, as well as those

---

[1] *Karl Marx: His Life and Environment* (London, 1939), bib. 24; MSB 411–22.
[2] Further biographical information may be sought in Michael Ignatieff, *Isaiah Berlin: A Life* (London, 1998), and Alan Ryan, 'Sir Isaiah Berlin (1909–1997)', *Oxford Dictionary of National Biography* (Oxford, 2004).

of the individuals with whom he became close (whether personally or professionally) and the spheres in which he moved. During his lifetime he professed to have little interest in his own accumulation of letters and other material, and found going through them in later years so distasteful that he avoided doing so as far as possible:

> As for Edmund [Wilson]'s letters: I feel terribly ashamed of what I am about to tell you: of course I received some, as you know, and marvellous some of them were – one I remember very vividly – it was a wonderful practical joke, in which, as you read page one you expect a rather horrifying conclusion, and as you turn the page there is a great surprise, and it is very funny indeed. I do not destroy letters, but I stuff them into sacks and drawers; they are totally unclassified and unordered, and it would take me at least two years to sort them out (this is equally true of letters from, e.g., T. S. Eliot), so I simply do not know how many letters I have, or where they are. This is a terrible confession and merely a further indication of the chaos and confusion of my life. Some sacks are in my mother's house, some in Oxford, some in Italy, and so on; will you forgive me? After my death all this may emerge, but I dread delving into my past: I once experimented with pulling out ancient letters, and my relationships with the authors had changed so much since, and the memories were so upsetting, that I never did it again.[1]

In 1996, ownership of the papers passed to Berlin's Literary Trustees, who in 1999 donated them to the Bodleian Library, in accordance with his wishes. The Library had become involved with the papers before this, having provided assistance (during Berlin's lifetime) with some initial sorting, particularly of the correspondence. This was partly in order to facilitate research already beginning, particularly that undertaken by Henry Hardy and Berlin's biographer, Michael Ignatieff. Some sense thus began to be made of the caches of papers in the cellar and other storage areas of Berlin's home. Further rationalisation of the archive took place in the course of editorial work by Hardy. Further personal papers, dating from Berlin's Presidency, were kept in Wolfson College, and other material was housed in his room at All Souls College. It was only when all these sets of papers were transferred to the Bodleian that work could begin in earnest on a comprehensive catalogue.

The papers attracted a major award from the Arts and Humanities Research Board, which allowed a full cataloguing project to be undertaken between 2001 and 2004. This enabled the material to be arranged and described using current international archival standards, and the resulting electronic catalogue is

---

[1] Letter to Elena Wilson about letters from Edmund Wilson, 10 May 1974; MSB 206/192.

available online via the Library's website to allow information about the papers to be as widely available as possible.[1] Direct links with the Isaiah Berlin Virtual Library, maintained by Henry Hardy and containing a wealth of information on Berlin and his work, are included to enable the user to access associated information readily, including a full bibliography, lists of broadcasts and interviews, and in some cases the texts of works.

The process of detailed sorting followed usual professional practice. An appraisal was undertaken so that the full scope of the papers could be determined. This enabled identification of the principal series of material, and the critical task of arrangement into a coherent order followed. Once the basic arrangement was complete, work could begin on the compilation of a detailed description of the archive. An electronic catalogue was constructed using Encoded Archival Description (EAD), in conformity with other catalogues of Western manuscripts at the Bodleian Library. The process of description included identification of significant writers in the correspondence series, noting the principal topics recurring throughout the papers, and marking up this information according to professional rules, to enable online searching of the catalogue. This will also facilitate the identification of papers of interest by those using the National Register of Archives (NRA), and make possible a direct link between such national resources and the local descriptive information.

The papers are arranged in six principal series of varying size and complexity, as detailed in the online catalogue. Of these, the major groupings of correspondence and of academic and literary research papers and publications are of greatest significance, and potential areas of research interest will be discussed here in relation to these. However, reference is made where appropriate to links between these series and to other papers of value for specific topics.

CORRESPONDENCE

The correspondence falls into four sections. The general correspondence is chronological and is extremely broad in scope, including personal letters to and from many of Berlin's close friends; exchanges discussing in detail questions relating to Berlin's views and writings on liberalism, the history of ideas and other matters of professional interest; and routine business and social correspondence. The letters of major correspondents are similar in scope. The family correspondence is dominated by letters between Berlin and his parents, including Berlin's original letters home, which returned to his possession after his mother's death.[2] These provide insight into Berlin's relations with his parents,

---

[1] http://www.bodley.ox.ac.uk/dept/scwmss/wmss/online/modern/berlin/berlin.html.

[2] L1 includes the majority of those written during the period covered, and L2 many of those from the subsequent period.

and are full of detail and comment. There are also letters between Berlin and his aunt, Ida Samunov, and a small quantity of letters between Isaiah and Aline Berlin, the majority remaining in the possession of Lady Berlin. The several groups of subject-based correspondence reflect the professional and personal concerns and interests of Berlin. At certain periods before, and more or less continuously from 1959, the correspondence series include carbon copies of Berlin's replies to incoming letters.

The letters of individuals with whom Berlin corresponded provide a natural resource for biographers and are supplemented by *éloges* and other appreciations of friends and colleagues, which provide considered and eloquent personal pen-portraits of individuals through Berlin's eyes. In the correspondence there are occasional similar descriptions, sometimes more candid because they were not intended for publication. Also there are more general recollections and memories of friends and acquaintances about whom Berlin received enquiries. Examples in the latter category include Adam von Trott, the anti-Nazi German patriot whom Berlin knew in the 1930s; and the spies Guy Burgess and (to a lesser extent) Donald Maclean. And there are contemporary comments on people he met:

> I could not resist curiosity and we went to call on [the art critic Bernard] Berenson at Vallombrosa. He is all that you think he is and his moral character is perhaps not above suspicion. But at 86 he is remarkable. His brain is very clear, his eye very sharp, his sentiments malicious. He [...] reminds one to talk to of no one so much as Freud (whom he despises). To like him is difficult, perhaps even to respect him, but in a curious way one can be fascinated by so much controlled rational self-love. [...] I was horrified by such appalling, walled-in, windowless self-centredness by which everything – history, art, religion, politics – is related to himself. But when he told me that the people above all that he liked to meet were persons immediately after defeat – defeated generals, fallen prime ministers, exposed crooks etc. – that was genuinely interesting – and when he talks about himself and his tastes he no longer poses, or falsifies I think. I went away with a slightly creepy feeling but not undisposed to see him again.[1]

POLITICS, CURRENT AFFAIRS AND SOCIETY

Berlin's wide circle of friends and acquaintances mean that there is much material in his correspondence to draw on for research into several aspects of society. Correspondents in the fields of politics, diplomacy and journalism include the politicians Douglas Jay, Harry d'Avigdor-Goldsmid and Keith

[1] Letter to Rowland Burdon-Muller about a visit to Bernard Berenson, 3 November 1950; MSB 268/79–80; L2 200.

Joseph; the diplomats Patrick Reilly, Gladwyn Jebb, Anthony Rumbold and Charles (Chip) Bohlen; and the journalists and commentators Joe Alsop, Philip Toynbee and Alistair Cooke. In addition, Berlin's contacts included many society figures such as Ann Fleming and Ava Waverley in the UK, and Susan Mary Patten (later Alsop), Nin Ryan and Alice James in the US. Also of interest are Berlin's comments on figures in this field, for example a report of a dinner party late in 1949 attended by Churchill which 'turned out to be a kind of meeting of the Conservative shadow Cabinet – I don't quite know why I was asked':

> Winston was splendid on the subject that what we need is greater multiplicity of choices – choices which may many of them be bad, but choices nevertheless. Lyttleton said that Lord Ancaster had delivered a fine speech in his Home County, saying that there was to be 'no *damned* nonsense about policies or anything of that kind', whereupon Winston remarked that Lord A. 'had the root of the matter in him' and generally carried on in a gay and remarkable manner. He obviously had not the remotest notion of who I was but I identified myself to his wife, with the result that some weeks later I received a Christmas telegram from him thanking me for my article in the *Atlantic* [*Monthly*] + an Xmas card reproducing *his* painting of Mte Ste. Victoire, whose crudity has to be seen to be believed: but I must say, [a] very fearless thing to do: you wdn't know he and Cézanne lived on the same earth.[1]

The article referred to was that by Berlin on Churchill.[2] The previous year, Berlin had given assistance to Churchill with his memoir, *The Gathering Storm*, and a draft of his comments includes the following:

> [...] the story, told, I imagine, for the first time in print of the events behind Mr Eden's resignation in 1938. I remember being told about it during the war by Foreign Office officials, & I seem to remember someone saying that after Mr Eden came back post haste from Grasse, he did get a formal reversal of the Cabinet decision rather in the teeth of Neville Chamberlain – although by that time it was all too late, Roosevelt had felt snubbed, & all the bad consequences followed.[3]

Commentary by Berlin on international events is also valuable. At the time of the Cuban Missile Crisis he happened to be in Washington and attended a dinner with the Kennedys:

---

[1] Letter to Rowland Burdon-Muller, 29 December 1949; MSB 268/43–4; L2 157–8.
[2] 'Mr Churchill', bib. 32; MSB 426/142–250; repr. in PI.
[3] Draft letter to Winston Churchill, 14 Feb 1948; MSB 116/209–10. The slightly different version sent to Churchill is at L2 43.

I was oversold to the new young Turks and, indeed, to the Grand Turk himself to such a degree that when I finally came to meet them and him their disappointment was acute and visible. I am really no good at a round-table discussion of ICBMs, of middle-range weapons, the strategic importance of Assam, or even the secrets of the British Minister of Defence. Geo-politics is in the air and the tension is enormous – that comes from the top. The President, to give him his proper title, is exceedingly 'withdrawn' as they say here in comparison to the outgoing FDR and he only has two gears: either business – if he sits next to the French Ambassador he talks to him immediately about what France should do about, let us say, Sékou Touré; [...] if he is compelled to speak to me he assumes me to be an expert Kremlinologist and wants to know precisely why Krushchev did or did not do that in Berlin; and so on [...]. Mrs K. is very different from what she is popularly assumed to be and one can talk to her quite genuinely.[1]

JEWISH AFFAIRS AND ZIONISM

Berlin's commitment to Zionism and Jewish affairs is a recurrent theme in his papers. His correspondence includes much material of relevance, including statements of his own position both in general and with regard to specific events. One such is a letter to Hansi Lambert in 1958:

That Arab rights have been trodden on – that a wrong to them has been committed – it seems to be morally shameful to deny. If you then ask me why I am pro-Zionist, it is because I think that where right clashes with right – or rather misery with misery – one must not think about rights, which always exist – whether those of the French and Germans or the Russians and Americans – but of some calm utilitarian solution which produces on the whole the best or happiest solution in the end. In human affairs I am prepared to adopt a Catholic standpoint, accept original sin, and agree that men are imperfect, and that whatever we do someone will suffer and no solution can be lasting. That being said, the reason for admitting the Jews to Palestine was that their misery has been too long and too great [...][2]

Several of Berlin's correspondents were deeply involved in this field, including Chaim Weizmann, the first President of Israel, a close friend of Berlin's. After Weizmann's death the link was maintained through friendship with his widow, Vera, and Berlin's involvement with the Weizmann Institute and Archives. Other correspondents in this area include in the political sphere the

---

[1] Letter to Noel Annan, 6 December 1962; MSB 247/76–8.
[2] Letter to baronne Johanna Lambert, 20 May 1948; MSB 154/305–10; L2 630.

civil servants and diplomats Jacob Herzog, Walter Eytan and Eliahu Elath; the Mayor of Jerusalem, Teddy Kollek; and the activist Meyer Weisgal; on academic topics in Israel and Britain Jacob Talmon, Chimen Abramsky, Meyer Verete and Nathan Rotenstreich; and influential Jewish Britons such as Dorothy de Rothschild, Victor Rothschild, and Isaac and Leonard Wolfson.

Berlin wrote on Zionism and Jewish affairs also. There are obituaries, appreciations and biographical accounts of Weizmann, Herzog, Weisgal and others; papers on historical figures and topics such as that on Disraeli and Marx;[1] and accounts of Berlin's own Zionist convictions and experiences.[2]

Evidence for parental influence on Berlin's Jewish identity and Zionism may be found in the papers of Mendel and Marie Berlin. These form an archivally distinct series of the papers, having originated from the family home in Hampstead, but the closeness of the links between Berlin and his parents means that there is much of relevance to his own life. The early family correspondence is of great interest for the link it provides to Berlin's Russian Jewish origins: it includes letters from his mother's family in Latvia before the Second World War. Relatives of Berlin's who were still in Riga in 1941 were exterminated, and the abrupt conclusion of this correspondence is a poignant reminder of this:

> It's already a long time since we had no letter from you and from the Samunovs. I do not think you have not written probably the post is not in order and I do not know whether my letter will reach you and when it will be but I beg you, if you will receive my letter please do wire me immediately about your health and Samunovs as well. About us I can say we are well Thank God Where is Shaya?[3]

ANGLO-AMERICAN RELATIONS IN THE SECOND WORLD WAR

Berlin's work for British Information Services in the United States during the period 1940–6 provides source material for this topic. Relevant material is to be found in correspondence with Herbert Nicholas and Lady Daphne Straight and in the general series; there is also comment of interest in Berlin's letters to his parents.[4] In addition, Berlin wrote some accounts of his experiences.[5]

---

[1] 'Benjamin Disraeli, Karl Marx, and the Search for Identity', bib. 118; MSB 483–5; repr. in AC.

[2] *Zionist Politics in Wartime Washington: A Fragment of Personal Reminiscence*, bib. 126; MSB 512–13; repr. at L1 663–93.

[3] The last extant postcard from Berlin's maternal grandfather Salman Volshonok, 8 August 1940; MSB 806/84.

[4] Selected examples of all these are included in L1.

[5] See L1, and the Introduction to H. G. Nicholas (ed.), *Washington Despatches 1941–45: Weekly Political Reports from the British Embassy* (London, 1981), repr. at L1 654–62; bib. 174; MSB 523.

The lecture on which one of these was based gave rise to correspondence about the extent of knowledge of the Holocaust in wartime Washington:

> I simply tried to tell the truth about how matters looked to me when I was in Washington, and the thing that seems most evident is that facts afterwards known in retrospect were either unknown or not known at all clearly at the time. You say that people are critical of the fact that I do not estimate the vehement propaganda of say, Wise or Silver [...] at its true worth – ignoring their manner of presentation etc., they were concerned about the horrors suffered by the Jews in Europe, more than Weizmann etc. I think everyone was upset by what they read and heard – but you are quite right in supposing that the holocaust – the real, unspeakable disaster [...] was not known, at least, in my world, until 1945.[1]

AKHMATOVA AND PASTERNAK

There is little contemporary material among his papers concerning Berlin's meetings with Russian poets. However, the significance of the encounters meant that Berlin was frequently asked about these occasions, and this results in considerable later correspondence on the topic. Berlin also wrote a moving account of these meetings.[2] Some contemporary correspondence relates to the publication of Pasternak's *Doctor Zhivago*,[3] which Berlin read in Russian manuscript on his 1956 visit, and found profoundly moving. While Berlin did write a short appreciation of this book, in general he cautioned against excessive publicity in the West because of the negative effect this might have on Pasternak's welfare, as in the points he made against a cover on Pasternak for Time & Life in 1958:

> *Time* & *Life* are regarded as the spearhead of the Cold War party in the West. For them to play up Pasternak's heroism & martyrdom, even in the literary section, is to align him with the enemies of the Soviet Union so openly, as not only to expose him to further dangers, but also to produce a violently anti-American reaction among the uncommitted Asians, European liberals etc. who may be anti-communist, but don't wish to feel allied to the bugbears of "Wall Street imperialists" & other reactionaries. [...] so support for, or playing up of, Pasternak's cause by openly anti-Soviet organs may compromise him finally – lead him sincerely & desperately to disavow such alliances – cause the wobblers & the uncommitted & the anti-communist left to think that perhaps the Soviet Writers Union *had*

---

[1] Letter to Sarah Groll, 17 November 1972; MSB 200/218–19.
[2] 'Meetings with Russian Writers in 1945 and 1956', in PI; bib. 169; MSB 522/1–207.
[3] Boris Pasternak, *Doctor Zhivago* (London, 1958).

to pillory *Zhivago* openly, if it was to be exploited by the "imperialist[s]" for their own wicked ends.[1]

The series of personal papers in the archive includes a few items reflecting the significance of his meeting and connection with Anna Akhmatova, including a copy of the poem from *Cinque* referring to himself, written in his own hand in Russian, probably not long after a copy in the poet's autograph was given to him personally on his departure from Leningrad in 1946.[2]

LITERATURE

Berlin counted numerous figures in the literary world among his close friends. Of greatest personal significance among these is his lifelong friend the poet Stephen Spender, with whom there is considerable correspondence, often enclosing drafts of poems, especially in the 1930s when Spender spent time abroad in Germany and Spain and was witness to events in those countries. Other correspondents include the writer Elizabeth Bowen, whose letters again are particularly valuable in the pre-war period when Bowen and Berlin were especially close. In one of their exchanges there is an account by Berlin of a visit to the home of Hugh Walpole:

> We went to tea there a few days ago: you know Mr Walpole? he says he admires your books immensely – a fat, rosy, happy largeish dimpled man came bouncing out to meet us, and then served tea coyly, like a shy provincial spinster, anxiously inquiring about milk and sugar. He bounded at once on to William Plomer & Mrs Woolf. He was proud & pleased about his knowledge of them, & spoke of them with a curious mixture of patronage & admiration. Mrs Woolf – who plainly persecutes him & plays him & turns him over & over – he said was a very humourous woman.[3]

Another facet of this area is Berlin's writings on and translations of Russian literary works: notably those by Turgenev. Of great significance also is Berlin's masterly essay on Tolstoy's view of history as depicted in *War and Peace*.[4]

---

[1] Manuscript original of 'Isaiah Berlin's points against Pasternak cover' enclosed with letter from Raimund von Hofmannsthal, 1958; MSB 155/271b–f; L2 762.

[2] MSB 784/3.

[3] Letter to Elizabeth Bowen, [14 September 1936]; MSB 245/56–60; L1 193. The papers include Berlin's original outgoing letters to Bowen, many of which (including this one) are printed in L1.

[4] 'Lev Tolstoy's Historical Scepticism' (later title *The Hedgehog and the Fox: An Essay on Tolstoy's View of History*), bib. 44; MSB 428.

MUSIC AND THE ARTS

Berlin's love of music was lifelong, and crops up in his writings in the form of reviews and occasional pieces for opera programmes, together with a more substantial article on Verdi.[1] There is also correspondence with individuals in the musical world: the composer and musical director Nicolas Nabokov, a close personal friend whose wildly eccentric letters are predominantly in Russian; the violinists Yehudi Menuhin (Berlin's distant cousin) and Isaac Stern; and the music critic Martin Cooper. And there is a vivid description of a visit to Oxford by Shostakovich in 1958, when the composer stayed at Berlin's home:

> His cello sonata was played by a young and very handsome cellist from Ceylon, he listened to it calmly, said to me that the cellist was good, and the pianist very bad (which was perfectly true), and complained to the cellist that he had played two passages incorrectly. The cellist flushed, produced the score, and S. saw that the score bore out the cellist. He could not think how this could be, suddenly realised that it had been edited [by] Piatigorsky, who had of course altered the score arbitrarily to please himself; this was the moment at which he came nearest to real rage, took out a pencil and violently crossed out Piatigorsky's forgeries, and substituted his own original version. After that his brow cleared, and he returned to his little corner.

This detailed account ends, as Berlin writes, on a sombre note:

> S's face will always haunt me somewhat, it is terrible to see a man of genius victimised by a regime, crushed by it into accepting his fate as something normal, terrified almost of being plunged into some other life, with all powers of indignation, resistance, protest removed like a sting from a bee, thinking that unhappiness is happiness and torture is normal life.[2]

ACADEMIC AND LITERARY
RESEARCH PAPERS AND PUBLICATIONS

Material for Berlin's written works forms a major portion of the papers. It includes research notes for specific works, together with successive drafts and proofs. Papers for published works have been arranged chronologically according to the date of publication, which enables correlation with Hardy's full bibliography of Berlin's works. Several works were based on earlier lectures or broadcasts, and usually the relevant lecture notes or broadcast transcripts

---

[1] 'The "*Naïveté*" of Verdi', bib. 110; MSB 476/8–99; repr. in AC.
[2] Letter to Rowland Burdon-Muller, 28 June 1958; MSB 269/113–14; L2 638, 640–1.

have been grouped with the further drafts preparatory to publication, reflecting the order of the papers as found. In some instances the research notes and papers are broader in scope than the work in question; Berlin appeared to group many of his notes by topic rather than by work. If sets of such notes were found together with relevant drafts they have been kept together in the archival arrangement.[1] Revisions for later editions have also been placed with papers relating to the original work, except where they form part of a substantially different publication such as *Four Essays on Liberty*,[2] which includes revised drafts of the component writings and a full new introduction.

The material in this section illustrates Berlin's tendency to revise obsessively and redraft his work. His eventual practice was to dictate a first version on to a Dictaphone.[3] This would be typed out for Berlin to make numerous and often substantial changes before retyping, a process that might be repeated several times. Even at the end Berlin seldom appeared completely satisfied with his efforts, and insisted on further changes at later stages in publication.[4]

Papers relating to Berlin's unpublished writings are arranged chronologically by date of compilation as far as possible. They include lectures, papers and broadcasts unpublished at the time of Berlin's death – although some have since been published through the continuing work of Henry Hardy, and this has been indicated. While most unpublished material was already known to Hardy, one substantial new item came to light during cataloguing, a work on the philosophy of language.[5]

These papers provide a rich source for the study of the development of Berlin's thought, through both individual works and successive writings on related topics. Predominant themes are works on liberalism and pluralism; the development of political thought both in general and through the study of individual philosophers and thinkers; works on philosophy, particularly represented among Berlin's early works before he turned to the history of ideas, but recurring later in writings such as those on historicism; and writings on the Russian intelligentsia and on Russian and Soviet political thought. There are also relevant exchanges in his correspondence, for example a letter to Herbert Elliston in which Berlin expounds some of his early thoughts on liberalism:

> I think that what I am pleading for is really what used to be called Liberalism, i.e. a society in which the largest number of persons are

---

[1] For example, the notes found with drafts of 'The Originality of Machiavelli', bib. 122; MSB 494–7; repr. in AC and PSM.

[2] *Four Essays on Liberty* (London and New York, 1969), bib. 112; MSB 477–80; repr. in L.

[3] Some of the original Dictaphone recordings survive and are at the British Library Sound Archive.

[4] For a detailed account of such an occasion, see Hardy's 'The Editor's Tale', L ix–xxxiii.

[5] MSB 568/146–260.

allowed to pursue the largest number of ends as freely as possible, in which these ends are themselves criticised as little as possible and the fervour with which such ends are held is not required to be bolstered up by some bogus rational or supernatural argument to prove the universal validity of the end. Everyone does, in fact, have purposes and values for which they live and for which they are occasionally prepared to die.[1]

The small section of juvenilia includes some school and undergraduate essays, and a story which is Berlin's earliest extant piece of work, the author then 'being 12½ years of age'.[2]

CONCLUSION

The rich and varied content of Isaiah Berlin's papers stands as a testament to his passion for life, for it documents his commitment to all things in which he became involved, whether professional or personal, moral or social. He placed a very high value on the importance of human relations: from this sprang his interest in the ideas which have shaped humanity as it is today, and the passionate concern he felt for its future. His personal beliefs and interests may be discerned throughout the papers he has left behind, and unite them into a coherent whole.

[1] Letter to Herbert Elliston, 30 Dec 1952; MSB 131/301–2; L2 350.
[2] Story fictionalising the murder of Moise Solomonovich Uritsky, depicted by IB as Soviet Minister of Justice, 1922; MSB 731/17–25; published as 'The Purpose Justifies the Ways', bib. 241; repr. in FL and L (see also L xxviii–xxix).

Elysian Schools

Isaiah Berlin

When this work was published in the *Oxford Magazine* in 1958, it was preceded by this editorial headnote: 'The following manuscript appears to have turned up in the Schools, though it is hard to say exactly how it can have found its way there. There is little evidence to show that this examination was ever conducted here. We have, however, consulted Professor Sir Isaiah Berlin about it, and he considers that, if it was, the candidates were dealt with as fairly as could be expected.' The *Oxford Magazine*'s typesetter appears to have corrupted the text at various points, but since the manuscript has not been traced, it has not always been possible to establish what the author wrote. The editor has done his best, but admits that a certain amount of apparent gibberish remains.

		Phil.	*Pol.*	*Econ.*
Aquinas, S. T.	Ampleforth & Campion Hall	$\alpha-$	$\alpha\gamma$	γ
Aristotle, Onassis	Winchester & New College	$\alpha\equiv$	$\alpha\equiv$	$\beta\beta\alpha$
Solid 1st; no imagination; becomes civil servant in Ministry of Education.				
Bentham, J.	Westminster & Queen's	β	$\alpha\beta$	$\beta\alpha$
Scrapes 1st.		(jejune)	(narrow)	
Burke, E.	Wellington & Trinity	$\gamma++/1$	$\alpha\beta/1$	$\gamma-/1$
Filmer, R.	Eton & Trinity	δ	δ	ε
Hegel, G. W. F.	Salem & St Antony's	$\gamma\alpha$	$\delta?\alpha$	β
Odd historical knowledge. Epigrams.				
Hobbes, T.	Malmesbury GS & Balliol	$\alpha\alpha\gamma$	$\alpha\beta\gamma$	β
Rusticated for writing nasty, brutish, short article (anonymously) in *Oxford Magazine*. Viva also short and nasty. Purged γ on Politics, but one examiner morally disturbed, and has nightmares.				
Hume, D.	Edinburgh Academy & Balliol	$\delta\alpha$	$\beta+$	$\alpha\beta$
Kant, I.	Bootham & St Catherine's	$\alpha-$	$\beta++$	$\beta?+$
Won scholarship to CCC, but wouldn't row in fourth boat, so went to St Cath's instead. Lived in tent in New Bodleian bicycle yard. Viva formal (very).				
Kautsky, K.	Prague & Oriel	β	β	β
Formal 2nd.				

		Phil.	Pol.	Econ.
Locke, J.	MGS & Lincoln	β+?+	β+?+	β+
Machiavelli, N.	Charterhouse, King's Coll. London & Univ.	δ++	α–	γ

Smooth.

| Maistre, J. de | Gordonstoun & Worcester (Besse Scholar) | γ+ | γδ | ε |

Hockey blue; not interested in academic work.

| Malthus, T. | King's, Canterbury, & Keble | βα | βγ (irrelevance) | α= |

| Marx, K. | St Paul's & Christ Church (cut by Jenny von Westphalen's brother's set) | δ | β? | ββα |

Long viva; intolerable Hegelian patter; no facts, except in Social and Economic History; given 3rd as compromise. Denounces examiners in *New Oxford Mail* (one issue only). Flies to America and becomes Professor in New School of Social Research; splits off to form New New School, etc.; scandals. Flies to England. Elected to Fellowship at pre-[undecipherable monosyllable] Balliol. Never heard of again.

| Montesquieu, C. S. de | Harrow & Magdalen | β+ | α= (Political Institutions) γ– (British History) | γβ |

Irish; *invents* elegantly and freely.

| Paine, T. | Bradford GS & Queen's | γ– | β= | δ |

Formal viva on best paper (Political Institutions) shows intimate knowledge of American Constitution and French Assembly. Long viva. Utterly fails to come up. 4th.

| Pareto, V. | Lausanne & Christ Church | δ | αγ | αβ |

Strong on Latin countries, but ill-informed on UK and US. Viva clear and vicious. Philosophers disagree.

| Plato, Robin | Eton & Christ Church | δα | δ | ε |

Birdwatcher; very British. Ploughs (no work).

| Rousseau, J. J. | St Paul's & Wadham | ε | εα | βδ |

| Socrates, Onassis | Privately ed. & St Catherine's |

This candidate's scripts were unfortunately lost (by an examiner who shall remain nameless), but a tradition persists among undergraduates that he was given α++/14. Viva'ed his Philosophy examiners from 10.30 to 2.30, at which point the search for one last truth was broken off when an examiner collapsed from extreme hunger and thirst and a gnawing doubt about the justification for boards, examinations, subjects, candidates, universities etc.

		Phil.	*Pol.*	*Econ.*
Sorel, G.	Paris & Ruskin	γ	γ – (on Labour movements, α–)	γ
Uncooperative. Propounds myths suitable for examiners.				
Spengler, O.	St Paul's & St John's	δ	β– (Political Institutions) γδα (History)	ε
Ploughs after long viva.				
Tocqueville, A. de	Eton & New College	β	βα	γβ
Toynbee, A.	Radley & Merton	δ	γ++ (Political Institutions) γ?α (History)	ω
Ploughs.				
Veblen, T.	U. of Minnesota & Magdalen	γ	β+ (Political Institutions) αγ (History)	αβ
Rhodes Scholar. Unhappy because rejected by Balliol. Viva short and improper; removed for leering at female examiner. 2nd.				
Webb, S.	MGS & Exeter	γ	ββα	β+?+
Potter, B.	Roedean & LMH	γ?+	ββα	β+?+

Identical marks on all questions except Morals. After investigation by Proctors it was established that no illicit collusion had occurred. Insisted on using numbered postcards instead of proper books for answers. Punitive vivas; examiners punished instead. Enormous erudition impressed economists; 'α' vivas on both Economic Organization and Economic History. Philosophers not shaken. 3rds.

For the Benefit of My Son
Mendel Berlin

I always thought it might be embarrassing. He said he was doing it, and I thought: He oughtn't to, and he'll probably write a lot of nonsense, and might write anything. I've never read a single line.

Isaiah Berlin talking to Michael Ignatieff in 1989[1]

EDITORIAL NOTE

The manuscript of Mendel Berlin's autobiographical memoir, of which the following text is a transcription, is sometimes very hard to read, and contains numerous personal names that are spelt sometimes inconsistently, occasionally eccentrically. East European Jews characteristically used a mixture of Hebrew, Yiddish and Russian names, with a range of diminutives in each language, so that establishing standard forms of their names is virtually impossible. Where Mendel Berlin consistently uses the same form, I have not changed it. Where his practice varies, I have standardised it, choosing the usual form, or the one that fits most naturally into the context of Isaiah Berlin's own practice. Otherwise only minor changes, mostly to punctuation and spelling, have been made in the interests of readability: more intrusive editing would have watered down the distinctive atmosphere of Mendel's prose.

Reference to the family trees on pages 316–19 may aid identification of the relatives Mendel Berlin describes. The trees include most of the family members referred to by Mendel, as well as other relatives not specifically mentioned by him.

The subheadings and notes are editorial. In the notes IB = Isaiah Berlin, MB = Mendel Berlin. Several of the notes derive from annotations made by IB on a transcript I provided him with late in his life.

Since I have no Hebrew or Yiddish, I have depended entirely on those whose know these languages for the transcription, transliteration, translation and interpretation of matter written in the Hebrew alphabet (used for both languages). Mendel's Hebrew is transliterated according to current modern Hebrew pronunciation; his Yiddish is transliterated according to the YIVO system. Yiddish is identified as such in the notes; other Jewish terminology can be assumed to be in Hebrew. I am extremely grateful to Gennady Estraikh, to the late Ofra Perlmutter, to Joseph Sherman and to Norman Solomon for generous expert help in preparing this document for publication. I am also very much in debt to Jennifer Holmes for her work on the family trees, and for timely help in the last stages of editing the memoir.

I STARTED several times to write down my autobiography and some facts of my life for the benefit of my son, but during the war I could not concentrate sufficiently; now, when the extinction of nearly all the members of my wife's and my family by the Nazis[2] has been confirmed, I feel the necessity for these records is real; the living link between the past and the future, the link who still remembers the past, is practically only myself.

I will begin with a few genealogical data. I believe that heredity is an important factor and good breeding counts for much: 'יחוס'[3] or belonging to a good family among Jews in Eastern Europe meant descent from a long line of rabbis and scholars, going back to some world-famous rabbi and scholar. Perhaps this is the best breeding of all, since it means that for generations spirituality and scholarship was the pervading element in the family and was put before material acquisitiveness and good living; also character was moulded on gentler and more moral principles.

SCHNEERSON ANCESTORS

I can trace the line of my paternal ancestors (incidentally also my wife's, since my father and mother-in-law were brother and sister) to the latter part of the eighteenth century. It begins with a certain R.[4] Baruch who settled in the little townlet of Liosno[5] in the Gouvernement of Mohilev (Могилевская Губерния)[6] c.1750. His origin I don't know; he is believed to have come from Austria or Galicia and was supposed to have descended from the מהרש'ל[7] (R. Solomon Lurie), a very famous rabbi and Talmudist of the sixteenth century. His son was the famous R. Shneur Salman[8] of Liadi (commonly known as the

---

[1] The date on which MB began writing his account, which eventually covered a period ending in the autumn of 1949.

[2] As far as is known, Mendel Berlin's father and Marie Berlin's father, brother and youngest sister, together with her paternal uncle, his wife and two of their three daughters, all died in 1941 during the Nazi occupation of Riga (see family trees for names). Other relatives died elsewhere in Europe.

[3] 'Yikhes' ('distinguished lineage').

[4] Depending on context, 'R.' in personal names stands either for 'Reb' (as here), a polite form of address used for adult males by Yiddish-speakers, akin to 'Mr' (except that it is used with the given name); or for 'Rav' (Rabbi, as in the next sentence: see note 7 below).

[5] Liozno, near Vitebsk in Belarus.

[6] 'Mogilevskaya Guberniya'.

[7] 'MaHaRSHaL', acronym for 'Moreynu Ha-Rav Shlomo Lurya' ('Our Teacher Rabbi Shlomo Luria' – or Lurie, as MB spells it), i.e. Solomon ben Yehiel (c.1510–74).

[8] A variant spelling of Zalman.

'Alter Rabbi'),[1] the founder of the חב״ד[2] system of Chassiduth. The family name of Schneerson[3] later has been derived from the name Shneur. He certainly was a most extraordinary and great man. His knowledge of the Jewish literature and Cabbolah[4] was vast; at a very early age he was a recognised talmudical authority, and in his search for further knowledge he wandered to the Maggid[5] of Meseritz, the pupil of R. Israel Baal-Shem,[6] and during his years of study there developed his system – a system which drew hundreds of thousands of pupils and admirers, and which split the Russian, Lithuanian and Ukrainian Jewry into two sects, the Misnagdim[7] and Chassidim, with a lasting influence on their character and make-up. He became a legendary figure to Eastern and particularly Russian Jewry. Because of his schism and the split among Jewry he was denounced by his adversaries to the Russian Government and the infamous III Division (Третье Отделение)[8] took up the case against him. He instituted the collection of money for the benefit of scholars and pious Jews in Palestine ([the] so-called 'רמב״ן'[9] – Rabbi Meir Baal Ness – collection) and one of his enemies' accusations was that he was collecting money for Turkey against Russia. The Russian administration put him in prison[10] in the notorious Petro-Paul Fortress in St Petersburg and he was only freed when after the assassination of Tsar Paul a more liberal spirit began in Russia with the ascent of Alexander I.

Notwithstanding the humiliations he suffered under the tsarist Government he supported the Tsar very effectively during the 1812 Napoleonic War. His contention was that while material and civic freedom will be the lot of the Jews under Napoleon, yet religion and spirituality will suffer under the liberating regime, and therefore the Tsar had to be supported. The intelligence system in the Russian Army was very poor, and the Rav mobilised his hundreds of thousands of followers (Chassidim) who lived all along the line

---

[1] sc. Alter Rebbe, Yiddish for 'Old Rebbe'. A Rebbe is the leader of a Hasidic sect.

[2] 'Chabad', acronym of 'chochmah, binah, da'at' ('wisdom, understanding, knowledge'). These are basic Cabbalistic terms central to Shneur Zalman's religious philosophy, and 'chabad' has accordingly become the designation of his (Lubavitch) sect of Hasidism (called Chassiduth by MB).

[3] Now sometimes spelled 'Shneerson'.

[4] i.e. Cabbala or Kabbalah.

[5] 'Preacher'. Rabbi Dov Baer, the Maggid of Mezhirech, died in 1772.

[6] Rabbi Israel ben Eliezer (c.1700–60), known as the Baal Shem Tov ('Master of the Good Name'), the founder of the Hasidic movement.

[7] Literally 'opponents', i.e. of Hasidism.

[8] 'Tret'e Otdelenie' ('Third Department' of the secret police).

[9] 'RaMBaN', usually the designation by acronym of Nachmanides, but here correctly interpreted as an acronym for Rabbi Meir Baal ha-Nes (Rabbi Meir the Master of Miracles, possibly the second-century sage), in whose name this fund was set up long before Shneur Zalman's time.

[10] Shneur Zalman was imprisoned twice, in 1798 and in 1801, and on both occasions released the same year. MB's account seems to be derived from family tradition.

of the advance of Napoleon's armies into scouts and spies, and news of the armies' movements, its provisioning and so on travelled quickly ahead of the armies and were regularly supplied to the Russian Army. Because of this he had to flee when the French army came near his residence in Liadi (between Vitebsk and Smolensk) and he was helped in his flight by the Russian Commander. During this flight in the Russian winter he died and was buried in Gadiaz (Гадязь, Полтавская губ.).[1] There is on record a letter by his son to one of his friends telling him how sure the Rav was of Russian victory, a letter written from Viasma before the French entered Moscow, and how serene he was in all his plight and misery, in full conviction of ultimate victory.

This is then our great ancestor. He was followed by his son, called רב האמצעי[2] (the Mitteler Rabbi) R. Dov-Ber, who continued his teaching, and he in his turn was followed by his son-in-law R. Menachem Mendel, called the 'Zemach Zedek'[3] (after the title of his work of talmudical and canonical Responsa). The wife of the Zemach Zedek – Mussa – is the one after whom your mother is named,[4] and I was named after the Zemach Zedek. The Zemach Zedek was also a grandson of the Alter Rabbi – a son of his daughter and thus also a member of the same Schneerson family. The Zemach Zedek had a large family – five sons and one daughter.[5] His sons – after his death – set up 'sees' of their own and divided his followers, who may well have numbered over half a million, among themselves. The eldest, R. Leib, was the rabbi of Kopustz, the second – R. Shneur Salman – of Liadi, the third – R. Samuel – continued at his father's see, Liubavitchi, the fourth – R. Baruch Schalom – was only an ordinary Rav, the 5th – R. Joseph – was somewhere in the Ukraine. The daughter was a particularly gifted woman and was invited by her father to all his 'Councils of State' along with her brothers. She married R. Shneur Schneerson, the son of Nachum Schneerson (who resided in Niestin – Ukraine), who was a son of the 'Mitteler Rabbi', and thus again intermarried in the family. She died young and left one son and three daughters. The eldest of her children was Frumma[6] – my and your mother's grandmother – who was brought up practically as a young orphan on her mother's side by her grandparents – the Zemach Zedek and his wife – and was therefore a favourite of theirs.

---

[1] 'Gadyaz', Poltavskaya gub[erniya]' ('Gadyaz' [now known as Gadyach], province of Poltava').

[2] 'Rav ha-Emtzai' ('the Middle Rebbe').

[3] 'The Plant of Righteousness'.

[4] In their naturalisation papers Mendel gives her name as Mussa Marie Berlin.

[5] MB's description of the number and birth order of the Zemach Zedek's offspring is not entirely accurate.

[6] Also Frooma or Frumme in the MS.

She looked after her younger sisters and brother – Chayetta[1] (Ethel?), who later married Shaya[2] Berlin, who originated from Vielish – near Vitebsk – and later settled in Riga. You did not know Shaya Berlin (as he died in 1908) but were named after him, but in your early childhood you knew Aunt Chayetta (whose hand you used to refuse to kiss). A second sister was Rivka-Slata, who married Moshe-Eleazar Levin of Vidzi, Gouvernement of Kovno, with whose son Baruch Levin your mother and I were very friendly in our early youth. Her brother was Baruch Schneerson of Vitebsk (of his children you have met when you were about 7–8 years of age in Staraya Russa[3] Schöne Lagovier of Moscow). Grandmother Frumma, whose name was increased to Frumma Sarah Deroza during an illness – as was the Jewish custom (משנה שם משנה מזל)[4] – had another half-brother, Leib Schneerson: her father Shneur Schneerson married a second time and he was the child of the 2nd marriage. He was Rav of Velish. Velish was the town, by the way, where there was at the end of the eighteenth century a blood libel,[5] and many families were kept for years in prison, among them the Berlins and Aronsons (of whom Mulia[6] Aronson is a descendant). Derzhavin (Держа́вин) the poet was for a time Governor-General of Bielorussia and he was partly responsible for the imprisonment of the Velish martyrs.

MENDEL'S FATHER AND HIS FAMILY

Grandmother Frumma was married to one Benjamin Zuckerman of Rudnia – a little town in the Gouvernement of Vitebsk – near Liubavitchi – her townlet of birth. The Zuckermans came from Mohilev and were a very good talmudical and rich family. Benjamin's father – Meyer Zuckerman – married into the family of one Binke in Rudnia who got enriched in one of the Russian wars as an army contractor (I am not sure, I believe his family was Rivlin). He was a Chassid, while the Zuckermans all were staunch Misnagdim, and Meyer thus became a proselyte to Chassidism.

The 'Binke' blood is the one streak of rather degeneration in the descendants of Meyer Zuckerman. Practically all the children of this marriage were not quite normal, feeble-minded, and it broke out in the later generations, as you quite well know. Grandfather Benjamin was extraordinary pious, ascetic

---

[1] MB calls her Chaete, Chaie-Et[t]e, Chaja-Ette (the spelling that appears here in the MS) or Chajete.

[2] Diminutive of 'Isaiah'. MB also calls him Schaie or Shaie. Shaya is the version usually used of IB.

[3] A spa town between Petrograd and Moscow.

[4] 'Meshaneh shem, meshaneh mazal' ('He who changes his name, changes his luck').

[5] IB adds: 'Jews were accused of using Christian blood, obtained by murder, in the preparation of the unleavened bread for the Passover.'

[6] i.e. Samuel: see L1 307, note 3.

to eccentricity, very good-natured but rather feeble-minded and confused. Your mother remembers him rather with a certain sympathy, remembering how in her childhood he used stealthily to sidle up to her and give her a pat on her head and murmur a few encouraging words. Grandmother Frumma was very strong-willed, had great strength of character and common sense. She could not very well get on with a feeble and non-consequential husband but in those days a divorce for such reasons was unthinkable. She took over the reins of the house, ruled it, worked for the living of the family. She had four children: the eldest, Schöne, married to Simon Jacobson (originating from Pogar near Dubno – District of Tchernigov); my father, Ber [Boris]; your mother's mother, Rodsia-Freude; and the youngest, Mendel Zuckerman. She had a draper's shop in Rudnia; used to travel to Moscow to buy the cloth, arrange for credits and so on; had several ventures in timber and forest work, often in partnership with her son-in-law Jacobson and the children of her uncle – R. Samuel, the rabbi of Liubavitchi – Salman-Aaron and Mendel Schneerson (the latter the father of Anna Oiserman), [and] her nephew – Salman Schneerson, the son of her brother Baruch. She never had any money worth while to mention; she could not inspect or control the forest work, but her partners used to take her in for her sound general understanding of affairs, her judgment and her firmness in times of crises, and her abounding energy. You must remember her, as she died rather old in Andreapol in 1916 or 1917.

Her later years she passed with her daughters, mainly your grandmother Rodsia-Freude Volshonok, whom she could domineer, although she was much fonder of her son-in-law Simon Jacobson, who had a gay sunny disposition and [was] of a speculative turn of mind, [and she was] always [more] friendly to his children than [to those] of her other son-in-law, Salman Izchok[1] Volshonok, your grandfather, who was an ascete, gloomy, always expecting inability to keep up his family, preaching gloom and austerity and therefore by nature not kindly to her liveliness and boisterous ways, and urging her daughter – his wife – to take more interest in life and to oppose his schemes of keeping her down, but outer decorum and respectfulness were observed by him to the utmost, both as to a mother-in-law and particularly to the granddaughter of the highly venerated and sanctified Zemach Zedek, who was for him the highest authority. My father you knew; he certainly had a streak in him of the 'Binke' blood, which explains his placidity, inactivity and dependability on others.

---

[1] The Hebrew version of 'Isaac', usually 'Yitzchak' among Hebrew speakers, appears in Yiddish in a form variously rendered as Itzchok or Izchok (MB's spellings), or Yitzchok.

MENDEL'S MOTHER AND HER FAMILY

In my parents' house the respected and ruling power was my mother. A few words about her antecedents: her father was the famous 'Lubliner Rav' or as some knew him 'the Ladier' ([after] the townlet of his origin). His father was a 'schochet'[1] in Liadi – a pious and simple Liubavitzer Chassid. My grandfather, his son – R. Shneur Salman Fradkin – was a precocious child, a prodigy. When 3 years of age he could read, and when he was 5 or 6 a stool used to be put up on the Almemar[2] and he did the 'Keriah' or reading of the Law out of a Sefer-Torah[3] with all the proper pronunciations and the 'neginah' (so-called Trop).[4] When he was 12 years of age he was already famous in all the neighbouring towns as a great Talmudist and an עילוי[5] – a prodigy. It was then the practice among Jews that very rich people used to find for their daughters poor learned and pious young men as husbands, and marriages were contracted at a very early age. A certain Glinternik of Czashniki near Vitebsk won the highest lottery prize in the Russian State Lottery – 200,000 roubles – which among the poor Jews of the Pale of settlement was an undreamt of fortune. He promptly sought and arranged for the poor prodigy from Liadi to marry his daughter – Chassia. The marriage did not prove a success, as the poor scholar had a very gentle unaggressive nature, while she was strong, aggressive and quarrelsome; still as all such marriages in those days the thought of dissolution never entered anybody's mind and loyalty between the spouses was very strong.

The particular characteristic of my grandfather was his prodigal memory. Books used to be sold by peddling booksellers; the scholars used to finger the leaves before buying them. These pedlars never liked my grandfather as he used quickly to turn over the leaves of any book he took in his hands, then refuse to buy it (because of poverty), as he could memorize the whole book and he had little further use for it. He became what is commonly known as a 'gaon', one of the greatest talmudical authorities of his time, and the pride of the Chassidim, who had not too many 'Lomdim'[6] among their members. He became Rav of Polotzk but later was called to Lublin, a call which, although he preferred Lithuania with its seats of learning and the nearness of his adored teacher, the Zemach Zedek, he could not resist. Lublin prided itself on always having the greatest rabbinic authority at the head of its

[1] Ritual slaughterer.
[2] Synagogue reading-desk.
[3] A manuscript copy of the Pentateuch written on a parchment scroll and used in the synagogue for the weekly readings.
[4] 'Neginah' means 'chant'; 'trop' ('emphases') is a Yiddish term for the musical notation in printed Torah texts.
[5] 'Ilui' ('genius in holy studies').
[6] Scholars of Torah and Talmud, holy studies.

Beth-Din.[1] The Lublin seat was not only of a Rav but Rav and Av-Beth-Din:[2] there was the famous 'Maharam' m'Lublin,[3] a famous rabbi called 'the Eiserne Kopf',[4] and the Lublin Cemetery was a shrine for worshipping pious and learned rabbis. The rabbinical position in Lublin was the most illustrious position among Polish and Lithuanian Jews; hence a call to that seat could not be ignored. To do justice to the Lublin Community they have issued this call to R. Salman of Liadi, despite the fact that he was a Chabad Chassid, while the Community were either Misnagdim or Polish Chassidim, who were very far from Chabad Chassidism, much more ignorant and superstitious, generally hating the Lithuanian Jews, whom they nicknamed – 'Litvak', a Zeilim Kopf.[5] They did it because he was the greatest scholar of his time and the tradition was that the greatest scholar available should preside over the Rabbinical Court of Lublin. This removal to Poland had a profound effect on his and particularly his children's life, as I hope to show later. He led a hermit's life among his books and writings. His bed was tucked away in his large study and he never left it even for his meals, except on Sabbath-Festivals, when he dined with his family. This study was close to the Synagogue, or as one would say now the Chapel, attached to his large residence. Even on Sabbaths he entered the Synagogue only for the period of the 'Reading of the Law', then withdrawing for further prayer to his study and only re-appearing at the end of the Service to bid 'Good Shabbas' to the Congregation. Sabbaths afternoons he used to deliver a discourse but this was about all his intercourse with the entire world; even ordinary rabbinical duties were carried out by his 'Dayanim'[6] sitting in his Synagogue – only complicated cases, often divorce cases, were listened to and adjudged by himself. He was in the habit of driving out often on afternoons outside the town, walk in the forests and fields and recite by heart parts of the Talmud.

My father soon after he married was taken as a sign of favour on these drives and walks, and my father recited as an example of my grandfather's extraordinary memory the fact that he used to ask him to hold a book and listen to his recital. On one occasion he left out purposely exactly a whole line (so well did he remember its position in the book) and my father naturally did not notice it, when he was upbraided for inattention. He was a very beautiful, a tall, erect, full figure with a white full beard, dark shining eyes, a straight well-formed

[1] Rabbinical law court.

[2] President of the court, a title given to the chief rabbinical judge.

[3] MaHaRaM is an acronym for Moreynu Ha-Rav Meir, Meir ben Gedalia of Lublin (mi Lublin) (1558–1616).

[4] Yiddish for 'The Iron Head', the nickname given to Rabbi Azriel Horowitz (c.1745–1815).

[5] sc. *tseylem kop* (Yiddish: 'head like a [Christian] cross', i.e. a hard-headed rationalist, a term of insult used by Polish/Hasidic Jews of Lithuanian [Litvak] Misnagdim).

[6] The judges of a rabbinical court.

nose and very soft spoken, dressed in a long black coat with a very broad silk girdle. He was very gentle. He got once angry with my uncle Shaya Berlin, when the latter told him of the piety of the Rav of Tchernigoff and used the phrase ער מורא האט פאר גאטט ווי פאר א גזלן.[1] How did he dare to make such a parallel! Notwithstanding his seclusion, he loved his children and used to show them great tenderness and care, with the result that he was simply adored by them. For their father they would go anywhere or do anything. My mother, as you well know, was not happy in her marriage, and she had already a good many modern notions, but when one-and-a-half years after her marriage she mentioned to her father her desire for a divorce, a simple frown on his face was enough to stop her from doing anything, not out of fear, as she related to me later – but how could she possibly annoy her beloved father?

I was born in his house in 1883.[2] In his old age, he realised his lifelong ambition to emigrate and settle in Palestine. He went first to Hebron, then was called to Jerusalem, as a kind of the Authority over the rabbonim there, and both the Ashkenazim and Sephardim accepted his authority. Shortly afterwards (must have been about the year 1898–99 – I don't quite remember) he died and is buried in Jerusalem. Characteristic of his unworldliness is the fact that when his son Ber (or Bezie) went through his books he found quite a number of currency notes scattered among the pages of his books; I believe it amounted to quite a number of thousands of roubles left there from time to time and forgotten.

He was certainly a man of extraordinary brainpower and phenomenal memory; any qualities that you may possess in this direction I venture to ascribe to inheritance from this grandfather. His family consisted of four sons: the eldest, Chaim, looked very much like him, a very dignified person, gentle and of few words. He married and lived in Proskurov, later in Warsaw. The second, Solomon, whom I never met, married in Galicia in Stanislavov and died very young: he was of the extremely pious type and a scholar. My grandfather, the Lubliner, in his work called תורת חסד[3] – responsa on the Schulchan-Aruch[4] שולחן ערוך[5] – mentions some of his contributions to this book. The cause of his death was over-zealousness in carrying out the religious ritual: plunging in a cold 'Mikvah'[6] during the winter, as a result he caught pneumonia and died. He was my mother's favourite brother. I still remember my mother's story in connection with him: when she was about to give birth to me, she fell asleep and

[1] Yiddish: 'Er hot moyre far gott vi far a gazlen' ('He is afraid of God as one might be of a bandit').
[2] According to his birth certificate, in 1884.
[3] 'Torat Hesed' ('The Law of Love').
[4] The Shulchan Arukh ('prepared table') was the definitive code of law drawn up by Rabbi Joseph Caro (1488–1575).
[5] 'Orach Hayyim' ('path of life'); the title of part 1 of the Shulchan Arukh.
[6] sc. *mikveh*, an immersion-pool for ritual purification.

dreamt that her brother Solomon was sitting at her bedside; he told her that if she will have a son he would like her to name him after him, and my mother promised him to fulfil his wish. When she awoke, she forgot the story. I was named (as usual on the eighth day) by my grandfather Menachem Mendel in honour of his revered leader, the Zemach Zedek. On the day after, my mother remembered her dream and burst out in tears when her father paid her a visit, bitterly resenting the non-execution of her promise in the dream to her brother. The Lubliner consoled her, saying no better name than the Zemach Zedek could be given to her first-born, and that when she will have a second boy she will then carry out her promise. My brother Lioma (Solomon) was born 10½ years later and the promise was carried out. Now you see the origin of my not too popular name.

Uncle Solomon, who took the surname Ladier instead of Fradkin as this was the one popularly attributed to his father and appearing in some of his official papers, founded a branch of the family in Stanislavov. I believe mother met once in Carlsbad or Marienbad my cousin, a son of Solomon – a very good-looking man. His third son was the above mentioned Ber or known in the family as Bezie, a rather bigoted religious fanatic who also emigrated to Palestine and lived with my grandfather there. There must be members of this branch in Palestine[1] (one son – Solomon – visited us about 1910 in Riga) and in the United States. There was a beautiful daughter who caught the fancy of a rich American young man, hence the American branch of the family. A fourth son was Izchok (called by the family Itzig), a highly nervous, excitable, kindly but quarrelsome man (apparently inherited from his mother) but of no consequence. He married a wife from Zamostie in Poland – his brother-in-law was the famous Jewish writer L. Peretz. I remember him coming to Vitebsk, which must have been nearly 50 years ago, in connection with some trouble about his military service. He answered his call to conscription in Lublin under the name of Ladier, but the authorities were searching for a man of the name of Fradkin who didn't answer the call. He must have been about 30 years of age then. He was a burden to my mother and constantly quarreled with my father. He left for Dvinsk to stay with the Apters, entrusted his money to my uncle Mendel Apter (Kadish's[2] father). I believe he never got it back, worked himself up into frenzy and died very young.

My mother had three sisters: the eldest was Devorah, whose first husband was a man Cohn (the father of her eldest son, Joseph Cohn), and who died of consumption only about a year or so after marrying her. She then married a rich widower – one Azriel Przepiórka – the father of her second son David, who as you know became a chess champion. Azriel Przepiórka died and left her

---

[1] IB comments: 'There are.'
[2] On Kadish Apter see L1.

a comparatively young but rich widow. She was a character. She was eccentric, good-looking, domineering, and used her good fortune to please her whims, something in the nature of the self-willed Russian помещица – так моя левая нога хочет.[1] She led what was then considered a life of luxury. She used to travel a lot and used to shock my very conventional aunt Chayetta Berlin when she met her in the fashionable watering places by her extravagant toilettes and her unorthodox ways. She thought her two sons would be rich enough never to need anything in life and brought them up without giving them any train- ing for an independent life and made of them what is commonly known as לאדיגנייהער בעל-הבית'ישע,[2] hence the taking to chess of David. I believe both Joseph Cohn and David Przepiórka must have perished in Warsaw, but one of Joseph's sons,[3] Max – an architect by profession and a very intelligent man – has turned up in Palestine (I don't know when he went there)[4] and was recently seen by Mr Halevy in Samunov's house, as one of their good friends.

Another sister – Zivia Apter – was a usual middle-class woman of no par- ticular merits or demerits. She married Mendel Apter, of whom grandfather was not fond, much of her own desire, because being in her twenties she was afraid she may get too old to wait much longer and I believe regretted it ever after. Mendel Apter was a mean man, close-fisted, boastful, and overawed her. His pride and boastfulness went so far as to resent that Dvinsk,[5] the town of his birth and domicile, was not the губернский город,[6] but was subordinated to Vitebsk, to which town he had often to repair in his capacity as army contrac- tor, and I remember as a young boy meeting him often in our house, where he stayed during his visits to Vitebsk, and often telling that he has it on highest authority that the seat of the district government is going soon to be trans- ferred to the more important town of Dvinsk. He was always short of finance and used to work on my mother's soft and sentimental nature to induce her to make my father accept accommodation bills for him and there was eternal trouble when the bills were presented on maturity to my father for payment and Apter more often than not failing to provide the necessary funds to redeem the bills. Notwithstanding these failures he succeeded time after time to make my mother persuade father to sign again, picturing lurid pictures of what will happen to his family if funds will not be found by way of discounting the bills. He and one of his sons were shot sometime in 1918/9 in Charkoff or Kieff in connection with black market food transactions. His sons – Solomon and

---

[1] 'Pomeshchitsa – tak moya levaya noga khochet' ('landowner – as my left leg wants', i.e. following every whim).

[2] Yiddish: 'balebatisher leydikgeyer', 'idle rich'.

[3] IB notes that Joseph's other son, Oscar, also went to Palestine.

[4] IB adds, referring to both sons: 'as officers in [Władysław] Anders's Polish Army'.

[5] Modern Daugavpils.

[6] 'Gubernskii gorod' ('administrative town').

Kadish – you know. My aunt Zivia died shortly before the 1939 war in Riga – a woman over 70 who always was ailing but looked with great care and selfishness after her health. Kadish's boastfulness and bustling are inherited from his father. There was another son, whose whereabouts I don't know.

The fourth and youngest sister was Rivka – a strapping, tall and fulsome woman, considered by lovers of oriental beauty as good-looking. She was very sensuous and pleasure-loving. She was first married to one Jacob David Landoberg, by whom she had her eldest son, Isaac Landoberg,[1] now in Palestine and a bodyguard of Dr Weizmann; a second son, Michael, whom my aunt disliked, considering him as having inherited his father's views (gambling and over-sexuality), became officially a Communist in Russia and died there a few years ago. She married later Izchok Ginsburg, a man of good family, who was once a rich man, living in Roslavl (Smolensk Govt) and engaged in the timber trade. He lost most of his money, emigrated to Riga where his father Simon lived before him (and was very well known as the protector and ходатай[2] for the Jews before the Authorities). He was a Chassid, pious, but I disliked him, having always suspected him of a certain shiftiness in character. They had a son, Simon Ginsburg, who lives now in Russia. He was a rather pampered young man. Later they moved to Leningrad, where my aunt died at the beginning of the 1917 Revolution, and Izchok Ginsburg moved to Moscow, where he recently died. He had quite a humorous turn of mind. He used to have in Moscow certain business deals with Kadish Apter, who was the smart one, while he, Ginsburg, was the reliable one. I remember him once making an appointment over the 'phone with Kadish and adding at the end, 'But be precisely on time, don't tell me afterwards that you were unavoidably detained by meeting in the street Мария Феодоровна[3] (the ex-Tsarina). This episode characterises both of them.

And now to return to my mother. I think you must still have a dim recollection of her. As I said before, the residence in Lublin, to which town she was brought when a child of three, had a profound effect on her. She, while really being a Russian woman, took on many characteristics of the Polish – love of clothes, quickness of temper, touchiness – but her character was very noble and honest, full of a sense of duty and good nature, although over-sentimentalised and romantic. This is partly due to her education. In Poland it was at her time quite normal for the young Jewish men only to be educated in a Jewish sense and to be entirely devoid of any European culture, while the young girls were sent to schools and pensions. She was sent to one of such pensions, where she was taught – besides Polish – Russian, German and French, was made to

---

[1] Later known as Yitzhak Sadeh, subject of a memoir by IB in PI2.

[2] 'Khodatai' ('intercessor').

[3] Mariya Feodorovna.

recite Russian and German poetry by heart and was attached to the romantic literature of her time. This school education planted in her a great respect for European culture and was responsible for her later insistence, despite the family opposition, to give her sons as good a general education as she could afford, to the detriment of their strictly Jewish instruction, and also made her look with respect on the few representatives of the Haskalah[1] whom she met. I suppose another cause was responsible for this attitude of mind: when very young, I suppose 16 or 17, she fell in love with a young man, an ardent Haskalah man in Lublin. It was unthinkable to speak to her father of such a union. The young man offered to run away but her attachment to her father forbid such a course and this early romance left a deep impression on her, particularly considering the very contrasting marriage which she entered at the age of 18.

There was nothing in common between my mother and father. She was stately, blond and beautiful (I especially remember her exquisitely shaped hands), and he diminutive, swarthy and ugly, she having a smattering of European culture and literature, reading books avidly, and he completely ignorant apart from Jewish learning, she dreaming about romance and happiness and he a matter-of-fact, lazy, not too clever man. She never saw him before the day of her marriage. My grandfather was blinded by his descent from the Rav's family (which was the equivalent of a Royal family), his knowledge of the Talmud (which by the way was not too profound, I suppose owing to his laziness), and the material prospects as the nephew and adopted son of the millionaire and Chassid, Shaya Berlin, who was himself married to the granddaughter of the Zemach Zedek. Of course, the father selecting a husband for his daughter, and not only not consulting her but even not showing him to her beforehand, was the usual practice among that kind of Jews in those days – 63 years ago. She cried, but a daughter of her age could not dream of revolting, but felt very unhappy. I was born before the first anniversary of their wedding and when soon afterwards she mooted to her father of the necessity of a divorce, my grandfather could not see any reason for it at all.

She lived the first 3–4 years of her married life in Lublin and my father, having to attend to business in Russia, used to come home only 2–3 times a year. I believe these long separations perhaps prevented a divorce. Soon afterwards my sister Hinde (self-styled Eugenie) was born and all her love and care were devoted to her children. I suppose these long absences of my father, which continued until they moved to Riga, when I was already adolescent, and the sole company and care of my mother partly explain my relationships with my parents.

---

[1] Jewish Enlightenment.

CHILDHOOD

I curiously still remember my very early childhood in Lublin, although I must have been not older than 4 years when my parents moved to Vitebsk. I can remember exactly the flat of my grandfather, and himself as well. He loved and played with me often. His room, though large, could not accommodate all his books, and some bookcases were placed in the adjacent room. I used to love to play with them, drop them with a noise on the floor, the way children behave; my mother used to run after me to remove me and the noise I made from the immediate neighbourhood of grandfather's sanctum; he often used to open the door and tell my mother to let me play and do as I like, which was a triumph for me. I remember when he was convalescing from an illness, he asked for me to be brought into his bed and play with me; I remember not to have been over-awed by him but to address him frankly and boldly.

My mother used to dress me in the most modern child's cloth available in Warsaw, whence they were sent to her irrespective of cost, but when I must have been about 3 years of age, on Sabbaths I was dressed in a long black silk kaftan reaching to my ankles and an embroidered skullcap. I remember having complained once to my grandfather that, unlike the grown-up people, they didn't put round me the traditional 'gartel', a sort of girdle. He took off his own broad girdle – somewhat similar to those worn by the catholic clergy – and wound it round me, nearly entirely enveloping the tiny tot. He was so devoted and worshipped the Zemach Zedek that I imagine the fact that a grandchild of his was at the same time a grand-grandchild of the Zemach Zedek must have been to some extent responsible for his partiality for me. I remember my mother telling that her elder sister Devorah was complaining that their father never showed a similar attachment to her sons – his grandchildren.

Of my grandmother I have scarcely any recollection and when later I found my mother in tears on her receiving news of her mother's death it didn't touch me at all, it was a person unknown to me who died. My mother I think must have inspired a certain feeling of strangeness and inferiority among her in-laws. When my father insisted, and possibly his uncle and aunt – the Berlins – who had a great influence with my grandfather, that the family must move nearer to my father's occupation, it was decided to move to Vitebsk, although his family (parents) were in Rudnia and the Berlins in Velish (soon afterwards or shortly before they moved to Riga), because the Lublinerke (as my mother was called) could not be tucked away in a little muddy townlet. On the way to Vitebsk the family passed a few weeks or months in Rudnia in my grandmother Frumma's house. There her two sisters-in-law – Schöne Jacobson and Rodsia-Freude Volshonok – were admiring her toilettes, such as they have scarcely seen before. She was accompanied by a kind of companion and nurse, Livscha (I still remember her name) from Lublin, to make easier for her transition into new surroundings and life. There your mother remembers me for the first time. Her memory is rather of an unpleasant moment. She was wearing some necklace, I tore it from her neck, and as usual both children started shouting and crying. Our grandmother Frumma, who appeared on the scene, chose to punish your mother – the innocent and rather victimised party. I suppose she was afraid of hurting my mother's feelings and this injustice provoked a very loud and lacrimous protest from your mother: מענדעלי איז א הייליגער אונד שמייליגער[1] – he is the aggressor and I am punished. She could for many years not forget this episode.

EDUCATION: RELIGIOUS AND SECULAR

My memories of Vitebsk really start from the time I was first sent to Cheder. I must have been about 5 years of age. I remember it was a very ceremonious occasion. The Melamed came to our house to fetch me, an Alphabet אלף בית[2] printed in very large letters was placed before me, strewn with sugar and candies, and I was supposed to kiss the letters by trying to lick the sweets off the paper. I was taught the first few letters and told to shout at them (שרייא קמץ אלף אָ, פתח [אלף] אַ) and so on)[3] with all my might. Refreshments were served and I was solemnly led away for the first time to the Cheder a few streets away, a semi-dark semi-basement room of the Melamed's abode. His name was פסח[4] and he was consumptive, and therefore very irritable, but he was the fashionable מלמד דרדקי[5] or elementary Melamed. In the same courtyard his mother-in-law kept a bakery, and I, along with the other pupils, used, out of my very scanty pocket-money, to buy nearly daily 'blinis' with butter, the whole thing coming to say 2 copeks or a halfpenny, but it tasted to us children deliciously. The Melamed himself used in the afternoon to accompany me home, and I remember how in the dark winter evenings I was muffled up to the tip of my nose, carrying in my heavily gloved hands a lantern with a candle in it to light the way and to avoid the snow-drifts or the too slippery icy road. On the way to Podvinnie – the street we lived – was a church and I was taught to make a wide semicircle to avoid touching the church's parapet, as an unholy place. This Melamed taught me only reading; he soon died and I

---

[1] 'Mendeli iz a heyliger und shmeyliger' ('Little Mendel is a holy-shmoly': the second epithet is just the usual Yiddish repetition with the shm- prefix, as in 'Oedipus, Shmoedipus').

[2] 'Alef bet' ('AB[C]').

[3] An instruction in Yiddish given by their teacher to children learning to read Hebrew: 'Shray "Komets alef oh, pasekh [alef] ah" etc.' ('Shout "Komets [with] alef – oh; pasekh [with alef] – ah" etc.'). *Alef* is a silent consonant; *komets* and *pasekh* are Ashkenazic pronunciations of *kamatz* and *patach*, the names of two Hebrew vowels.

[4] 'Pesach' ('Pascal').

[5] 'Melamed dard'ki' ('teacher of small children').

was handed to another Melamed, Joseph-Leib der Melamed, who lived much further in the less fashionable part. My mother did not quite like him, because he was exceedingly pious and too old-fashioned and not too popular among the richer parents, but my father insisted, just because he was an old-fashioned Melamed. He was also given to beat his pupils. I stayed for a few years with him. I believe, fearing my mother, he never laid his hands on me until one day I must have tried his patience too much and he struck me, and this was the end of my visiting his Cheder. His wife was herself baking bread, of course, rye-bread, the staple food of the poor Jews, and I still remember the overheated stuffy atmosphere, smelling of freshly baked bread, and the great delight of buying from her a part of a loaf for 1 copeck (a farthing) and eating it hot – fresh from the oven, no doubt very indigestible but heavenly palatable. Of course, sanitation was entirely absent and all needs were satisfied in the open courtyard, warm or cold, dry or wet. There was a competition between the pupils in drawing patterns on the white snow when letting water.

This Melamed had a great influence on me. He tried to communicate his piety to his pupils; this was done by reading parts of a certain medieval pious book ראשית חכמה.[1] I remember vividly the awe struck into me when the chapter שבעה מדורי גיהנום[2] was read out and embellished. All the punishments were enumerated, the heat of the hellish fire estimated 60 times stronger than the ordinary fire, and the appropriate punishment for particular sins described in horrifying detail. I used to go home in a very subdued mood and wonder what expects me in the world to come, very frightened of committing any sin mentioned in this book. He also worked on the children's love of the fantastic. A month or so before Purim we were taught the Megillath Esther[3] with many embellishing commentaries. If I remember rightly it was the Targum R. Jonathan ben Uziel[4] (one of the Tannaim)[5] which especially appealed to the children's sense of the fantastic. There were descriptions of Ashmodai[6] capturing King Solomon, while the Ashmodai sat disguised on Solomon's throne, Solomon meanwhile wandering round the world and utilising his knowledge of the language of birds and trees to give him his bearings and taking advice from all sorts of creatures, the ultimate discomfiture of Ashmodai and so on, stories of Haman having to bathe Mordecai and offering to the enfeebled

---

[1] 'Reshit chochmah' ('beginning of wisdom').

[2] 'Shiv'ah m'dorei Gehinnom' ('seven dwellings of hell'): the sinner must pass through the seven stages of hell, and suffer a different punishment in each.

[3] 'Scroll of Esther', the biblical Book of Esther, which is read from a scroll on the festival of Purim.

[4] It is more likely to have been Targum Sheni on Esther, an Aramaic paraphrase of the book.

[5] Aramaic: Early Rabbinic sages, authors of the Mishnah.

[6] The king of the demons.

Mordecai his back to step on to reach the saddle of the King's horse and so on. This was fortified by little booklets given us describing the wonder deeds of several obscure medieval saints known as the hidden 36 Zadikim[1] (ל"ו ניקעס),[2] the little book known as שבחי הבעש"ט[3] the acts of the Besht. The boys were also made to start the day with the morning prayers in a minian (מנין),[4] one of the boys acting alternatively as the Chazan;[5] later מנחה and מעריב[6] were said in the same order. When the month of Elul came – the one before the New Year – teaching in the Cheder was only until lunchtime; the afternoon was devoted to medieval books on penitence, then about late in the afternoon one went to the Synagogue for the 'Mincha'-service and the beautiful summer evening between 'Mincha' and the first stars appearing. When the 'Maariv' service was said, the synagogue turned into a lecture or study room, a 'shiur' or lecture was given by an elderly member of the congregation, usually a Melamed, on the current 'sidrah', Midrash or 'Ein Jacob'.[7] I used to love it, because of the mass of 'Hagada' and the whole atmosphere; after 'Maariv', which was quite late, one went home. I was a 'masmid',[8] particularly loved the prophets, and used (although there was never any home work given) to re-read at home chapters of the prophets and sometimes learning them by heart. With non-Jewish 'shkozim'[9] one never came into contact, also friendship with the other boys of the 'Cheder' was confined to the Cheder, as one passed from early morning till late in the evening. I vividly remember having to pass an empty space where stray dogs were wandering and I was once bitten by a dog. Since that day passing these few yards was always agony to me and I retained fear of dogs till quite late in life. Playing with a dog or cat was generally considered unbecoming for a Cheder-boy. In the summer between פסח[10] and שבועות[11] – seven weeks – one had to go every Saturday afternoon to the Melamed's house far away in the outskirts and there a

---

[1] Thirty-six 'hidden' or unknown just men upon whom the world rests (not medieval saints, as MB thought). 'Zadikim' means 'righteous men'.

[2] Yiddishism derived from Hebrew: 'lamed-vovnikes' ('thirty-sixers').

[3] 'Shivhei ha-Besht' ('[in] praise of the Baal Shem Tov'), a hagiographic collection of tales about the deeds and teachings of the Baal Shem Tov (by acronym, 'the BeSHT'; see 266 above, note 6).

[4] 'Minyan' ('number', 'prayer quorum'): MB gives the word first in transliterated form and then in Hebrew. The quorum is ten adult male Jews, the minimum for congregational prayer.

[5] Cantor.

[6] '*Mincha* and *ma'ariv*', afternoon and evening prayers.

[7] *Sidrah* is the portion of the Torah read that week in the synagogue. Midrash and *Ein Yaakov* are collections of *aggadot* (homilies and legends interpreting biblical texts: MB's 'Hagada').

[8] Diligent scholar.

[9] An abusive Yiddishism for Gentile boys.

[10] 'Pesach' (the Festival of Passover).

[11] 'Shavuot' (the Feast of Weeks).

chapter of the 'Ethic of the Fathers' was taught; it was considered too light fare to waste a week's day on it, when more serious matters had to be learned. Thus one really had only half a day in the week for rest.

During my Cheder period at Joseph-Leib's Cheder my mother thought it was time to start on my non-Jewish education. School was out of [the] question, as the Cheder could not be given up, so a private teacher was engaged, a young very nice girl – Moina Schalil – who taught me reading and writing Russian, arithmetic and later German – the gothic script. I had to visit her 2–3 times a week in the intervals between Cheder – the Cheder break for lunch was usually between 2–4 and lunch was sent to me to the Cheder at 2 o'clock, after which I went to my teacher and then back to Cheder, so that on those days I was away from home from 9 in the morning till 8–9 in the evening. Then at home teacher's home-work had to be done. I really worked very hard then. My Melamed looked very disapprovingly on my extraneous lessons, he used to call them טרפה־פסול,[1] and when sometimes my mind was not all riveted on the page of Talmud which he was expounding and he noticed it, his remark 'apparently your head is full of the טרפה־פסול'. This was another reason my mother thought it was time for me to leave this intolerant zealot and at the age of 9½ I was taken away from him, not without regret, as I rather liked him, and handed to a new 'Melamed' – Koppel the Melamed – who was considered more up to date. He allowed time for non-Jewish learning, then he taught among other things Hebrew Grammar (דקדוק)[2] which very strict Chassidim considered unnecessary and rather smacking of 'Haskalah'. Otherwise he was quite as orthodox and steeped in the study of the Talmud as the others. He also had new methods of punishment. Instead of beating his pupils he used to put them into a corner with a 'метла'[3] in hand. I was the youngest among his pupils. The others treated me rather condescendingly, particularly as I could not take much part in their conversation, which was, as I remembered afterwards, erotically tinged, but of which I had no idea at the time.

The summers we used to pass on a 'Datcha'. Villages next to town, say 2–5 miles from the fringe of the town, had specially built primitive villas, which the better-to-do townspeople used to hire for the 3–4 summer months. I recollect these 'datcha' times still with pleasure. They brought me nearer to nature. The village was surrounded by forests, where I used to go picking berries and mushrooms, finding little brooks where wild raspberries used to grow. There was a river and I went fishing, boating and bathing. I went swinging on the village roundabouts. I finally learned horse-riding, usually by unharnessing the

---

[1] 'Terefah-pasul', commonly pronounced 'treyf-posl' ('unclean and forbidden object'), a term of condemnation applied by the strictly obervant to secular books.

[2] 'Dikduk' ('grammar').

[3] 'Metla' ('broom').

butcher's cob, on which the butcher used to bring the 'kosher' meat from town, and while the butcher-boy made his rounds among the villas I enjoyed tremendously bareback riding on his horse. Of course I still had to go to Cheder, but less assiduously, only say 2 times a week. When the butcher came to take me back to town on his cart, back one had to walk 4–5 miles or more, occasionally begging a lift from some village peasant returning from town. Twice a week 'Koppel der Melamed' used to come out to us to the datcha, gave me a lesson in the evening, another one in the morning before he left. Twice a week after Cheder I also visited my 'lay' teacher. So even the summer vacancies were not quite free of work.

For the first time during this datcha period I came into contact with girls, children of the neighbouring 'datchniki', with whom I played, and I remember vividly falling madly in love with one little girl with black curls, the daughter of a neighbour called Schalil. Of course, it was love in secret. I made all kinds of excuses to meet her as often as possible and to play with her without ever giving any vent to my romantic feelings. When 'Elul'[1] approached, usually mid-August, one went back to town and one resumed the arduous Cheder life. A week before the 'New Year' Selichot[2] began – penitentiary prayers in Synagogue, usually about 1 a.m. or early in the morning, about 5–6 o'clock. From the age of about 10 I used to go these services, and wait then for the morning prayers with the שופר[3] at the end, and the grave, serious mood prevailing among the congregants also took possession of me. Of course, when the ימים נוראים[4] came, practically all the 24 hours were devoted to prayer, recitals of the Psalms and learning.

About the age of 10–11 my mother used to take me to the theatre on the rare occasions when she went, usually to the displeasure of her friends, among them Sonia (Schenke) Schneerson, later Mrs Lagovier, who didn't like the little boy in the box among them. I still remember two plays which impressed me then very much: a visiting celebrity – Kozielsky – in Hamlet and Gutzkow's 'Uriel d'Acosta'. By the time I was 10 or 11 I could read Russian with facility and I was reading voraciously. I still remember a scene: one Friday night I was reading late, perhaps 1 o'clock in the morning, Grigorovitch's 'Anton Goremyko' – a very sloppy romantic description of the life of the Russian serfs – and my sympathy and pity for Anton was so great that I could not help bursting out in very loud crying. I woke up the whole household, which was fast asleep. I was

---

[1] Month preceding the festival of Rosh Hashanah, the Jewish New Year.
[2] The prayers offered during the all-night or early-morning services (called Selichot, 'penitential prayers') before Yamim Noraim (see note 4 below).
[3] 'Shofar' ('ram's horn').
[4] 'Yamim noraim' ('the Days of Awe'), i.e. the ten high holy days from Rosh Hashanah to Yom Kippur.

also reading some Hebrew books, mainly brochures by Ben-Avigdor (an author scarcely known today), Kalman Schulman, who translated 'The Mysteries of Paris' (מסתר פריז),[1] and a work of his of quite a different nature, מוסדי עולם[2] ('Foundation of the World'), a sort of geography of the world. But my main and voracious reading was Russian.

At about the age of 12 my Cheder life was finished, partly because my mother (who was in charge of my education) decided more time must be spared for my general education and partly because an uncle of my mother – the brother of her father – Levi-Izchok Fradkin – got impoverished and my mother decided to engage him as my Hebrew and Talmudic tutor as a full-time job. Hence I started having daily lessons in general subjects from better tutors, based on the syllabus of the classical gymnasium,[3] but still every spare hour – morning, noon or evening – was spent in delving into the 'sea' of Talmud and its commentators. For days I did not go out into the street at all, my every minute being occupied with studies. To enter the gymnasium was thought both undesirable, as this would mean an end of my Hebrew studies, and also desecration of the Sabbath and impracticable owing to the numerus clausus.[4] I was to become an 'extern' – which meant sitting annually for examinations at the gymnasium for the respective form (or class) with a view of finally getting an 'attestal of maturity' (аттестат зрелости)[5] which would open the way to an university in Russia or abroad. Best tutors of the gymnasium, particularly in classics, were employed at a remuneration then thought exorbitant, something like 5 roubles an hour, but my mother, however strained her circumstances, would not spare anything to give me an adequate education. Her early studies in a 'pension' in Lublin gave me an immense respect for European culture. I am grateful to her to this day, as otherwise my time would be fully occupied with Hebrew studies, and whatever little culture I possess is due to her and her energy and her valiant struggle with my parental relatives, who looked on my education as preparing me to become a 'goy'.[6] My Hebrew studies, as I said above, were not neglected and I was considered quite proficient in Talmud and so on, which I continued to study regularly until the age of nearly 19 or 20.

I had very few friends: really only one, Zalman Gurewitsch – a relative on the paternal Zuckerman side who was studying on about the same lines as I. With him when I was about 13 or so we started going to the theatre, of course in the gallery – the entrance fee was something like 25 copeks – 6 pence. Still

---

[1] 'Mistrei Paris', i.e. *Mistere Pariz* (Vilnius, 1857), Schulman's Hebrew translation of Eugène Sue's novel *Les Mystères de Paris* (1842–3).

[2] 'Mos'dei Olam': sc. the Hebrew book *Mosdei Eretz* (Vilnius, 1877).

[3] Secondary school, in preparation for university.

[4] Quota (of Jews).

[5] 'Attestat zrelosti', school-leaving certificate (akin to the French *baccalauréat*).

[6] Literally 'Gentile', hence 'unbeliever'.

we went to operas, plays and developed quite a taste for it. My barmitzvah, for which I was taught by my uncle and tutor – Levi-Izchok – to deliver a learned dispute on the controversy between the Maimonides and the ראב״ד [1] ('Raavad'), was marred as two days before it my twin brothers – Leo and Samuel – were born and the festivity had to be abandoned, much to my annoyance. The only person who ever listened to my very pilpulistic and learned discourse was my uncle and future father-in-law, who happened to pass Vitebsk at the time and who, I supposed out of kindness, asked me particularly to recite it to him. I remember I was grateful, as the learning by heart of the dissertation took quite a lot of time and became redundant. My brother 'Lioma' – Solomon – was born about 3 years earlier when I was 10 and I remember his arrival quite upset me, as I ceased to be the בן יחיד,[2] the only son, and thought less attention and love would from now onwards be lavished by my mother on me.

I must here say a few words about my uncle Levi-Izchok – my tutor. He was a gentleman and saint. He was poor but cared little about it, and he taught me with love and great care. He tried to implant in me (alas, in vain) an inclination to austerity, to avoid superfluous food and luxuries, as diverting a man from true obedience to the Divinity, good manners, used to buy me multicoloured crayons and similar things to encourage diligence in learning the Talmud, and I always had a real and great respect for him.

My mother tried even to teach me music: a young fiddler was engaged to teach me the violin, but my ear was too bad and I never learned anything; also perhaps it was considered a luxury and too little time and attention was given to it. I soon abandoned with relief the violin, although I regret until today that I did so, as I always thought that even indifferent playing is a great comfort and pleasure.

ISAIAH BERLIN, SENIOR

When I was 15 or 16 years of age I was sent to Riga. The 'extern' examinations were supposed to be fairer outside 'the Pale of Settlement'. I failed at my final examination on maths and physics. I could not draw a steam engine and I was not too good at algebra. I never liked maths. I remained for ever in Riga. I was staying with my grand uncle and grand aunt – Shaya Berlin. To describe them really needs a lot of time and paper. They were the millionaires of the family, made their money in timber, chiefly by buying in his young days forest estates with the land, which have in course of time grown enormously in value. Shaya B. was practically the first Jewish timber exporter and saw-miller in Riga, which business he started about 1880. Before then, and even for some time afterwards, the Jews bought forests, worked out the timber, floated them to

---

[1] 'RaAVaD', Hebrew acronym for Rabbi Avraham ben David (of Posquières) (1125–98).
[2] 'Ben yachid' ('only son').

Riga and sold the raw timber to the 'Taitschen' – the Baltic Germans – among whom were a few Englishmen, such as Armitstead, Addison, whose business it was to saw them up in their mills, sell abroad, chiefly to England, charter ships, travel abroad and so on. This was too much for the old-fashioned Jewish timber merchants, who lacked the culture, knowledge of languages to carry on an international trade.

Shaya Berlin was the first who ventured into this trade, engaging for his external relations an old-fashioned German, who failed in his own business but who knew all the ropes about timber export. Some years later he was followed by other Jews, who thought what one Jew can do, another can do as well if not better, and the old-fashioned unhurried profitable timber export business became a keenly competitive, at times a cut-throat, business, squeezing the German patricians nearly out of it. For this purpose he bought a sawmill in a suburb, The Red Dvina (Rote Düna), and engaged a large staff of employees, mainly Jews. In those days the feudal system was still existent in the relations between the owner of the business and his employees. He could maltreat them, shout at them and use them for his private purposes at any time of day or night. He lived on a floor above his office and the senior officials, such as Süskind Berlin (Rachmilevich's[1] and Lionel Schalit's grandfather),[2] your grandfather Salman Izchok Volshonok, Victor Volshonok, my father, who was the summer months in Riga, myself or any relative happening to be there gathered at his midday dinner in his house, and there was even 'a court fool' standing by the table – one Chaikel (Хайкель)[3] Malatzky, at whose expense the gathered company tried their witticisms. This Chaikel was in the habit to make his ripostes the next day as he was rather a nit-wit, and got his proper answers after discussing the arrows directed at him at midday with his wife at night, and this added to the hilarity of the company.

Shaya Berlin was a very interesting type. Born and bred as a pious Chassid, he had however a very gay and generous nature, liked a glass of wine with his dinner, took only a general interest in his business and left the day-to-day work and all routine work to his managers. At 11 o'clock all merchants gathered on the 'bourse'[4] for about three-quarters of an hour, while the necessary business was

---

[1] IB comments: 'Well known to me.' Solomon Rachmilevich (usually 'Rach', as below) (*c.*1892–1953), a Russian Jewish intellectual born in Riga and living in exile in London, was a close and influential friend of IB, whom he met through the Schalits. In his preface to his book on Marx IB thanks Rach for his help. He also said: 'He was the first person who gave me a taste for ideas in general, interesting ideas *telles quelles*' (interview [no. 6] with Michael Ignatieff). See also Michael Ignatieff, *Isaiah Berlin: A Life* (London/New York, 1998), 424.

[2] In fact Lionel Schalit's great-grandfather.

[3] 'Khaikel', diminutive of 'Khaym' (Chaim).

[4] Stock Exchange.

conducted by his managers. He spent his time among the puffed-up German 'patricians' – owners of old business houses and members of civic and other public offices – making malicious jokes directed at their dignity, and assumed superiority over the Jewish merchants. Nevertheless he was very popular for his uprightness in business and generosity, and known to everybody in town, which after all had a population of 400–500,000 inhabitants. The droshki-drivers used to know him by name and drive up to him whenever he was in the street: 'Herr Berlin, kann ich Sie nach Hause fuhren?'[1] When your mother was a baby of perhaps 6–7 years of age and lost her way in the streets, she went up to a bank-porter and asked her way to Shaya Berlin's house. Of course she was not only properly directed but led to it by one of the high-ups in the bank. Whenever she mentioned that she was a niece of Shaya Berlin she found better treatment and a certain respect. Although disapproved of by his surrounding, he scarcely ever passed an evening at home, went out to restaurants and theatres and nightclubs with his German cronies, under the pretext always of having to meet and entertain them for business reasons. A pathetic figure was then his wife, aunt Chayetta – sitting alone in a chair in the vast drawing room, singing quietly in a minor key and waiting up for him until midnight and later. He was very philanthropic, contributed generously to public, mostly orthodox, funds and was the recognised undisputed leader of orthodox Jewry in Riga.

He used to go annually to Carlsbad, suffering from diabetes, and mother tells a story of an old poor Jew, who asked her there when the old Mr Berlin is coming and told her his story that for years he is coming to Carlsbad to take the cure and all his expenses have regularly been paid by Shaya Berlin. This year Mr Berlin seems to be late in arriving and he is in despair. The man was a total stranger to him. There was a special register of poor relations all over Russia containing hundreds of names to whom twice annually subventions were sent regularly without failing. Those who were near relatives practically lived on his generosity either by direct gifts or by lending them money for business, which was rarely repaid. To his employees, however, he was in accordance with the times an old-fashioned employer, addressing them as servants, demanding unwavering obedience and even conformity to Jewish orthodoxy. Besides his town flat, he had a house near his mill occupied only early in the spring and late in the autumn for a few weeks. Still every employee had to appear on Sabbaths and Festivals at his private synagogue. On the other hand no employee was ever dismissed, however inefficient he was. Victor Volshonok, who was sent to his mill to reorganise it, dared, during his absence abroad, to dismiss a couple of men who were no good and were hindering the business. These men wrote to Shaya complaining and immediately came the reply and demand for their

---

[1] 'Mr Berlin, can I drive you home?' A droshky (Russian *drozhki*) is a type of horse-drawn carriage.

re-instatement – nobody dares remove any of his men. On his death he left everybody a legacy equivalent to 3 years' salary, but woe to the man who dared answering back when shouted at by him however undeservedly.

His business mind was also set on big operations and he disdained occupying himself with everyday sales or attending to the post. This was left to the staff, but he was not lazy. He rose at 6 in the morning, half past seven or earlier was out of the house in his pair and coach, going to his mill or railcar-factories with which he was connected and making an inspection like on parade, back to his office, to the bourse, to his lunch, an afternoon nap and then descending to his office, writing his private letters and open to be consulted by his managers, or cracking jokes or stories with his visitors, supper and his night rounds. He was deeply religious, but no hypocrisy or 'scheinheiligkeit',[1] and above all no austerity. His high living was partly responsible for his death at a not over-ripe age of 67 – in 1908.

His wife, who loved him passionately, was just the opposite: miserly, bad-natured – her poorer relations were supported by him, but when they had to apply for help they contrived to see him in her absence – refusing to accompany him to his friends and relatives, illiterate, quite clever but malicious, music-loving but refusing to go to the opera, only sometimes being persuaded by him, exploiting her relations, whom in later years she used to take abroad with her as companions. Your mother when quite a young girl went one summer with her for a couple of months and never having been in Europe before rather looked forward to it with eagerness and anticipation but had to suffer a lot from her, only your mother's character was even then, when she was in her teens, strong enough to force relations which made the journey tolerable and in the end even pleasurable for your mother.[2] She would neither give money nor spend much on herself. She survived her husband by 9 years and died in Tver in 1917, all her money being subsequently lost in the Russian Revolution. She did not spend it in her lifetime or let others enjoy it, and when forced, being childless, to leave it to her near relations, must have enjoyed posthumously the fact that they could not enjoy it.

I dwelt for so long on Shaya and Chayetta Berlin, because they were the pivot round which the family's life ran. My father when a small boy was adopted by them, and then the name of Zuckerman was altered to Berlin. He was brought up in their house and his marriage arranged by them. My grandfather – the Lubliner Rav – must have obtained from Shaya Berlin a promise to look after them financially and my father's timber business was always financed by Uncle Shaya. My father must have lost several times what was then considered

---

[1] IB translates as 'pseudo-saintliness'.
[2] Crossed out here: 'She could not in her illiteracy read names of streets or of shops, but developed a sense of finding her w[ay]'.

fortunes and many a time uncle used to plead with him to desist from business, which he never understood, and for which he only worked when it was promising, and neglected when it turned difficult and troublesome – to leave business well alone and draw all he needed for his upkeep just so, but my mother was strongly optimistic, believing after each business disaster that she will find another working partner for my father and earn her living by earning and not by remittances. When uncle died, he left a sum in trust for my father from which the executors should pay sufficiently for a decent living, knowing full well that if he left him money it will take a comparatively short [time] for my father to lose it in business. Unfortunately the Russian Revolution confiscated this quite considerable trust, to which was added an even larger sum by my aunt, who died at the beginning of the Revolution. He also left legacies for myself and my brothers and sisters. This legacy certainly helped me in starting business on my own. But apart from my father, there was my father-in-law, who was a nephew, Simon Jacobson, another nephew, Mendel Zuckerman (my father's brother), who all in one way or another depended on the good will of uncle Shaya, and this of course all added to his feeling of omnipotency. When I came to Riga, I passed about 5 years of my adolescent life in their house, the first 2 or 3 years studying, sitting for examinations each spring at the Stadtgymnasium[1] for my 'extern' examination.

STARTING WORK

Another factor then came into my life: my love for your mother. This started when I was still a boy really. I was nearly 3 years younger and I don't think I was taken seriously by her. I used to suffer awfully when she went about with other suitors – and there were several of them – and for a few years had to bear it silently, being both shy and not hopeful of response. This passion finally decided my career as a businessman. My mother intended me for the professions – a doctor, a lawyer, anything not to be in business, where she had such bitter experiences with her husband. When I was nearing my last gymnasium examination, I was mortally afraid that, having to enter an University and go away from Riga for 4–5 years, your mother will most likely marry somebody (as her parents were desperately trying to do) and my chances will be gone for ever. When therefore Uncle Shaya insisted that I should enter his business and not go to an University I gladly agreed, very much to my mother's chagrin. I used to go on Sunday afternoons to the 'Red Dvina', where your mother's family lived, have supper there, and mostly stay overnight (I remember in discomfort having to sleep on chairs put together in the sitting room), but happy to have been able to pass an evening in your mother's company.

[1] Town secondary school.

The staff in Shaya Berlin's office did not like my entry at all, feeling a favourite of the boss having been put in. Still I suffered it gladly, worked very hard, studied languages, which were necessary for an export business, book-keeping and so on, improved my awful handwriting (no typewriters having yet been in use in Riga) and in the course of about 2–3 years, although I was very young, worked myself up to the position of the manager of the export branch of the business and having been given procura – the right to sign for the firm – which was considered a symbol of great confidence similar to power of attorney.

I was taken by my uncle, I believe in 1904, on his first journey abroad, to help as interpreter and secretary, and made a tour of Germany, Holland, Belgium and England. I remember having bought my first top-hat, which was considered then the necessary headgear for somebody visiting the City of London. I remember vividly my forebodings when, crossing for the first time the Channel from Calais to Dover, I was approached by a steward and could not understand a single word of his English, which must have been broad Cockney, and there I was, supposed to act as interpreter to my uncle, who did not understand a single word of English. However, after a few days in London, I somehow managed to understand and to be understood, and partly, owing to my uncle not understanding a word, guessing and making up my own interpretation.

From London we went to Paris where a few gay days were passed. Paris was then really gay and interesting. Of course, I had no connection with the intellectual life of Paris then, but the life in the restaurants, on the boulevards, in cafés, theatres and night resorts was really lively and nothing like what it has become in the interwar years. From Paris we went to the Riviera for a couple of months; it did my French a good deal of good. In spite of his wealth, Shaya Berlin would not dream of taking a sleeper from Paris – this was not within his spending, although in Paris he did not mind how carelessly and lavishly he spent. Ordinary 2nd class carriage was good enough for a Jew, and I remember how early at dawn I was awakened by my uncle saying 'Hurry, everybody else is asleep in our compartment we can put on Tallis and Tephillin[1] and pray', and so we did. The Riviera, after my only experience of country life near Vitebsk and Riga, enchanted me. It must have been a particularly warm and sunny winter. The mountains, the sunshine, the street singers awakening me in the morning with a serenade of 'Santa Lucia' under the hotel window (Hotel du Parc), Monte Carlo with its dazzling figures, the battles of flowers – it all looked to me so dazzling, so beautiful.

We stayed there for a couple of months. Of course, I had no company, except my uncle's few old cronies, so I took to reading the Russian literature forbidden in Russia. I read then for the first time Tolstoy's 'Исповедь',[2] the 'Iskra'

---

[1] Prayer shawl (also 'tallith') and phylacteries.
[2] 'Ispoved" ('confession').

leaflets.[1] When my aunt noticed me reading 'forbidden' literature she was hor-rified, and when on the return journey, which carried us past Genoa, Milan and Switzerland, she pretended to have noticed a police sleuth who looked several times into our compartment, no doubt spying for an empty seat, but who in her own mind was watching me and therefore the whole company, her included. Shortly before, the papers reported that Gotz was arrested in Italy and turned over to the Russian authorities. Therefore she was particularly frightened dur-ing the traversing of Italy, and our previous plans to stop at Genoa and Milan and tour these two towns had to be abandoned and the carriage not to be left until the frontier – Chiasso – was behind us. And of course she was terribly cross with the young 'revolutionary' – me – for having succumbed to the illicit pleasure of reading unsuitable literature and endangering the freedom of the whole family. It sounds ridiculous now, but characterises the times.

We entered Germany and stopped at Frankfurt-on-Main. We tried to spend Passover at Bad Homburg, but the Jewish restaurant of the famous Braunschweig, famous all over Germany as the best Jewish eating place, was not opened yet, and [we] returned to Frankfurt to pass the holiday there. It gave me some little inkling into the German-Jewish life. My uncle had friends among the Frankfurt prominent Jews; we visited the 'Breuer' – ultra orthodox – Synagogue during Passover and I still remember the hypocritical German-Jewish customs. Frankfurt had an 'eruv' (a device permitting the carrying of things on Sabbaths) and when it rained the worshippers came to Synagogue with open umbrellas, but would not shut them themselves, this being an act not permitted on Sabbath or Jomtov[2] (it being considered equivalent to building an אהל[3] – a tent), and the Aryan porter performed this for every worshipper, and opening it again when leaving Synagogue if the rain still persisted.

COURTING MARIE

This concluded my 'grand tour' and after Easter I left alone for Riga, the old people going on to Carlsbad. I was glad to return to meet your mother again, hoping to impress her with my newly acquired knowledge of Europe, to which she as yet has never been. Your mother was managing her parents' house, as you know; your grandmother (mother's mother) was never a housekeeper or capable of looking after her children properly and your mother was in charge of everything, of the family purse, looking after her sisters and brother, order-ing them about, keeping the house in order and being the mistress of the house, in fact. Her knowledge of house economy and striving after order and cleanliness in the house came from her contacts with German neighbours,

[1] *Iskra* (the *Spark*) was a Marxist newspaper edited by Lenin.
[2] sc. *yom tov* ('good day'), used of religious holidays.
[3] 'Ohel' ('tent').

particularly the family of Wallenburger, an old patrician German who came down in the world and was employed by Shaya Berlin as a person bringing in 'Europeanism' into his business and representing the firm outwardly. He lived next door to mother's house – both houses belonging to Shaya Berlin's mill. The Wallenburgers, although anti-Semites as all Riga Germans, took to mother, she being an attractive intelligent little girl and ready to imitate the German ways. There she learned how to keep house in a German economic way, how to sew and mend and keep everything scrupulously clean and demand value for money. One of their girls, Meta, was her great friend. Still, when she took her out to the German opera house, she carefully bought two seats, *non*-adjoining, so as not to be seen by her German friends, who might be in the theatre, sitting too close to a Jewish girl. Their son Robert was, I believe, in love with mother, but of course no serious affair could be thought of by both parties, the gulf between German and Jew being far too wide.

Mother left school early. In fact she placed herself in school: her parents would never have done it. But after the 4th class she had to leave, the management of the house demanding it, and with it went many of her dreams, particularly her desire to develop her musical talents. She had a beautiful voice and I feel sure if she had been taught she would develop into a magnificent singer. She was very good-looking, vivacious, clever, and knew all the women's tricks, and had no lack of admirers. All young men employed at Shaya Berlin's mill nearby were at her feet. She had, I believe, also some non-Jewish admirers. Later on, had she not been oppressed by the whole orthodox Jewish atmosphere and her father, she undoubtedly would have chosen herself a husband among her admirers, but she dared not go as far. I know that the late Lev Schneerson was her admirer and she was also carried away by him. He lived in Kreutzburg – a few hours from Riga – was a railway contractor in a big way, was the lion of the Society, sang, spent lavishly and so on; but, alas, he was not religious at all, in short, a 'goy', and as such she knew could not be acceptable to her father. There was an Ingenieur[1] Zaitlin in Riga, where the relations were even closer, again the same reason. Sometimes I was taken in by your mother in her confidence. I often wondered whether she did not discover my feelings towards her and I was torn between a desire to appear at least 'fair' and my jealousy. Her father also brought her proposals for שדוכים,[2] but there my advice, when sought, was easier to give, as no feelings on her part were involved and the specimens for the most part were poor, except for one Joshua Blumenthal (a younger brother of the London Blumenthal), who was clever, well-read in German literature, and a singer – a field in which he had common interests with mother. When he married later and became a very shady businessman in his endeavours to get

---

[1] 'Engineer'.
[2] 'Shiduchim' ('matches').

rich quickly, mother still maintained that, had she married him, he would have
been kept on the straight path and would not be so consumed by a passion to
get money at any price. With all her hard commonsense she was very romantic
and I remember her devouring the German romantic literature of her time.

During that time she was once taken abroad by our rich aunt – Chayetta
Berlin – to Carlsbad and some 'bad' [1] in the Schwarzwald. I suppose she must
have jumped at the idea to go once abroad, which on her own she could never
then achieve. It was a hard time for her, to be a companion to a rich capricious
old aunt, grudging the young girl every pleasure, and not having enough of her
own money to dress adequately or to buy her own pleasures; but with her eternal tenacity she fought for at least partial freedom, and in the German Kurort [2]
had a host of young admirers, of whom one at least offered her marriage, but
aunt would of course even not listen to it. I remember I felt very miserable during the couple of months of her absence. When I saw them off at the station
in Riga, I returned feeling very miserable and lonely and wept for hours out of
sheer youthful misery.

So it went on until 1905 when the first Russian Revolution took place. My
sister Genia and cousin Rosa Jacobson took what they supposed to be an
'active' part in it. I don't know actually what they did but I suppose it must
have consisted merely in hiding some 'proclamations' and similar literature.
They were led by an Armenian, Atabekoff, who I believe later in 1917 took a
really prominent part in the Revolution somewhere in Russia. Mother was
also in sympathy, but I don't think that she did anything. When the liquida-
tion of the Revolution began, which was particularly severe in Livonia under
Meller-Zakomelsky, my sisters thought it wise to disappear for a time and went
to Warsaw. Genia went to stay with Joseph Cohn (my cousin, brother of the
chess player David Przepiórka), who disliked it immensely. Why should he be
mixed up with alleged 'revolutionaries'? My mother went there and I decided
one day to go there to see my mother and discuss my feelings to your mother,
feeling that something must be done. Mother was very appreciative and promised every help. Although she liked your mother, still I believe in her heart [she]
thought that I was capable of making a more brilliant, particularly a more rich,
match, and I believe was dimly afraid of your mother's domineering character,
but she was exceedingly romantic and, having herself had a frustrated romance
in her youth, was all on my side, and some time afterwards, encouraged by our
relatives, I went down to 'Rote Düna' – your mother's domicile – and made her
a proposal, which I was encouraged by all her family would be accepted. To my
consternation, horror and also shame (since the purpose of my visit was known
to the whole family), I was turned down. Mother had a gruelling time from her

[1] 'Spa'.
[2] 'Health resort'.

parents, except, I believe, grandmother Frumma, who sympathised with her in not accepting me if she did not want to. Anyhow my courtship was finished for several months. That summer Joseph Cohn's family came for the summer to the Riga seaside – Dubbeln – and I passed many evenings with Joseph's wife, Bolbina. I was after all very young, inexperienced, and Bolbina must have taken a special pleasure in keeping me away from meeting your mother. By the end of the summer – in fact on the eve of Tisha B'av[1] – I had an intimate conversation with mother and the intimation of the renewal of my proposal came in some form from her. We became engaged, kept it from the family for a day until over Tisha B'av (your grandfather Volshonok was abroad and he was telegraphed).

I remember now with what mixed feelings I got engaged: on the one hand it was the culmination of my desire and passion for years, on the other hand I had a feeling that mother accepted me only after calculating that she has after all to get married and she might do worse than accepting me. No doubt the estrangement between my first proposal in the spring and the decision at the end of the summer had something to do with her decision. Mother went to Warsaw to prepare her trousseau, stayed with the Cohns, the relations with whom were not too good, but who in those days would dream of staying in an hotel when one had near relatives in the same town! I started thinking of improving my economic position in view of the oncoming responsibilities. I was getting a salary from Shaya Berlin, somewhere about 100 roubles a month (only about £10), which [was] then considered quite good, but could draw on his cashier for all my actual needs. In fact all my 'trousseau' (men in Jewish circles then also made clothes, and bought a lot of personal things before marriage) was paid by him. I then took on an agency for insurances from London from Price Forbes – representing Lloyds – and this augmented very considerably my income. Grandfather promised a dowry of 10,000 roubles to mother. I never asked for it before marriage, so if he would have chosen to refuse it, he could have done so, but he paid 8,800 roubles, apparently finding it financially inconvenient to go beyond.

MARRIAGE AND FATHERHOOD

We married in Riga on ניסן ר'ח[2] 1906 – 14 March 1906. The wedding was a grandiose one, in the Hall of the 'Kleine Guilde [sc. Gilde]' – one of the medi-aeval guild-buildings – with several hundreds of guests. Over 20 uncles were present, all the rabbonim of Riga, relatives coming from near and far, and the dinner and luncheon parties spreading over a whole week. We took furnished rooms and for the summer went to the seaside – Strand. By next spring 1907 a

---

[1] Tisha B'Av (the ninth day of the month of Av) is a fast day commemorating the Destruction of the Temple in Jerusalem.

[2] 'Rosh Chodesh Nisan' (the first day of the month of Nisan).

child was to be born. The delivery was extremely difficult, mother was in agony for 3 days and finally it had to be extracted and was dead. It was a girl. Mother fell ill with puerperal fever, an illness of which in those days only one in thousands survived – her life was for many days in very grave danger, her strength was kept up by constantly plying her with champagne, port and brandy, but her will to survive was very strong. I remember a professor from Königsberg was summoned to her. One of his questions to her: 'Was denken Sie, werden Sie leben?' 'Gewiss'[1] was her answer. I was in despair and beyond myself. Later I developed some heart trouble – the result of those fateful days. Finally the crisis arrived and she started slowly to recover. Before that we have already taken and furnished (practically beyond our meagre means) a flat in Albertstr[aße].[2] Late in the summer mother went for a cure accompanied by my mother to Franzensbad. I was sent also for a cure to Kissingen, and as I still had to stay in Riga it was arranged that I should visit mother in Franzensbad, stay with her for a while, and then we both would proceed to Kissingen.

An incident here will show you how little consideration rich people took then of their employees. Shaya Berlin was in Bad Nauheim taking his cure. He knew exactly my movements and when I arrived in Franzensbad after midnight a telegram was already waiting for me to proceed immediately without any delay to Nauheim, giving no reasons. I have not seen mother for quite a time – she left Riga scarcely able to walk – and here I arrived after 12 at night and had to take the next train, about 7 in the morning, for Nauheim. Shaya was a sick person, heart trouble – according to this telegram I expected the worst. On my turning up in the evening in Nauheim I found he had to write a letter and telegram denouncing certain options which he was foolishly persuaded to give on some of his estates, and he had not sufficient command of the language to write them himself; and for all that a peremptory telegram, evoking the worst expectations, was sent summoning me in the presence, and not taking the slightest note of my family or any anxiety caused to them.

Anyhow, some time later mother joined me in Kissingen. I went to Sturzburg to meet her and she immediately burst into tears: the Franzensbad doctor told her she never could have children. I comforted her as best as I could and we passed a nice short time in Kissingen. Afterwards we had an invitation from Shaya Berlin to pass a couple of weeks with them in Homburg where they took a villa. Previously however I was to visit to Liubavitcher Rebbe (father of the present) to consult him whether to travel round Europe to sell timber. I got the Rebbe's consent to do so and we were anticipating an European tour of our own. A little illustration of our Chayetta Berlin's parsimony: in Wiesbaden was a famous Jewish restaurant to which we used [to go] for the midday meal.

[1] 'Do you think you will survive?' 'Certainly.'
[2] 'Albert Street'. The flat was on the top floor of no. 2a.

For the evening our aunt thought it much too expensive to pay for 5 persons daily (my mother also came there), so she used to buy some bread and tinned food and prepare a cheap meal at home. We, the two young ones, were healthy and had a good appetite, and often stole away to have a meal at the restaurant by ourselves for our own account. Sometimes the old man – Shaya – stealthily joined us, finding some excuse to get away, and had a meal with us, but the old woman must not know it – and they were multi-millionaires!

From Homburg we went to Bieberich [sc. Biebrich], down the Rhine in a pleasure-boat to Cologne, and then continued our journey to Antwerp and to Holland, stayed [for] Rosh-Hashana in Scheveningen, went on and passed Yom-Kippur[1] in Paris and Succoth[2] in London. I already had been in all these places before, but for mother it was her first visit to 'Europe' except her one visit a few years before to Carlsbad and a Kurort in Baden. This was instead of our honeymoon journey.

I was made in the meantime manager of Shaya Berlin's business (there was a kind of directorate – your grandfather managing estates and forests, Victor the mill and internal sales, I export, finance and general management of office). In the summer [of] 1908 Shaya Berlin died. I stayed on managing the winding up of the business for two more years. In the meantime on 6 June 1909 you were born, also after a very difficult confinement and with mechanical aid[3] (hence your left arm muscle weakness – the spot the pincers squeezed it). My financial position, in accordance with the values of the times, improved considerably. I was making good profits out of my insurance London agency, turned my money into good investments, and was increasing my capital steadily. Also Shaya Berlin left me some 20,000 roubles. When Shaya Berlin's business was wound up, his mill and business was bought up by his nephews – Beinus and Leib Berlin, both millionaires – with small shares for Leib Berlin's son-in-law Dr Lourie and myself, who were to manage it.

This was a troublesome year, as the Berlin heirs – particularly Beinus, a most incalculable, unreliable, dishonest man and liar – were intolerable, not only to me but also to his nephew Dr Lourie. The result was that this firm was dissolved with the help of Leib Berlin, who was really only keen to set up his son-in-law Lourie, husband of his only daughter, in business; and in January 1912 we set up our own business, Lourie and myself as equal partners, under the style: I. Lourie, M. Berlin & Co. – both putting in equal sums of money as initial capital – 50,000 roubles each – any further money necessary to be provided by the richer partner, Lourie. There was no great need for it, as the credit

---

[1] The Day of Atonement.
[2] The Feast of Tabernacles.
[3] IB deletes 'and with mechanical aid' and substitutes 'Caesarian', mistakenly. His was a forceps delivery.

of the firm was very high – we could obtain all we needed from the banks. This pleased me as it was giving me equal status, and the business flourished from the beginning and became one of the leading timber firms in Riga. This was the happiest time of my life, happily married, a lovely baby, and a prosperous and respectable business. I travelled a good deal abroad, England included, in the interests of my business. The summers were passed on the Riga strand. I was no longer under the tyranny of Shaya Berlin, and I was helping in arranging for my father a business to be able to live without depending, as he always used to, on the benevolence of Shaya Berlin. But, alas, it did not last long.

LEAVING RIGA

In August 1914 the First World War broke out. Riga became immediately blockaded. I had the foresight to provide myself with a substantial sum in cash, so that we did not suffer from a closing of the banks and credits which lasted quite for a few months. Lourie joined the army in his capacity as a doctor, although he scarcely remembered anything of his medicine. The business started giving me quite a lot of trouble, particularly a Max Gurvitch, to whom I have advanced money on timber lying in Maksaticha near Tver. I mention this as this led later to prosperity. In Riga I had a large stock at the mill of a certain Kremmert; this stock was greatly diminished by a fire which broke out in May 1915. This led to very much trouble. The Russian armies were then in Lithuania and the C. in C., the Grand Duke Nicolai Nicolaevitch, egged on by his Chief of Staff – a rabid anti-Semite, Januschkewich – issued an order that all Jews living in Lithuania and Curland, bordering on the battlefields, must leave forthwith, all of them, for the interior, as all Jews were suspect by him of espionage. So a merciless eviction started, not even the madhouses were permitted to keep their inmates, and cattle trucks were passing daily with Jews, old and young, healthy and sick, permitted to take with them only bare necessities. Riga was threatened in the same way. A Jewish special committee was formed, and only by bribing the then Governor-General of Riga, the notorious General Kuzlov, was disaster to the 30,000 or more Riga Jews averted, though the menace was in the air all the time.

At this time the fire at the mill occurred. I have no doubt that the mill owner Kremmert had a hand in it, as he was interested to clear the yards to enable him to start his mill running, which was impossible while all available storing space was occupied by my goods. Possibly to avert suspicion from himself, he sent an anonymous denunciation to the police that Berlin, that is I, already worried by the absence of his richer partner Lourie in the Army, and menaced as a Jew with deportation, thought of an excellent way to turn his goods, which cannot owing to blockade be exported, to ready cash by putting fire to his yards. In the atmosphere reigning then in Riga, this sounded plausible enough, and this denunciation, repeated by constant reminders from public telephone boxes to the Chief of the Criminal Police, gave me a good deal of worry and sleepless nights. It also influenced the several insurance companies who had to deal with the settlement of my claim, aggravated by non-existence of a market value for goods for which no market then existed. Riga also became menaced militarily. The Germans were only 30–40 miles from Riga. I then decided to send you and mother away to Andreapol (near Velikie-Luki), where I had a business, and a certain Katznelson, a very smart and clever man, my manager there, and myself decided to go to St Petersburg to deal with the head offices of 6–7 insurance companies (who had to compensate me for the fire loss) in an atmosphere less poisoned than Riga. The denunciation to the police, owing to Victor's acquaintance with the Chief of the Criminal Police and a douceur, was not proceeded with. I think even now that my decision was a wise one. I reached in a short time a settlement with the insurance companies and became possessed of cash which enabled me to entertain new business in Russia proper.

In Riga I left my father-in-law in charge of my business. Soon, however, a few bombs dropped by the Germans frightened him and he also left for Andreapol, leaving Izchok Samunov in charge of the business. From there started my business association with Izchok. He resided in Riga until the beginning of 1917 and was helpful in getting away the Riga very valuable timber stock to several railway companies and war organisations for cash. When this was in a large measure accomplished, he came to Petrograd with Ida,[1] to which city we then migrated from Andreapol. My timber business, inland now instead of export, prospered, and one felt very little the effects of the war. There was until early 1917 no food or any other shortages; anti-Semitism in Petrograd, apart from friction with the Police about the right to reside, which was easily smoothed over, one scarcely felt, and life went on nicely in our flat on Vasily Ostrov.[2] You had by that time Wansky as a teacher and kind of mentor, and also other Hebrew teachers, such as Rav-Rebe, the Ros-Jeshiva of Ponewesh[3] (Reb Ber), but very few children to play with.

THE FEBRUARY REVOLUTION

Then the February 1917 Revolution came. I remember very clearly that it came really quite unexpected not only by me, but by the majority of the people. Since November rumblings started. Miliukov made his famous speech in the Duma, adumbrating the possible treachery of the Empress Alexandra Feodorovna. The speech went round in roneo-ed copies, was avidly read, the 'progressive block'

---

[1] Ida Samunov (1887–1985), IB's maternal aunt.

[2] Vasil'evsky (St Basil's) Island.

[3] sc. Rosh Yeshivah (principal of a talmudic academy) of Ponevezh (modern Panevėžys) in Lithuania.

in the Duma became a bit bolder, but this was all very far from a revolution. The front was, owing to winter conditions, inactive; there was no particular scarcity of food in Petrograd, possibly owing to defective transport and winter road conditions; bread in particular might have been temporarily somewhat scarce, but really there were no hunger conditions. Demonstrations of working men started, also not on a big scale, and all of a sudden one morning I heard noises in the street below.[1] Looking out of a window I saw masses of people marching, workmen and soldiers intermingled, singing revolutionary songs, and soon one heard that the tsarist Government disappeared and the Duma took over command of the situation, unprepared and certainly not expecting to have to do so.

I have not the slightest doubt that had the Russian throne been occupied by a stronger man than Nicholas II, not so much under the evil influence of his wife, a more intelligent and better-informed one, this revolution would never have occurred, and how different the history of the world would have been! Had Nicholas followed Rodzianko's advice and nominated a 'responsible ministry' comprised of Octobrists, Cadets and perhaps a sprinkling of more left elements such as 'Trudoviki' and so on, instead of challenging every thinking intelligent man by nominating a crass reactionary nonentity such as Prince Golitzin, the Revolution would not have taken place. Alas, the old saying, 'Whom the Gods wish to punish, they deprive first of common sense', proved again true and is another proof that the march of history is influenced not only by the inevitable course of economic development, but to a large extent by personalities. Still, I don't jot down my memoirs to discourse on politics, so let us get on.

My feelings were a mixture of elation at the fall of the hated tsarism and fear for the future. Still one walked as on air, the people were friendly, practically very little violence was in evidence, meetings were taking place everywhere, the famous tribunes of whom one only heard before were now addressing mass gatherings to the resounding 'huzzas' of the hearers, and one expected a new free world to begin. The liberals – the Cadets – also did not realise the situation and particularly the mood of the army. Miliukov made very strong declarations about the right of Russia to the Dardanelles and Constantinople, and soon street demonstrations were marching with banners: 'Down with the capitalist ministers', 'Down with Miliukov Dardanellski'. Miliukov, Gutshkoff and [a] few others were dropped and soon the ineffectual Prince Lvov was replaced as Premier by that windbag Kerensky. The Bolsheviks with Lenin and friends were admitted to the country and this was the first step toward the Bolshevik Revolution in October. The triumphant and happy mood of the February Revolution soon changed to new dissatisfaction. The Petrograd garrison who

[1] IB comments that he had the same experiences.

were made to believe they were the heroes of the Revolution lost all sense of discipline (particularly so after the famous Prikas[1] no. 2 of the Petrograd Soviet issued by Sokolov), were selling matches and other things in short supply at street corners, and one decisive element in the October success of the overthrow of the provisional Government was the propaganda disseminated among them, [which] was that they were to be sent to the front to replace other regiments too long kept at the front. Anything to avoid to change their comfortable and easy life in Petrograd against going to the front, even if it involved the storming of the Winter Palais – seat of the Government – and certainly not conscious ideological convictions.

To return to our private life – my business with the Windava–Rybinsk Railway Company went on and profits in roubles increased: they were not much depreciated yet. Suddenly towards the end of May an English voice in English called me up on the telephone (and conversations in foreign languages were forbidden over the 'phone then). It was George Payne from London, who arrived from Scandinavia where he just married Sygne (sister of Steen Giebelhausen, who became a millionaire out of ship-owner's profits in Copenhagen) as his second wife. He came to Russia to find plywood, badly needed in wartime England and to be exchanged against some textiles shipped or to be shipped from England via Scandinavia. I never had great faith in Payne's ability and integrity and also was too preoccupied with my internal lucrative timber business to wish to engage in a business I knew very little of and the pitfalls of which were unknown to me. I at first declined all Payne's blandishments. However, I met him often in the company of his newly acquired stepson – Bruun – a son of Sygne from her first marriage, and spent many evenings together in Petersburg's nice restaurants. Your mother and you left for Staraya Russa for something like six weeks and I had time to meet him often. One evening he brought me to a party in Bruun's flat. In the meantime his barter arrangement of plywood against textiles fell through and he found himself in embarrassment, having bought plywood and sent it to Archangel for shipment to England, but no rubles to pay for it. Partly hoping it may turn out a sufficiently good business, partly desiring to help Payne out, I took over this consignment from Payne, something like £7–8,000. The deal went through smoothly and I realised a very good profit on it. In the meantime the July disorders occurred in Petrograd – troops with Bolshevik banners and slogans marched through the streets, the Kerensky Government took fright. Within a few days these [dis]orders were quelled but the atmosphere became tense.

I started thinking that it might not be a bad idea to convert some money into sterling in London by shipping plywood. I bought through Payne and sold

---

[1] sc. Prikaz ('Order').

some more plywood, and went on with it in ever greater measure, right till October. This by mere chance, of which, had not Payne turned up in Petrograd, and had he not got into difficulties, necessitating my intervention, I have not thought myself at all. In fact, my father-in-law disapproved of it strongly because he thought it would interfere with the regular business, distracting my attention and resources. So little did many people then fear the consequences of the Revolution and anticipate the swift advent of the Bolsheviks and destruction of the capitalist class! Shipping of the timber demanded frequent journeys to Archangel and I then ask Izchok Samunov, who only shortly before then came to Petrograd from Riga (where he attended to my Riga timber interests for a remuneration) to go instead of me to Archangel, in return for which I offered him 10 per cent of the profits. Thus it was that my partnership with Izchok started.

A very unpleasant episode occurred in the meantime. On a return journey from Andreapol one morning (during the Kornilov episode) I found that, during the night before, men from the Counter-Espionage office visited our flat, on the Vasily Ostrov – which also housed our office – searched the flat thoroughly and took away a lot of books, papers, check-books and cash, and left an address where I was to call. I could not think of any reason until I visited the Counter-Espionage office, found there Payne's stepson sitting, and when I addressed him, I was told sternly I must not converse with prisoners. He was accompanying Payne to Archangel and he was alleged while there to speak to some sea captains and try to find out information. For several days I had to submit to interrogations until I was able to establish my innocence and that I had nothing but business relations with Payne and his stepson. Payne in the meantime was also searched and taken by a convoy of soldiers round the town, slept a night in the Commandatur with several Korniloff officers, taken round again by some soldiers and not being able to speak a word of Russian knew nothing at all. While he passed the British Embassy on the Angliisky N'noy[1] he simply ducked into the Embassy building and the porter barred the way to the soldiers, pleading the extraterritoriality of the Embassy. The soldiers remained for hours sheepishly on the pavement and walked away. The Embassy arranged for him for exit visa and he left via Finland, however was sent back from the frontier, because on one of his envelopes was jotted down the address of the Counter-Espionage Bureau, given by men, where he had to go to collect his impounded papers. Finally, Payne left and crossed the frontier just a very short while before

---

[1] 'English Embankment' (though the exact transcription of the second word is very uncertain). The British Embassy was in fact at that time at 4 Dvortsovaya naberezhnaya (Palace Embankment). Further to the west this embankment was then (as now) called 'Angliiskaya' (MB seems not to decline the word), after an intervening 'Admiralteiskaya' section. MB may have forgotten at what point the name changed.

the Bolshevik coup d'état. I was left to deal alone with various plywood contracts, shipments etc. A quite large amount (about £20,000 or more) was laden into two ships in Archangel, which on the outbreak of the Bolshevik coup were detained in port, and I thought this sum was lost, as one didn't dare even to make enquiries. By a sheer piece of luck and good fortune, these boats were smuggled out of Archangel in the early spring of 1918 by the British Admiralty and I received payment for them in due course.

I dwelt at length at this plywood episode of June–October 1917 because this unexpected and at the beginning unwanted and very grudgingly accepted business was to decide my further course of life and incidentally yours. Had this not happened I should not have any money abroad, and particularly not in England, and would not have gone to live in England – most probably would have stayed in Riga and took up there my old business, and you would have gone to school there, and Heaven's know whether any of us would have been alive there or, if alive, very likely another 'Häuflein of Elend' (a bundle of misery) – the name which some Germans were calling the poor Russian-Jewish students in the pre-1914 period in Berlin. I look upon it as an act of Providence.

THE OCTOBER REVOLUTION

In Petrograd in the meantime the Communist Revolution triumphed and all ex-bourgeois like myself wandered about in anxiety and misery. We moved from Vasily Ostrov to Angliisky Prospect in order not to live where my office used to be and where I was known as 'bourgeois beast'. I burned all papers relating to my trading with England in order not to be forced to sign a cheque on London and to be taken in custody to prevent me from stopping the encashment of such a cheque, as I heard happened to several people who exported goods and were presumed to have 'valuta' abroad to their credit. My business with Moscow–Windava Railway went on under a new form: instead of being suppliers, we were made a kind of contractor but called 'уполномоченный по доставке лесных материалов'[1] (plenipotentiary for the production of timber materials). The State, [i.e.] the nationalised Railway Company, provided expropriated forests; we organised the work; all wages and transport, also all materials, were paid by the Railway under their control; and for our organisation, which included all salaried staff, offices, travelling and all overhead expenses, we were given 12 per cent of the amount of wages paid. The Company also provided many products paid out to the peasant-workmen in lieu of monetary wages, as roubles did not attract any work – distributed on a strict scale, so much per each unit of work done. We were given all facilities of State employees, exemption from military service, certificates that we were State workers

---

[1] 'Upolnomochenniy po dostavke lesnykh materialov'.

and therefore exempt from all other work, levies etc. This was a great help as it included us among those useful and working for the State, not to be rounded up in mass searches etc.; also the facility to travel, even in special railway carriages, when travel to ordinary mortals was nearly prohibited, and thus the possibility to bring from the country some food otherwise unobtainable in big towns; but also put us under the special vigilance of the Che-ka[1] to watch that food and produce given for distribution in lieu of wages went exactly as instructed, that work was properly carried out, and a special Ve-che-ka (Всеросс[ийская] Чрезвыч[айная] Комиссия)[2] agent attached to us. I was at Headquarters in Petrograd (now called Leningrad), and Samunov in Maksaticha – a station between Bologoie and Rybinsk – the centre of the actual forest work. At the head of all the organisation was Sergei Alexeevitch Ivanov – the head of the Materials Dept of the former Railway Co., a very clever and able man, a full-blooded monarchist and reactionary, but very clever, adaptable, ready and able to work efficiently to protect his skin and indirectly protecting the skins of all of us who worked under him, fully understanding that otherwise he is bound to fail.

The times were getting very thin, rations consisted of 1/8 lb. for ordinary people, and ¼ lb for us privileged brain workers, of dark indigestible bread mixed with straw and some dried fish (вобла).[3] A few titbits were distributed from time to time. Shortages increased and from the second part of 1918 real hunger reigned. Were it not for the supplies which I either brought myself from visits to Maksaticha or parcels sent by occasion by the Samunovs, I think we could scarcely have survived the cold and hungry 1918–19 winter. I remember still now with what greedy eyes I surveyed a bit of white bread, baked by your mother from some small supply of flour I have obtained, but which was reserved exclusively for your consumption, a small growing child, and which we both – grown-ups – did not dare to touch ourselves, as the quantity was not sufficient for the child alone. On another occasion I got hold of a piece of horseflesh which I consumed with the greatest of satisfaction. I remember also an occasion when I have returned from Maksaticha with a sackful of food. The train was late, got into Leningrad 2 or 3 in the morning, I had a heavy skunk fur coat over me; in Leningrad, as it sometimes happened in its maritime climate, it was thawing when I have arrived. After having dodged, by some obscure exits well known to me, the Che-ka guards of the station (who usually took away any food), I found myself in the street with the prospect of walking the 2–3 miles to Angliisky Prospect home in the middle of the night, but, unable to carry

[1] The Cheka was the Soviet secret police force, so called after the initials (ч к – che ka) of its Russian name (which means 'Emergency Commission'), 1917–22.

[2] 'Vseross[iiskaya] Chrezvych[ainaya] Komissiya' ('All-Russian Emergency Commission').

[3] 'Vobla'.

the exceedingly [heavy] fur coat and the heavy sack full of produce, after each few steps I had to rest and was nearly ready to drop the fur coat in the street, but certainly not the sack, on which our survival depended. It took me several hours to make the 2–3 miles home.

Another occasion when the house was searched by seamen for some flour, which was apparently stolen from some naval barracks, but bought by the chairman of our house-committee – a tsarist general – and distributed among the other bourgeois inhabitants of the house. The position was desperate, we had our sack of flour, could not dispose of it, and the search party was already in the flat below us and bound any minute to come to us. The sack was hidden on a balcony, covered by the snow which lie several feet on the balcony. The search party duly arrived, went through every nook and cranny, [and] finally was leaving, when one of the men chanced on the balcony and must have seen the sack, but was decent enough not to report it, but only made a gesture to mother, as if to say, 'I know the secret but, well, I won't give you away.' Had he talked, we would promptly have been bundled off to the Gorochavaia (Leningrad HQ of the Che-ka).

Several times I was summoned to the Gorochavaia, fully expected to be arrested, took each time a piece of bread in my pocket, as for the first day or two one was not given any food, but talked myself each time successfully and was allowed to go home. The worst was when Victor Volshonok, whom I took on as one of my aides and put to work on a small station near a forest not far from Leningrad, was arrested and brought to prison to Leningrad. He was denounced on trumped-up accusations by an employee of his – Rothschild – who was at the same time a secret agent of the Che-ka. I was warned by Gorinov – another of my railway friends and chiefs – and promptly left for Moscow, where I hid myself for a fortnight until the worst will be known. Rothschild and other agents did come to my office, searched it, and stole a considerable amount of money which I have kept quite legitimately in my safe and for the keeping of which the authorities gave an appropriate certificate. After this theft I felt safe to return to Leningrad, and after a few weeks, with the help of [an] intermediary who distributed some bribes, succeeded in freeing Victor.

Next summer we lived in a pension in Povlovsk, and were already working on obtaining papers to enable us to leave for Riga, where the Latvian Republic was established and recognised by the USSR as an independent State. The GPU (the renamed Che-ka) suddenly surrounded the pension and begun a search. I run out to the verandah with some of your mother's jewellery and hid them in some flowerpots. When the search was finished, the jewellery was gone. A woman living in the pension approached mother and told her that she knew who took the diamonds, and that for a ransom she could recover them for us. We badly wanted to recover them, as this was the currency we were expecting to live on when we shall reach freedom in Riga, but were frightened of provocation, and also to admit that we could procure the vast amount of money demanded as ransom. Finally we decided to take the risk and recovered everything. We also recovered the diamonds which were lying in the sealed bank safe and which the Government was expected to open and take away. This was another grave risk taken, as provocation was round every corner. We paid in kind by buying with some part of the recovered stones.

You we kept shielded as much as we could, we did not send you to school, but took tutors, as you well remember, into the house; there [is] where your basic Hebrew knowledge comes from. Whatever food we had went for you, and people in the queues used to make offensive remarks to your mother like 'With such a fat boy you can scarcely need more food.' We might even have tried to escape from Russia much earlier than we actually did, as we felt like in a prison, but were always afraid that the child – that is you – might in his innocence talk on the way and we shall be caught. Finally, in October 1920, we were able to leave Leningrad for Riga legitimately as refugees from Riga. Your mother's knowledge of Lettish helped a great deal both in being recognised as Latvians by origin and in crossing the Russo-Lettish frontier. The Samunovs were left in Maksaticha and later Leningrad as being my substitutes, as otherwise I could not have obtained my release from the work for the Railway Co. We left everything in our flat as it was, also all business and monies, taking with ourselves the permitted amount of 3,000 Romanov roubles per person.

One was happy to go, even without anything, and one felt as prisoners must feel when the prison gates are opened. It was not the lack of food, the discomfort, cold or very primitive conditions of life which made one crave to leave the country, [so much] as the feeling of being imprisoned, no contact with the outside world, the spying all round, the sudden arrests and the feeling of absolute helplessness against the whim of any hooligan parading as a Bolshevik. One's ear was cocked the whole night to listen to a car which stopped near the door of the building one lived in, as at night every car was practically a Che-ka car, and if one heard it stopping near one's house, it meant a search is being started somewhere and somebody carried away to death or endless imprisonment and torture, as everything one did was against the law, or generally because you belonged to the former possessing or intellectual classes. That psychological state of getting nervous at the sound of a car stopping outside at night continued for many years afterwards in the security of London, and I used to be drawn to the window to investigate, though I was fully aware that this is London and no Che-ka cars pursue you here in the stillness of the night.

RETURN TO RIGA

We travelled for 10 days in cattle trucks, loaded with all kinds of household goods and all kinds of people, stopping for hours or full days at some large stations, such as Pskov, and just continuing unexpectedly without any time-table, and leisurely. You can imagine the comfort of it, there being no wash-ing or sanitary arrangements in the truck, and having to wait for the next stop, sometime for hours, to satisfy one's physical needs. On the way we bartered salt and candles for bread or egg or something else edible. In Ostrov (the frontier) we were searched for four hours, nothing was detected, and finally arrived in Reshitza – the sorting and delousing Latvian station. Letts were permitted to proceed to Riga, while Jews had to disembark at Reshitza.

Now a great disillusion took hold of us. We were thrusting forth from the slavery of the Soviets into the free, liberal Europe, as we knew it before 1914, and there we were met at the very door of this civilised world by a new anti-Semitism, as even pre-1914 Russia did not practise it. Still, nothing could be done, we had to pass the night in a cold, unheated barracks, went to a Russian steam bath for delousing, and started to find our way about the camp. People told us that one waits here for a week or longer until the Lettish control officials verify your statements about your former residence in Latvia. I wired to Riga but received no satisfaction. Suddenly I was approached by one of the con-trol officials who apparently knew me by sight or name (which was very well known) in Riga, and made me an offer that for a certain sum things could be expedited and we might be able to leave for Riga the same evening. Although frightened of possible provocation, I felt so dejected and degraded in this camp that I have readily agreed and the man carried out the bargain.

We left the same night for Riga in a crowded 3rd-class carriage huddled in a corner. We got so depressed ourselves by the journey in the cattle truck, the sojourn and the treatment in Reshitza that we even did not dream of taking up 2nd-class tickets, which was a mistake. In the carriage some Letts made dis-paraging remarks about Jews and your mother used this time her knowledge of the Lettish language to her disadvantage. She made a spirited rejoinder that in Russia at least the Jews were not treated in such an abominable way and that such remarks would not have been permitted there. In the morning one of the Letts complained to the military control who passed the train that this Jewess here was a Communist, and that she prefers Russia to Latvia, adding on no doubt a good deal which she never said, with the result that instead of stepping off the train as free citizens of a free country, coming out from the slave country, mother was taken under police escort to the Police Station and arrested, being led in full daylight as a criminal over the streets. While still at the station two plain cloth men approached me, who was free, by the mere chance of not understanding a word [of] Lettish and therefore not taking any part in the night altercation, and said they were detectives travelling in the same carriage, overheard the whole conversation and [were] ready for a consideration to assist in freeing mother. I again paid and got mother off within an hour or so.

This was our greeting to free and democratic Latvia. This bribe and the one in Resitza left me with scarcely any money, and I was not sure that the quite considerable amount of sterling lying to my credit with the Bank in London was at my disposal, as rumours were spread before our departure from Leningrad that monies due to Russian citizens were confiscated by the British Government in payment of Russian defaulted State debts. So I had to be very careful and we even did not spend on a cab from the station, or rather the police station where we have got landed, and walked quite a long way to the house of Shaya Berlin,[1] who offered us very kindly hospitality and waited for us at the station, and whose offer under the circumstances we greedily accepted. The same day (a Friday) I cabled to my bank in London enquiring as to the freedom of my account, and got a reply the same evening which set my mind at ease, and we soon transferred ourselves to the house of Uri[ah] Berchin, who let us a room in his house and where we also could have our meals.

Anyhow from that moment we started breathing more freely. There was no need for me, as I thought, to look for immediate employment at any remuneration, and I could start thinking about engaging in my old timber trade. I soon find some business and make some profit, and we decided finally to go away from Latvia. As to where to go, we were not yet quite decided, but thought first to try London, where our money was lying and was now safe. I was to go first and find out whether we could settle in London and you and mother were to follow. Before I left, the old story in the train was revived again. Mother was summoned to the counter-espionage office (who also dealt with politicals) and it transpired that her enemy in the train to Riga repeated his denunciation of her to this authority, accusing the police of having covered up a 'Communist' dangerous woman. I went with her and the officer there assured me there was nothing in it and that I could safely go away; nothing would happen to her. I left, but soon after my departure she was sent for again and was advised, if she wanted to avoid trouble, to leave Latvia. This was a very friendly advice. I could not get so quickly the visa to London. Victor got her and you a visa to Berlin, and in fact a day or two after she has left, soldiers came to arrest her. In Berlin you waited a few days until I got you the visa, which was granted on the strength of Mr Bastable of the Arundel House School having accepted you as a pupil.

[1] Presumably yet another member of the late Shaya Berlin's extended family.

IN ENGLAND

Finally in March[1] 1921 you arrived in London. I remember you running off the ship's gangplank in your Russian fur overcoat and fur cap, looking a strange but lovely sight. I have in the meantime prepared for us a flat in 1 St James' Square,[2] Surbiton. You could not speak a word of English; still only a few days after your arrival I have sent you to Bastable's school. You must have felt very awkward, never having been to school before, and also without a word of English. Still you must soon have adapted yourself – this was about March 1921 – as at the end of the July term you got the first prize, of all things in English. I remember the first word you have asked me after a few days school was the meaning of the word 'swop', and I went along the High Street with you to search for a sweet, the name of which you didn't know but which you would recognise at sight – it was a toffeeapple.

For Passover we went to Brighton and stayed in a very mediocre Jewish boarding-house off the Parade. You saw a bicycle in a shop and although you could not ride there was no persuading you to postpone. You have set your heart on it – the bike had to be bought. It rotted later away in Upper Addison Gardens. That summer mother broke her ankle in Berrylands Road, Surbiton, to which house[3] we moved early after our arrival, and was immobilised for several months, during which time our lease of Berrylands Road expired and we had to move to 'Maydene', a house in Surbiton.[4] Mother's leg demanded her moving to a nursing home for a lengthy time to London, and Mrs Bastable took you in for a couple of weeks out of pity. I think it had a good influence on you; you quickly learned several of English customs and manners and by Christmas 1922 [sc. 1921] you left Arundel House School for good, stayed with us for a month or so at the [Royal] Palace Hotel Kensington, and then we all moved into 33 Upper Addison Gardens. You were taught by a coach – Mr Crouch – in preparation for entry into Westminster School, and also had your Hebrew teachers, one of whom, Mr Tessel I think, must have remained in your memory for some time.

It was then that you told me your one and only lie in your life – you said you went to Mr Crouch, while in fact you did not go to him. The fact was not an important one, but it has upset me very profoundly. I thought you were incapable of telling a lie and here you've told me one. I made you a scene, very painful to me and I believe which also must have impressed you (as only recently you

---

[1] The most likely date is 20 February.
[2] In fact, 1 St James's Road.
[3] No. 8.
[4] In Effingham Road, Long Ditton, Surbiton.

have reminded me of it). It was a childish impulse and it suffered a shock and had its consequence.

While Westminster was ready to admit you and Mr Crouch only pleaded (for your own sake, as he said) to change your name from Isaiah to Jim or James, I felt[1] that for a foreigner and a Jew Westminster might be, for the first year or two anyhow, not a very comfortable place, and it might affect your sensibility rather badly, and got you in instead into St Paul's School.[2] I still think it was a wise decision, except that St Paul's didn't have the same social mark as Westminster. Very soon you won a Junior Scholarship and acquired friends at school. I think this would not have been as easy at Westminster. Your school life was smooth and not eventful. From Junior you acquired a Senior Scholarship and your tuition at school cost me a very trifling sum. Your Jewish studies also proceeded apace and you have acquired a very tolerable and useful knowledge of Hebrew and the Bible. Talmud never from the Petrograd days appealed to you and this is a pity, since its knowledge would have given you a deeper insight into Judaism. You have read the modern Hebrew poets, such as Bialik, and I think this as well as some of your friendships gave you a sympathy for Zionism, which shaped to some extent your 'Weltanschauung'.

In 1928 you won a Scholarship in Oxford and entered Corpus Christi College, also carrying a leaving exhibition from St Paul's, so again I cannot complain that your education was expensive. Your four years in Oxford were, I think, on the whole, happy ones. You have acquired friends, some of them, I think, for a lifetime, and English culture became part and parcel of your life. Nearing the end of your undergraduate life, thoughts of a career naturally entered your head and you will remember your journey with me to Manchester for an interview with C. P. Scott, with the idea for joining the *Manchester Guardian*. It must have been in 1931. I don't remember this interview to have been a very successful one (and how well that it was so). On your return you found a letter from your College Tutor, Mr [W. F. R.] Hardie, imploring you to abandon the thought of a journalistic career and to prepare yourself for the examination to 'All Souls'. I think this letter must have influenced [you] very much. In the spring of that year I visited you in Oxford and you were agitated by the problem of whether to apply for a job at (if I remember well) Exeter College. You were not keen on joining Exeter, but did not think that any of the Colleges which you fancied would take you. Still, you decided to wait and the opportunity of a lectureship at New College occurred, which you took.

Soon afterwards the examination at All Souls took place. I don't know how you felt but possibly you were more encouraged by some of your friends, particularly Hardie. I was sure in my mind that a College known for their great

[1] IB changes to 'you felt – because of this recommendation'.
[2] IB crosses out 'and it might [...] badly', and adds here 'where you had a friend'.

selectivity, full of bishops and statesmen, will not plump for a foreign-born Jew. There I believe was scarcely a Jew ever on record having been a Fellow of All Souls.[1] And I believe the first reaction of Lord Chelmsford, the Warden, after your examination, was 'I hope *he* will not join our College.'[2] I remember having written to you, in order to soften the blow of the expected rejection, that your election could only be a miracle, and that miracles nowadays don't happen. The reply next day was a telegram from you: 'A miracle has happened.' I think the moment when [Goronwy] Rees was sent to see you and inform you of your success must have been one of the proudest in your life. I remember old Lenanton of J. P. Morgan & Co. telephoning me to congratulate, in the belief that I was not fully conscious of the honour and importance of election to an All Souls Fellowship, trying to explain to me what it meant and how impressed he was, knowing your antecedents. The *Jewish Chronicle* devoted an article to this important event in the Jewish Community and the Chief Rabbi wrote to congratulate you (addressing you, if I remember correctly, as 'Irving' Berlin).[3] This election established your position in Oxford.

In the meantime I established slowly and cautiously my timber business in London. I was rather timid, so soon after the catastrophic fall of values after the First World War, to go all out myself, and Mr Bick entered into a partnership with me. Izchok Samunov also arrived in 1922 in London and he had one-third in my share of the business. We developed a business in Riga, employing my uncle Victor Volshonok as the local manager, and dealt mainly with the Russians in timber. Soon we joined in this business with the Schalits, who were operating on a big scale with the Russians. This developed into a large and profitable business and we prospered, although I and particularly your mother felt that we are throwing away the profits on too many partners, particularly Bick. This business took me on very frequent journeys to Riga, Berlin, France, Holland and Belgium. [After] some years I established a business in Finland in partnership with a Finn, Paanonen, building a planing mill, which however turned out a disaster; this was followed by establishing a pit-props business in Finland under the management of Mulia Aronson, and it became a very lucrative business right until the beginning of the war in 1939.

In the meantime the Schalits got into financial trouble and the joint Russian business via Riga came to an end in 1932. This in turn led to breaking up of the partnership with Bick and I finally got emancipated from the multiplicity of partners. Samunov also left in 1934 for Palestine and ceased to be a partner in

---

[1] There was none.

[2] This anecdote is told in various forms. IB usually reported the Warden as having said, as IB left his interview, and not intending that IB should hear him, 'At least we don't have to take *that* one!' IB annotates Mendel's version here: 'not quite accurate'.

[3] True: for this episode see L1 41, notes 7–8.

the business. In 1932, when the Russian business in partnership with Schalits ended, the timber business for a while went down considerably, and it was then that I started the bristle business with Syder and Selzer, who were the experts, and I was the financier. This looked a moderate business in the first few years, but giving quite a lot of trouble, as Syder had a very speculative nature, just the opposite of mine, and always loaded us up with too large stocks of goods. Syder died in 1938, and at the time of his death we were left with a very heavy stock, worth considerably less than its cost price, and things looked rather gloomy. Also the Riga business which we started in 1934 together with Katz, but since 1937 alone without Katz, turned out badly, mainly because of Volshonok's not skilful management, following the trend of others but less smart in following the others' tricks, and also owing to a great extent to very heavy taxation in Latvia – heavy not because of the rate of taxation, but owing to a deliberate policy of the Latvian authorities to mulch by all legal or illegal means Jewish businesses, and the partiality of the Latvian Courts in cases of appeals. Only people who bribed the officials got off lighter. Those, like Volshonok, who could not play this game bore all the burden and therefore profits there in a legitimate manner were practically impossible. I was burdened in 1938/9 with heavy guarantees to the banks for monies lent to the Riga business, while the assets were by far not sufficient to cover all this indebtedness. It looked as if I will have to dip my hand deeply in my pockets to cover all the losses. This state of affairs made me very gloomy and worried in the second part of 1938 and right till August 1939.

Then the war started and things began to change. Riga, being cut off, worried me less; while some of the Riga banks managed to get out of me a few thousand pounds against my guarantees, the Russian occupation of Riga put an end to any further demands from there, and the bristle stocks which worried me in London began to appreciate in value, and by 1940 I found myself in a position to have recovered the losses on stock and even making a profit on them. This went on till 1942 when bristles came under Government control, but at prices ruling at the time, which put my stock at a premium. In 1940 the blitz destroyed about £70,000 worth of bristles, for which compensation was paid. This eased the financial position but decreased the profits in that portion of stock, had they been left intact, as happened to the saved stock.

These changes put me again on a solid economic and financial basis, which was threatened to a large degree in 1938/9. Life however was not easy when in 1940 the bombing of London started, and particularly night bombing. For weeks on end one could scarcely snatch more than a few hours' sleep, early in the morning. The best part of the night we had to pass in a tiny shelter, without sleeping accommodation, in the cellar of the house, or on duty at the

ARP[1] post, where I was a warden. After a few months we scarcely could stand it and went for a holiday to Llandudno. I used to go up to London twice a week – an ordeal in those days owing to the bombing and overcrowding of trains. Still the days and particularly nights passed in Llandudno gave one's nerves a rest. In June or July[2] 1940 you left for America. Our anxiety was great until we heard from you that your boat arrived safely. I understood from you afterwards that your few months in New York from July till October were not happy ones.

In October we received a cable from you from Lisbon that you were on your way back to England. Great excitement! I packed my things and went to see you on your arrival in Oxford. Mother, who naturally was as keen, if not more, to see you after the fateful months July–October 1940, joined us only a few days later. You arrived on שמחת תורה.[3] The following day was Saturday and she stuck to her principles and would not travel until the following Sunday. This was the beginning of our installing ourselves in your rooms in Oxford for the next 4½ years until a couple of months before the end of the war. This arrangement was, anyhow for me, a happy one. Although I regularly passed two nights a week in London, attending to my air-raid warden's duties, the possibility of passing five quiet nights every week and sleeping soundly, also weekends and Wednesdays in the atmosphere of Oxford and its serenity, undoubtedly contributed to our surviving the horrid war years with minds and bodies comparatively sound and being able to resume normal life. Abbé Sieux's [sc. Sieyès'] dictum 'J'ai vécu' can be appreciated only by those who survived those years 1940–45 in bombed London. True, I caught early in 1941 an unpleasant illness – inflammation and disorder of the gall bladder, which galled my life for nearly three years – but had we stayed in London I doubt whether it would not have led to much more serious consequences. Mother, whose fortitude and strength of character are beyond admiration, still keeps on saying that the rheumatic state of her legs has been much aggravated by the dampness of the Oxford climate, her quarters there in a Holywell ground floor in Mrs Hall's house, and principally by her having to pass innumerable hours in the underground kitchen of New College House (preparing meals for me because of the strict diet I was put on), does not quite realise what the alternative would have been had we both continued to stay in our house in London. Probably we would not have been alive today, or like many of our acquaintances developed heart diseases or thrombosis which proved fatal shortly after the war was over.

[1] Air-Raid Precautions.

[2] 10 July.

[3] 'Simchat Torah' ('Rejoicing of the Law') is the celebratory festival that marks the conclusion of the annual cycle of public readings of the Torah and the beginning of a new cycle. The celebration forms part of the holiday of Shemini Atzeret ('Eighth Day of Assembly') which concludes the festival of Succoth.

Of course, we could have gone to another more salubrious place or even in Oxford find quarters [providing] more suitable accommodation, but knowing, as I do, the 'laissez-faire' and conservatism of our characters, the most likely thing is that, had you not settled us in Oxford, we would have stayed in London with the result I mentioned above.

On 1 January 1941 you went to Bournemouth to join a plane from there for Lisbon and from thence to New York. We accompanied you and for 8–9 days we stayed together as the weather was too bad for the plane to take off. You were not too happy there. I remember the nearly nightly telephone calls from Miriam Rothschild teasing you about your going away, and we felt it, and of course the perilous journey worried us. Your decision to go turned out very wise and proper. Imagine your staying on through the war years in Oxford, or perhaps having to take some minor and very uncongenial government office. It would have not only repressed you but possibly sapped your great vitality and you would have shrunk inwardly, turned you perhaps into a hack. Instead, thanks of course to your gifts and personality, you grasped the opportunity and developed enormously in America. You must have done very good work for the Government, or you would not have been so praised and appreciated, but you have done good work for yourself. You have enlarged and expanded your personality, came into contact with a greater and larger world than academic Oxford, you have seen how things are 'cooked in the kitchen' and convinced yourself that 'не боги горшки обжигают'[1] and gained a great deal of self-confidence. You have obtained a knowledge of politics and diplomacy and cannot so easily be led up the garden, as many academicians were and are. Knowledge of the world and life are great acquisitions.

Your several visits to England during that time were sources of great pleasure to us, but also of great anxiety owing to the hazards of wartime travel. Particularly was this the case in 1942, I believe, when, after having received your usual cheerful cable announcing safe arrival in New York, I was rung up by Rach, advising me to buy an *Evening Standard* where there were some news of you. His tone was so funereal that I hastened to obtain a copy and there were the news that you were taken ill and had to be transferred from the airfield to a hospital (which turned out to be not quite true). Mother, who already went to Paddington Station to catch a train to Oxford, and whom I was to join at the station, was hastily recalled by me back to our London house and we frantically started telephoning to your Ministry – at that time the Ministry of Information – to obtain news and information. About 10 p.m. that night we had from them the news that a Mr Thomas[2] visited you in

---

[1] 'Ne bogi gorshki obzhigayut', a Russian proverb that continues 'a te zhe lyudi' ('It is not the gods who make pots, but men themselves').
[2] Ben Thomas: see L1 411, note 2.

hospital and that you were as well as you could be. This sacramental English phrase can mean anything you like. We only knew that you were alive, but that is all. An idea struck us, to telegraph to Dr Weizmann, who was then in New York, to enquire about you, and we shall never forget his kindness in sending us such a reassuring cable that we really started believing that you were not in great danger. You yourself were very good in cabling and writing us reassuring letters making light of the whole affair. Still for 10–14 days we passed through great anxiety and worry. You [had] contracted pneumonia owing to an open window in the Shannon Hotel, where you had to wait a night for the next New York plane. Our great consolation at several times when we worried about you was only that you were not in London under the bombs, particularly knowing that when you were in London during air raids you never took cover and exposed yourself fearlessly (and perhaps foolishly) to all possible dangers. We sometimes read articles and remarks about you in the papers, filling us always with justifiable, and in parents so understandable, pride.

My greatest excitement during the war was: 1) on that fatal [22] June 1941 when the news came of Hitler's attack on Russia and 2) in 1945 when the first atom bomb fell on Hiroshima. Although I never believed (neither did you, I remember clearly) in a German victory and not even in an invasion of Britain (a belief not based on logic but somehow intuitive), the moment I have heard of Germany's involvement in Russia, the conviction of ultimate victory grew to a certainty, which all the later Russian reverses could not shake. The immensity of Russia, her teeming millions, her comparative indifference to huge losses of human lives have always bogged down her enemies and, I am afraid, will continue to do so. Having gained this certainty, one's outlook immediately changed and it remained only a question of time and sacrifice, but the dawn was no longer in any doubt.

The news of the atom bomb left me breathless. I am afraid in this instance my imagination ran away with me. I imagined wars will henceforward become unthinkable, simply physically impossible, the application of atom power to civil life a matter of a short period, coal and oil will become superfluous, cheap power, heat and light attainable with only little human effort, and a millennium in consequence in the not too far distance. Alas, this illusion did not last long, or perhaps it still may turn out not so illusory?! Who can tell as yet! I remember Rach 'phoning soon after the publication of the news. I spoke very excitedly. Mother who stood nearby asked what is the excitement all about, and I telling her, 'You don't know yet, this is the greatest news, a new world is coming and much happier one' and so on. The armistice in May 1945 did come less as a climax, because the end of the war was in the air for several weeks and the celebrations were certainly less exciting and frantic than on 11 November

1917 [sc. 1918]. Bombing has already stopped about 6 weeks before the armistice and people became less nervous.

You arrived soon after the armistice, expecting to be sent to Potsdam. However Mr Eden intervened and you were left out. You were very disappointed. You passed a few months with us, then went to Moscow for four months – a time, I think, you greatly enjoyed. Your curiosity in many respects could be satisfied. You had an opportunity of meeting my brothers and sister and their families, all very novel and out of the ordinary. Your knowledge of Russian affairs, their literary and cultural activities [were] much clarified and I think this visit, the books you acquired there and the interest roused in you was the cause to a large extent of your concentrating on past Russian ideas and literature, and led you finally to lecture on these subjects in Harvard in 1949.

In the meantime I was sent out in September 1949 as a member of a Government Commission to Germany to study and report on possibilities of exploiting German forests for British needs. I was over six weeks in Germany in Bad Oeynhausen near Minder. I had some opportunity to see all the damage done to Germany and to meet several Germans in the timber industry. Even then one could see that their only regret was that they lost the war, but certainly not regret for the war or the Nazi regime. I remember a visit to the estate of Prince Bismarck in Holstein outside Hamburg. We first called on the Chief Forester, who still could not suppress his German haughtiness and arrogance, but the Prince himself came, very charming, speaking a perfect English. He bowed and said 'Bismarck'. I inclined slightly and said 'Berlin'. I could not help thinking how different such an encounter would have been before the war. On the way from Bad Oeynhausen to Hamburg we passed Lineburg [sc. Lüneburg], and I attended for a few hours the Military Court trying the Belsen Camp murderers. I never saw a more beastly calm arrogant face than that of Ilse Koch. Some Jewish victims, giving evidence, were led round the long dock to identify the culprits, and when one pointed his finger to Ilse her stare at him made him falter and tremble. Germans one met on the Autobahn were all sulky, with hostility in their eyes. I had to make a trip to Vienna (which however finished outside Eisenach as already the Russians were putting all obstacles in the way of the Anglo-American army men traversing their zone), and, hurrying back from Eisenach to Frankfurt for the night, our car containing two people was for long stretches on the Autobahn, flanked by forests, the only vehicle on the road. One really felt danger lurking from the dark forests and one instinctively put on a foot on the accelerator to reach Frankfurt before complete darkness.

FAMILY TREES

These notes explain the conventions adopted in the three family trees that follow.

Persons in italics appear with more detail elsewhere.

Only selected members of these extensive families are shown.

East European Jews did not adopt fixed surnames until well into the nineteenth century; so the earliest generations of the Schneerson family are shown without surnames, and some later family members with alternative surnames (as in the Fradkin family).

Given names are even more complicated. Any given name may, at different times and in different places, appear in a multiplicity of forms. (See Editorial Note at 264 above.) The names given in the trees are mainly Yiddish for the earlier generations, including that of IB's grandparents; later names are those used by IB.

The versions of names given here are not always identical with those used by Mendel Berlin in his memoir, sometimes because of differences in transliteration.

THE BERLIN FAMILY

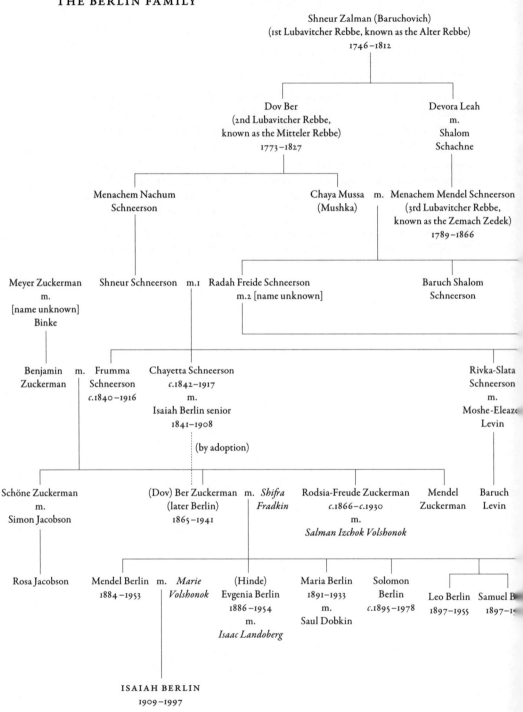

Shneur Zalman (Baruchovich)
(1st Lubavitcher Rebbe, known as the Alter Rebbe)
1746–1812

Dov Ber
(2nd Lubavitcher Rebbe,
known as the Mitteler Rebbe)
1773–1827

Devora Leah
m.
Shalom
Schachne

Menachem Nachum
Schneerson

Chaya Mussa
(Mushka)

m.

Menachem Mendel Schneerson
(3rd Lubavitcher Rebbe,
known as the Zemach Zedek)
1789–1866

Meyer Zuckerman
m.
[name unknown]
Binke

Shneur Schneerson

m.1

Radah Freide Schneerson
m.2 [name unknown]

Baruch Shalom
Schneerson

Benjamin
Zuckerman

m.

Frumma
Schneerson
c.1840–1916

Chayetta Schneerson
c.1842–1917
m.
Isaiah Berlin senior
1841–1908

Rivka-Slata
Schneerson
m.
Moshe-Eleaze
Levin

(by adoption)

Schöne Zuckerman
m.
Simon Jacobson

(Dov) Ber Zuckerman
(later Berlin)
1865–1941

m.

*Shifra
Fradkin*

Rodsia-Freude Zuckerman
c.1866–c.1930
m.
Salman Izchok Volshonok

Mendel
Zuckerman

Baruch
Levin

Rosa Jacobson

Mendel Berlin
1884–1953

m.

*Marie
Volshonok*

(Hinde)
Evgenia Berlin
1886–1954
m.
Isaac Landoberg

Maria Berlin
1891–1933
m.
Saul Dobkin

Solomon
Berlin
c.1895–1978

Leo Berlin
1897–1955

Samuel B
1897–1

ISAIAH BERLIN
1909–1997

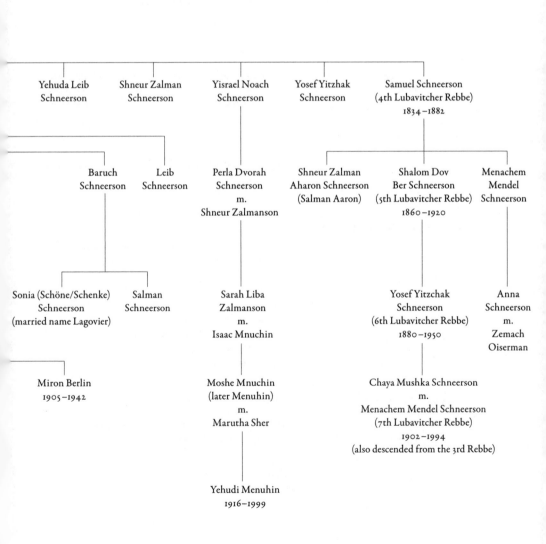

Yehuda Leib
Schneerson

Shneur Zalman
Schneerson

Yisrael Noach
Schneerson

Yosef Yitzhak
Schneerson

Samuel Schneerson
(4th Lubavitcher Rebbe)
1834–1882

Baruch
Schneerson

Leib
Schneerson

Perla Dvorah
Schneerson
m.
Shneur Zalmanson

Shneur Zalman
Aharon Schneerson
(Salman Aaron)

Shalom Dov
Ber Schneerson
(5th Lubavitcher Rebbe)
1860–1920

Menachem
Mendel
Schneerson

Sonia (Schöne/Schenke)
Schneerson
(married name Lagovier)

Salman
Schneerson

Sarah Liba
Zalmanson
m.
Isaac Mnuchin

Yosef Yitzchak
Schneerson
(6th Lubavitcher Rebbe)
1880–1950

Anna
Schneerson
m.
Zemach
Oiserman

Miron Berlin
1905–1942

Moshe Mnuchin
(later Menuhin)
m.
Marutha Sher

Chaya Mushka Schneerson
m.
Menachem Mendel Schneerson
(7th Lubavitcher Rebbe)
1902–1994
(also descended from the 3rd Rebbe)

Yehudi Menuhin
1916–1999

THE FRADKIN FAMILY

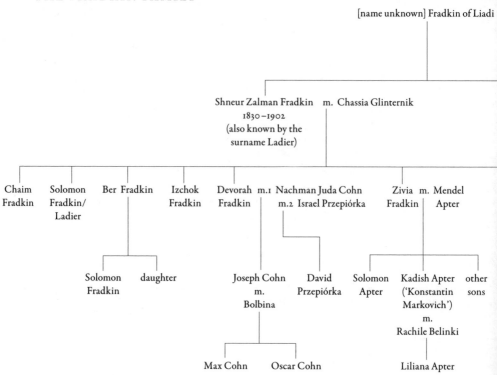

[name unknown] Fradkin of Liadi

Shneur Zalman Fradkin m. Chassia Glinternik
1830–1902
(also known by the
surname Ladier)

Chaim Fradkin | Solomon Fradkin/Ladier | Ber Fradkin | Izchok Fradkin | Devorah Fradkin m.1 Nachman Juda Cohn / m.2 Israel Przepiórka | Zivia Fradkin m. Mendel Apter

Solomon Fradkin | daughter

Joseph Cohn m. Bolbina | David Przepiórka

Solomon Apter | Kadish Apter ('Konstantin Markovich') m. Rachile Belinki | other sons

Max Cohn | Oscar Cohn

Liliana Apter

THE VOLSHONOK FAMILY

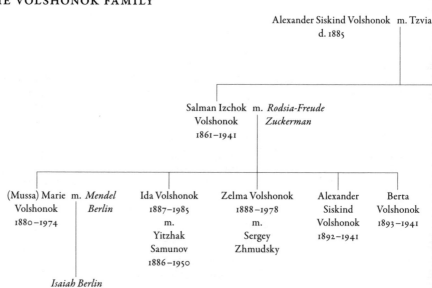

Alexander Siskind Volshonok m. Tzvia
d. 1885

Salman Izchok m. *Rodsia-Freude*
Volshonok   *Zuckerman*
1861–1941

(Mussa) Marie Volshonok 1880–1974 m. *Mendel Berlin* | Ida Volshonok 1887–1985 m. Yitzhak Samunov 1886–1950 | Zelma Volshonok 1888–1978 m. Sergey Zhmudsky | Alexander Siskind Volshonok 1892–1941 | Berta Volshonok 1893–1941

Isaiah Berlin

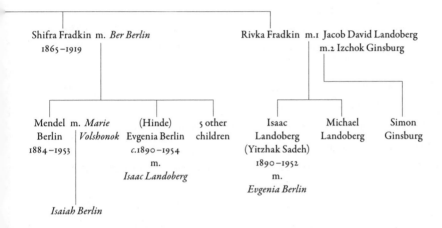

Levi-Izchok Fradkin

Shifra Fradkin m. *Ber Berlin*
1865–1919

Rivka Fradkin m.1 Jacob David Landoberg
m.2 Izchok Ginsburg

Mendel m. *Marie*   (Hinde)   5 other
Berlin   *Volshonok*   Evgenia Berlin   children
1884–1953   *c.*1890–1954
m.
Isaac Landoberg

Isaac   Michael   Simon
Landoberg   Landoberg   Ginsburg
(Yitzhak Sadeh)
1890–1952
m.
Evgenia Berlin

Isaiah Berlin

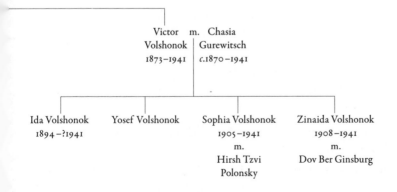

Victor   m.   Chasia
Volshonok   Gurewitsch
1873–1941   *c.*1870–1941

Ida Volshonok   Yosef Volshonok   Sophia Volshonok   Zinaida Volshonok
1894–?1941   1905–1941   1908–1941
m.   m.
Hirsh Tzvi   Dov Ber Ginsburg
Polonsky

The Contributors

Noel Annan (Lord Annan, 1916–2000) was Provost of King's College, Cambridge, 1956–66, Provost of University College, London, 1966–78 and Vice-Chancellor, University of London, 1978–81.

Shlomo Avineri is Professor Emeritus of Political Science at The Hebrew University of Jerusalem.

Isaiah Berlin (1909–97) was Chichele Professor of Social and Political Theory, Oxford, 1957–67, and the Founding President of Wolfson College, Oxford, 1966–75.

Mendel Berlin (1884–1953), Isaiah Berlin's father, was a timber merchant in (successively) Riga, Petrograd and London.

James Billington has been Librarian of Congress since 1987.

Alfred Brendel is a concert pianist and writer.

Joseph Brodsky (1940–96) was a poet, critic and translator, awarded the Nobel Prize for Literature in 1987.

Ian Buruma is a writer and lecturer and has been Henry R. Luce Professor of Democracy, Human Rights and Journalism at Bard College, New York, since 2003.

Humphrey Carpenter (1946–2005) was an author, broadcaster and musician.

James Chappel is a doctoral student at Columbia University, New York.

Joshua Cherniss is a doctoral student at Harvard University.

G. A. Cohen was Chichele Professor of Social and Political Theory, Oxford, 1985–2008.

Alistair Cooke (1908–2004) was a journalist and broadcaster who wrote and presented *Letter from America* for over 50 years.

George Crowder is Professor in the School of Political and International Studies, Flinders University, Adelaide, Australia.

Katharine Graham (1917–2001) was publisher of the Washington Post 1969–79.

Steffen W. Groß teaches economics and the history of ideas at Cottbus University in Germany.

Samuel Guttenplan emigrated to the UK a few years after working with Berlin in 1966. He is now Professor of Philosophy at Birkbeck, London, and Executive Editor of the journal *Mind & Language*.

Stuart Hampshire (1914–2004) was Grote Professor of Philosophy of Mind and Logic, London, 1960–3, Professor of Philosophy, Princeton, 1963–70, Warden of Wadham College, Oxford, 1970–84, and Professor of Philosophy, Stanford, 1985–91.

Henry Hardy, a Fellow of Wolfson College, Oxford, is one of Isaiah Berlin's Literary Trustees, and has edited many of his books.

Nicholas Henderson was British Ambassador to Poland, 1969–72, Germany, 1972–5, France, 1975–9, and the USA, 1979–82.

Kei Hiruta is a doctoral student at Wolfson College, Oxford, writing on concepts of pluralism in mid-twentieth-century political thought.

Jennifer Holmes is a researcher and genealogist, and co-editor, with Henry Hardy, of Berlin's letters.

Michael Hughes is an archivist at the Bodleian Library, Oxford. He is the author of the Library's catalogue of Isaiah Berlin's personal papers.

Michael Ignatieff's authorised biography of Isaiah Berlin was published in 1998. Formerly Carr Professor of Human Rights Practice at Harvard, he is now Leader of the Canadian Liberal Party and MP for Etobicoke-Lakeshore, Toronto, Ontario.

Aileen Kelly is Reader in Intellectual History and Russian Culture at Cambridge University and a Fellow of King's College.

Bryan Magee is a philosopher, critic of the arts, author and broadcaster and was an MP 1974–82 (Labour) and 1982–3 (SDP).

Avishai Margalit is Professor Emeritus at The Hebrew University of Jerusalem, and became George F. Kennan Professor at the Institute for Advanced Study, Princeton, in 2006.

Alan Montefiore was a Fellow and Tutor in Philosophy at Balliol College, Oxford, for thirty years, and is now President of the London School of Economics.

Serena Moore, née Denholm-Young, a.k.a. Sally, has been Henry Hardy's Assistant since 1998.

Anatoly Naiman is a Russian poet and author. In the 1960s he was Anna Akhmatova's literary secretary. He is the author of the memoir *Remembering Anna Akhmatova* (English edition 1991), and his novel *Ser* ['Sir'] (2001), from which his contribution is extracted, was shortlisted for the Booker-Smirnoff Prize.

Peter Oppenheimer is an economist and Emeritus Student (i.e. Emeritus Fellow) of Christ Church, Oxford. He was President of the Oxford Centre for Hebrew and Jewish Studies 2000–8, and a Director of the *Jewish Chronicle* 1986–2006.

Beata Połanowska-Sygulska works in the Department of the Theory and Philosophy of Law at the Jagiellonian University in Kraków, Poland. Her book *Unfinished Dialogue*, co-authored with Isaiah Berlin, was published in 2006.

Anthony Quinton (Lord Quinton) was a Fellow of All Souls College, Oxford, 1949–55, Fellow and Tutor in Philosophy at New College 1955–78, and President of Trinity College 1978–87.

Nick Rankin is a writer, broadcaster and radio producer.

Alan Ryan was Professor of Politics, Princeton, 1988–96, has been Warden of New College, Oxford, since then, and Professor of Politics, Oxford, since 1997.

Arthur Schlesinger, Jr (1917–2007), a historian, was Albert Schweitzer Professor of the Humanities, City University of New York, 1966–95.

Robert Silvers was co-editor of the *New York Review of Books* 1963–2006, and is now sole editor.

Charles Taylor was Chichele Professor of Social and Political Theory, Oxford, 1976–81, Professor of Political Science and Philosophy, McGill, 1982–98, and has been Professor of Law and Philosophy, Northwestern University, since 2002.

Patricia Utechin (1927–2008) was Isaiah Berlin's personal secretary, 1963–5 and 1972–97.

Leon Wieseltier is a writer and critic, and has been literary editor of the *New Republic* since 1983.

Bernard Williams (1929–2003) was Knightbridge Professor of Philosophy, Cambridge, 1967–79, Provost, King's College, Cambridge, 1979–87, and White's Professor of Moral Philosophy, Oxford, 1990–6.

Robert Wokler (1942–2006) was a historian of political thought who taught at Oxford (Magdalen College), Reading, the London School of Economics, Manchester (1971–98), Budapest, Exeter and Yale universities.

Evan Zimroth is a writer, mainly on Jewish topics, and Professor of English and Jewish Studies (and the Associate Director of Jewish Studies) at Queens College, City University of New York. She was one of the core organisers of the the week-long celebration of Berlin's birth in his home city of Riga in June 2009.

Index